Meso-Organizations and the Creation of Knowledge

Meso-Organizations and the Creation of Knowledge

Yoshiya Teramoto and His Work on Organization and Industry Collaborations

Edited by Caroline F. Benton,
Frank-Jürgen Richter, and Toru Takai

FOREWORD BY IKUJIRO NONAKA

Westport, Connecticut
London

Library of Congress Cataloging-in-Publication Data

Meso-organizations and the creation of knowledge : Yoshiya Teramoto and his work on organization and industry collaborations / edited by Caroline F. Benton, Frank-Jürgen Richter, and Toru Takai; foreword by Ikujiro Nonaka.

    p. cm

  Published in honor of Teramoto.

  Includes bibliographical references and index.

  ISBN 1–56720–613–1 (alk. paper)

    1. Strategic alliances (Business) 2. Business networks. 3. Knowledge management. 4. Interorganizational relations. 5. International business enterprises—Management. I. Benton, Caroline F., 1961– II. Richter, Frank-Jürgen. III. Takai, Toru, 1958– IV. Teramoto, Yoshiya, 1942–

HD69.S8M47   2004

658.4′038—dc22   2003057985

British Library Cataloguing in Publication Data is available.

Library of Congress Catalog Card Number: 2003057985
ISBN: 1–56720–613–1

First published in 2004

Praeger Publishers, 88 Post Road West, Westport, CT 06881
An imprint of Greenwood Publishing Group, Inc.
www.praeger.com

Printed in the United States of America

The paper used in this book complies with the Permanent Paper Standard issued by the National Information Standards Organization (Z39.48–1984).

10 9 8 7 6 5 4 3 2 1

Contents

Foreword

Knowledge is receiving much attention lately as the source of sustainable competitive advantage for corporations. However, knowledge itself does not provide competitive advantage. It is the creation and utilization of knowledge in a more effective manner than the competition that leads to competitive advantage. Knowledge integration is essential to these processes.

Of course, there have been many theories related to knowledge integration within an organization; with regard to product innovation, it has been considered the key to competitive advantage. Existing theories regarding innovation-related knowledge integration, however, presume the creation and utilization of knowledge in a single organization—which has become extremely difficult even for major corporations. In the global marketplace, we find that corporations with highly specialized knowledge, such as Intel and Solectron, have been able to build competitive advantage by executing the highest global standards of operation at each link in the value chain. For this reason, large corporations form alliances with specialist companies to increase their level of knowledge and seek new competitive advantage.

Small and midsized corporations are also building competitive advantage by forming new network relationships against a background of open source technology that go beyond *keiretsu* relationships. This trend is not limited to companies. Advancements in information technology are also being made by networks of individual entrepreneurs who develop new businesses at speeds that large corporations cannot match. These entrepreneurs, who at times are competitors and at other times allies of large corporations, use the resources of these businesses as their own infrastructure to grow.

Today, corporations must consider the use of external resources to build sustainable competitive advantage from the stage of strategy establishment. That is, it is necessary to go beyond the logic of a single organization's strategy by linking and integrating multiple organizations and individuals in order to adapt successfully to the market and build competitive advantage.

Such linkages among organizations have been discussed in network and alliance theories. In the field of sociology, rather than management, research on networks of individuals has been accumulated. However, there has been a lack of comprehensive research on diverse networks consisting of individuals and corporations that use knowledge resource as the analytical framework.

In this sense, this book attempts to present new interdisciplinary theories regarding the linkages of external and internal resources of individuals and organizations. Businesspersons who are dealing with intercorporate relationship issues will benefit significantly from this book.

Ikujiro Nonaka
Professor
Hitotsubashi University

Introduction: The Rise of Meso-Organizations

Caroline F. Benton, Frank-Jürgen Richter, and Toru Takai

We dedicate this book to Yoshiya Teramoto, a Japanese scholar of business and management who marked his sixtieth birthday in 2002. Although he continues to be a highly energetic and productive scholar, a group of his former students, friends, and colleagues arranged this book to honor not just this occasion but also his career as one of the most important scholars in the field of interorganizational arrangements and networks in Japan and abroad. We give various examples from growing research on networks to which he has been a great inspiration. He has established a theory of interorganizational economics mainly centered on joint ventures, strategic alliances, cross-shareholdings, and other forms of interorganizational arrangements such as the Japanese *keiretsu*.

Teramoto's recent work is directed toward analyzing the current malaise and decadence of Japan, which is now in its longest recession of the post–World War II period. Most attempts to reform the country have failed and even the so-called Koizumi reforms that have been instilled by Prime Minister Koizumi upon his taking office in 2001 have not lead to much-needed results yet.

Without creative ideas and purposeful interventions, the Japanese economic system cannot survive indefinitely. This failure stems from macroeconomic malfunctioning and—more importantly—from the country's cultural environment, which has been inhibiting domestic corporations' ability to respond to dire microeconomic issues. For example, the culture of consensus and social contract has made new initiatives and the rise of Anglo-Saxon style entrepreneurship extremely difficult. Due to this conjuncture, theoretically imaginable solutions (e.g., a more aggressive monetary policy or new bilateral and unilateral trade arrangements with its Asian neighbors) are meaningless in terms of their practicality. A sustainable solution must tackle the root causes of the Japanese failure caused by its economic, social, and cultural systems of obedience to seniority, the male gender, group interests, and inherited power, and must consider nontraditional, extra-group, and cross-boundary networking to sustain competitive advantage in this era of ever increasing sophistication of knowledge and global markets.

In advocating a dynamic approach to the study of networks, Teramoto's work and this book concentrate more thoroughly on transforming organizational structures and on creating knowledge than other former mainstream studies of networks have. We hold that the character of the new industrial societies of Asia is one of continuous innovation by linkage across, rather than within, the borders of specific industries. By carefully combining resources located within and outside the organization, Asian industries and firms have steadily advanced innovation across the spectrum of industry and have formed innovative networks that advance the creation and distribution of knowledge.

We coin the term *meso-organizations* for such endeavors that are able to go beyond traditional boundaries and define these formally as networks of individuals and organizations that view the environment as extensions of themselves and do not operate as self-contained entities. This allows them to go beyond traditional organizational, group, or national boundaries to capitalize on diverse sources of knowledge through free exchange with all sectors of the marketplace, fading the boundary between micro-socioeconomic issues (business) and macro-socioeconomic issues (societal). We propose that meso-organizations offer a good medium for creating and using knowledge as they perceive the plurality of knowledge more easily and are able to react more sensitively to environmental changes.

Our theory of meso-organizations differs from transaction cost theory and current networking theory in that it addresses the issues of changing membership, fading organizational and sector boundaries, and knowledge creation and utilization processes, whereas traditional transaction cost theory emphasizes single nonrepeatable transactions and the processes of negotiation and execution of resource exchange between economic agents in a nondynamic manner.

The relationships among members of a meso-organization are much more involved and intricate than acknowledged by traditional theories in three essential characteristics. First, these theories approach and analyze networks and alliances as a means to share capital, tangible and human resources so that physical limitations are overcome and financial efficiency is achieved, whereas meso-organizations, such as the Human Genome Project, are formed to pool and create knowledge. Second, the membership of traditional networks are mainly profit seeking enterprises and corporations while emerging networks bring together individuals, nonprofit organizations, and government agencies as well as other businesses. Third, traditional theories deal with networks that are fixed in space and time; contracts are drawn and deals are made between limited numbers of partners for prearranged deliverables and outcomes. In contrast, the memberships of recent networks are ephemeral in that individual and organizational memberships are dynamic (not necessarily less devoted) and flexible in their participation. Thus, the networks are more loosely tied, although each instance of participation can be relatively highly involved to achieve knowledge creation. For example, the eBay community, the largest on-line auction venue in the world, is comprised of autonomous individuals and businesses that actively and willingly contribute their physical and knowledge resources at their own will and discretion.

YOSHIYA TERAMOTO: A PIONEER IN THE HISTORY OF NETWORKS

Yoshiya Teramoto was born in 1942 in Nagoya, a large metropolitan prefecture located in the central region of Japan. He earned his master's degree in business from Waseda University in 1967. After working for Fujitsu, a leading Japanese electronics manufacturer, in its business planning department, he completed his doctorate work from the same university in 1972. He has since held faculty positions at Meiji Gakuin University, Tsukuba University, Hokkaido University, and at the School of Knowledge Science at the Japan Advanced Institute of Science and Technology. Currently, he is a professor at the Graduate School of Asia-Pacific Studies at Waseda University.

In Japan, Teramoto is best known for his pioneering work studying organizational networks. During the 1980s, his research focused on networking among companies from different industries and found that inter-industry cooperation led to higher levels of knowledge. He studied business associations that brought together companies from different industries, and observed that networking among small to midsized corporations promoted fusion of knowledge and expertise for further innovation.

In the late 1980s, Teramoto began investigating networks of large corporations. His interest in these major corporations was born from the realization that the hierarchical relationships that controlled Japanese corporate groups, such as the major *keiretsu*, were no longer valid in the changing emerging environment. In these groups, parent companies controlled and grew their subsidiaries and affiliates on a one-to-one basis, forming a star-shaped structure of group control. However, with the intensification of global competition and the move toward consolidated accounting in Japan, the traditional domestic management style that focused on the performance of the parent company could not fully realize the potential of the corporate group as a whole. Teramoto's research suggested that parent companies must develop a holistic strategic initiative for the group, and move away from managing their groups based on a one-to-one relationship with their subsidiaries.

During the end of the 1990s, Teramoto shifted the focus of his research toward knowledge management with the recognition that knowledge is the key managerial resource in today's society. Accumulated knowledge, he proposes, not only goes into the development of corporate output (products and services) but also guides the manner in which a company will gather, process, and use its resources and how it will manage and build its organization. He states that in the new competitive environment, knowledge networks are the essential source of new information. Such knowledge networks import and accumulate diverse tangible and intangible resources from the market in general and process these to create new value that is in turn given to the market in the form of new products and services.

Teramoto's recent work reflects on the very heart of Japan's malaise. He proposes to break up the traditional *keiretsu* system in a radically different way as practiced and pursued by Japanese businesses and policymakers. Since the outbreak of the Asian crisis in 1997, the boundaries of the *keiretsu* system have been fading with mergers of certain entities of the leading Mitsubishi, Mitsui, Sumitomo, Fuyo, Sanwa, and Daiichi Kangyo groups. The banking sector, in particular, is consolidating and abandoning the traditional boundaries between *uchi* (within the *keiretsu*) and *soto* (outside the *keiretsu*). (Daiichi Kangyo Bank merged with Fuji Bank of the Fuyo Group this year while Mitsui Bank and Sumitomo Bank merged last year. Sanwa Bank merged with second-tier bank Tokai Bank this year, as well.)

Unfortunately, these mergers have not led to a rise in the competitiveness of the affected firms or the economy in general. Teramoto's solution goes one step beyond these mergers: he proposes "revolutionary networks"—a concept that assumes elements of *soto* to first destroy a given order before rebuilding from scratch. The remaining financial strength of Japanese banks should not be misused to artificially create national champions in order to serve national pride. Rather, banks should merge with foreign entities to absorb revolutionary cells, which could revitalize the weakened body of the Japanese patient. Also, companies like Sony, Honda, and Fujitsu might even consider transferring their headquarters from Tokyo to New York or another foreign metropolis. Such a move would allow Japanese companies to become real multinationals. Revolutionary networks will help to readily contain dramatic changes and adjustments.

As noted, Teramoto's work has evolved from studying small to midsized companies to large corporations and then on to understanding knowledge networks that influence and are influenced by business and corporate governance models. These phases in his research are tied by the common theme of organizational innovation through knowledge creation and utilization. Through collaborative efforts of former students, this book aims to present the next step in Teramoto's research by describing the emerging phenomenon of meso-organizations, or knowledge networks that are blurring societal barriers.

Yoshiya Teramoto has always been intellectually on the move. He has selected his own track through the academic system and has formed a school of thought that has brought him wide recognition in Japan and abroad. We also must not forget that his high reputation in Japan comes not just from his research; his style and charisma have also won him an enviable place in the local student folklore of "who's hot" among teachers in Japanese higher business education. His breathtakingly open-minded and unique perspective has captivated businesspersons and researchers from diverse fields. He continues to teach and write on diverse topics at Waseda University. Examples of his major works are *Network Power* (1990, NTT Shuppan: Tokyo), *Power Middle* (1992, Kodansha: Tokyo), *Gakkushu Suru Soshiki* (Learning Organization, 1993, Doyukan: Tokyo), *Nihon Kigyou no Corporate Governance* (Corporate Governance of Japanese Corporations, 1997, Seisansei Shuppan: Tokyo), *Chishiki Shakai Kozo to Jinzai Kakushi* (Structure of Knowledge Society and Human Resource Innovation, 2000, Nikka Giren Shuppan: Tokyo), and *21 Seiki Ni Okeru Chishiki Network to Kigyou Model No Sogo Shinka* (The Co-evolution of Knowledge Networking and Corporate Models in the 21st Century, 2000).

CONTENTS OF THE VOLUME

This volume is organized into four parts. Part 1, "Creating Knowledge-Based Organizations," comprises chapters that sample issues faced by knowledge-creating organizations. Chapter 1 examines the theoretical roles and implications of entrepreneurship in the start up stage of a business. It finds that the role of entrepreneurs is to create knowledge and social capital and shifts the focus of study of entrepreneurs' roles from the predominant resource-based perspective to a knowledge creation-based view. Chapter 2 quantitatively studies the relationship between R&D strategy and knowledge-based networking and addresses the process of knowledge evolution in commercial R&D. Chapter 3 brings the concept of trickster, an abstraction used in cultural anthropology, into the field of management. The trickster, as a knowledge transformer, freely crosses boundaries and links different worlds to challenge the old existing order.

Part 2, "Catalyzing Knowledge Exchange among Individuals and Organizations," addresses the ubiquitous phenomenon of individual participation in profit-generating networks. Chapter 4 investigates empirically how and to what degree personal ties in Japan are used for information sharing and how they influence business performance. It presents a model of a management production function that integrates multiple information networks. Chapter 5 recognizes that open-structured organizations and networking are beginning to play a more significant role in knowledge-based economics by collecting knowledge and wisdom from individuals, institutes, and corporations. It is proposed that trust and reputation encourage and stimulate the activities of an academic society, while order and command determine the behavior of members in hierarchical organizations such as large corporations or military troops. Chapter 6 discusses how the Open Source movement evolved in major companies and is transforming conventional R&D strategies. It clarifies knowledge creation of engineers in a network through a case study of Open Source.

Part 3, "Linking Knowledge among Organizations," deals with networking among corporate and/or nonprofit organizations. Chapter 7 studies how global organizations promote competence and reform through linkage among group companies. It also suggests that in this age of advanced information technology where competition can come from any area of the globe, no corporation can afford to remain satisfied with status quo; for global success, it is necessary for managers to focus on building a network that actively assimilates subsidiaries to dynamically optimize knowledge creation capabilities. Chapter 8 clarifies the skills required of companies for building a mobile network of partnerships that matches tactics and strategy, with a focus on the Japanese automobile industry. It confronts the changes occurring in the traditionally stable *keiretsu* relationships of Toyota and shows how an independent parts supplier was able to build competitive advantage through broad based networking. Chapter 9 develops a theory for managing federated networks that are defined as inter-organizational collectivities composed of legally independent affiliates. It is suggested that effective federated networks strive to match their strategies with their capabilities and that the capability-deployment processes that generate the dynamics of exploration and exploitation enhance network effectiveness.

Part 4, "Engaging Knowledge Globally," is a collection of chapters that address the issue of global knowledge management in meso-organizations. Chapter 10 discusses aspects of globalization and merger and acquisition activities that impinge upon organizations. The chapter moves freely between the academic notions of leadership, trust, and other aspects within the ruminations of organizational behavior. Throughout the chapter it is stressed that there is a need for individuals in firms to "chat" to promote organizational learning and knowledge management across local, national, and international boundaries. Chapter 11 describes the new global competitive environment, which is characterized by a combination of competition and cooperation (coined "coopetition"), and submits that national and organizational culture, as well as organizational competencies and alliance drivers, are crucial variables in today's business setting. Chapter 12 is a systematic view of the theory of corporate internationalization strategies. It is argued that in addition to the three traditional logically interrelated forms of corporate, business, and functional strategies, a metastrategy, which lays out the entrepreneurial or future activity of a firm, must be considered to accord theory with the real situation we find in today's internationalization process.

In summation, this volume pulls together many influential contributors to the theory of networks. Their writings represent substantial intellectual input to the areas of networks and knowledge creation within networks.

PART I

Creating Knowledge-Based Organizations

CHAPTER 1

Entrepreneurship as Knowledge and Social Capital Creation: Theoretical Analysis of the Startup Stage of Firms

Jin-ichiro Yamada

INTRODUCTION

This chapter theoretically examines from diverse viewpoints the roles of entrepreneurs during startup. With globalization accelerating, the competitive relationships between individuals, firms, regions, and nations are becoming increasingly complex and interlocked regardless of their size or development levels; industrial structures are also changing. Many firms are under pressure to adjust to the acceleration of technological innovation and the diversification of customer needs by applying proper lifecycles to their products and services and to orchestrate both internal and external resources to create new knowledge through trial and error. At the same time, the surviving and operational states of individual firms, as well as industrial clusters, are diversifying.

Under such globally and locally competitive circumstances, there have been discussions on the strategic growth of small- and medium-sized firms as entities to promote diversified socioeconomic dynamism and on the importance of entrepreneurial activities as a foundation for venture creation. In addition, enablers to enhance the vitality of entrepreneurs have been discussed frequently in terms of relationships with the supporting foundations of the local economy and industrial clusters. This chapter examines the theoretical roles and implications of entrepreneurship, which is a key concept for understanding future socioeconomic changes, and attempts to move away from the traditional resource-based view to a knowledge creation-based view, while focusing on the startup stage of ventures.

In the creation of a new firm, the vision of the founder must be reflected in specific strategic domains (area), which, however, cannot be established through one person's single, drastic decision-making. Instead, these are created by the elaborate editing of knowledge through complex chain reactions. In this process, not only the traditional industry-university linkages but also multidimensional partnerships with investors and customers are thought to play a vital role; however, the conditions and circumstances of this process have not been discussed much, either theoretically or systematically. This chapter attempts to derive a new hypothesis in this regard, focusing on past literature and surveys.

ORGANIZATIONAL ECOLOGY MODEL AND THE RESOURCE-BASED PERSPECTIVE

Firms at their startup have been studied from a very wide range of perspectives. The enablers of a growing organization have been examined from the multiple viewpoints of various fields of research. Studies on the determinants of organizational growth can be roughly divided into two perspectives according to which factors of organizational growth are more emphasized, internal or external factors. One is the perspective based on environmentalism, which is characterized by studies based on viewpoints of organizational lifecycle or organizational ecology (Quirin and Cameron, 1983; Whatten, 1987; Hannan and Freeman, 1989). The other is the resource-based view of the firm. Studies based on the former provide extremely important viewpoints because there are many firms whose growth is largely influenced by the environmental factors present during their early stages of operation that sometimes lead them to bankruptcy regardless of their own efforts. Many immature firms are likely to face numerous risks beyond their control. Because the degree of growth is influenced by environmental factors, such an environmental framework is an invaluable perspective for the study of new ventures.

These studies are based on the assumption that short-term organizational changes, as emphasized in strategic theories, may be unlikely because of institutional inertia and organizational influences. The organizational lifecycle model—as expressed in birth, development, and bankruptcy—emphasizes various factors that are intricately linked to activities of a group of firms. Therefore, the growth of an organization is attributable to random consequences of environmental selection and interaction. In actuality, the survival rates of organizations, which are subject to competition as a result of environmental selection as well as variable factors including the transition of market size, largely fluctuate at early stages of operation. This phenomenon is attributable to lower customer reliability due to the weak institutional inertia and the limitation of available resources as well as to lack of experience (Hannan and Freeman, 1989).

Although organizational analyses based on environmentalism provide deeper insight into the surviving factors of firms at their startup stage, they seem not to address the major driving forces behind organizational growth. In contrast, the perspective that places greater stress on internal factors of an organization is examined in a series of studies that focus on organizational growth theories. Such studies support the traditional life-cycle model whereby each organization goes though several growth stages by trial and error (Penrose, 1959; Haire, 1959; Greiner, 1972). These growth-based organizational studies, derived from an organizational viewpoint that focuses on the acquirement, accumulation, and distribution of resources are also called the "resource-based view of the firm," and helped accumulate empirical knowledge on the diversification of firms in the 1970s and the 1980s (Rumelt, 1974; Wenerfelt, 1984; Mahoney and Pandian, 1992). If each firm possesses core management resources as advantageous organizational assets, the resources enable the firm to achieve great operational success if effectively used. This resource-based view of the firm also greatly influenced studies of firms' startup (Chrisman, 1999).

As in the case of high-tech firms, where empirical studies often focus on original technology development and fund procurement, these views assume that the existence of dominant resources and technology is a prime prerequisite for the birth of a new firm. To be sure, it is not easy to create a new firm and achieve remarkable growth in an established economy. The proper accumulation and distribution of management resources may be equally important for small- and medium-sized firms. Firm-specific management resources derived from its founders or business administrators tend to determine the startup process of a business as well as its early performance because an owner of scarce resources is more likely to obtain profits. Therefore, each new venture focuses on accumulating specific management resources through unique business development. In addition, because it is difficult for other firms to imitate or acquire through market dealings such path-dependent and firm-specific management resources, they can be an important advantage over existing large firms.

This approach toward the startup and growth processes of a firm is derived from the resource-based growth theory of Penrose (1959). Internal factors that drive the long-term growth of a firm are assumed to be unutilized resources. Such resources originally have various potential uses, and as Penrose (1959, p. 77) points out, they can be turned into utilizable resources for specific functions by properly directing them according to the entrepreneur's knowledge.

The founders or business administrators of a firm are expected to play their entrepreneurial role of creating new utilizable resources by interpreting and exploring new business opportunities and conceiving new combinations of existing resources. They are, in other words, the creators of new knowledge in that they sort out available resources and reinterpret them from new perspectives to create new value. It is the master utilization of resources, as well as entrepreneurial confidence and vision with regard to the behaviors of other firms and consumers, that can truly influence the knowledge of members of an organization. However, the resource-based view of the firm tends to disvalue the diversification of management resources and that such resources are created through human knowledge and beliefs.

ENTREPRENEURS AND BUSINESS OPPORTUNITIES: INNOVATION, RISKS, PROACTIVE ACTIONS

To fully understand the startup process of a firm, not only the processes of collecting and accumulating resources but also the entrepreneurial role of providing innovative processes that allow a new business to be created and developed must be considered. Each firm tries to eliminate variables with environmental risks and utilize its internal as well as external resources for a certain goal. Therefore, it is necessary for a firm to approach such resources from both sides.

The concept of entrepreneurship is defined in many ways. It is often pointed out that the conceptual framework of entrepreneurship is not always clear (Low and MacMillan, 1988; Shane and Ventakaraman, 2000). In the broadest sense, entrepreneurship is defined as activities to promote socioeconomic stabilization and effective utilization of resources by stimulating socioeconomic progress, creating new values, and providing employment opportunities. This concept is considered to have three major characteristics in terms of entrepreneurial activities.

Entrepreneurs are likely to take proactive action with risk bearing to promote innovation (Miller, 1983; Covin and Slevin, 1991). First, most prior discussions on entrepreneurship focus on innovation factors. Repetitious and routine activities of an organization are fundamentally changed through innovation to create a new environment and in principle it is entrepreneurs that play such innovative roles. The second aspect of entrepreneurship is risk bearing. Entrepreneurs are likely to take great risks to explore business opportunities and promote innovation. Knight (1921) places greater stress on this aspect of entrepreneurship. As she points out, there is no guarantee that developed products will sell in the real market economy. Thus, to respond to such markets, entrepreneurs must confront this uncertainty because they are under pressure to behave based on their speculations, which are not always correct. According to Knight, it is entrepreneurs that effectively cope with uncertainties. Combining the foregoing discussion on innovation, taking innovative action ahead of others is always accompanied by risks that are different from those of routine activities because mere knowledge obtained through experience may not be sufficient to cope with this uncertainty.

The third characteristic of entrepreneurship is its proactiveness (taking action ahead of competitors), or gaining insight into market opportunities through proactiveness. While the foregoing discussion on innovative activities emphasizes the execution phase, the proactive aspect places greater stress on insight into market opportunities to induce innovations. Kirzner (1973), among others, insists on the importance of such insight. Assuming that the knowledge of those trying to enter the market is insufficient, he believes that there are always opportunities to gain unknown profits and that the role of entrepreneurs is to identify and utilize such business opportunities ahead of others.

However, these theories cannot completely explain the mechanisms of such proactive activities as a pursuit of innovation and risk bearing in entrepreneurial processes. Stance or attitudes toward business opportunities as well as the motives of entrepreneurs for starting an enterprise are also important factors to be examined. Because identifying business opportunities is closely related to motivation, such a dynamic process must be explained (Kirzner, 1997). It is known that motivation has a great influence on the survival, growth, and profitability of newly created organizations (Bird, 1988; Kats and Gartner, 1988; Norris and Carsarud, 1993; Scott, 2000).

Entrepreneurial motivation is formed through rational and analytical thinking in social, political, and economic contexts and through instinct and holistic thinking based on individual backgrounds, personalities, and abilities (Bird, 1988). How they recognize and understand business opportunities largely depends on prior knowledge and context (Scott, 2000). In general, there are three kinds of entrepreneurship: novice entrepreneurship, serial entrepreneurship, and portfolio entrepreneurship. The mode of information searching and its direction and quality in each category largely vary depending on individual experiences and skills (Cooper et al., 1995; Westhead and Wright, 1998, 1999). Although the behavioral traits of each entrepreneur have both internal and external factors, there is no doubt that his/her knowledge system has a great impact on the way the entrepreneur encounters and understands various resources.

To become an entrepreneur is, so to speak, a trial-and-error learning process of obtaining knowledge and creating something new through various activities (Minniti and Bygrave, 2001). Such entrepreneurial activities should be understood as process-conscious activities rather than a single event. Entrepreneurial opportunities are more like dynamic, long-term opportunities, which may change throughout the career of each entrepreneur. In fact, it is known that there are entries into certain businesses from various other fields according to the potential career lifecycle of each entrepreneur (Harvey and Evans, 1995). Starting up a business, acquiring necessary skills and experience, and understanding market opportunities are totally different activities. However, human activities are essentially based on partial ignorance and uncertainty and the relationship between entrepreneurs and business opportunities should be understood together with changes in their knowledge structure, interactions, and numerous environmental obstacles. In this sense, entrepreneurship is a painstaking, long-term process. What keeps this process going are the high-level emotional energy and motivation of entrepreneurs themselves, interactions with the social and economic environments, and their networks.

MOTIVATION OF ENTREPRENEURIAL ACTIVITIES AND SOCIAL NETWORKS

There are two approaches to the study of the motivation of entrepreneurial activities: the emotionally deterministic approach and the socially deterministic approach. One of the pioneer studies based on the former that provided a micro-analytic framework is "Achievement Motivation" by Macreland (1961), who statistically identified the causal relationship between economic progress and achievement motivation. However, as Kets de Vries (1977) points out, this approach is an oversimplification because it overlooks the fact that various experience-based processes interplay between high achievement motivation and entrepreneurial traits; therefore, the point of the argument has shifted to the social environment surrounding entrepreneurs (Bygrave, 1989; Gartner, 1988, 1989). Researchers now consider that entrepreneurial activities are not directly induced by high achievement motivation but through interactions with social factors that support and promote independent enterprises.

This macro-approach can be divided into studies that attempt to attribute environmental factors that give rise to entrepreneurs gregariously and encourage economic success to various cultural traits of specific locations or ethnic groups and studies that shed light on institutional factors such as labor markets. For example, the opportunity structure theory (Kim, Hurh, and Fernandez, 1989; Fernandez and Kim, 1998), which focuses on the occupational choice of immigrants and independent enterprises, regards the differences of language, nationality, and educational background as factors that alienate such people from the labor market. While the opportunity structure theory focuses on alienating factors of the labor market, Pennings (1982a,b) statistically identified the direct relationship among the economic growth rate of an urban area, the number of universities, and the clustering phenomenon of startup small- and medium-sized businesses of a specific field and noticed that growing industrial agglomeration promotes entrepreneurial activities and facilitates flows of technology and human resources. Kat (1991) also showed in his study that growth in the number of small- and medium-sized businesses in the early 1970s is attributable to the rapid increase of entrepreneur training programs in the late 1960s all over the United States.

These micro and macro approaches should be systematically examined within the framework of the interdependence of entrepreneurial activities and the environment. This framework implies the diversity of the situations of each entrepreneur. Each entrepreneur does not develop or utilize business opportunities in a void, for instance. Thus, entrepreneurs are not so much independent decision-makers as entities that function in social networks (Aldrich and Zimmer, 1986; Aldrich, 1999).

Entrepreneurship is often said to be a network activity (Birley, 1984). Expansion of a network is indispensable to firms at their startup stage (Relnolds, 1991). As Granobetter (1973) puts it, economic activities are at the same time social activities. A business network is not a mere part of a social network but is born from a complex, rich social network. For entrepreneurs, human relations are always a resource. For example, venture capitalist funds are not resources per se, but will have a value depending on the knowledge of the entrepreneurs who encounter and utilize such funds. The ability to create new knowledge by combining internally and externally acquired knowledge is thought to be an innovative ability that affects the success of small- and medium-sized firms (Lippariri and Sobrero, 1989).

There are two kinds of networks for entrepreneurs: formal networks (investors, accountants, lawyers, SBA) and informal networks (family, friends, business contacts). Such networks may gradually develop from small and individual ones to extended networks and vice versa (Dubini and Aldrich, 1991). Social networks are regarded as a united whole of emotional and physical solidarities and are thought to have instrumental as well as expressive value in that potential profits may be gained through such networks (Kanai, 1989). Prior studies assume that the density, reachability, and diversity of a network determine a time and space framework within which entrepreneurs as entities of "bounded rationality" (Cyert and March, 1963) can communicate with each other (Dubini and Aldrich, 1991).

Cooper and colleagues, (1995) in their survey of actual conditions, looked at entrepreneurs' information searching activities and found that the actual conditions of such activities vary widely depending on whether they have prior knowledge about the business area they are entering and whether they have confidence in their success. Entrepreneurial activities do not result from a single decision or process but are a diachronic process based on multiple decisions and actions. In addition, the entrepreneurial network before and after starting a particular enterprise is not led by a single entity and should be understood from multiple viewpoints of various entities and their organic interactions. The reason why a certain network lends impetus to creation is thought to be because it provides opportunities to newly combine heterogeneous ideas, promote their realization, and create new activities and potentials through interactions. The importance of networking, the specific roles of key players, and their interactive processes need to be examined.

ROLES OF STARTUP TEAMS AND THEIR SOCIAL INTERACTIONS

The major characteristic of studies on entrepreneurial activities at the startup stage is that they tend to be extremely practical and normative in analyzing factors required for startups and their gradual development (Vesper, 1989; Bygrave, 1994; Timmons et al., 1987; Timmons, 1994). Five factors are identified as essential to startups: technological know-how; product/service ideas; personal contacts; physical resources; and customer orders (Vesper, 1989). Although the combination of these important factors in the best order can be considered a normative model, there is no doubt that such a combination varies depending on individual activities for various entrepreneurial opportunities and interactions. Because these factors are closely interlinked, it is difficult to precisely distinguish the factors from each other and it is also considered as less reasonable and proper that linkages of the factors should be formulated into several fixed patterns (Van de Ven et al., 1984). In addition, there are three issues that entrepreneurs are likely to confront at their startup stage: potentially profitable ideas; effective sales development plans; and fund procurement, all of which can be combined into one issue: the necessity of effective and persuasive business plans. That is why so many prior studies discuss the necessity of proper business plans and research into know-how.

In the formation process of a firm, it is naturally the founder that has always attracted the attention of researchers for his/her key role and that has been analyzed as a major factor of operational success. However, the focus of discussion has recently shifted from the entrepreneur himself as an independent hero acting in a social network to the formation of an entrepreneurial team and its roles (Cooper, 1986; Vyakarnam et al., 1997). Timmons and colleagues (1987) point out that a startup team with the entrepreneur as a key person plays the main role in applying proper resources to a particular business opportunity and that such activities can be clarified in an overall business plan. Thus, a startup team is a group of people who practically participate in forming a business together with the founder.

Although startup teams are highly valued in the evaluation process of venture capital firms, their theoretical examinations are hardly adequate (Timmons, 1994). Traditional organizational theories argue that the foundation for organizational homogeneity and inertia is built by the primary group or the leader of a new organization who imprints a sense of value at startup in the members of the organization. But there is no further development in these theories (Selznich, 1957; Stinchcom, 1965). Also in empirical studies, there is no further development of the hypothetical discussions of the correlation between the scale of a startup team and entrepreneurial performance (Van De Ven et al., 1984; Cooper et al., 1989; Kazanjian and Rao, 1999). However, many empirical studies support the view that a firm established by a team tends to achieve greater success than an individually established firm (Cooper and Bruno, 1977; Bird, 1989; Doutriaux, 1992; Vyakanrnam et al., 1997). The main roles of a startup team are to orchestrate various resources required for startup so that they complement each other and to set up and carry out business plans. Conceiving a business plan is essential to enrooting the philosophy and values of the entrepreneur in the team, implementing various strategies and operation, and determining financial and investment directions (Dollinger, 1999). However, it is not easy for entrepreneurs to collect various heterogeneous resources widely from social networks to set up long-term, attractive themes of activities and to implement them. The whole process is not a simple linear process of good inputs producing good outputs.

In this respect, there is a series of studies that argues that social interactions are essential in the formation of a new venture (Eisenhardt and Schoonhoven, 1990; Francis and Sandberg, 2000; Lechler, 2001). These studies insist on the importance of friendship, affections, and confidential relationships and point out that emotional or psychological energy has been less valued in recent discussions of strategies and management. They hypothesize that if collaborative experiences are shared among the members of a startup team, the process of decision-making is quicker and involves many heterogeneous members, which leads to constructive conflicts. The team is thought to serve as a medium of task performance so that the accumulation of social interactions has various functions such as facilitating communication and coordination, cross-subsidization, and sharing of norms. Lechler (2001), for example, used a quantitative evaluation model to reason that the higher the quality of social exchanges of a startup team, the more customer-satisfactory its business planning will be.

The argument that the main role of a startup team is to design strategic business plans has two connotations in terms of strategic and organizational theories. Business plans allow the entrepreneur, using relationships with his/her social network, that may become easily confused at the startup stage, to function for specific purposes and to draw a line marking the boundary with the outside. In the process of organizational growth, promoting resource exchanges and drawing a distinct boundary through information collection and sense making are essential (Kats and Gartner, 1988). Based on their business plans and future vision, those involved in the startup can "capture a new reality different from that of repetitious and routine activities through socially-shared knowledge" (Berger and Luckman, 1967).

Kagono (1988) points out that entrepreneurship refers to the activities of changing the existing business paradigms and to the editing mechanism of structuralizing various kinds of knowledge for the creation of a new business. He argues that the prime role of entrepreneurs is not only to utilize business opportunities, which have already existed prior to the formation of a new venture, but also to actively connect the establishment of the new organization with future or unknown opportunities. The other connotation is that future strategic directions are clarified by business plans at startup. Most prior discussions focus on the collection of resources and risk bearing, and what coordinates such activities is entrepreneurs' leaning ability and continuous organizational knowledge creation. The breadth and depth of each entrepreneur's vision in the longer term is possible from the diversified knowledge of the members of the startup team and the scale of its network.

Each entrepreneur's utilization of various kinds of information and resources and his/her emotional energy are synchronized through various social interactions so that a mere business idea can be turned into a new business concept. Kanai (1994) assumes that entrepreneurs' motivations to create something and their business concepts determine their interpretation and utilization of management resources, insisting that mere business ideas and accessibility of such resources are not sufficient conditions for startup. The strategic business concept of a startup team makes it possible to utilize various resources without using past industrial practice established by existing large firms, providing a crucial advantage for new ventures.

DEFINITION OF CORPORATE DOMAIN AND DOMAIN CONSENSUS

According to discussions in the field of business administration, each firm recognizes its own business and defines it in the rapidly changing corporate environment (Drucker, 1954; Meyer, M. W., 1975; Hofer and Schendel, 1978; Abell, 1980; Sakakibara, 1992; Yamada, 2000a,b). Drucker (1954) is thought to be the first to pose one of the most important questions for firms: "What business are we in?" He takes the case of Sears as an example in his book to point out that any business is created and managed by humans and entrepreneurial activities cannot be defined and explained in terms of the profit maximization alone.

The concept of corporate domain shows the sphere and directions of corporate activities. Determining what idea or goal to pursue, what kind of customers to deal with, and what products or services to provide internally or externally may greatly influence the activities, surviving rate, and growth of each firm and the quality of its activities (Hofer and Schendel, 1978). Abell (1980) attempted to define the concept of business domain from the three aspects of customer segmentation, customer function, and technology. He attempted to modify the traditional two-dimensional way of defining the concept such as technology versus markets or products versus missions for easier description and comparison of domain changes.

In defining business domains at the startup stage, superior innovation needs to be sought in the sense that the core entrepreneurial activity of producing new products or services is based on such a definition. However, the way of defining specific business domains must not be arbitrary or one-sided. Domains can be operational only if the organizational stance toward them is accepted by those who provide support. Therefore, domain consensus, which provides shared awareness for both insiders and outsiders, needs to be obtained between each firm and society, and between the members of an organization and their customers (Thompson, 1967; Sakakibara, 1992).

Domain consensus is a socially reached agreement on what activities a particular firm will or will not perform. In this sense, obtaining domain consensus is definitely a prime task for entrepreneurs at startup. Well-established domain consensus is essential for the initiation of any entrepreneurial activity. Therefore, to understand and analyze the organization process of a firm at its startup stage, complex exchanges and communication processes between those involved in the startup must be examined. In other words, the complex structure and process of social interactions between each organization and society, not to mention among the members of the organization, must be considered (Figure 1.1).

In addition to the entrepreneur himself and his partners, various individuals and organizations with their own speculations participate in a

Figure 1.1
Basic Definition of Domain Consensus

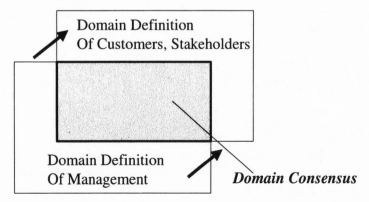

startup. These include venture capitalists, bankers, local universities, supporting administrative agencies, potential customers, and mentors. The differences between their speculations or expectations tend to give rise to a domain gap. This domain gap, in the broad sense, refers to the nonconformity between the administrators of a startup and the external environment with regard to business domain (Sakakibara, 1992). However, the fact that domains are defined and their gaps arise shows that there are active social interactions between various entities inside and outside startup teams for consensus. By examining this process in detail, startup teams may identify several patterns of diversification in their primary task of obtaining social validity for their parent organization, supporting groups, potential customers, and various other involved parties (Figure 1.2).

Burgelman (1988) insists that strategic building should be understood as a social learning process and, in the case of an in-house venture, provides a framework in which strategic concepts for new businesses are institutionalized and recognized. Developing new business concepts, after identifying business opportunities and enhancing organization abilities, requires constant learning and the interplay of recognition, business activities, and hindsight rationalization. This social learning process can resolve the previously mentioned domain gaps present at the startup stage.

Corporate domains established at the startup stage show each organization's cognitive structure of the internal and external environments. When facing environmental diversity and uncertainty, each organization

Figure 1.2
Dynamics of Domain Consensus in a Startup Team

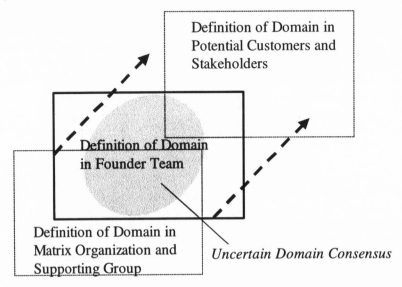

tends to create a new environment (Weick, 1979, 1995). Domain gaps arising from the diversity of information present in the environment can be a dynamic source of learning and knowledge for emerging organizations.

The behavior of entrepreneurs and their startup teams should be examined in terms of domain consensus building and interactions with the environment. The analysis of social interactions within the startup team alone cannot adequately explain their dynamics. However, the environment here refers to a specific location. Therefore, the social context of entrepreneurs should be examined based on regional characteristics and interactions with the active environment in its own context.

THEORY OF LEARNING REGIONS: INDUSTRIAL AGGLOMERATION AND CLUSTERS

The necessity of new firm creation has recently attracted great attention from the standpoints of regional economy and communities (Dorfman, 1983; Piore and Sabel, 1984; Maillat and Lecog, 1992; Morgan, 1997; Romanolli and Schoonhoven, 2001). With globalization accelerating, the competitive relationships between individuals, firms, regions, and nations are becoming increasingly complex and interlocked regardless of their levels. In the changing industrial structures, long-term, regional programs, policies, and strategies have been discussed to avoid deterioration of the regional economy. Specifically, there have been many studies on industrial agglomeration as a background of startups. The concept of industrial agglomeration has been newly recognized as an effective analytical measure.

The phenomenon of industrial agglomeration itself has long been studied in terms of technology transfer, innovation, development of subsidiary industries, economical use of machinery, presence of skilled laborers, and cost minimization (Marshall, 1937; Weber, 1922). There are many other quantitative studies dealing with this concept such as those dealing with urban growth theories based on business groups, models of industrial location (Beckmann, 1968), models that apply Williamson's concept of transaction costs to industrial agglomeration (Scott, 1988), and the self-organizational cluster formation model in a space-time framework (Krugman, 1996). These studies mainly discuss spatial patterns of industrial locations in terms of economic rationality. Paradoxically, as globalization accelerates, the source of continuous competitive advantage is more likely to derive from local factors such as local knowledge, linkage, and motivation.

For example, the flexible specialization theory of Piore and Sabel (1984) explains local industrial communities that guarantee the handing down of their technological foundations and skills to the next generation to permit large-variation and small-lot production, adopting the case of the textile industry of Prato, which is called "the third Italy." They point out the importance of the relationship between firms and various externalities relating to culture, society, and systems of the agglomeration, which may not be converted into transaction costs in their narrow sense. Harrison (1992) finds the key to distinguishing between neoclassical agglomeration theories and recent agglomeration theories in the "embeddedness" (Granoveter, 1985) of entrepreneurial activities in the society, culture, and relationship among firms. The reason the roles of networks, culture, and society in entrepreneurial activities attracts so much research attention is that regional industrial systems are important. These have been examined by many researchers including Dorfman (1983) and Saxenian (1995), who adopted two cases of high-tech industrial agglomeration: Silicon Valley and Route 128 in Boston. Using the case of Silicon Valley, they point out the advantage of open networks, regional culture, and industrial structures that support such networks.

In recent years, a growing number of studies have focused on learning and knowledge creation to explain the advantage of regionalism and industrial agglomeration. Although the production sites of manufacturing industries are increasingly moving away from urban centers to suburbs, local cities, and developing countries, certain high-cost regions in advanced economies still keep their competitive edge. This phenomenon clearly shows that learning and knowledge creation are not easily transferred to other regions, therefore providing the advantage of regionalism and agglomeration.

There have been remarkable studies with regard to regional learning and knowledge creation. The local milieu theory by GREMI, a European research group, represented by Camaguni (1991), the learning region theory suggested by Florida (1995), the collective learning process theory by TSER Network (Keeble, 1998; 1999), and studies by P. Maskel (1998) and Boekema et al. (2000) are examples. These studies regard social infrastructure and learning environment in a region as the determinants of competitiveness and innovation and suggest that proximity, R&D, and industry-university linkage and the sharing of implicit knowledge are factors. The organizational knowledge creation theory by Nonaka and Takeuchi (1995) is also frequently applied to various studies in the regional contexts.

These studies highlight the relationship between industry-supporting organizations and new firms with the potential of becoming star players in the region. Both in American (Dorfman, 1983; Feldman and Florida, 1994; Saxenian, 1995) and European cases (Morgan, 1997; Keeble et al., 1999; Scott, 1999; Collinson, 2000), the roles of supporting organizations are remarkable. There are three major infrastructures in a learning region: physical and communicative infrastructure, production infrastructure, and the human infrastructure (Florida, 1995).

Porter (1998) points out that while there have been frequent discussions on the influence of economic policies, studies from the viewpoint of location itself tend to be disvalued. He emphasizes that a "cluster"—a state in which related firms and organizations are concentrated in a specific geographical area—has a positive effect on midterm success. A cluster is a concentration not only of similar firms producing finished products or services but also of distributors, manufacturers of complementary products, government, universities, think tanks, and vocational training schools all of which provide professional training, education, information, research, and technical support. The plenitude of such organizations is likely to determine the scale and sophistication of the cluster. Entrepreneurial activities in such a cluster usually aim at enhancing production efficiency and innovation. The basic functions of clusters are sophistication of accumulated technologies and effective utilization of human and financial resources for R&D (Porter and Stern, 2001).

According to Porter (1998), the growth of industrial clusters depends on the competitive environment of firms, demand conditions, material (input resources) conditions, and supporting industries. This view is also consistent with that of Trist (1983) who considers the focusing and development of domains as an important factor in interorganizational relations. Most researchers agree that in such an agglomeration or cluster, universities play a vital role as a medium promoting communication among various firms and other players.

Starting up in a certain region means a domain selection for the firm. Establishing regional domains to promote a certain clustering pattern is as important a midterm strategic decision for the firm as the process of determining its own domain at startup. In this case, the entity that makes such a decision is inevitably the aggregation of various individuals and organizations, including administrative officers of the local government, governors, residents of the community, core firms, and NPOs. Therefore, domain gaps arise due to complex power games and interest differences. Under such circumstances, universities are expected to play a main role in resolving these gaps. However, in Japan, universities are facing difficulties in achieving their own domain consensus.

THE UNIVERSITY-INDUSTRY RELATIONSHIP AND THE PRISONERS' DILEMMA

Attention is being focused on the roles of local universities for encouraging startups and improving innovativeness of localities themselves (Branscomb, Kodama, and Florida, 1999). Also, with attention concentrating on the importance of knowledge as a factor for economic vitalization (Drucker, 1993; Nonaka and Takeuchi, 1995; Leonard-Burton, 1995), universities must inevitably play a role in enhancing the flow of knowledge across organizations. However, there have been few theoretical studies with regard to universities (Merton, 1973; Rosenberg and Nelson, 1994).

The university-industry linkage includes education and collaborative research and is now recognized as one of the most important issues for revitalizing industries. First, the university-industry linkage is greatly affected by each country's history and is not a recent phenomenon of the United States. According to Mowley and Rosenberg (1989), universities, mainly those with agricultural science and engineering departments, were established in each state of the United States based on the land offers of the Morrill Act of 1862. These universities were committed to supporting local industries. The university-industry linkage in the United States was reformed in the mid-nineteenth century during the Second World War, when large-scale government investments were made to support them. Recently, universities tend to make their own profits (Etzkowitz, 1999).

However, the university-industry linkage in Japan is not firmly established despite the long history of 120 years or more of Japanese universities (especially state-run ones). Great controversy regarding this linkage arose during the student rebellions in Japan after the late 1960s and has led to a taboo regarding university-related links (Kobayashi, 1998). Another significant consequence of this controversy was that Japanese enterprises made more positive and consecutive investments in American universities than their American counterparts in Japan (National Academy of Engineering, 1996).

However, in the 1980s, both the Japanese government and industry were forced to change their policies as a result of the Japan-U.S. trade friction, technological friction, and the criticism of "free riding on basic research." The Japan Federation of Economic Organizations pointed out in 1980 the necessity of the university-industry linkage to encourage innovative engineering developments. Also, the Industrial Structure Council of the former Ministry of International Trade and Industry proposed a "technopolis concept" that gathers high-tech industries and institutions. The concept has played an important role in the Japanese regional expansion policy by improving local knowledge-intensive industries and housing conditions (Suzuki, 2001). Many study groups were sent to the United States and Europe by government organizations and a number of reports on university-industry linkage were published. The necessity of improving the structure of production and basic research through university-industry linkages was widely recognized for promoting Japanese original technology, as opposed to importing and applying technology from the United States and Europe, which was commonplace after the war (Hashimoto, 1999).

Institutions of higher education, particularly universities, should play an important role in the production of knowledge in each country. Comparing research and development investments in the United States, Germany, France, the United Kingdom, and Japan, it is Japan that makes the largest investments in universities (National Institute of Science & Technology Index Project Team, 1997). R&D investments by both the public and private sectors exceeds 3 percent of the GDP in Japan. In truth, however, despite the consensus on the necessity of university-industry linkage, the flow of funds from the private sector to universities is remarkably low in Japan compared with other key countries (Sakakibara, 2000). As a result, universities, which depend on indirect public funds, are likely to have little direct interaction with industry.

Nevertheless, there were some changes among the main players in university-industry collaborative work during the high economic growth period in Japan (Kobayashi, 1998). The systematic utilization of university-industry research doubled from 1992 to 1998 (Sakakibara, 2000). Although there are signs that such joint research is likely to grow, it is the small- and medium-sized firms, rather than large ones, that are currently playing an important role, reflecting the fact that approaches to regional vitalization are moving away from policies that focus on attracting plants of big firms and toward policies for endogenous development through fostering vitalization of existing industries and supporting the formation of new industries. The university-industry linkage is changing from one between a few big enterprises and many universities throughout the world into one of multiple internal linkages with a broader but smaller base. The Japanese-style system, which has been effective despite its extreme informality compared that of the United States (Florida and Cohen, 1999), is in a transition stage during the current period of protracted economic recession.

The university-industry-government linkage is valuable not only for cross-industrial exchanges but also for efficiency. First, universities and research institutes have sophisticated and state-of-the-art know-how including basic research. Second, because universities and public institutions have networks different from those of industry and social credibility, they may be able to create connections to obtain information and know-how at home and abroad. Third, objective broader viewpoints of universities and research institutes may enable better judgment on the possibility of technological developments or commercialization of products. The use of opinions from people outside of profit-seeking domains may be extremely valuable; firms may be able to create social value as well.

However, the results of a survey showed that university-industry linkage is far from the expected level with regard to stability and information disclosure. Because mutual confidence has not reached the expected level, domain gaps have remained unfilled for the most part (survey commissioned by the Small and Medium Enterprise Agency, 1999; Ijichi, 2000). Ijichi (2000) points out that a sharp distinction between public and private interests may exist in university-industry interactions and argues that there is a need to confront issues of non-profitability in management. Assuming that there are two types of positive and passive attitudes in collaboration, the four situations shown in Table 1.1 can be assumed.

In this table, the university-industry relationship in joint development is considered. Industry requires multifaceted perspectives on experiments of new technology, while universities require sufficient funds to support research. Industry clearly has the options of purchasing technology from the market or of developing and manufacturing products internally. But they also have the third option of working with research institutes or universities. Universities can opt to obtain public or private sector funds for research (Table 1.1).

Cell IV organizations in Table 1.1 exhibit the similar form of collaboration through traditional market transactions as cell I organizations. It is important to note, however, that there is also a strong likelihood for cell I and cell III organizations to do so as well. This suggests that an industry or industrial firm might expect remarkable achievements from R&D collaboration through its preferential treatment (providing funds) of a certain research sector, while the research sector might not expect much from the collaboration and might be ready to abandon its relationship with industry, thus providing sufficient information.

Universities tend to be generally passive toward their relationships with industry, even though they can obtain funds for research. Industry, on the other hand, tends to be positive toward this relationship even though the results may be extremely poor. One side is willing to build a collaborative relationship without receiving sufficient information from its partner, while the other side is ready to terminate the relationship while obtaining

Table 1.1
Prisoners' Dilemma in Industry-University Relationships

		University	
		Defect	Cooperate
Corporation	Defect	I (2, 2)	II (4, 1)
	Cooperate	III (1, 4)	IV (3, 3)

sufficient support and information. This causes a disparity in the bargaining power of the two sides. The research sector, which is in an advantageous bargaining position, tends to achieve reasonable research results, while industry, in a disadvantageous bargaining position, may need to restrict the flow of information to its partner and seek an alternative relationship with a partner from another sector to restore its bargaining power. In other words, cell I should be valid.

This situation resembles the "prisoners' dilemma." Suppose the values in parentheses show achievements attained (research-sector value on the right; industry value on the left). If either a university or an industrial organization attempts to establish such a relationship, the targeted partner is likely to be passive, suggesting that it may be more advantageous to seek an alternative partner in another market. It may also be advantageous for industry entities to continue to obtain new technology in traditional market transactions. Thus, even if it is obvious that achievements attained from a university-industry relationship are more fruitful than those attained from traditional market transactions, such a relationship is not always formed due to lingering suspicions.

Industries also tend to overestimate the merits from market transactions, while universities tend to have a strong expectation of receiving public funds. In addition, attainable achievements from university-industry collaboration may be uncertain and there may be conflicts concerning allocation of results. Achievements from a university-industry relationship may be equivalent to obtaining new technology or completion of a prototype. However, in reality, it ranges from new technology to insights into a new market, whose value is found in the collaborative process. Also, innovation does not always occur through such a cumulative process of knowledge creation and it is difficult to predict the rate of innovation from a university-industry relationship. Furthermore, if achievements are not equally allocated when innovation is successful, the partner that ends up with less may not agree to future collaboration.

Therefore, there are three patterns of conflicting factors in the process of establishing a university-industry relationship when a domain gap cannot be filled. These are:

1. possibility of insufficient performance (cells II and III),
2. adherence to traditional market transactions based on organizational habits (cell I),
3. uncertainty of attainable achievements (cell IV).

With these factors in mind, it is necessary to consider other factors to overcome these obstacles and establish domain consensus.

SOCIAL CAPITAL AND KNOWLEDGE COMMUNITIES

Innovation through university-linkage provides a base for discussing regional entrepreneurial activities and economic growth. However, for such a linkage to function, various entities including entrepreneurs, researchers, investors, and policy makers must be deeply rooted in the social network of innovative knowledge creation. The domain definition of each entity must also be self-organized based on mutual trust. The importance of mutual trust developed through the social interactions of startup teams was discussed earlier in this chapter. There are also several studies that place greater emphasis on the concept of social capital to explain the importance of the knowledge community in different sectors (Bourdieu, 1986; Coleman, 1988; Taylor and Singleton, 1993; Fountain, 1998; Brass and Labianca, 1999; Baker, 2000). Social capital, as a core community resource, is thought to reduce transaction costs (Taylor and Singleton, 1993).

Coleman (1988) defines social capital as private and public entities that enrich individual lives "by voluntarily transferring their own resources or their control over such resources to others." This definition provides an important perspective for further discussions. Social capital reduces transaction costs by developing regularity and standards of conduct within a network and promotes mutual cooperation and knowledge exchange and creation. Social capital can thus determine the quality of network relationships.

The role of social capital in a certain region can also be discussed in terms of the maturity of entrepreneurial infrastructure that is a base for spontaneous growth of new ventures (Flora and Sharp, 1997). Specifically, industry-university linkage is a complex process different from that of linear models for R&D that follows basics, application and development sequence. To capitalize on various business opportunities, entrepreneurs must explore various methods of directly assessing, for example, customer requests and proposals from production sites. This requires networking and communication so that more sophisticated knowledge and basic research can be used and so that the latest implicit knowledge can be exchanged through contacts with universities.

Universities play a key role in accumulating high-quality knowledge and are a central part of regional industrial clusters where various entrepreneurial activities are performed. University-industry relationships are three-dimensional, linking education, research, and business creation—all of which complement each other. Although each has its own time span—long-term, mid-term, and short-term, respectively—they are considered to be closely related (Figure 1.3).

The educational function is the most basic dimension of the university-industry linkage. Education services offered by a university include not

Figure 1.3
Three Dimensions of Industry-University Linkage

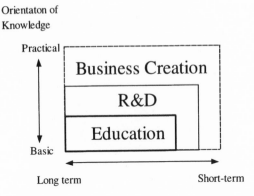

only conveyance of basic knowledge and enhancement of students' mental faculties but also application of practical knowledge. The former is a common function of universities. In terms of the latter, universities have internship programs that provide on-site knowledge regarding firms and administration. The education linkage is the most important of the three because the function to complement the flexibility of a social network depends on the reputation built by abundant human capital including university graduates (Penning, Lee, and Witteloostuijn, 1998; Florida and Cohen, 1999). R&D that disvalues the long-term process of building mutual trust and the short-term expectations and business investments may induce erroneous decisions and also hinder effective policy making and management strategies.

Except in rare cases, fruitful university-industry exchanges can be achieved only if domain consensus is reached and if those involved are confident of carrying out their expected roles. Based on the demographic data of Dutch accounting firms for over 100 years, Penning and colleagues (1998) conducted an empirical study and reported that the bankruptcy rate of firms immediately after their startup was as high as 61 percent, which is comparable to that of firms older than 15 years and clearly shows the weakness of social and human capital. Social capital may be the key ingredient for startup teams for technological know-how.

In the process by which new knowledge is created from external communication relationships in different contexts or conditions based on industry-university networks, differences arise depending on whether such exchanges take place in their true sense or not. Merely providing places in their artificial or superficial sense may not lead to the creation of practical knowledge communities. Although relevance to social capital is not necessarily clarified, there are several studies on this issue (Nonaka,

1998; Itami, 1999; Kanai, Asizuka, and Ishida, 1999; Kanai and Ishida, 2000; Baker and Obstfeld, 1999; Nonaka, Toyama, and Nagata, 2000; Kurogh, Ichijo, and Nonaka, 2000).

Baker and Obstfeld (1999) argue that social capital is built through entrepreneurial activities. According to them, opinion gaps arise when various entities including entrepreneurs are linked in turn to the development of a network. Two kinds of strategies are likely to be conceived: nonconsolidation strategies that focus on short-term profits by denying linkages to other entities and consolidation strategies that attempt to gain advantages by filling the gaps among such entities. They analyzed this point and claimed that providing long-term cross-subsidization should lead to the formation of social capital.

Nonaka (1998) and Kanai (2000) used the concept of *ba,* a Japanese word meaning "place(s)," to explain the foundation for effective creation, distribution, and interaction of knowledge. *Ba* is defined as a dynamic context, the sharing of space and time under conditions determined by interactions. There are the physical *ba,* the virtual *ba,* and the mental *ba* based on experiences or ideologies. Itami (1999) and Kanai and colleagues (1999) identified five determinants of *ba:* membership, agenda, sensory codes, information carriers, and collaboration incentives.

There are two hypotheses on the causal relationship between *ba* as a knowledge community and social capital. One view is that superior knowledge communities are created from certain heterogeneous entities of social capital. The other is that the driving force of superior knowledge communities creates social capital. This potentially reciprocal relationship shows that efforts to endlessly seek new differences and meanings among entities is the source of vitality in networks of entrepreneurial entities and that their commitment to such activities based on their spontaneous motives is the most important factor.

MULTI-DIMENSIONAL VIEW OF ENTREPRENEURSHIP

The creation of *ba* requires knowledge sharing among individuals regardless of their titles, or in some cases, when they are released from their duties. Teramoto (1990) points out the importance of diversifying combinations of resources as openly as possible and of enhancing dynamics by internalizing the power base of external resources while externalizing internal resources in the implementation of networking. This is an extremely fragile process. Kurogh and colleagues (2000) points out that the process of knowledge creation and sharing requires love, trust, care, commitment, and direct management.

In recent years, there has been a series of studies that attempt to include the important activity of creating social capital and communities in the scope of entrepreneurial roles (Henton, Melville, and Walesh, 1997; Leadbeater, 1997; Brinckerhoff, 2000; Yli-renko, Autio, and Sapienza, 2001; Luchio, 2001). Henton and colleagues (1997) proposed the new concept of civic entrepreneur, which combines the two important American traditions of entrepreneurship and community activity. Civic entrepreneurs function as a medium to create collaboration networks of businesses, government, educational organizations, and communities. They are not necessarily involved in starting a business but have a leading role in forming communities that support startups.

For example, Frederic Terman (Saxenian, 1994) helped developed the foundation for a region of technology and industry and built a community of engineers and researchers on the periphery of Stanford University. Later, his efforts led to an extensive industrial complex called the Industrial Park. The Park has grown to become one of the largest industrial regions in the United States and provided the foundation for Silicon Valley today. In addition, the Smart Valley initiative led by Bill Miller at Stanford University, which aims at promoting business and personal exchanges, has been implemented to cope with the restructuring of industries in Silicon Valley. He established a nonprofit organization, Smart Valley Public Corporation, as a core entity for the area and has been an active leader of change. The civic entrepreneurial activities of Terman and Miller should be clearly distinguished from their traditional roles as supporters or coordinators of entrepreneurs. The communities built by their activities have helped entrepreneurs start new business but from their standpoint, this is the product of their carrying out their own domain definitions.

It should be noted that social activities, including regional community formation, are performed not only through the creation of firms but also through the creation of NPOs (nonprofit organizations). In general, NPOs are different from businesses in that they are based on different organizational principles and their profits are not redistributed to their members. However, in many cases, it is difficult to draw the line between business-type NPOs and sociocentric NPOs because both types have the same mission of resolving social problems. Therefore, organizational types are usually determined based on the direction of entrepreneurial activities. In addition, those who utilize business power and present a new scheme to resolve social problems that may include community disruption are called social entrepreneurs (Leadbeater, 1997; Brinckerhoff, 2000). They address various social issues including welfare, education, environment, poverty, community redevelopment, aid to developing countries, and revitalization of towns or regions.

Besides businesspersons, researchers and administrators sometimes serve as leaders of regional innovation, before and after business creation, providing necessary support. How they are understood in terms of entrepreneurship depends on what activities are emphasized. This multi-dimensional view of entrepreneurship is not new. In his detailed case study, Ostrom (1965) regards the role of the administrative body in resolving the problem of ground water basins as that of public entrepreneur. He clearly distinguishes this activity from those based on pure economic motives. Similar discussions are found in the Kanai case study (Kanai, 1980), which examines the innovative process of administrative organizations and successful university-industry collaboration (Kanai et al., 1999).

While greater emphasis has been placed on the one-sided, self-interested aspect of entrepreneurships, researchers, particularly in Britain and the United States, have been focusing on the view of entrepreneurship based on expansive, social motives (Kanai, 2000). For industry-university-government linkage to function substantially as the foundation for regional economic revitalization, multi-dimensional entrepreneurship, which includes civic, social, and cultural factors, must be positively rooted in the region. One of the reasons why this process is stagnant is because society's stance toward entrepreneurial activities tends to be resource-based and boundaries are drawn among economic, public, and industry activities.

Lousbury and Glyn (2001) point out in their research paper on cultural entrepreneurship that corporate culture as well as social and institutionalized capital are key factors and argue that entrepreneurs develop their views toward business based on their own situations, establish their reputation as an intangible asset, and obtain necessary external resources to achieve fortune. Henrekson and Rosenberg (2001) compare and analyze the entrepreneurial activities of university researchers in Sweden and the United States. These studies show the importance of having a multi-dimensional perspective on entrepreneurship.

Entrepreneurship is a creative, and at the same time, destructive activity that develops new domains through knowledge creation. However, there are various approaches and motives for establishing domains. Although somewhat deviating from the main discussion, Florida and Cohen (1999) assume that intellectual workers are motivated not so much by material or financial incentives as by honor, involvement, and social meaning. This assumption might also be suggested of entrepreneurial activities at startup.

CONCLUSION

This chapter theoretically examined the startup stage of firms from multiple viewpoints and draws the following hypothetical conclusion. The primary role of entrepreneurs at the startup stage is to properly acquire knowledge and create social capital. Traditional studies on the role of entrepreneurs at the startup stage tend to be extremely practical and normative in examining necessary resources and their gradual growth. In most cases, they merely list indispensable management resources and insist that such resources should be obtained in social networks whose scale and density vary depending on the stage of development.

This chapter attempts to shift the focus of entrepreneurs' roles from the predominant resource-based perspective to the strategic-domain perspective based on the knowledge-based view, assuming that the use of any management resource depends on the interpretation of entrepreneurs or startup teams. The multi-dimensional examination of this chapter identifies two basic roles of entrepreneurs (Figure 1.4). First, entrepreneurs clearly define their corporate domains, contemplate the gaps between various interested parties rooted in the region, and obtain their consensus. This process is necessarily accompanied by knowledge creation in knowledge communities within a social network.

The second role of entrepreneurs at startup is to create or obtain the social capital necessary for establishing their domain and building consensus. Various interested parties including involved supporters have their own domain definitions based on their own contexts. Their activities may be based on public interest and they may become estranged and lapse into disruption as seen in the "prisoners' dilemma." This is particularly true of collaboration, or supporting activities, by different sectors or industries. Therefore, social capital, which serves as the driving force behind such activities, is an essential condition for the creation and functioning of knowledge communities as practical units.

The theoretical implications of this study are as follows. The formation

Figure 1.4
Regions and Domain Consensus from the Multi-Dimensional Viewpoint of Entrepreneurship

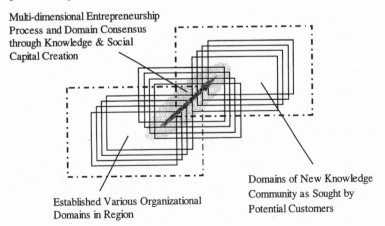

Multi-dimensional Entrepreneurship
Process and Domain Consensus
through Knowledge & Social
Capital Creation

Established Various Organizational
Domains in Region

Domains of New Knowledge
Community as Sought by
Potential Customers

of new ventures is based on knowledge creation theory, which differs from traditional management and operation theories. The process of organization formation includes domain establishment for new products and services. Nothing comes from nothing in socioeconomic activities; there must be various organizations or networks in the region to enable the creation of new firms. Various kinds of knowledge and technology and the interactions between entities with different purposes promote the creation and growth of organizations, which in turn affects regional economics. In the reverse situation, the disruption of the domain consensus of existing organizations causes domain gaps, leading to new knowledge conceptions and entrepreneurial activities.

While modern capitalism has become pervasive and people's sense of value has diversified, communities are often disrupted and problems arise that existing administrative bodies cannot cope with. To resolve these social problems, the situation in which government and administration monopolize associated markets may be changed with the development of multidimensional linkages among entrepreneurs, administration, and NPOs. To understand this trend theoretically, it is necessary to reexamine the activities of entrepreneurs and other interested parties, arising from the gaps or overlaps of defined domain. Even for the successful case of one startup or one NPO activity, the multidimensional view of entrepreneurship requires analyses of domain gaps and consensus from various viewpoints including organizational and strategic.

As for practical implications, domain gaps and consensus building are two important issues for the management of relationships between entrepreneurs and various interested parties. There is knowledge that cannot be obtained from the mere combining of the perspectives of promising technology and expanding markets. Although various heterogeneous entities and the interactions of their knowledge are often emphasized in the discussions of how superior knowledge communities are created, managers or entrepreneurs who own or create social capital itself should also be included in this argument.

This study merely sets out to provide hypotheses. The assumptions and arguments in this chapter need to be examined in the future based on empirical studies. There are still many issues remaining, including the analysis of strategic domains in comparison with spontaneous entrepreneurial activities in a region and the activities of an immigrant or international type, and the roles of entrepreneurs in the domain change to guarantee long-term growth.

REFERENCES

Abell, D. F. 1980. *Defining the Business: The Starting Point of Strategic Planning*. New Jersey: Prentice-Hall.

Aldrich, H. 1999. *Organizations Evolving*, Sage Publications.

Aldrich, H., and C. Zimmer. 1986. "Entrepreneurship Through Social Networks." In *The Art and Science of Entrepreneurship*, edited by Donald L. Sexton and Raymond W. Smilor, 3–23, Ballinger. Reprinted in Howard Aldrich in collaboration with Ellen R. Ouster, Udo H. Staber, and Catherine Zimmer, *Population Perspectives on Organizations* 24, Acta Universitatis Upsaliensis. Studia Oeconomiae Negotiorum, Sweden.

Baker, W. 2000. *Achieving Success Through Social Capital*. Jossey-Bass Inc.

Baker, W. E. and D. Obstfeld. 1999. "Social Capital by Design: Structures, Strategies, and Institutional Context." In *Corporate Capital Liability*, edited by Roger, T. A., A. J. Leenders, and Shaul M. Gabbay. Kluwer.

Beckman, M. J. 1968. *Location Theory*. Random House.

Berger, P. L. and Luckman, T. 1967. *The Social Construction of Reality: A Treatise in the Sociology of Knowledge*. New York: Doubleday.

Bird, B. J. 1989. *Entrepreneurial Behavior*. Glenview, IL: Scott Foresman and Company.

Bird, B. J. 1988. "Implementing Entrepreneurial Ideas: The Case for Intention." *Academy of Management Review* 13, no. 3: 442–453.

Birley, S. 1984. "The Role of Networks in the Entrepreneurial Process." *Journal of Business Venturing* 1: 107–117.

Bourdieu, P. 1986. "Forms of Capital." In *Handbook of Theory and Research for the Sociology of Education*, edited by J. C. Richards. New York: Greenwood Press.

Branscomb, Lewis M., Fumio Kodama, and Richard Florida, eds. 1999. *Industrializing Knowledge: University-Industry Linkages in Japan and the United States*. Cambridge, MA: The MIT Press.

Brass, D. J., and G. Labianca. 1999. "Social Capital, Social Liabilities, and Social Resources Management." In *Corporate Social Capital and Liability*, edited by R. T. Leenders and S. M. Gabbay, 323–338. Boston: Kluwer Academic Publishers.

Brinckerhoff, P. C. 2000. "The Benefits of the Social Entrepreneurism Model." In *Social Entrepreneurship*, ch. 2, Wiley.

Burgelman, R. A. 1988. "Strategy Making As Social Learning Process: The Case of Internal Corporate Venturing." *Interfaces* 18, no. 3: 74–85.

Bygrave, W. D. 1989. "The Entrepreneurship Paradigm (I): A Philosophical Look at its Research Methodologies." *Entrepreneurship: Theory and Practice* 14, no. 1: 7–26.

Bygrave, W. D. (ed.). 1994. *The Portable MBA in Entrepreneurship (MBA Series)*, John Wiley & Sons Inc.

Camaguni, R. (ed.) 1991. *Innovation Networks: Spatial Perspectives*. London: Behaven Press.

Chrisman, J. J. 1999. "The Influence of Outsider-Generated Knowledge

Resources on Venture Creation." *Journal of Small Business Management* 37, no. 4: 42–58.

Coleman, J. C. 1988. "Social Capital in the Creation of Human Capital." *American Journal of Sociology* 94: 95–120.

Collinson, S. 2000. "Knowledge Networks for Innovation in Small Scottish Software Firms." *Entrepreneurship and Regional Development* 12: 217–244.

Cooper, A. C. 1986. "Entrepreneurship and High Technology." In *The Art and Science of Entrepreneurship*, edited by D. L. Sexton and R. W. Smilor. Cambridge, Massachusetts, Ballinger.

Cooper, A. C. and A. V. Bruno. 1977. "Success among High-Technology Firms." *Business Horizons* 20, no. 2: 16–22.

Cooper, A. C., et al. 1995. "Entrepreneurial Information Search." *Journal of Business Venturing* 10: 107–120.

Cooper, A. C., et al. 1989. "Entrepreneurship and the Initial Size of Firms." *Journal of Business Venturing* 4: 317–332.

Covin, J. G. and D. P. Slevin. 1991. "A Conceptual Model of Entrepreneurship as Firm Behavior." *Entrepreneurship: Theory and Practice* 16, no. 1: 7–25.

Cyert, R. M. and J. G. March. 1963. *A Behavioral Theory of the Firm*. New Jersey: Prentice-Hall.

Dollinger, M. 1999. *Entrepreneurship: Strategies and Resources*. New Jersey: Prentice-Hall.

Dorfman, N. S. 1983. "Route 128: The Development of a Regional High Technology Economy." *Research Policy* 12: 299–316.

Doutriaux, J. 1992. "Emerging High-Tech Firms: How Are Their Comparative Start-up Advantages?" *Journal of Business Venturing* 7, no. 4: 303–322.

Drucker, P. F. 1954. *The Practice of Management*. New York: Harper and Brothers Publishers.

Drucker, P. 1993. *Post-capitalist Society*. New York: Harper Business.

Dubini, P., and H. Aldrich. 1991. "Personal and Extended Networks are Central to the Entrepreneurial Process." *Journal of Business Venturing* 6: 305–313.

Eisenhardt, K. M., and C. B. Schoonhoven. 1990. "Organizational Growth: Kinking Founding Team, Strategy, Environment, and Growth among U.S. Semiconductor Ventures, 1978–1988." *Administrative Science Quarterly* 35: 504–529.

Etzkowitz, H. 1999. "Entrepreneurial Science in the Academy: A Case for the Transformation of Norms." *Social Problems* 36: 14–29.

Feldman, M. P., and R. Florida. 1994. "The Geographic Sources of Innovation: Technological Infrastructure and Product Innovation in the United States." *Annals of the Association of American Geographers* 84: 210–229.

Fernandez, M. and K. Kim. 1998. "Self-Employment Rates of Asian Groups: An Analysis of Intra Group and Intergroup Differences." *International Migrant Review* 32: 654–681.

Flora, J. L., and J. Sharp. 1997. "Entrepreneurial Social Infrastructure and Locally Initiated Economic Development in the Nonmetropolitan United States." *Sociological Quarterly* 38, no. 4: 623–644.

Florida, R. 1995. "Toward Learning Region." *Futures* 27: 527–536.

Florida, R. and W. M. Cohen. 1999. "Engine or Infrastructure? The University Role in Economic Development." In *Industrializing Knowledge: University-Industry Linkage in Japan and the United States,* edited by L. M. Branscomb, F. Kodama, and R. Florida. MIT Press.

Fountain, J. 1998. "Social Capital: A Key Enabler of Innovation." In *Investing in Innovation,* edited by Lewis Branscomb and James H. Keller. MIT Press.

Francis, D. H., and W. R. Sandberg. 2000. "Friendship within Entrepreneurial Teams and its Association with Team and Venture Performance." *Entrepreneurship Theory and Practice* 25, no. 2: 5–26.

Gartner, W. B. 1989. "Some Suggestions for Research on Entrepreneur Traits and Characteristics." *Entrepreneurship Theory and Practice* Fall: 27–37.

Gartner, W. B. 1988. "Who is an Entrepreneur? Is the Wrong Question." *American Journal of Small Business* 17: 22–29.

Granovetter, M. 1973. "The Strength of Weak Ties." *The American Journal of Sociology* 78, no. 6: 1360–1380.

Granovetter, M. 1985. "Economic Action and Social Structure: The Problems of Embeddedness," *The American Journal of Sociology* 91, 481–510.

Greiner, L. E. 1972. "Evolution and Revolution as Organizations Grow." *Harvard Business Review* 50, no. 4: 37–46.

Haire, M. 1959. "Biological Models and Empirical Histories of the Growth of Organizations." In *Modern Organization Theory,* edited by M. Haire, 272–306, New York: John Wiley and Sons.

Hannan, M. T., and J. Freeman. 1989. *Organizational Ecology.* Harvard University Press.

Harrison, B. 1992. "Industrial District: Old Wine in New Bottles?". *Regional Studies* 26: 469–483.

Harvey, M., and R. Evans. 1995. "Strategic Window in the Entrepreneurial Process." *Journal of Business Venturing* 10: 331–347.

Hashimoto, T. 1999. "The Hesitant Relationship Reconsidered: University-Industry Cooperation in Postwar Japan." In *Industrializing Knowledge: University-Industry Linkage in Japan and the United States,* edited by L. M. Branscomb, F. Kodama, and R. Florida. MIT Press.

Herenkson, M., and N. Rosenberg. 2001. "Incentive for Academic Entrepreneurship and Economic Performance: Sweden and the United

States." In *The Wealth of Knowledge*, edited by S. Sorlin and G. Tornqvist.

Herenkson, M., and N. Rosenberg. 2001. "Designing Efficient Institutions for Science-Based Entrepreneurship: Lesson from the US and Sweden." *Journal of Technology Transfer* 26, no. 3: 207–231.

Hofer, C. W. and D. Schendel. 1978. *Strategy Formulation: Analytical Concepts.* West Publishing Co.

Ijichi, M. 2000. "Conflict of Interest in Interactions between University and Industry: An Analysis Based on Patent Data and the Management in Selected Countries." *Organizational Science* 34, no. 1: 54–75.

Itami, H. 1999. *The Management of Ba.* NTT Shuppan.

Kagono, T. 1988. *The Cognitive Theory of Organization.* Tokyo: Chikura Shobou.

Kanai, K. 1980. "The Comparative Case Study of Innovation Process in Organizations." Unpublished PhD dissertation, Kobe University, Graduate School of Business Administration.

Kanai, K. 1994. "The Mechanism for Promoting Entrepreneurship." In *Regionalization of Science and Technology Resources in the Context of Globalization*, edited by K. Gonda, F. Sakauchi, and T. Higgins. Tokyo: Industrial Research Center of Japan, 331–341.

Kanai, K., I. Asizuka, and S. Ishida. 1999. "Formation and Evolution of Venture Network in Region." The Creation of Fast Growth High-Tech Ventures: Experience in the USA, the UK and Japan Working Paper, International Conference in Osaka Chamber of Commerce and Industry, 5 August 1999.

Kanai, K., and S. Ishida. 2000. "Accumulation Process of Regional Industry and Entrepreneurship: Case Study of Sapporo Valley." Entrepreneurship on the Technology Frontier in the USA, the UK and Japan Working Paper, International Conference in Vanderbilt University, 14 October 2000.

Kanai, T. 1989. "Entrepreneurial Networking: A Comparative Analysis of Networking Organizations and Their Participants in an Entrepreneurial Community." Unpublished PhD dissertation, Sloan School of Management.

Kats, J., and Gartner, W. B. 1988. "Properties of Emerging Organizations." *Academy of Management Review* 13, no. 3: 429–441.

Kazanjian, R., and H. Rao. 1999. "Research Note: The Creation of Capabilities in New Ventures—A Longitudinal Study." *Organization Studies* 20, no. 1: 12–142.

Keeble, D. and C. Lawson (eds.) 1998. "Collective Learning Process and Knowledge Development in the Evolution of Regional Clusters of High Technology SMEs in Europe." Report on Presentations and Discussions, Goteborg Meeting of the TSER European Network, ESRC Center for Business research, University of Cambridge.

Keeble, D., C. Lawson, B. Moore, and F. Wilkinson. 1999. "Collective Learning Process, Networking and 'Institutional Stickiness' in the Cambridge Region." *Regional Studies* 33: 319–332.

Kets de Vries, M.F.R. 1977. "The Entrepreneurial Personality: A Person at the Cross-Road." *Journal of Management Studies* 14, no. 1: 34–57.

Kim, K., W. Hurh, and M. Fernandez. 1989. "Intra-Group Differences in Business Participation: Three Asian Immigrant Groups." *International Migrant Review* 23: 73–95.

Kirzner, I. 1973. *Competition and Entrepreneurship.* University of Chicago Press.

Kirzner, I. 1997. "Entrepreneurial Discovery and the Competitive Market Process: An Austrian Approach." *Journal of Economy Literature* 35, no. 1: 60–85.

Kobayashi, S. 1998. "The New Stage of Industry-University Linkage." *Higher Education Journal* 16: 107–118.

Krugman, P. 1996. *The Self-Organizing Economy.* Blackwell Publishers.

Kurogh, G. V., K. Ichijo, and I. Nonaka. 1996. *Enabling Knowledge Creation: How to Unlock the Mystery of Tacit Knowledge and Release the Power of Innovation.* Oxford University Press.

Leadbeater, C. 1997. *The Rise of the Social Entrepreneur.* Demos.

Lechler, T. 2001. "Social Interaction: A Determinant of Entrepreneurial Team Venture Success." *Small Business Economics* 16: 263–278.

Leonard-Burton, D. 1995. *Wellsprings of Knowledge: Building and Sustaining the Sources of Innovation.* Harvard Business School Press.

Lippariri, A., and M. Sobrero. 1989. "The Glue and the Pieces: Entrepreneurship and Innovation in Small-Firm Networks." *Journal of Business Venturing* 9: 125–140.

Lousbury, M., and M. A. Glyn. 2001. "Cultural Entrepreneurship: Stories, Legitimacy, and the Acquisition of Resources." *Strategic Management Journal* 22, no. 6–7: 545–564.

Low, M. B., and I. C. MacMillan. 1988. "Entrepreneurship: Past Research and Future Challenges." *Journal of Management* 14, no. 2: 139–161.

Lucio, B. 2001. "Self-Organizing Process in Building Entrepreneurial Networks: A Theoretical and Empirical Investigation." *Human Systems Management* 20, no. 3: 209–223.

Macreland, D. C. 1961. *The Achieving Society.* Van Nostrand.

Mahoney, T., and R. Pandian. 1992. "The Resource Base View within the Conversation of Strategic Management." *Strategic Management Journal* 13: 363–380.

Maillat, D. and B. Lecoq. 1992. "New Technologies and Transformation of Regional Structures in Europe: The Role of the Milieu." *Entrepreneurship and Regional Development* 4: 1–20.

Marshall, A. 1937. *Principle of Economics.* Macmillan Press.

Merton, R. 1973. *The Sociology of Science.* University of Chicago Press.

Meyer, M. W. 1975. "Organizational Domains." *American Sociological Review* 40: 599–615.

Miller, D. 1983. "The Correlates of Entrepreneurship in Three Types of Firms." *Management Science* 29, no. 7: 770–791.

Minniti, M., and W. D. Bygrave. 2001. "A Dynamic Model of Entrepreneurial Learning." *Entrepreneurship Theory and Practice* Spring: 5–16.

Morgan, K. 1997. "The Learning Region: Institutions, Innovation and Regional Renewal." *Regional Studies* 31, no. 5: 491–503.

Mowley, D. and N. Rosenverg. 1989. *Technology and the Pursuit of Economic Growth.* Cambridge: Cambridge University Press.

National Academy of Engineering. 1996. *Foreign Participation in U.S. R&D: Asset or Liability?* National Academy Press.

National Institute of Science and Technology Project Team (eds.) 1999. *Science and Technology Trend Report 2000.* Tokyo: National Institute of Science and Technology Policy.

Nonaka, I. 1998. "The Concept of 'Ba': Building a Foundation for Knowledge Creation." *California Management Review* 40, no. 3: 40–54.

Nonaka, I. and H. Takeuchi. 1995. *The Knowledge-Creating Company: How Japanese Companies Create the Dynamics of Innovation.* Oxford University Press.

Nonaka, I., R. Toyama, and A. Nagata. 2000. "A Firm as a Knowledge-Creating Entity: A New Perspective on the Theory of the Firm." *Industrial and Corporate Change* 9: 1–20.

Norris, K., and A. L. Carsarud. 1993. "Entrepreneurial Intentions: Applying the Theory of Planned Behavior." *Entrepreneurship and Regional Development* 5: 315–330.

Ostrom, E. 1965. "Public Entrepreneurship: A Case Study in Ground Water Basin Management." Unpublished Ph.D. dissertation, University of California–Los Angeles.

Pennings, J. M. 1982a. "Organizational Birth Frequencies: An Empirical Investigation." *Academy of Management Journal* 2: 63–79.

Pennings, J. M. 1982b. "Explaining Variation in Rate of Entrepreneurship in the United States 1899–1988." *Journal of Management* 27: 120–144.

Penning, J. M., K. Lee, and A. V. Witteloostuijn. 1998. "Human Capital, Social Capital, and Firm Dissolution." *Academy of Management Journal* 41, no. 4: 425–440.

Penrose, E. T. 1959. *The Theory of Growth of the Firm.* Revised ed. White Plains, NY: Sharpe.

Piore, Michael J. and Charles F. Sabel. 1984. *The Second Industrial Divide, Possibilities for Prosperity.* New York: Basic Books.

Porter, E. M. 1990. *The Competitive Advantage of Nations.* Free Press.

Porter, E. M. 1998. *On Competition.* Harvard University Press.

Porter, E. M., and S. Stern. 2001. "Innovation: Location Matters." *Sloan Management Review* 20: 28–36.

Quinn R., and K. Cameron. 1983. "Organizational Life Cycles and Shifting Criteria of Effectiveness: Some Preliminary Evidence." *Management Science* 29, no. 1: 33–51.

Relnolds, P. D. 1991. "Sociology and Entrepreneurship: Concepts and Contributions." *Entrepreneurship Theory and Practice* 16, no. 2: 47–70.

Rosenberg, N. and R. Nelson. 1994. "American Universities and Technical Advance in Industry." *Research Policy* 23: 323–348.

Rumelt, R. P. 1974. *Strategy, Structure and Economic Performance.* Cambridge, MA: Harvard Business Press.

Sakakibara, K. 1992. *The Strategy Theory of Corporate Domain.* Tokyo, Chukou Shinsho.

Sakakibara, K. 2000. "University-Industry Relationships and Knowledge Production Systems: The Case of Japan." *Organizational Science* 34, no. 1: 45–53.

Saxenian, A. 1994. *Regional Advantage.* Harvard University Press.

Scott, A. J. 1988. *Metropolis: From the Division of Labor to Urban Form.* Berkeley: University of California Press.

Scott, S. 2000. "Prior Knowledge and the Discovery of Entrepreneurial Opportunities." *Organization Science* 11, no. 4: 448–470.

Selznick, P. 1957. *Leadership in Administration.* Harper and Row.

Shane, S., and S. Venkataraman. 2000. "The Promise of Entrepreneurship as a Field of Research." *Academy of Management Review* 25, no. 1: 217–226.

Stinchcomb, A. 1965. "Social Structure and Organizations." In *Handbook of Organizations,* edited by J. G. March, 142–193. Rand-McNally.

Suzuki, S. 2001. *The Study of High-Technology Oriented Development Policy in Japan.* Minerva Shobou.

Taylor, M., and S. Singleton. 1993. "The Communal Resource Transaction Costs and the Solution of Collective Action Problems." *Politics and Society* 21, 2: 195–214.

Teramoto, Y. 1990. *Network Power.* Tokyo: NTT Press.

Thompson, James D. 1967. *Organizations in Action.* New York: McGraw-Hill.

Timmons, J. A. 1994. *New Venture Creation,* 4th edition. Richard Irwin.

Timmons, J. A., D. F. Muzyka, H. H. Stevenson, and W. D. Bygrave. 1987. "Opportunity Recognition: The Core of Entrepreneurship." *Frontiers of Entrepreneurship Research* 409–475.

Trist, E. 1983. "Referent Organizations and the Development of Inter-Organizational Domains." *Human Relations* 36, no. 3: 269–284.

Van de Ven, A. H., R. Hudson, and D. M. Schroeder. 1984. "Designing

New Business Startups: Entrepreneurial, Organizational and Ecological Considerations." *Journal of Management* 10, 1: 87–107.

Vesper, K. H. 1989. *New Venture Strategies*. Prentice Hall.

Vyakarnam, S., R. C. Jacobs, and J. Handelberg. 1997. "Formation and Development of Entrepreneurial Teams in Rapid-Growth Businesses." Paper presented at Frontiers of Entrepreneurship Conference, Babson College.

Weber, M. 1922. *Uber den Standori der Industrien*. Verlag von J.C.B. Mohr.

Weick, K. E. *Sensemaking in Organization*. Sage Publication.

Weick, K. E. *The Social Psychology of Organizing*. McGraw-Hill.

Wenerfelt, B. 1984. "A Resource Based View of the Firm." *Strategic Management Journal* 6: 171–180.

Westhead, P., and M. Wright. 1999. "Contributions of Novice, Portfolio, and Serial Founders located in Rural and Urban Areas." *Regional Studies* 33, no. 2: 157–173.

Westhead, P., and M. Wright. 1998. "Novice, Portfolio, and Serial Founder: Are They Different?". *Journal of Business Venturing* 13: 173–204.

Whatten, D. A. 1987. "Organizational Growth and Decline Process." *Annual Review of Sociology* 13: 335–358.

Yamada, J. 2000a. "Empirical Study on the Transforming Process of Corporate Domains from the Viewpoint of Knowledge Editing Management." Unpublished Ph.D. dissertation, Graduate School of Economics and Business Administration and Faculty of Economics and Business Administration, Hokkaido University.

Yamada, K. 2000b. *The Strategy and Organization of New Business Development: An Analysis of Constructing Prototype and Changing Domain*. Tokyo, Japan: Hakutou Shobou.

Yli-Renko, H., E. Autio, and H. J. Sapienza. 2001. "Social Capital, Knowledge Acquisition, and Knowledge Exploitation in Young Technology-Based Firms." *Strategic Management Journal* 22: 587–613.

CHAPTER 2

Composite Knowledge for High-Tech Corporations: Knowledge Evolution and Strategies in Research and Development

Syuichi Ishida

INTRODUCTION

This chapter has three objectives. The first is to analyze the process of knowledge evolution in the knowledge-creating activities of commercial research and development from a meso-organizational perspective. The second objective is to examine R&D in terms of knowledge evolutionary capabilities based on a specific case in which R&D organizations participating in knowledge-creating activities achieved earlier commercialization of a product than other organizations in a corresponding industry. The final objective is to examine the relationship between basic R&D strategies and the networking of knowledge creation, the core environment for R&D activities, and to gain new insight into the issues of knowledge evolution in R&D assuming that the factors that determine the direction of R&D are the collective strategies of each R&D organization.

This chapter mainly discusses R&D aimed at product innovation and knowledge creation as seen in laboratories. In the cycle of the innovation process, the fluid phase (Utterback, 1994) is addressed, while the process innovation phase is excluded from the scope of the discussion because the frequency of knowledge exchange among R&D organizations decreases during this phase, weakening the role of networking in knowledge-creating activities.

The chapter will first present an analytical framework according to each research objective after examining constitutive concepts. It will then discuss the relationship between the factors that promote knowledge evolution and R&D strategies based on case studies and patent analyses to establish theories and derive practical implications.

EXAMINATION OF CONSTITUTIVE CONCEPTS AND ANALYTICAL FRAMEWORKS

R&D Knowledge

R&D knowledge is utilized mainly for technical decision-making and is defined as the aggregation of data and information required for R&D. Most of the R&D knowledge that is examined in this chapter is shared among R&D organizations through patents, professional literatures, and mass media. Even with existing products, a considerable part of R&D knowledge is shared within the same industry through reverse engineering,[1] although there are some interpretative differences.

R&D knowledge is constantly reorganized and changed through combination with new knowledge. In general, fragments of knowledge, such as physical laws, are first formed at R&D institutions and organizations and are then associated with each other to accelerate the systematization of such knowledge leading to product commercialization. In addition, R&D knowledge is transmitted to many other R&D organizations in various forms of association. Therefore, R&D knowledge is an input as well as an output resource that is exchanged among R&D organizations.

Knowledge Networking

The concept of "networking" is clearly distinguished from "a network" in this chapter. Most past studies (Burt and Minor, 1983; Birley, 1985; Teramoto and Kanda, 1984; Beckmann, 1993) regard networks as a mere linkage of organizations and focus on their structure. Networking, in contrast, is an effort to purposefully utilize a network and is recognized as a subjective connection of willed individuals or organizations with certain purposes (Lipnack and Stamps, 1982). Therefore, the networking of knowledge-creating activities in R&D examined in this study not only involves linkages of R&D organizations through R&D knowledge but also includes efforts to transmit and receive useful R&D knowledge.

How can the networking of knowledge-creating activities in R&D, or knowledge-based networking, be defined? The knowledge-based networking assumed in this study is a connection of R&D organizations and is also a scientific paradigm where various kinds of knowledge and worldviews are shared through R&D activities.

The scientific paradigm suggested by Kuhn (1962) and Price (1965) is equivalent to a framework of thinking, a worldview, or a research model. Based on this scientific paradigm, scientists exchange R&D knowledge with each other, promoting isomorphism of thought and worldviews. Dosi (1982) suggested that the concept of "technological paradigm" refers to a model or pattern for a solution to technological problems that is based on specific principles derived from natural scientific views of the world. The subjects who act according to this technological paradigm include not only scientists but also all members who participate in technological problem solving, including engineers of production technology and sales engineers.

Although these scientific and technological paradigms are useful concepts for discussing the macroscopic progress of technology, they have limitations in explaining innovation induced by R&D organizations that intentionally transmit or receive R&D knowledge. In this chapter, the new concept of "knowledge networking" is proposed where worldviews, models, and patterns of problem solving are shared and R&D knowledge is transmitted and received within the networking of knowledge-creating R&D organizations.

The transmission and receipt of R&D knowledge among organizations participating in networking are rarely obvious. In most cases, R&D knowledge is shared widely through professional literatures or patents, so neither the transmitter nor the receiver are aware of such sharing. This networking covers not only particular industries in specific fields of R&D but also related universities and research institutes including public laboratories and science journalists.

Characterized by its loosely connected system (Weick, 1976), knowledge networking is a self-organized network organization (Teramoto, 1990). Unlike mere aggregations, it can also be defined as the entire transmitting and receiving system by which R&D knowledge is exchanged in a loosely connected association of high mobility of information across boundaries. More specifically, knowledge networking is the entire system of transmitting and receiving R&D knowledge through all media and institutions such as academic circles, patents, mass media, collaborations, informal exchanges of information among researchers, and products.

Knowledge Evolutionary Capability

Since the mid-1980s, the concept of organizational capabilities has been attracting considerable attention among researchers who developed resource-based management strategies (Wernerfelt, 1984; Barney, 1986; Prahalad and Hamel, 1990; Grant, 1991). Because the traditional methods of examining strategy planning (Hofer and Schendel, 1978; Miles and Snow, 1978) and competitive strategies (Porter, 1980) do not adequately discuss the organizations that actually develop strategies, the concept of organizational capabilities has recently gained influence.

Organizational capabilities can be discussed in terms of the inability to imitate, learning characteristics, and sustainable competitive advantage.[2] Takahiro Fujimoto (1999), in his study on the evolution of production systems focused on original resources and abilities of a firm and expressed organizational capabilities as corporate competitiveness that is the source of corporate power. He then included evolutionary capability[3] in his analysis of competitiveness. Evolutionary capability creates routines required for corporate activities and builds new abilities. Kogut and Zander (1992) discussed the ability necessary for utilizing the knowledge accumulated inside an organization. However, most of these studies merely discuss knowledge management, using the organization as the analytical unit, and do not consider the ability built through relationships with external organizations and the roles of R&D organizations and individual researchers.

In light of these discussions on organizational capabilities, this chapter defines knowledge evolutionary capability as the ability to evolve R&D knowledge into new knowledge through the networking of R&D organizations. This knowledge evolutionary capability is also regarded as a nonroutine, advanced-learning process by which new knowledge is created.

R&D Themes

Based on various R&D cases,[4] this chapter focuses on R&D themes that are addressed not by a single R&D organization, but are widely shared through knowledge networking. R&D themes are also regarded as the most powerful driving force behind the evolution of R&D knowledge.

The driving force behind the evolution of R&D knowledge has been discussed generally by contrasting demand pull and technology push (Myers and Marquis, 1969; Belassa and Nelson, 1977; Mowery and Rosenberg, 1979; Pavit and Soete, 1980). The process by which R&D knowledge is converted to know-how or tacit knowledge (Nonaka and Takeuchi, 1995) is well understood. However, as pointed out by Rosenberg (1976), it is also important to note that know-how and tacit knowledge also help find various problems and issues that need to be examined thus conversely contributing to the evolution of R&D knowledge.

R&D themes, in some cases, present existing problems or issues. In other cases, they indicate problems or issues based on know-how and tacit knowledge associated with products and services. Therefore, R&D themes can be defined as research objectives that address predominating problems or issues shared by the entire knowledge networking.

R&D Strategies

This study will clarify the relationship between R&D strategies and knowledge networking in order to derive some practical implications for R&D management.

Numerous R&D organizations are thought to be taking advantage of knowledge networking for specific R&D themes. Because the domain of R&D activities differs between R&D organizations, each organization is assumed to have its own R&D strategies.

However, in actuality, mainstream strategies or so-called "dominant designs" (Abernathy and Utterback, 1978) exist in particular industries or businesses where various R&D strategies are intermingled. In order to understand this phenomenon, it is necessary to clarify the relationship between the strategies of each R&D organization and the evolution of knowledge in the exiting networking of organizations.

Consequently, the purpose of examining R&D strategies in this study is to identify not only the environmental factors of knowledge evolution in knowledge networking but also the subjective factors of the R&D organizations participating in the networking. Once such subjective factors of R&D organizations are clarified, implications for effective implementation of strategies based on the knowledge evolutionary capability of each organization in the knowledge networking can be derived.

Analytical Perspective of the Knowledge Evolution Process

Recently, the evolutionary perspective of the innovation process has become popular among researchers who discuss innovation in terms of strategic organizational innovation (Tushman and Romanelli, 1985; Fujimoto, 1999). The characteristics of this evolutionary approach to R&D and technological innovation differ from those of the conventional dynamics model of innovation (Abernathy and Utterback, 1978; Utterback, 1994) in the following respects.

First, the conventional dynamics model of innovation focuses on one technology or product that has gone through a single process, while the evolutionary perspective also considers innovation streams (Tushman and O'Reilly III, 1997) in more than two heterogeneous innovations and covers various innovations within a firm, including all trial and error involved in peripheral technologies and products. It also attempts to identify the processes of variation, selection, and retention of technology and products. Knowledge evolution in knowledge networking is then examined on the basis of the following assumptions.

The traditional evolutionary model always involves explanatory logic of variation, selection, and retention. Knowledge evolution in knowledge networking is assumed to go through the process shown in Figure 2.1. In this figure, (1) indicates the process by which specific knowledge is selected from some variations,[5] while (2) shows the process by which R&D organizations acquire and accumulate R&D knowledge through knowledge networking. The accumulated R&D knowledge is then learned by the members of the R&D organization who in turn create new R&D knowledge through higher order learning processes.[6] (3) shows the process by which new variations are created on the basis of accumulated knowledge.

The knowledge evolutionary capability of an R&D organization is analyzed with the following assumptions. First, each R&D organization promotes knowledge evolution on the basis of its own strategies and learning systems while knowledge evolution in knowledge networking proceeds on the basis of a different set of logic. Each organization evolves its knowledge by transmitting and receiving R&D knowledge to and from other R&D organizations within the network.

In the case study outlined in this chapter, knowledge evolution in both the knowledge networking of the target industry and an R&D organization (Sony in this study) participating in the network will be examined. Examination of knowledge evolution in knowledge networking is, in other words, a macroscopic analysis.

R&D organizations participating in knowledge networking reciprocally transmit and receive R&D knowledge and are assumed to have their own evolution processes. Because analyzing knowledge evolution in each R&D organization means to view the networking microscopically, it is called a "micro process."

RESEARCH METHODS AND SUBJECTS

As for the research method, an actual case of R&D will be examined using the aforementioned constitutive concepts and analytical frameworks. The case adopted for the study is based on comprehensive materials composed of interviews (oral and by e-mail) with researchers, production engineers, planners and sales representatives, professional literature, mass media information, and Internet information.

Figure 2.1
Analytical Framework of Knowledge Evolution

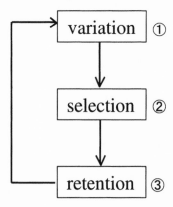

Figure 2.2
Knowledge Networking of R&D Organizations

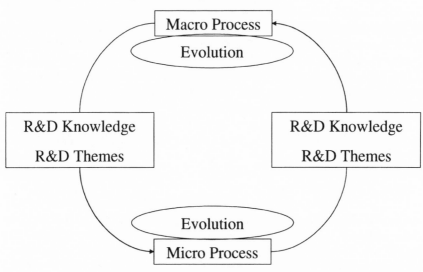

This study also adopts a single-case method that focuses on a particular field of technology. Because the case study contains information on more than two R&D organizations, it can also be regarded as an embedded-type case study (Yin, 1984). Case studies are often criticized in terms of such criteria as (1) internal validity (model validity), (2) validity of constitutive concepts (consistency of concepts with data), (3) reliability and repeatability of test results (repeated observations), and (4) external validity (utilization of other samples). Internal validity can be achieved by presenting adequate descriptions of the case and eliminating variations in perspectives as counter hypotheses. Validity of constitutive concepts can be achieved by employing various heterogeneous data. In this chapter, the case is analyzed in light of these criteria. According to Numagami (2000), although any study in the field of natural science must be evaluated in terms of reliability and repeatability of test results and external validity, meeting these criteria is not required for social science, because it is difficult to make valid judgments based on these criteria unless an immutable law is proved to be dominant. Therefore, this chapter discusses the case in light of only the validity of the internal model and the constitutive concepts.

This chapter adopts the R&D case of lithium ion batteries as a research subject. In this field, there is intense competition between major products and the evolution of R&D knowledge is accelerating with continual innovation. With the use of lithium ion batteries becoming widespread, the battery industry has grown to become the third largest key device industry in Japan next to the semiconductor and liquid crystal industries. Under such circumstances, R&D is being promoted on a large scale in response to rising demand for high-performance and low-cost among equipment manufacturers. In addition, it is anticipated that a wealth of materials will be developed further for lithium ion batteries (such as for their electrodes). Thus, R&D of lithium ion batteries, which utilizes a wide range of knowledge, is an ideal research subject for examining the evolutionary phenomenon of R&D knowledge.

CASE STUDY OF THE KNOWLEDGE EVOLUTION PROCESS

Macro Process

Since lithium ion batteries were first developed at U.S. research institutions (mainly at universities) in the years before 1970, various private organizations have conducted R&D on these batteries. Figure 2.3 summarizes the evolution process of R&D knowledge according to various themes that have emerged over time. The following is a prehistory of battery R&D.

Supported by electrochemical theories, lithium has long been regarded as the ultimate material for batteries and trial production of lithium batteries has been conducted repeatedly at the laboratory level since the late 1950s. Originally, Harris and Kratochvil (1974) wrote a paper on organic electrolytes, which drew the attention of researchers. Based on this paper, R&D for practical application of the battery was started by NASA.

In the 1970s, development of secondary batteries,[7] such as Ni-Cd batteries, was promoted in the battery and consumer electronics industries. In Japan, following this trend, Sanyo Electric and Matsushita Battery took the lead in developing lithium-based secondary batteries, creating a great deal of knowledge in material technology. During this period, numerous research projects on metal lithium and lithium alloy were conducted and many R&D organizations adopted experimental systems. Although Steel and Armand (Gool, 1972) proposed the idea of a "rocking chair,"[8] which utilizes lithium in ions, no R&D organization adopted this approach at that time.

In the 1980s, R&D for lithium-based secondary batteries was further accelerated by rising market demand for high-capacity batteries and the accumulation of related technologies. Many companies, including newcomers such as Sony, began R&D to create a battery system that would determine basic structure. Among these, Asahi Chemical Industry got a head start. In 1987, the company posted on the open patent bulletin[9] its battery system that employed negative electrode carbons, $LiCoO_2$ positive electrodes, and organic electrolytes. The system is now widely used for lithium ion batteries.

Sony also adopted the system and succeeded in applying it to actual products in 1990. It is important to note that the information Asahi Chemical Industry posted on the open patent bulletin was received by many other R&D organizations including Sony and served as key R&D knowledge. Besides, the materials used for the negative and positive electrodes, as well as for the electrolytes, described on the bulletin had potential for variations. For example, when Sony was pursuing commercialization of the battery, three kinds of material were available for the negative electrode: hard carbon, soft carbon, and graphite. The company ultimately chose hard carbon and commercialized the battery.

As shown in Figure 2.3, various dominant R&D themes arose at each stage of knowledge evolution, resulting in a large variety of R&D knowledge. Some of the variations were dismissed while others were retained.

Micro Process

The next issue is how each R&D organization participating in the knowledge networking improves its R&D performance. In this section, the micro process, which is the internal process of knowledge evolution in each R&D organization, will be examined.

Figure 2.3
Knowledge Evolution Process: Macro Process

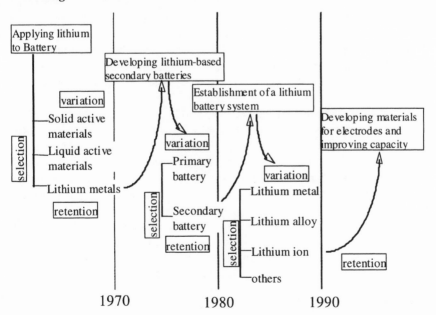

Figure 2.4
Typical Case of Micro Process

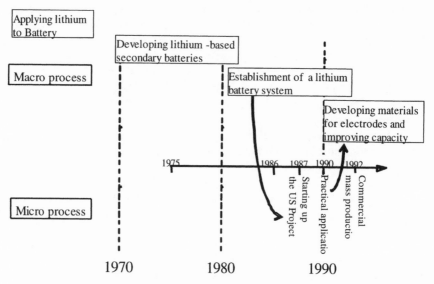

Figure 2.4 shows the knowledge evolution process of Sony's R&D, which led to the first successful practical application of lithium ion batteries. It was at the stage of "Establishment of a lithium battery system" as shown in Figure 2.3, that Sony actually started R&D on the battery. At this stage, the company pursued practical application of the battery by forming a top management-led project called the U.S. project.

Figure 2.5 shows the details of the U.S. project. The project, based on the theme of "Establishment of a lithium battery system," first selected six variations out of the many that were discussed in the knowledge networking. Among these were metal lithium and lithium alloy, which were initially adopted by Matsushita Battery and Sanyo Electric and the lithium ion battery system proposed by Asahi Chemical Industry. Sony named these US11–US61 and promoted their R&D in parallel by organizing a project team for each. The company gave a high degree of discretion to each team to encourage autonomous operation and systematic selection of R&D knowledge (high degree of discretion and organizational autonomy).

Although US41 and US61 were ultimately retained after the selection process, there were no decisive criteria to adopt one from the other, because both had certain advantages that were too important to dismiss. US41 used metal lithium and theoretically had high capacity. US61, on the other hand, was a rocking chair type that used oxide lithium and had the best stability, although its capacity was lower than that of US41. Therefore,

Figure 2.5
Knowledge Evolution Process: Micro Process

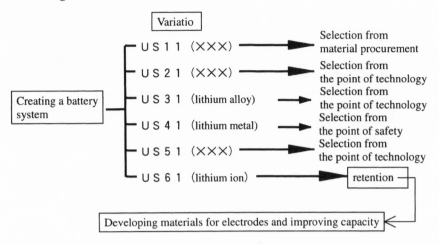

it was extremely difficult to select one from the other (future course of technology development).

Meanwhile, a different manufacturer ventured to put a US41-type battery on the market for the first time. However, the battery caused a serious accident resulting in personal injury. Those involved in the industry including the R&D staff at Sony were shocked because they had had no doubt about the feasibility of its commercialization. This accident, coupled with public concerns, forced researchers to abandon R&D on the US41 (social systems) battery.

Therefore, during this period, much of the R&D knowledge creation completely shifted to oxide lithium (clarification of selection criteria).

Sony, thus, shifted its R&D focus to the US61 battery, which was expected to be used with combination cameras. During this period, therefore, R&D was not only affected by scientific arguments but was also promoted by practical application to products from which new selection criteria were created. At this stage of R&D, which stressed practical application to products, various selection criteria were created including strict safety standards, short-circuit prevention standards, and electric charging and discharging standards. Based on these, the company accumulated a great deal of know-how related to electric charging and discharging with such technological achievements as the invention of electronic safety devices, improvement of the separator for short-circuit prevention, and embedding of PTC elements. Such R&D knowledge was subsequently shared with other R&D organizations within the same knowledge networking through patents, professional literature, and scientific journals. Again, this shared knowledge helped create new R&D themes.

Although Sony was a newcomer in the battery industry, it succeeded in obtaining new R&D knowledge through the US project. The company transmitted this R&D knowledge throughout the organization to establish a learning process of a higher order for new capabilities (deep understanding of R&D knowledge).

While R&D knowledge scattered over a networking is considered to be explicit knowledge, it may be viewed as tacit knowledge in the context of products. In this respect, the US project served as an integrator of such scattered knowledge to promote explicit knowledge (promotion of explicit knowledge).

Through this process, R&D knowledge was accumulated at each R&D organization leading to the retention of the revolutionary framework. This series of processes helped Sony not only to quicken the commercialization of lithium ion batteries but also to promote the evolution of R&D knowledge within the knowledge networking.

Since the US project, Sony has been addressing new technological issues concerned with improving the quality and capacity of electrode materials, while grasping the future course of R&D in the networking (early setting of technological themes).

In summary, each R&D organization in the micro process receives R&D knowledge scattered over knowledge networking and internally establishes R&D themes based on these. The receiver then utilizes the knowledge to create new R&D knowledge and transmits this back to the networking.

FACTORS THAT PROMOTE KNOWLEDGE EVOLUTION AND THEIR IMPLICATIONS

The foregoing analyses show that that R&D knowledge evolves according to R&D themes that vary over the course of time in knowledge networking. This section assumes that adding "creation of new themes" to the traditional knowledge evolution process shown in Figure 2.1 may further promote knowledge evolution.

The themes thus created also evolve in the sequence of R&D. Figure 2.6 illustrates this evolution of R&D themes in the case of lithium batteries. As shown in the figure, there is a significant correlation between the evolution of R&D themes and the transition of knowledge networking, which clearly shows that the evolution of R&D themes helps create new lifecycles of evolution.

In addition, the result of the case study identifies several important aspects at each stage of the knowledge evolution as shown in Figure 2.7. These aspects not only make the process of knowledge evolution more

Figure 2.6
Evolution of R&D Themes

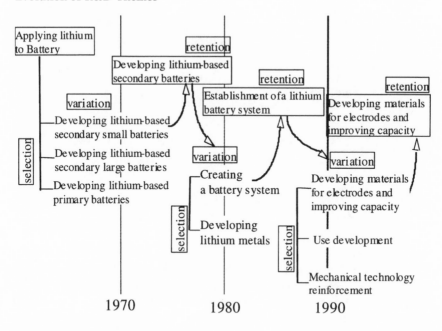

efficient but also contribute to the creation of new knowledge for continual innovation.

R&D STRATEGIES AND KNOWLEDGE NETWORKING

This section examines the relationship between the R&D strategies of each R&D organization and knowledge networking.

One of the main issues of R&D activities today is how each organization promotes R&D within its relationships with other organizations. For example, the recent phenomenon of increasing mergers and R&D consortiums shows that organizations are trying to reduce R&D costs.

Mowery and Teece (1996) argue that proper management and costs are indispensable to information transfer and utilization for R&D, while some researchers insist that the costs related to information transfer are virtually none (Teece, 1987; Mowery, 1983; Mowery and Rosenberg, 1989; Cohen and Levinthal, 1990). However, the interpretation of information differs between the former and latter groups. The information referred to by the former group is highly mature and utilized in specific technology. In order to transfer such information among organizations it must be shared in the form of tacit knowledge, as pointed out by Nonaka and Takeuchi (1995).

Figure 2.7
Ideal Management to Promote Knowledge Evolution

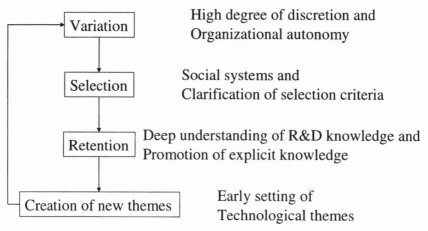

The latter, on the other hand, limits information to explicit knowledge that can be shared extensively among organizations. In this case, the internal accumulation of transferred information largely depends on each organization's interpretive framework.

This chapter's stance is positioned between these opinions; R&D knowledge assumed are data and information that basically require no transfer costs but need proper management for utilization. Indeed, interviews with on-site R&D engineers showed that they received R&D knowledge through professional literature and patent information at low costs and that each R&D organization's originality is reflected in their utilization. Thus, explicit knowledge utilized in specific fields of R&D will be turned into tacit knowledge once it is applied to products or production. This chapter refers to the knowledge required for application to products and production as "knowledge parts."

The position of this chapter can be distinguished from the viewpoints of traditional technology-based innovation studies as follows. First, classical innovation models (Abernathy and Utterback, 1978; Mansfield, 1988; Kline and Rosenberg, 1986) assume that products and production are based on the achievements of basic research. In addition, according to the fundamental proposition of March and Simon (1958) on organizational quality, the organizations that undertake innovation and routine operation must be differentiated from each other in order to promote innovation. Today, most studies on technical economies and R&D management accept these basic assumptions.

Also, many classical studies focus on the self-complete process of R&D in a single firm. In the analyses of such processes, a sequential model of basic research → application → products, where each phase corresponds to an organization, is often proposed. This suggests that R&D strategies are also based on such a model. This model is applicable to self-contained R&D for products whose technology is relatively constant. However, in light of today's R&D environment, the innovation process must be considered in relation to external organizations (March and Simon, 1958; Cohen and Levinthal, 1990) and new innovation models and model-based R&D strategies need to be developed.

Sakakibara (1993a,b) and Dumas and Watanabe (1993), in their comparative studies of R&D in Japan and the Unite States, found that frequent exchanges between R&D organizations accelerate isomorphism. In this context, isomorphism can be considered equal to the homogenization of human resources, values, and behavioral patterns. In addition, the framework of thinking of researchers may also be homogenized. The concept of isomorphism has been developed mainly by DiMaggio and Powell (1983) and Meyer and Scott (1983) as an institutionalized perspective of interorganizational relations. The institutionalized perspective places emphasis on interorganizational culture and values to explain justification of relations and the resulting isomorphism. Although isomorphism of knowledge has not been discussed in past studies, it is clear that such isomorphism will decrease the originality of each R&D organization, resulting in the homogenization of R&D knowledge.

In light of the above issues, the relationship between R&D strategies and knowledge networking will be examined in the next section based on case and quantitative studies.

CONCEPTUAL FRAMEWORKS FOR UNDERSTANDING R&D STRATEGIES AND KNOWLEDGE NETWORKING

In order to discuss R&D strategies, the three basic competitive strategies suggested by Porter (1980) are employed in this study. These are cost leadership, differentiation, and concentration. First, the concept of cost leadership is less effective in discussing laboratory-level R&D because scientific logic sometimes prevails over business logic in such activities. Therefore, in order to enhance the effectiveness of R&D strategies based purely on business logic, it is more appropriate to focus on the concepts of differentiation and concentration. In this chapter, expanding to other segments, which corresponds to differentiation, is called "diversification" and is defined as the attempt to expand one's area of research and product range. On the other hand, narrowing the range of segments, which corresponds to concentration, is called "focusing," and is defined as the attempt to confine one's efforts to specific areas of research and product ranges.

In discussing company-level R&D beyond the laboratory, R&D activities for marketing products (application) must be distinguished from purely academic activities (theorization). The process by which theorization provides the foundation for know-how and tacit knowledge of products and services (Nonaka and Takeuchi, 1995) can be understood by the sequential model of R&D. Likewise, it is important to note that, as pointed out by Rosenberg (1976), application helps identify problems and issues that need to be examined and greatly contributes to the evolution of R&D knowledge. The driving force behind the evolution of R&D knowledge has been discussed in terms of the two extreme ideas of demand-pull and technology-push, which have also helped to clarify the concepts of theorization and application.

Theorization here means building models to understand each phenomenon based on cause-and-effect relationships. In most cases, such models are not built by a single R&D organization but by coordination among R&D organizations through the networking assumed in this study. In light of specific phenomena, theorization can be understood to be activities such as producing professional literature and promoting patent applications. This paper thus considers that interactions between theorization and application are the essence of R&D strategies.

ANALYTICAL METHODS

This section first examines several cases of R&D in the lithium ion battery industry over the past ten years and then analyzes related patents to complement the case studies.

The several cases during the 10-year period from 1988 to 1998 that are addressed in this study are examined according to the revolutionary perspective shown in Figure 2.1. The reason for limiting the study to this period is that there are few patents from the early 1980s because of the greater emphasis placed on academic research during this period when each firm started full-scale R&D on such batteries.

In order to examine the cases from multiple viewpoints, the effectiveness of R&D strategies in knowledge networking and the actual R&D strategies implemented by each organization were analyzed on the basis of the conceptual framework shown in Figure 2.8, where the evolution of R&D knowledge and knowledge networking influence each other.

Case Studies on R&D

The R&D strategies of Sony that contributed to establishing the de facto standard for lithium ion batteries greatly influenced knowledge networking during the early stage of battery development. After commercializing the battery, the company set four important goals to further promote R&D:

Figure 2.8
Conceptual Framework for Research

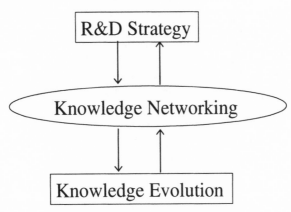

development of electrodes, improvement of safety, improvement of capacity, and improvement of durability. Among these, the company's sensitivity to safety and commitment to negative electrodes were particularly strong.

Sanyo's approach to the battery was utterly different from that of Sony. The company's material technology for positive electrodes was more advanced (theorization). As seen in its professional literature, the company was actively working on next-generation materials for positive electrodes when Sony started full-scale marketing of the battery in 1992 (theorization). In addition, Sanyo exclusively employed graphite for negative electrodes, which had gained more academic support (focusing). At this time, the crystallinity of graphite was higher than that of the non-graphitizable carbon materials adopted by Sony and many researchers advocated the use of graphite. Sony decided that it would be difficult to control graphite up to the stage of practical application because of the difficulty involved in selecting a suitable electrolyte for graphite electrodes. For that reason, the company adopted easy-to-control non-graphitizable carbon and succeeded in achieving earlier practical application of lithium ion batteries (application). Thus, Sanyo's decision to select the negative-electrode material was made in spite of the more advanced technology of the positive-electrode material, which ultimately delayed marketing of its battery until 1993. Although such material selection strategies were based on academic theories and did not assume commercialization and mass production, they served as the driving force behind the subsequent competition from Sanyo to increase capacity.

On the other hand, the R&D strategies of Matsushita Battery show no remarkable characteristics. However, the company's area of research was the broadest in the industry (diversification). Judging from its professional literature and patents, although the company has the ability to apply its technology, it always follows the strategies of other companies in introducing new products and technologies.

In AT Battery, a joint venture between Toshiba and Asahi Chemical Industry with jointly managed production plants, the technology of negative-electrode materials was more advanced because Asahi Chemical Industry had sophisticated technology related to carbon materials. In the early 1990s, it became well known in the knowledge networking that AT's carbon materials effectively improved safety and companies competed to evaluate the materials. Backed by such material technology, AT Battery, without having a firm grasp of mechanical safety and electronic control, became the second company in the industry to start mass producing the lithium battery. Even after mass production began, the company kept its faith in its materials and promoted R&D that focused on material technology. Asahi Chemical Industry also owns nine important patents, which are considered to be the basic patents for lithium ion batteries, an issue that has emerged recently. Thus, attaching importance to patent strategies is another characteristic of AT's R&D strategies. The joint venture between Asahi Chemical Industry and Toshiba can be regarded as a strategic partnership to focus on the production and sales of lithium ion batteries (focusing). Asahi Chemical Industry is a manufacturer of materials and chemical products and had no product lines on which to mount batteries. Toshiba, on the other hand, was lagging in R&D for lithium ion batteries. Therefore, the two companies promoted knowledge evolution by adopting strategies that would systematically combine mass production and R&D while utilizing each other's merits.

Finally, Japan Storage Battery, one of the oldest companies in the battery industry, established a joint venture called in 1997 GS-Melco-Tech with Mitsubishi Electric. Like AT Battery, GS-Melco-Tech focused on production and sales of batteries although it was established five years later. In 1993, Japan Storage Battery succeeded in commercializing lithium ion batteries and became the third company in the industry. As seen from its professional literature and patents, the company's battery producing technology was never inferior to that of other companies. However, because Japan Storage Battery specialized in battery production and had no product lines on which to mount batteries internally or within its group, it was virtually impossible for the company to conduct application R&D for the battery as Sony did.

Patent Analysis

Based on the above cases, the number of patent applications related to the important fields of technology of capacity, safety, negative electrodes, positive electrodes, and cycle property by the five major companies in the lithium ion battery industry over the past ten years was counted sequentially. A correlation analysis between these fields, which were the five parameters that Sony's R&D strategies focused on, was then conducted. In this sense, the main purpose of this analysis is to identify differences in R&D strategies between Sony and the other companies. This section does not aim to identify causal relationships between patent fields but attempts to analyze the R&D strategies of major industry players based on these.

Figure 2.9 compares the correlation coefficients between the five fields based on the number of patent applications by the five companies. These figures were derived from calculating the correlation coefficients between the fields after counting the number of patent applications from 1988 to 1998 by company and field.

For most companies, high correlations are observed between capacity

Figure 2.9
Correlation Coefficients among the Five Fields

Matsushita (N=1593)

	Capa	Posi	Nega	Safety	Cycle	Total
Capacity		0.802**	0.811**	0.770**	0.280	0.852**
Positive			0.958**	0.770**	0.609*	0.990**
Negative				0.683*	0.589	0.973**
Safety					0.097	0.771**
Cyclic						0.616*
Total						

SONY (N=1024)

	Capa	Posi	Nega	Safety	Cycle	Total
Capacity		0.963**	0.965**	0.830**	0.847**	0.963**
Positive			0.999**	0.877**	0.937**	0.997**
Negative				0.887**	0.934**	0.998**
Safety					0.867**	0.902**
Cyclic						0.948**
Total						

** p<0.01
* p<0.05

SANYO (N=854)

	Capa	Posi	Nega	Safety	Cycle	Total
Capacity		0.594	0.650*	0.278	0.505	0.722*
Positive			0.859**	0.485	0.706*	0.926**
Negative				0.788**	0.668*	0.967**
Safety					0.317	0.664*
Cyclic						0.791**
Total						

AT Battery (N=675)

	Capa	Posi	Nega	Safety	Cycle	Total
Capacity		0.970**	0.898**	0.475*	0.813**	0.935**
Positive			0.971**	0.583	0.806**	0.977**
Negative				0.623*	0.780**	0.965**
Safety					0.569	0.722*
Cyclic						0.864**
Total						

** p<0.01
* p<0.05

GS Battery (N=374)

	Capa	Posi	Nega	Safety	Cycle	Total
Capacity		0.960**	0.921**	0.608*	0.571	0.913**
Positive			0.977**	0.695*	0.563	0.963**
Negative				0.724*	0.503	0.961**
Safety					0.347	0.844**
Cyclic						0.608*
Total						

** p<0.01
* p<0.05

1. Capacity
2. Positive Electrode
3. Negative Electrode
4. Safety
5. Cycle Property
6. Total of each element

and the other fields with a significance level of less than 5 percent. This may be because the technology of improving capacity scientifically depended on the technology of negative electrodes, and each company realistically had to address this issue. However, Sanyo Electric shows a different pattern from the other companies with only a slight correlation observed between negative electrodes and capacity. As mentioned previously, Sanyo had more advanced technology in the field of positive electrodes and focused on applying its leading-edge materials to positive electrodes. Therefore, there is a strong correlation between material technology for positive electrodes and related factors of material science (theorization).

Sony and AT Battery show high correlations between cycle property and the other fields with a significance level of less than 1 percent. Sanyo exhibited correlations in some fields with a significance level of less than 5 percent. Cycle property is an important field of technology because it serves as a measure for estimating the durability of a battery after repeated charging and discharging. Therefore, promoting R&D by effectively linking the technology of cycle property to capacity and electrodes was the key to commercialization (application). The reason Sony and AT show high correlations between cycle property and the other fields is because they succeeded in earlier commercialization and mass production of the battery and already had R&D systems based on existing products (focusing).

Matsushita Battery, on the other hand, adopted strategies that focused on basic research of lithium ion batteries and has made major academic achievements since then (theorization). In addition to lithium ion batteries, the company has such competing product lines as nickel cadmium batteries and nickel hydride batteries (diversification). Because such an approach does not confine R&D efforts to lithium ion batteries, stagnation of each R&D may be induced.

CONCLUSION

Based on actual case studies of R&D for lithium ion batteries, the relationship between knowledge evolution and R&D strategies was examined. The result shows that the process of application, which leads to early commercialization and mass-production, was an important factor in promoting knowledge evolution. It also suggests that business conditions such as market logic and constraints of management resources are selection criteria in knowledge evolution and that it is important for each company to internally accumulate knowledge created at the stage of commercialization or mass production at a basic level. In addition, R&D knowledge at a practical level can build some sort of entry barrier to R&D in the industry. Such knowledge is also considered to have a great impact on further creation of practical knowledge as seen in the improvement of cycle property technology.

From the start, Sony targeted products on which to mount batteries while AT adopted R&D strategies aimed at mass production (focusing). Only these two companies succeeded in taking the leadership in battery technology by enhancing capacity and convenience of products at an early stage. However, as R&D matured, Sanyo and Matsushita adopted strategies to expand the area of research as well as range of product applications (diversification) and are now gradually taking the leadership in the industry.

In summary, by utilizing knowledge networking strategically, it is possible for each R&D organization to accumulate its own R&D knowledge and form invisible entry barriers of knowledge. Furthermore, the degree of connection between theorization and application in R&D, together with either the focusing or diversifying of research area, may determine the originality of the R&D knowledge to be accumulated and must be carefully considered in implementing R&D strategies.

The following two major hypotheses are derived from this study.

1. The degree of connection between theorization and application in R&D may determine the originality of the R&D knowledge to be accumulated.
2. The concepts of focusing and diversification may help provide a systematic understanding of networking and strategies in R&D.

ACKNOWLEDGMENT

First, I would like to congratulate professor Yoshiya Teramoto on his sixtieth birthday. He provided useful guidance on forming the main concept of this study. This study was supported with the Japanese Ministry of Education and Science's Grant-In-Aid for Scientific Research, Encouragement of Young Scientists Type-A, No. 13730092. I would like to sincerely thank professor Teramoto and all those who provided assistance. Finally, I would like to appreciate Mrs. Hiroko Takeuchi for the end of this chapter.

NOTES

1. This means to evaluate a product by disassembling and analyzing it.
2. According to the classification of Grant (1991) and Barney (2001).
3. Fujimoto (1999) expressed evolutionary capability as "ability building capability."
4. Refer to Hughes (1983), David (1985), and Weinberg, et al. (1994).
5. For this process, this chapter does not assume survival of the fittest as outlined by traditional evolutionary theory.
6. Double loop learning (Argyris and Schon, 1978) is assumed.

7. A secondary battery is equivalent to a rechargeable battery.

8. The innovative idea of achieving battery reactions by the movement of ions without using a lithium alloy.

9. Because the details of any invention are first posted on the open patent bulletin before patent rights are enforced in Japan, the bulletin is an effective means of evaluating the technology levels of other R&D organizations.

REFERENCES

Abernathy, William J. and James M. Utterback (1978). Patterns of Industrial Innovation, *Technology Review*, 80 (7), pp. 40–47.

Argyris, Chris and Donald A. Schon (1978). *Organizational Learning*, Addison-Wesley.

Barney, Jay B. (1986). Strategic Factor Market, *Management Science*, 32 (10), pp. 1231–1241.

Barney, Jay B. (2001). *Gaining and Sustaining Competitive Advantage, 2nd ed.*, Prentice-Hall.

Beckmann, Martin J. (1993). Knowledge Networks, *The Annals of Regional Science*, 27, pp. 5–10.

Belassa, Bela and Richard R. Nelson, eds. (1977). *Economic Progress, Private Values, and Public Policy: Essays in Honor of William Fellner*, Elsevier North Holland.

Birley, Sue (1985). The Role of Networks in the Entrepreneurial Process, *Journal of Business Venturing*, 1, pp. 107–117.

Burt, Ronald S. and M. Michael J. Minor, eds. (1983). *Applied Network Analysis*, Sage.

Cohen, Wesley M. and Daniel A. Levinthal (1990). Absorptive Capacity: A New Perspective on Learning and Innovation, *Administrative Science Quarterly*, 35, pp. 128–152.

David, Paul A. (1985). Clio and the Economics of QWERTY, *American Economic Review*, 75, pp. 332–337.

DiMaggio, Paul J. and Walter W. Powell (1983). The Iron Cage Revisited: Institutional Isomorphism and Collective Rationality in Organizational Fields, *American Sociological Review*, 48, pp. 147–160.

Dosi, Giovanni (1982) Technological Paradigms and Technological Trajectories, *Research Policy*, 11, pp. 147–162.

Fujimoto, Takahiro (1999). *Evolution of a Manufacturing Systems at Toyota*, Oxford University Press.

Gool, W. van, ed. (1972). *Fast Ion Transport in Solids: Solid State Batteries and Devices: Proceedings of the NATO Sponsored Advanced Study Institute on Fast Ion Transport in Solids, Solid State Batteries and Devices, Belgirate, Italy, 5–15 September*, American Elsevier.

Grant, Robert M. (1991). The Resource-Based Theory of Competitive Advantage, *California Management Review*, 33 (3), pp. 114–135.

Harris, Walter E. and Byron Kratochvil (1974). *Chemical Separations and Measurements: Background and Procedures for Modern Analysis*, Saunders.

Hofer, Charles and Dan Schendel (1978). *Strategy Formulation: Analytical Concepts*, West Publishing.

Hughes, Thomas P. (1983). *Networks of Power: Electrification in Western Society, 1880–1930*, John Hopkins University Press.

Kline, Stephen J. and Nathan Rosenberg (1986). "An Overview of Innovation." In Ralph Landau and Nathan Rosenberg eds., *The Positive Sum Strategy*, National Academy Press.

Kogut, Bruce and Udo Zander (1992), Knowledge of the Firm, Combinative Capabilities, and the Replication of Technology, *Organization Science*, 3, pp. 383–397.

Kuhn, Thomas (1962). *The Structure of Scientific Revolutions*, The University of Chicago Press.

Lipnack, Jessica and Jeffrey Stamps (1982). *Networking*, Run Bernstein Agency Inc.

Mansfield, Edwin (1988). "Industrial R&D in Japan the United States: A Competitive Study," *American Economic Review*, 78 (2), pp. 223–228.

March, James G. and Herbert A. Simon (1958). *Organizations*, John Wiley & Sons.

Meyer, John W. and W. Richard Scott (1983). "Centralization and the Legitimacy Problems of Local Government." In John W. Meyer and W. Richard Scott eds., *Organizational Environments: Ritual and Rationality*, Sage, pp. 199–215.

Meyers, Sumner and Donald Marquis (1969). *Successful Industrial Innovation*, National Science Foundation (NSF 69–17).

Miles, Raymond E. and Charles C. Snow (1978). *Organizational Strategy, Structure, and Process*, McGraw-Hill.

Mowery, David C. (1983). Economic Theory and Government Technology Policy, *Policy Sciences*, 16 (2), pp. 27–43.

Mowery, David C. and David J. Teece (1996). "Strategic Alliance and Industrial Research." In Richard S. Rosenbloom and William J. Spencer eds., *Engines of Innovation*, Harvard Business School Press.

Mowery, David C. and Nathan Rosenberg (1979). The Influence of Market Demand upon Innovation, *Research Policy*, 8, pp. 103–153.

Mowery, David C. and Nathan Rosenberg (1989). *Technology and the Pursuit of Economic Growth*, Cambridge University Press.

Nonaka, Ikujiro and Hirotaka Takeuchi (1995). *The Knowledge-Creating Company*, New York: Oxford Press.

Numagami, Tsuyoshi (2000). *Toward an Action System Theory of Management*, Hakuto Shobo (in Japanese).

Pavit, Keith and Luc Soete (1980). "Innovative Activities and Export

Shares." In Keith Pavitt, ed., *Technical Innovation and British Economic Performance*, Macmillan.

Porter, Michael E. (1980). *Competitive Strategy*, Free Press.

Prahalad, C. K. and Gary Hamel (1990). The Core Competence of the Corporation, *Harvard Business Review*, 68 (3) pp. 79–91.

Price, Don K. (1965). *The Scientific Estate*, Belknap Press of Harvard University Press.

Rosenberg, Nathan (1976). *Perspectives on Technology*, Cambridge University Press.

Sakakibara, Kiyonori (1993a). R&D Cooperation among Competitors: A Case Study of the VLSI Semiconductor Research Project in Japan, *Journal of Engineering and Technology Management*, 10, pp. 393–407.

Sakakibara, Kiyonori (1993b). Angela Dumas and Shinji Watanabe, The New Product Trajectory: The Japanese Context of Product Innovation, Paper Presented at The Design Management Institute's Fifth International Forum on Design Management Research & Education, Symposium Proceedings, pp. 168–177.

Teece, David J. (1987). *The Competitive Challenge*, Harper & Row Publishers.

Teramoto, Yoshiya (1990). *Network Power*, NTT Publishing Co, Ltd. (in Japanese).

Teramoto, Yoshiya and Makoto Kanda (1984). Network Organization and Technological Innovation: Techno-Mixing Groups in Smaller Firms, Discussion Paper, 84–01, Meiji Gakuin University.

Tushman, Michael L. and Charles A. O'Reilly III (1997). *Winning through Innovation: A Practical Guide to Leading Organizational Change and Renewal*, Harvard Business School Press.

Tushman, Michael L. and Elaine Romanelli (1985). Organizational Evolution: A Metamorphosis Model of Convergence and Reorientation, *Research in Organizational Behavior*, 7, pp. 171–222.

Utterback, James M. (1994). *Mastering the Dynamics of Innovation*, Harvard Business School Press, pp. 57–78.

Weick, Karl E. (1976). Educational Organizations as Loosely Coupled Systems, *Administrative Science Quarterly*, 21, pp. 1–19.

Weinberg, Steven (1994). *Dreams of a Final Theory*, Pantheon Books.

Wernerfelt, Birger (1984). A Resource Based View of the Firm, *Strategic Management Journal*, 5, pp. 171–180.

Yin, Robert K. (1984). *Case Study Research: Design and Methods*, Sage Publications.

CHAPTER 3

Creating Social Knowledge with Business Tricksters

Aki Nakanishi

INTRODUCTION

At present in the twenty-first century, we are in the midst of a process that will create new social knowledge with the fusing of boundaries. The Internet has become a household word and a radical transformation of business paradigm has been observed in the current advent of a knowledge-based network society of accelerating digitalization. This transformation process of business and social paradigms is perceived as "creation of new knowledge" in this chapter, and the role of "knowledge transformers," the main actors of this creativity, will be interpreted with a focus on the concept of "trickster," an abstraction used in cultural anthropology and other disciplines.

The trickster is a knowledge transformer who freely crosses boundaries and links different worlds. He/she (or it) challenges the old existing inflexible order, destroys it, and creates a new world. In the knowledge-based network society of today we have to transcend the existing paradigm by fusing boundaries and creating new social knowledge. Thus, it is absolutely essential to fully examine the significance of this knowledge transformer who plays an important role in creating a new world. This chapter examines in detail the knowledge transformer as a trickster. This type of trickster required by a knowledge-based network society is then clarified by juxtaposing a number of specific examples.

Because this chapter adopts different disciplines such as cultural anthropology and psychoanalysis, the approach taken here is more descriptive than normative and more interpretive than empirical. Thus, this article itself is a trickster of the organization theory and challenges to create a new paradigm—meso-organization theory.

BASIC UNDERSTANDINGS OF A TRICKSTER

What Is a Trickster?

Stated in simple terms, a trickster is a rascal who appears in myths, legends, and ancient folklore in all parts of the world. This concept of a trickster was developed within structuralist, cultural anthropology and Jung psychology. One of the most extensive works of research concerning tricksters is *The Trickster* (1956) by anthropologist Paul Raddin, which studied the Native American trickster. In the preface of this book, Raddin defines the trickster as follows.

Trickster is at one and the same time creator and destroyer, giver and negator, he who dupes others and who is always duped himself. . . . He knows neither good nor evil yet he is responsible for both. He possesses no values, moral. . . . yet through his actions all values come into being. (Raddin, 1956, Japanese edition, 1972, p. xxiii)

In cultural anthropology, trickster stories among Native Americans in North America and tribes in Africa are extremely important for relating myths of creation and the origins of communities. Additionally, Hermes of Greek mythology, Susanoonomikoto of Japanese mythology, animals that trick or solve problems in folklore, and others can be cited as typical examples.

In particular, Hermes can be said, in a certain sense, to have an existence similar to that of a trickster. Understanding the characteristics of Hermes may provide the key for considering the trickster phenomenon we discuss. Therefore, a brief introduction follows.

Hermes is the last of the so-called 12 Olympic gods. He is the son of Zeus, the king of the gods of the world. He is the messenger of Zeus and shuttles between the gods of the heavens and people of the earth. Additionally, he is also called Pushcoponpos, a guide of the dead, and entices humans to the realm of the dead. Consequently, Hermes serves as the protector of travelers and merchants who travel to many worlds.

Hermes is also a god extremely proficient in evil and there is the well-known story in which he uses a clever trick to steal a cow from the pasture of his older brother Apollo, the god of the sun. Because of this, Hermes is also considered to be the god of thieves, swindlers, and impostors.

Japanese cultural anthropologist Masao Yamaguchi (1975a) summarized Hermes's characteristics as a trickster god as follows.

1. Uniting of opposites such as large and small, and old and young
2. Subversion of the order through theft and deception

3. Appears at various places with surprising swiftness
4. Creation of paths through new combinations
5. Tying different worlds as a traveler, messenger, and herald
6. Accomplishing conveyance between heterogeneous items through such acts as exchanges
7. Constant movement, introduction of new aspects, no fear of failure, and turning such into a laugh

The trickster is an archetype in C. G. Jung's psychology and is used as an important concept when discussing collective unconsciousness. Jung asserted that not only is there individual unconsciousness in a person's heart, as stated by Freud, there is also a common "collective unconsciousness (universal unconsciousness)" that exists in mankind. The archetype serves as a pattern of this collective unconsciousness. In addition to the trickster, there is anima (an inner feminine part of the male personality), animus (an inner masculine part of the female personality), the great mother who swallows up everything at birth, and the wise old man, who is symbolic of knowledge.

According to psychologist Hayao Kawai (1982), the trickster in Jung psychology is explained as follows.

1. The trickster creates the next new system by destroying a system while playing a huge prank. An unforeseen connection is created while engaging in destruction, so the trickster often appears in myths of creation.
2. The trickster has a duality of destruction and construction. In the tale of the trickster, the plot progresses from "ossification of the system, which leads to destruction for improvement, which in turn causes new couplings." Therefore, there is a close relationship with creativity.
3. The trickster has an immature, childish personality and often appears on the edge of consciousness in the form of an animal not yet developed as a human.
4. In myths and ancient folklore, the trickster is the forefather of a tribe and he is often known as a hero who generated much technology and culture, which ignited the tribe.
5. The trickster awakens causes within the sleeping unconsciousness and drives them to the surface of consciousness by running riot and thereby stimulates development of a new culture.

Who Is a Trickster?

The concept of a trickster is also often used in literature and drama. For example, the court jesters and elves that appear in the plays of Shakespeare are interpreted as being tricksters. In the genre of history, there are also many examples of Socrates and Christ being portrayed as tricksters.

In the modern business world, entrepreneurs can be seen as tricksters.

Anita Roddick, who is the founder of The Body Shop, played the part of a trickster to establish her cosmetic business. She is not only a successful entrepreneur in the business world but also a passionate social activist, against animal testing, and an environmentalist. She is fully committed to both worlds and The Body shop has realized many new concepts and knowledge such as fair trade between advanced and developing countries, recycling of bottles and packages that are sold in the shop, and new product development processes that don't involve animal testing. These are the fruits of fusing the boundary between business and nonbusiness.

Another entrepreneur example is Richard Branson, head of 150 or so enterprises that carry the Virgin brand and, at the same time, a famous adventurer who holds the speed record for crossing the Atlantic Ocean by boat. He still hopes to be first to circle the globe in a balloon. He never stops pursuing his dream and make the most of his resources. His adventurous spirit compells him to challenge business giants. Virgin Airlines and Virgin Cola are ambitious tricksters that stirred established industries where big companies reign and govern. Branson always enjoys both business and adventure challenges and transcends the framework of conservative management.

A trickster is not always an individual person. Groups, collectives, organizations, and institutes can function as a trickster. In this sense, The Body Shop and Virgin can be seen as tricksters of existing business fields. In Japan, Yamato Corporation, which challenged the former Ministry of Transport (now combined into Ministry of Land, Infrastructure and Transport), the heart of regulation and administrative licensing for transportation industry, is a typical example.

The concept of trickster becomes more fully developed by interpreting relationships to real phenomena. Here, the role and function of a trickster is viewed from the perspective of a knowledge-based network society.

Where and When Does a Trickster Act?

It is not enough to singularly analyze the trickster. There are many other actors in the drama played out by the trickster. In the story in which the trickster performs, the triangular relationship between a king (authority figure), a community, and a trickster can most certainly be seen.

The king is the personification of existing knowledge, and he reigns over the community as an authority figure and ruler. Stated in terms of a business organization, the equivalent is the president, chairman, and other top executives. The leading companies of industry and government agencies that have licensing authority also have similar positions.

The people of the community are the subjects who are controlled by the king and who accept the existing culture and values and live their lives in accordance with this paradigm. When an organization is viewed as a stage for this trickster drama, the constituent members, employees and supervisors, are the members of the community.

The trickster is simultaneously the destroyer of the existing order of the community and the creator of a new order. Additionally, the trickster is often portrayed in stories as a cultural hero who causes the creation of new knowledge (technology and systems) in the community, or as someone who acquires the position of king or wise man.

The manifestation of the trickster is often a person with an immature, childish personality or a small, weak animal such as a rabbit or squirrel. He/she, on the other hand, cunningly and shrewdly uses knowledge to challenge traditional order, authority figures (gods and kings), and the people of the community who adhere to them.

The trickster does things that are inconceivable under existing knowledge systems held by the community and teaches people who are focusing on existing order and norms.

In the trickster drama, there is the dual structure of cast members and spectators, or the audience, of the play. This dual structure is extremely important for understanding the essence of the trickster phenomenon. The latter at times go up on the stage and become cast members in the story. In the business world, the existence of shareholders, customers, competing companies, and other external stakeholders cannot be ignored.

Stated in a more active sense, the people of the community are self-governed and active selectors of knowledge. Whether existing knowledge will be maintained to justify and sustain the king (authority figure) or the trickster's new knowledge spreads depends on the decision they make. Naturally, the people of the community select the knowledge that is most appealing. Additionally, it's not just a simple choice between the existing knowledge or the trickster's knowledge because a third knowledge set can be created through association. Conversely, active participation of the community is an essential condition for creation of this third set of knowledge.

The knowledge-based network society makes it easy for spectators to participate. The Linux operating system (OS), built through open sourcing, is a typical example. It should be noted that Linux, which is currently being developed and improved, is also being incorporated into systems of existing large companies that emphasize reliability. If Linus Torvalds and the core development team are viewed as tricksters, companies, such as Microsoft, which provide existing operating systems, are "authority figures," user engineers are the collective body of people, and this group of companies are the spectators and the audience in this drama. In this sense, companies' choice of using Linux can be interpreted as direct participation in the story by spectators who previously waited for the story to unfold and have now chosen the knowledge of the trickster. Consequently, the overall structure of the trickster drama can be shown in the following figure.

Boundaries are an essential concept to the trickster phenomenon. Boundaries are "primary multi-dimensional concepts such as inner and outer, life and death, deciduous and flowering, culture and nature, fixed and mobile, arable and arid, and fertile and barren" (Yamaguchi, 1975b, p. 81). The trickster crosses and transcends boundaries. For example, Hermes is a messenger between the world of humans and the world of the gods. In the real world, entrepreneurs also cross and fuse the boundary between business and nonbusiness worlds.

The trickster sometimes exists within a community but he/she also moves freely without being restricted by a border. The trickster transcends borders and exists on the periphery of the existing community. He contrasts with and undermines the culture and thought of the center.

BUSINESS TRICKSTERS IN THE KNOWLEDGE-BASED NETWORK SOCIETY

The previous sections outlined the basic concepts and framework of the trickster. However, what we are discussing is a knowledge-based network

Figure 3.1
Basic Structure of the Trickster Drama

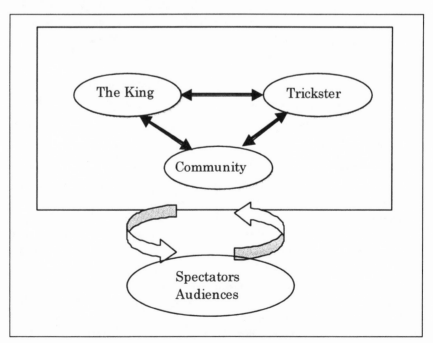

society not ancient myths or feudal societies of the middle ages. While keeping that in mind, we will examine a number of trickster-like phenomena in the modern business world. It is known that the world evolves through cyclic emergence of trickster-like people who challenge existing knowledge systems and of consumers and citizens who welcome them and the maturation of knowledge.

Here we can describe tricksters who challenge and create new social knowledge by exploiting digital technology to transform old business paradigms.

The IT Revolution and Manufacturing Renaissance in Japan

Tricksters tend to be small and fast. Incs, a small company with about 140 employees, has attracted attention by producing metal molds for cellular telephones and other products in less than a quarter of the normal time frame. Thus, Incs can be considered a trickster of the IT revolution.

The IT revolution is also an era of speed. In an industry like cellular telephones, where product lives are measured in months, the time span from development to mass production determines success or failure. Incs substantially shortened the period from development to production of metal molds for prototyping by employing an information transfer system that uses absolutely no paper. They call this their "rapid prototyping system." Despite its small size, Incs is the world's leading company in cellular telephone metal molds.

The company, established in July 1990, was the first domestic company to eliminate diagrams from all processes including product design, trial production, and metal pattern production—a feat that it accomplished by the end of 1998. Digital processing was realized through the use of computers. Incs kicked off this new revolution by combining the heterogeneous knowledge of synthetic resin laser-forming technology, three-dimensional CAD technology, and computer information and telecommunications technology. Incs calls this an "intellectual industrial revolution." Additionally, this intellectual industrial revolution resulted in the information industry. Incs defines the information industry as "an industry in which intent is conveyed through computers and networks." Mr. Shinjiro Yamada, the company's president, explains it as follows on the company's home page: Just as loom-weaving became automatic weaving through mechanization, this revolution will begin by turning the existing mass-production industry into an information industry. For example, current mass-production and development processes progress through design, specifications, trial production, and metal pattern processing to convey "the desire to produce a certain kind of good." We convey this intent as in the form of three-dimensional data and are developing a system for instantaneous conveyance to all processes using computers and networks. A completely new manufacturing industry with explosive production capacity will soon emerge through linkage of systems that convey intent, using computers and networks, to conventional machines.

Shinjiro Yamada, president of Incs, was born in 1949. He was first employed by Mitsui Mining & Smelting, where he was responsible for automotive parts design. While at this company he saw how the Big Three automobile manufacturers in Detroit were substantially shortening development processes through the use of next-generation, three-dimensional CAD and laser-forming technologies when he visited the United States in 1988. It can probably be stated that this was the primal experience that drove Mr. Yamada to establish Incs.

Full-scale use of next-generation, three-dimensional CAD became prominent since the development of Boeing 777. The internal structure of three-dimensional items can be represented as data. Easily visualized new product prototypes (called solid models) are combined with the basic three-dimensional specifications on screen. Products can be created using data by changing a number of variables. Additionally, trial production can be accomplished by using the created data to control laser beams for hardening of resins.

Prototypes are created at the Solid Reality Center, the company's Design Division in Kawasaki City, by hardening complex shapes using laser beams on fluid beam-hardening resins. Specifications and design information for trial products are not contained on paper-based design blueprints. Rather, digital data is sent from the design center in Tokyo. Not even one person is involved in trial production. Only a small number of young employees with dyed hair watch the computer. Oil-stained processing machinery, which was essential for production of metal molds until quite recently, cannot be seen at the company's plant in Ota-ku, Tokyo, a region with many small and medium-sized companies.

It is safe to say that the manufacturing strength of Japan, which peaked in the 1980s, came from the area of product development. The important characteristic of which has been the close cooperation between large companies and smaller firms in upstream and downstream processes and functional divisions. Adjustments of product concept, design, and trial production are carefully coordinated by the larger company and engineers use the design blueprints as information sources. Skilled operators at smaller companies accomplish precision trial production and metal pattern production based on extensive experience. However, this process has not been necessarily efficient.

One of the major reasons for this is the problem of blueprint creation. Blueprints must be created for trial production of metal molds after product design. The concept diagram created by the design division, product design diagram created by the specifications division, and metal pattern design diagram created by the metal pattern division exist independently and there has been no guarantee that these diagrams completely agree. Ultimately, products are three-dimensional but can be represented only in two dimensions on the paper diagrams. A diagram written in this manner is difficult to understand in conceptual terms and the intent of the designer and specification specialist often cannot be fully reflected in it. Also, problems, such as in parts, are discovered only when prototypes are being produced from these diagrams. Fixing these problems requires extensive communication, time and cost.

However, models created using next-generation three-dimensional CAD have integrated digital data. Therefore, there is not the ambiguity of diagrams. Additionally, data transfer between processes and computer simulations during design are easy. Incs realized a paperless design and production environment by linking these data series.

There was, however, another problem. Until quite recently, the final stage of metal pattern production required the skills of an experienced operator for detailed finishing. Incs saves skills that can be universally understood as technologies, by scientifically analyzing the skills of these operators to ensure continuity.

Incs has about 150 employees, 120 of whom are in their twenties. The average age of employees is 24.5, which is extremely unusual for metal pattern manufacturers who traditionally require experienced operators. At present, the average age of Japan's metal pattern makers is 52.5. Incs does not have a single operator in the original sense of the word.

Skilled metal pattern techniques generally require a number of years to acquire. It is not an overstatement to say that the skilled craftsmen of small companies supported the base of Japan's manufacturing industry. As opposed to this, Incs reduced training time to almost a month for part-time employees by creating jobs that can be handled by computer.

"We don't make them make decisions, and we don't fully polish their skills," and "it's alright if they leave after two or three years" says President Yamada about human resources. His statement seems to run counter to the values of lifetime employment and long-term training and development of human resource management in large established Japanese companies. Incs is not only a technical trickster but is also a trickster in terms of Japanese management.

We often think that the everyday lives of people working in organizations tend to revolve around organizations. The theory of the organization is central to this idea and home life, leisure, and community activities are driven to the periphery. However, the fact is that we belong to multiple, diverse communities and all of us have a private life. This is called "multiple affiliation" (Teramoto and Nakanishi, 2000). Incs's human resource management is believed to facilitate employees' multiple affiliations.

Many young people demand self-actualization outside the workplace.

These people work happily under the idea that "the organization is the organization, and I am me," and their existence transcends the simple two-dimensional human resource management theory of white collar and blue collar that has prevailed to the present. Incs employees call themselves "industrial citizens," people that make industry their work.

Incs is an industrial organization that is mounting a challenge to transform knowledge related to the production of goods by combining information technology and manufacturing technology. Japan has a global market share of approximately 45 percent of metal mold manufacturing. If this small, young company takes off while large companies continue to slump, this will indeed be a new story of trickster success.

Creating an Interactive World Fusing Communication Technologies

In a knowledge-based network society, each and every person will personally have the tools for networking. With this in mind, future development of cellular telephones as personal communication terminals becomes the focus. If legendary tricksters who are messengers between different worlds realize this, what will happen?

Incs is the largest company in metal molds for cellular telephones. We will consider cellular telephones from the perspective of the trickster phenomenon.

NTT DoCoMo announced its "i-Mode" cellular telephone service, which allows connection to the Internet, on February 22, 1999. Until then, you had to use a personal computer connected to a network, or a mobile terminal connected to a telephone line, to get on the Internet. As a result, it wasn't possible to access the Internet from anywhere at anytime.

i-Mode uses a dedicated browser installed on cellular telephones and allows net surfing, mobile banking, e-mail, and other services without connection to a personal computer.

The i-Mode service, which was expected to have 2–3 million units in service within the first fiscal year, exceeded 5 million units during this period. Sales continue to expand strongly at the rate of 20,000 units per day. Diffusion of i-Mode is causing the cellular telephone and Internet market to exhibit growth again. For example, the number of cellular telephone subscriptions in Japan exceeded 50 million units by the end of March 2000, and surpassed the number of subscribers for conventional, stationary telephones. Additionally, Japan ranked fourth in the world in terms of cellular telephone diffusion at the end of 1999 and is substantially pulling away from the United States.

NTT DoCoMo is a subsidiary of NTT, the king (authority figure) of Japan's telecommunications industry. How did it come to play the role of trickster? If i-Mode had debuted as a conventional information terminal, this would probably not have been achieved. The person who planned the i-Mode concept and brought it to life was Mari Matsunaga, who was scouted while she was the managing editor of Recruit's *Travail* magazine.

Mari Matsunaga was born in Sasebo, Nagasaki. She joined Recruit in 1976 during the employment crunch caused by the oil crisis of the mid-1970s. In 1986, she successfully revived the company's Employment Journal, which was in the red at that time, and she was appointed managing editor of *Travail* in 1988 in recognition of that success. She decided to move on in 1997 when she received an offer to "plan the content of a new information transmission business" from NTT DoCoMo. She developed i-Mode's content as the manager of the Planning Office of the Gateway Business Department of the Mobile Multimedia Promotion Division.

Matsunaga immediately began to work on the basic i-Mode concept when she moved to NTT DoCoMo. Required personnel were recruited through the first open recruiting drive NTT DoCoMo ever had. Additionally, she drew on her outside contacts from her Recruit years by talking with magazine editors and writers to flesh out the concept by receiving their frank assessments (Matsunaga, 2000).

Viewed from the standard operating procedure of a large company like NTT, this method was inconceivable. Product development in large companies was often done by selecting talented personnel from within the organization, conducting detailed market analysis a project, summarizing this in a report, and submitting it to decision-makers. However, this internal orientation increases the homogeneity of knowledge and there is the danger that the richness of the concept will be lost.

Matsunaga mixed different kinds of knowledge by assembling people from different fields to create the i-Mode concept. In that sense, it can be said that she was a trickster in NTT's organization.

Additionally, content specifications were opened to the public by NTT DoCoMo when i-Mode service commenced. These specifications are based on HTML, the most common basic language used for creating Internet home pages. Therefore, it was easy to build. In short, users can make their own sites.

It can be said that i-Mode is personal and interactive. These two characteristics are at the base of all services offered by i-Mode, such as the individual sites mentioned above, e-mail, mobile banking, and location confirmation through linkage to car navigation systems.

The "i" of the i-Mode logo is the image of the "i" in Japan's Tourist Information system. Anyone can use this system to obtain travel information. Although said to be relatively simple, connection to the Internet using a personal computer requires a number of settings. Additionally, telephone bills and ISP fees must also be considered. In contrast, the i-Mode service can be used by simply pressing the "i" key on the cellular telephone. The fee is a set charge of ¥300 per month and packet telecommunications charges based on data volume rather than connection time. For example, checking one's bank balance using i-Mode costs ¥20 to ¥30 on average, which is a rather competitive figure.

The i-Mode service has made it possible for anyone to use the Internet. If we define the "first Internet" as the network used by researchers and engineers at universities and research institutes, the "second Internet" as that used by businesses, and the "third Internet" as that used by the general public and students through diffusion to households, then it is not an overstatement to say that the emergence of i-Mode, which allows anyone to use the Internet anywhere at anytime, is the arrival of the "fourth Internet."

A Digital Trickster on the Net

We will introduce the case of Napster, a music software, as our final and supreme example of a trickster. The software and the company with the same name is at the center of a fierce debate between the world's music industry and Internet participants. There are proponents and opponents on both sides. In any event, Napster makes it clear that conventional business models cease to function in a knowledge-based network society.

Napster is a trickster that helped fuse the boundaries of existing music and digital industries. While the Linux phenomenon occurred primarily in the realm of the digital operating system industry, Napster challenged the music industry, one that was ordered and more historically established. In this sense as well, studying the case of Napster is important in clarifying the drama of the trickster in a knowledge-based network society that will culminate in fusion of boundaries.

Napster, which debuted in June 1999, rapidly spread primarily among college students. It is said that the number of users surpassed the 10-million mark in just eight months. Napster's company headquarters is located in San Mateo, California. The company's logo is a little kitty—appropriate for a trickster—wearing headphones.

Napster is file-sharing software developed by Shawn Fanning, a 19-year-old student at Northeastern University. Stated in simple terms, when users exchange MP3 files, their machines become file servers. Music fans input the song artist they desire and click the desired version to download the song for free. In short, users use the search and download system of the Napster server to directly connect their computers, which allows file sharing. Napster's system only facilitates searches of MP3 on the Net; not even one music file is contained on the servers of the Napster Company.

A major characteristic of digital technology, which is emerging as the core of intellectual property, is that duplication and exchange are now extremely simple. The problems caused by Napster arise from this fact.

MP3 is an audio file format that allows simple compression and sending of files, which has emerged as the de facto standard on the Internet. With MP3 files, people can save their music files on computers and exchanges them with friends on the Internet.

The problems created by Napster largely pertain to two points. First, there is the legal problem of copyright infringement with music files that are duplicated and exchanged. This has evolved into a legal fight that has embroiled the music and media industries. Second, there is the technical problem of network overload due to the huge capacity of files exchanged. College students, who were the core users, used Napster through their campus' network environment. Because of these problems, one-third of American universities prohibited students from using Napster to download files from school servers by the second half of 2000.

The suit filed by the Recording Industry Association of America (RIAA) against Napster touched off a huge debate. The RIAA asserts that the music business is beginning to be damaged by diffusion of Napster, which allows free exchanges of music, primarily among young people. Therefore, the RIAA filed suit against Napster to stop it from conducting business because "damage of $3.0 billion will occur in six months if this continues." At the end of July 2000, the U.S. District Court accepted the contentions of RIAA that intellectual property rights had been infringed and issued a preliminary injunction that essentially suspended Napster's services. However, Napster immediately petitioned the U.S. Court of Appeals for a stay of the order, which was granted. For the moment, suspension of business orders has been deferred.

The heart of the Napster dispute hinges on whether Napster is viewed as a hero of the new digital age or a scoundrel who infringes copyrights in creative activity. For example, the assertions of artists can also be divided into two camps. Fred Durst, vocalist of the hard rock band Limp Bizkit, supports Napster and asserts that its technology is a unique method for spreading music to many listeners. Limp Bizkit is on a free nationwide U.S. tour in conjunction with the Napster Company. Durst explains his viewpoint as follows.

We're now in the Internet age. However, there are some people who want to fight this. Those people are folks who derive their livelihoods from standards and practices of the record industry. It is only they who are afraid and feel threatened. (http://www.hotwired.co.jp/news/news/culture/story/20000426204.html)

However, there is also a group of artists who are antagonistic toward Napster. For example, the rock band Metallica filed suit against Napster in April 2000 for copyright infringement and unfair business practices. Additionally, rap music pioneer Dr. Dre also filed suit against Napster during the same period, demanding the deletion of his music from Napster's directory because his copyrights were being violated.

Many surveys have been published concerning Napster's impact on the music industry but their contents diverge widely. In a survey commissioned by the RIAA in May 2000, the results showed that "sales fell at CD stores in college areas that can be connected to high-speed networks" and "music software purchases by teenagers are declining." On the other hand, Jupiter Communications of the United States, an electronic commerce research company, surveyed on-line music users and according to the results released at the end of July 2000, "the percentage of users of Napster and other file exchange networks who purchase music tends to be higher than that of people who do not use these services." Additionally, when people who "spend less than $20 for music in three months" were surveyed about their music purchases after using music sites, the results indicated that those 18 to 24 years of age maintained the same level of purchasing and other age groups actually increased their purchasing. It is asserted that music is more accessible through use of the Internet, which produces a synergistic effect of expanding purchases of CDs.

In addition, the peer-to-peer (P2P) file-sharing technology provided by Napster has generated interest from Intel and other players in the digital industry. In sharing by conventional file servers, the load is concentrated in one server as the center. However, users on the Internet will be able to use their PCs as file servers if Napster's technology is used. Pat Gelsinger, chief technical officer of Intel's Architecture Group, says that peer-to-peer technologies broadened through Napster "will become a new frontier in computer usage." This is the new wave of the Internet, and will cause billions of dollars in cost reductions for companies.

Originally, the basic idea of the Internet was peer-to-peer. Napster, which debuted against a backdrop of increasing sophistication of networks and improved performance of nodes (computer software and hardware), has stimulated many people to rediscover the distinguishing characteristic of the Internet. In peer-to-peer networks, information transfers are accomplished between individual computers. Therefore, information does not travel through a central network and processing tasks can be handled among these computers. Of course, a central network can also participate in this processing. In a word, it means decentralization, or a world of multiple centers and the opposing concepts of center and periphery are eliminated. It is axiomatic that a knowledge-based network society is a decentralized society of multiple centers. In such a society, everyone is at the center and everyone is also on the periphery. Napster's peer-to-peer sharing technology and this concept will spread in the future as well.

If we thoroughly focus on decentralization, Gnutella may be a more appropriate example than Napster. If Napster is seen as intermediary software for file searches and exchanges, then Gnutella is transmission software for file searches and exchanges. Gnutella issues a search request among user networks connected to the Internet and this search request is transferred until the file is found. The major difference between Napster and Gnutella is that Napster is operated as a business and a server for searches clearly exists while Gnutella is not operated as a company. Consequently, it is extremely difficult to target Gnutella for regulation and litigation. Because of this, Napster tends to be an easier target as a vulnerable startup venture.

This debate confirms that Napster has a trickster-like duality. The heart of the Napster dispute hinges on whether Napster is viewed as a hero of the new digital age or a scoundrel who infringes copyrights in creative activity. The trickster has the dual significance of destruction of the existing order and creation of new values. Consequently, the trickster is evil for the defenders of the existing order, and a hero for people who desire new values.

For Napster, it is clear that the RIAA represents the existing system. Additionally, the assertions of artists as members of the collective body are also divided into two camps. While there is the rock band Metallica, rap producer Dr. Dre, and others who have sued Napster, there is also Limp Bizkit of Roderick, Prince, and others who criticize the existing system and support Napster.

In addition to players in a drama with Napster as the trickster, the RIAA as the authority figure, and artists, music lovers, and music consumers as the collective body, spectators and audience who have exercised caution have also begun to participate in this story. The prime example is German media giant Bertelsmann, who, backed by ample funds, entered into a strategic cooperation agreement with Napster. Bertelsmann is exploring the potential of a new music delivery business through conversion of Napster's services to fee-based services. Additionally, from a technical perspective, there is Intel, who has shown interest in Napster's peer-to-peer technology.

Table 3.1 summarizes the series of phenomena surrounding Napster from 1999 through March 2001. While Napster has been forced to curb services at present due to a judgment in the U.S. District Court, it is exploring new business opportunities. A movement of users to similar sites that are said to be Napster clones has been observed.

The U.S. Appeals Court demanded that Napster delete music product files for which the RIAA held copyrights but also stated that the decision of the U.S. District Court, which ordered suspension of business operations, went too far. This means that unrestricted sharing and exchange of copyright-free products is permissible on the Internet. This line of reasoning may be natural in the digital industry but it is difficult to understand in the music industry with its present logic. Thus, it is difficult to gauge how the decision will alter the scenario of Napster's trickster drama.

However, it will be virtually impossible for the music industry to sur-

Table 3.1
Series of Actions Concerning Napster: As of March 2001

June 1999	Napster is unveiled on the Internet.
December 1999	The Recording Industry Association of America (RIAA) files suit for copyright infringement and loss of business opportunities of $3.0 billion a year.
February 2000	A movement to prohibit use of Napster emerges at universities throughout the United States. The University of Southern California adopts a policy of non-prohibition.
April 2000	The rock band Metallica sues Napster and three universities, including the University of Southern California.
May 2000	Dr. Dre files suit because Napster refused his demand to delete music files.
July 2000	The U.S. District Court accepts the contentions of the RIAA and issues a preliminary injunction to suspend business operations. Napster immediately petitions the U.S. Court of Appeals for a stay of the order, which is granted.
August 2000	Interest is expressed in Napster s P2P technology at Intel s Developer Conference.
October 2000	German media industry giant Bertelsmann enters into a business cooperation agreement with Napster. A fee-based service business is explored.
February 2001	The U.S. Appeals Court acknowledges Napster s copyright infringement in its appeal decision, but remands the order for suspension of business to the U.S. District Court. Napster presents a $1.0-billion settlement offer to plaintiff record companies.
March 2001	Napster suspends services for songs to which plaintiff RIAA owns the copyrights. Filtering is upgraded. There is an increase in users moving to other similar sites.

vive solely on the basis of the existing industrial order in the knowledge-based network society of the future. The trickster functions to link heterogeneous worlds. Napster binds the digital and music industries by fusing the boundary. At present, we are in the midst of a process that will create a new knowledge paradigm with this boundary fusion.

NEW VERSION OF THE TRICKSTER DRAMA

Actors

The three cases examined above may be discussed from other perspectives such as innovation theory (Schumpeter, 1926; Christensen, 2000) and/or knowledge creation theory (Nonaka and Takeuchi, 1995). But our trickster perspective focuses on actors and their relationships.

The leading characters of the trickster drama in these cases are summarized Table 3.2. In every case, a triad of trickster, king (as the representative of existing order), and community (as the selectors of knowledge) can be seen. Spectators and audiences are also observed in the drama. Even though all three cases are ongoing stories, the tricksters who are challenging existing paradigms have created new social knowledge, the communities are accepting it, and the actions taken by spectators and audiences will determine the respective epilogues.

Created Knowledge by Fusing Boundaries

In these cases it is speculated that the tricksters fuse technological and industrial boundaries to create new social knowledge. In the first case, Incs has linked IT (information technology) and MT (manufacturing technology), fused these technologies, and created a paperless rapid prototyping system. NTT DoCoMo has integrated Internet technology with cellular phone services, developed i-Mode service, and rapidly brought about diffusion of browser phones. Napster has mixed music distribution systems with computer technology and its P2P file-sharing service has spread so rapidly on the Internet that it is now stirring legal controversy. In short, the trickster fuses the boundary between existing knowledge A and B to create new knowledge C. Table 3.3 shows the summarization of the new social knowledge created by the tricksters.

ESSENTIAL REQUIREMENTS OF THE TRICKSTER IN A KNOWLEDGE-BASED NETWORK SOCIETY

Characteristics of the Trickster as a "Knowledge Transformer"

What characteristics do tricksters have in a knowledge-based network society? The tricksters of the twenty-first century show the symbolic char-

Table 3.2
The Actors of the Trickster Drama

Trickster (Key person)	Incs (Shinjiro Yamada)	NTT DoCoMo (Mari Matsunaga)	Napster (Shawn Fanning)
King (Existing knowledge that is the target for the trickster)	Japanese big companies (Manufacturing /management System)	NTT itself (Organizational culture and climate, SOP of product development)	RIAA and conservative musicians (Copyright business and policy)
Communities	Cellular telephone manufacturers	Development team, cellular phone users	College students that love and/or consume music, radical musicians
Spectators and audiences	Manufacturers that want to be agile.	ISPs and contents providers	Media companies like Bertelsmann. Computer-related companies like Intel

Table 3.3
Created Knowledge and Fused Boundary

Trickster	Incs	NTT DoCoMo	Napster
Created knowledge (knowledge C)	Rapid prototyping system	i-Mode Service	MP3 file-sharing service, Napster
Fused boundary (knowledge A and knowledge B)	Manufacturing technology and information technology	The Internet technology and cellular phone service	Computer technology and music distribution

acteristics that all tricksters have. These are (1) swiftness, (2) flexibility, (3) fragility, and (4) ambiguity. If one lacks one of these four characteristics, he/she (or it) is not a trickster.

Swiftness

Speed is the essential characteristic handed down from tricksters of old mythology. However, it is axiomatic that the present time frame is different from that of the quiet age presented in mythology.

Swift does not mean hasty. However, when speed is required, there is sometimes immaturity. Immaturity makes development possible. The trickster grows by communicating with the cast (king and people of the community), as well as through the support of spectators. Rapid promotion of a forum for the transformation of knowledge is important to increase the speed of growth.

Flexibility

The trickster in a knowledge-based network society must also have a fully flexible existence. There must be flexibility of thought to consider things from multiple perspectives through distancing in order to create new business opportunities. Stripping a trickster of flexibility means he/she is no longer a trickster.

Along with this flexibility of thought, flexibility of action is also necessary. The actions of a swift and flexible trickster are the basis for producing mutual and creative synergy among the king, community, and audience. Various things evolve with this mutual synergy. In short, there is mutual evolution. The trickster not only changes the community—he/she must also change himself/herself.

Fragility

The trickster never has an omnipotent existence. Rather, it is better to say that he/she has an extremely weak and fragile existence. This is a common characteristic of knowledge resources.

However, weakness leads to cleverness. The trickster challenges existing knowledge not with power but with wisdom and tactics. In the network society of today, big and powerful may not necessarily be the best way to go. Rather, this environment may be tailored for the tricks of small and weak tricksters.

Ambiguity

The trickster has basically an ambiguous existence. There are two different types of ambiguity in this sense. First, the subject has many aspects and is understood from many facets. Second, while the subject has a single aspect, differing views are possible depending on the viewing party.

A specific example of the second is the previous Napster example. The trickster in a knowledge-based network society must fully recognize his/her own ambiguity and act aggressively. This promotes mutual association with the stratified knowledge around the trickster.

The Activity Arena of the Trickster

Finally, we will discuss the activity arena of the trickster in a knowledge-based network society. As used here, "arena" may be comparable to the Japanese *ba*, which means "the continuum in which multiple bodies interact." Thus, the concept of arena is formed by time, space, and multiple bodies and their interactions. The actors in the trickster drama are, of course, the cast—the trickster, king, people of the community—and the people who watch the play, the audience. We already saw in detail how the scenario of the knowledge transformation drama changes depending on how these actors interact.

There are largely three conditions that facilitate the transformation of knowledge in a knowledge-based network society. These are (1) openness: open borders, (2) freedom: self-governing actors, and (3) dialog: rich communication.

Openness

In knowledge-based network society, existing boundaries are being fused. Rather than merely transcending boundaries, the future role of the trickster will be more active opening and fusing of boundaries.

Because the arena has open borders it promotes the participation and withdrawal of many bodies to make the creation of new knowledge possible. Additionally, the knowledge created is transported by the trickster to other arenas, which become seeds for further creation of new knowledge.

Freedom

Freedom is required in all interactions a trickster to achieve his/her potential. Other bodies also must have self-governing existences. A knowledge-based network society is a society formed by these self-governing behavioral bodies.

Consequently, in the arena where a trickster acts in an organization or society, there must be flexible systems that provide freedom and autonomy. The actors are evaluated from the perspective of their knowledge transformation activities. From this point of view, it is important for society and organizations to create an age-free, gender-free, and barrier-free environment that is based on knowledge.

Dialog

The third condition of the activity arena of the trickster is promotion of dialog. Even if the borders are open and freedom is promoted, the play will not begin without dialog between the bodies. As shown by the example of the Internet and cellular telephones, it is certain that knowledge-based network societies overflow with diverse media for dialog.

However, the problem is not the media itself. Rather, the problem is the contents that make the dialog possible. How effectively that context can be created will determine the success or failure of a knowledge-based network society.

REFERENCES

Christensen, C. M. 2000. *The Innovator's Dilemma*. Harvard Business School Press.

Kawai, H. 1982. *Yume to Mukashibanashi no Shinsou Shinri* (Depth Psychology of Dreams and Folk Tales). Shogakukan.

Matsunaga, M. 2000. *i Mode Jiken* (A Case of i Mode). Kadokawa-Shoten.

Nonaka, I. and Takeuchi, H. 1995. *The Knowledge-Creating Company: How Japanese Companies Create the Dynamics of Innovation*. Oxford University Press.

Raddin, P., K. Kereneyi, and C. G. Jung. 1956. *The Trickster—A study in American Indian Mythology*. Routledge & Kegan Paul.

Schumpeter, J. A. 1926. *The Theory of Economic Development*. Oxford University Press.

Teramoto, Y. and A. Nakanishi. 2000. *Chisiki Shakai Kouchiku to Jinzai Kakushin: Shutaikeisei* (Creating Knowledge Society and Human Resource Innovation). Nikkagiren Shuppansha.

Yamada, S. *A Word from the President.* http://www.incs.co.jp/overview/
overview.html. (2000. 8. 25) accessed.
Yamaguchi, M. 1975a. *Douke no Minzokugaku* (Folklore of the Fool).
Shincho-sha.
Yamaguchi, M. 1975b. *Bunka to Ryōgisei* (Culture and duality). Iwanami-
Shoten.

PART II

Catalyzing Knowledge Exchange among Individuals and Organizations

Information Dissemination and Learning through Social Networks: The Changing Role of Personal Ties in Economic Relations in Japan

Andreas Moerke

This chapter investigates empirically how and to what degree personal ties (which are referred to as networks in this chapter) in economic relations in Japan are used for information sharing and how they influence economic results. The analysis concentrates on the top management of 77 of the largest corporations from the manufacturing sector. Whereas the connection between director dispatch and economic results has been investigated quite often, this chapter takes not only current dispatches but also experiences from previous job experience in other organizations into account. By doing so, information networks between firms and other organizations are shown. A unique database, compiled from about 10,000 biographies, is the basis for several indices measuring the density of personal relations at the disposal of the boards of directors in the firms under discussion. Further, a model of a management production function, which integrates multiple information networks and shows how they react with each other and how they influence economic results, was developed and applied.

INTRODUCTION

The main question of this chapter is to investigate how social networks affect economic results. It will be tested whether (and to what degree) Japanese firms utilize the social networks of their top management for information exchange and learning—and therefore for business reasons. Naturally, anecdotal evidence has been cited many times and there are several papers concentrating on current director dispatch, but to the best of my knowledge, investigations of current and previous links and experiences are missing. This chapter represents an attempt to fill this gap. The political and economic implication of this investigation is clear: To know whether, and to what extent, it is necessary for a foreign company in Japan to build-up a dense network for successful action in the market.

To answer these questions, the board of directors of 77 of the largest firms from the automotive, electronics, machine tool, and pharmaceutical industries were investigated from the years 1986 to 1998. For each individual executive (about 10,000 in all), the biography found in the annual report (*yuka shoken hokokusho*) was coded and analyzed. Five different networks (kinds of personal ties) were taken into account: links to Japanese corporations from the same group, corporations outside the enterprise group in Japan, corporations in foreign markets, financial institutions, and the state bureaucracy. For each of these networks, an index was developed that expresses not only the character of the ties (current dispatch or historical connection), but also the nature of the hierarchy inside the board of directors. By doing this, it can be demonstrated how the density of the various networks develops.

In addition, because in a corporation people interact and influence each other, it seems clear that the networks do not exert influence on the firm separately, but in combination. That is why in a subsequent step, the networks were integrated into a management production function. The model used was developed by Martin Beckman and starts from the premise that in every hierarchical organization control inputs from higher managerial levels influence the productivity (output) of the levels beneath. This was applied to our firms, assuming that not only control input, but also that knowledge spillover enhances productivity. This holds especially true for Japanese corporations because the board acts as managerial body for the rest of the company. By doing so in this manner, a regression model was employed as a means of estimating the mutual influence of networks on economic results.

It is a common view that economic structure of a company matters. Based on a method developed at the Science Center Berlin, four groups of firms were differentiated: horizontal (*keiretsu*) firms, independent firms, core firms at the top of a group, and subsidiaries/owned firms. Each of the personal ties (networks) was analyzed for each of these groups. By doing so, this chapter is able to show that, for example, in the case of a vertically organized group, the core firm somehow is responsible for the relationship management of the whole group. Differences between horizontal *keiretsu* firms (from the famous "big six") and independent firms are relevant to not only ties within the same group but also to the appointment of outside directors or ex-bureaucrats.

This chapter is constructed as follows. First, several hypotheses on the existence and depth of personal ties (social networks) that were derived from the literature are presented. Then, the dataset is explained and the definitions of the several indices used are clarified, along with explanations of the subgroups of firms and of the functions of the board of directors. An empirical analysis follows, while the last paragraph summarizes the findings and draws a conclusion.

PERSONAL TIES (NETWORKS) OF THE TOP MANAGEMENT—HYPOTHESES

Japan is a network society characterized by a network structure of industry as well as by placing immense importance on personal ties that attach every player in the framework. These personal ties are manifold and complex based on "old boy"' networks from schools and universities, connections resulting from work inside organizations, and friendships and long-lasting customer relationships. As these relationships are frequently used for information exchange and also lead to business connections, they should not be underestimated. So, in terms of investigating Japanese firms, it is necessary to know what kind of personal ties the board of directors, the main governing and deciding body, has. Much research has been done on director dispatch—the way other firms and organizations secure their interests by sending managing personnel to certain firms. As explained previously, this chapter goes beyond that scope and investigates personal networks of firms in several dimensions focusing on their function as information intermediaries and providers of knowledge. To cope with this topic, the following hypotheses were extracted from previous research and were then tested.

Hypotheses Related to Inter-Firm Networks in Japan— Inside and outside the Group

A crucial hallmark for inter-firm networks in Japan was—at least until recently—stable and concentrated ownership with cross-shareholding. Cross-shareholding was used as a measure to protect the firms from takeovers (i.e., disabling an important function of the capital market). Research on this topic is most often linked with discussion on company groups (*keiretsu*).[1] Because of the different character of inter-firm ties, however, it is necessary to differentiate between horizontal and vertical dimensions.

Horizontal Dimension (Horizontal and Independent Companies)

In horizontal groups, such as Mitsui and Mitsubishi, shareholding is reciprocal. By holding each other's shares, companies signal their willingness to act as a group. Independent companies are also linked with other firms through reciprocal (matrix) (Schaede 1994: 293) shareholding. This can be understood as a sign that the firms are willing to maintain long-term relationships. This holds true for director dispatch or information networks, as understood in this framework. Lincoln and colleagues (1992: 561) claim that when the relationship between firms is horizontal, the numbers of executives involved is smaller but that there is a reciprocal exchange rather than a one-way movement. Therefore, I will test this claim:

H1: In horizontal relationships, intra-group ties are weak but equal.

H2: On the other hand, independent companies have stronger, outside personal ties.

Vertical Dimension

In vertically integrated groups, shareholding is more likely to be hierarchical in structure, making these groups more comparable with Western governance mechanisms (Schaede 1994b: 292). By holding a certain percentage of the shares of group companies, the core firm secures its control rights. Because Lincoln and colleagues (1992: 561) claimed that when "the relationship between the firms is vertical in nature, it is common to send at any one time several executives of the core firm, e.g., the purchaser, to the supplier firm." I tested hypothesis 3.

H3: In vertical relationships, owned companies ("vertically integrated firms") have a substantially higher number of directors from intra-group firms than the core-firm of the group.

Reasons for Director Dispatch

The role of director dispatch as a mechanism for governance is stressed when linked with a company's (bad) performance. According to company literature, directors are dispatched when return ratios go down (Ito and Hoshi 1992; Kang and Shivdasani 1995), in the case of worsening share prices (Kaplan 1994; Kaplan and Minton 1994), when sales drop or the number of employees decreases (Abe 1997), or—generally speaking—in the case of bad performance (Lincoln et al. 1996). Therefore, I tested the following hypothesis.

H4: Good business results are connected with less dense inter-firm networks.

Hypotheses Related to Inter-Firm Networks with Non-Japanese Firms

With the ongoing internationalization of Japanese companies, there has been increased interest in questions relating to the success of Japanese management practices and the feasibility of adopting them. On the other hand, with deregulation, fading stable stock ownership, and the long-lasting economic crises, the number of mergers with and acquisitions of Japanese firms has grown. This has resulted in a substantial share of stocks held by foreigners—foreign firms, pension funds, and even individuals. If one applies the previously-mentioned findings to the analysis of international business relations, one has to inquire about the nature of director dispatch and networks between Japanese and foreign firms. Therefore, I tested the following hypothesis.

H5: Personal ties (networks) with non-Japanese firms are increasing.

Furthermore, it is interesting to observe how the different characteristics of group relations affect the links with foreign firms and markets. Following the views of Albach and colleagues (2001), which are that in a vertical group, the core firm is responsible for the relationship management of the whole group, one would expect core firms and independent firms to have the highest level of connections to foreign firms/markets.

H6: Personal ties with foreign companies are mostly built up by core firms, acting for their entire groups, and by independent firms.

The last question is, of course, how all of this relates to the economic success of corporations. Following Lincoln's argument, major shareholders dispatch personnel in the case of insufficient results. Therefore, I tested the following hypothesis.

H7: Strong personal ties (networks) with foreign firms have a positive influence on business results.

Hypotheses Related to Networks Involving Financial Institutions

Naturally, creditors have an incentive to monitor the firms they finance and to act when things are going wrong. The literature on financial institutions in Japan[2] often suggests that banks take countermeasures in case of economic failure. One regularly used method of monitoring a firm is the dispatch of personnel to the management or to the board of directors of that firm.[3] Dispatching directors offers an opportunity to obtain information and to discipline the management that did not achieve the performance level expected.[4] On the other hand, director dispatch is not only done in times of insufficient economic results. Because bank-firm relationships in Japan have tended to be rather long-term, they are expected to reduce monitoring costs and are, therefore, customary. To check which view is the more appropriate, I examined the following hypothesis.

H8: Personal ties with financial institutions are strong when performance is low.

Taking into consideration that the financial structure of large Japanese corporations has been shifting tremendously from bank loans to relying on capital markets for money supply (Moerke et. al 2000), one would expect that the firms in this sample are loosening their ties to financial institutions, especially to banks (the so-called *ginko banare*, cf. Yabushita 1995). This is tested with hypothesis 9.

H9: Over the time investigated, personal ties to financial institutions tended to grow looser.

Hypotheses Related to Networks between State and Industry

The connections between industry and state bureaucracy have a long and intense history in Japan. Without a doubt, industrial policy[5] was one of the main factors underlying the economic development of Japan after Word War II. Although various ministries were involved, the former Ministry of International Trade and Industry, (now the Ministry of Economy, Trade and Industry) is doubtless the best known (Johnson 1989). But there are more institutions influencing firms: public corporations (*kodan*), for instance, or organizations such as the Japan External Trade Organization (Göseke 1997). Using a full range of measures, from legal to informal (the famous *gyosei shido*, cf. Foljanty-Jost 1989), bureaucrats try (or tried) to coordinate and influence firms.

Among the features for which Japan is known, the transferal of retired bureaucrats to private industry (called *amakudari*—literally, descending from heaven) has been the most important. "In the 1950s and 1960s, when the Japanese economy was highly regulated and corporations were, accordingly, highly dependent on ministerial 'benevolence,' *amakudari* was a very strong mechanism to ensure firms' compliance with ministry wishes." (Schaede 1994: 290; with a similar statement, Tsutsuumi and Yamaguchi 1997: 59)

There is a vivid discussion in the literature about the question of which side accelerates the *amakudari* process. One perspective is that "there is a strong 'push' from the ministry" (Aoki 1988; 267, with a similar statement, Johnson 1989; or Usui & Colignon 1999). The opposite view, that the enterprises take the initiative in employing ex-bureaucrats, is taken by Calder (1989), Rixtel (1995), and Rixtel & Hassink (1998). I tested the following hypothesis.

H10: It is the state institutions and other bureaus (and bureaucrats) that push corporations to employ ex-bureaucrats. Therefore, regardless of economic results, enterprises have to employ ex-bureaucrats and maintain relationships with the bureaucracy.

Concerning the several types of connections a firm may have with other firms, there should be several patterns of relationships. According to the writings of Usui and Colignon (1997 and 1999), *keiretsu* firms are a favorite destination for ex-bureaucrats for *amakudari*. Furthermore, taking up the interpretation that core firms are responsible for the relationship management of their group, I tested the hypothesis.

H11: *Amakudari* patterns are connected with group membership patterns. Core firms and *keiretsu* firms are the main target for ex-bureaucrats.

DATA SET AND DEFINITIONS

For this investigation, I examined financial data and directors' personal data. The financial data came from the Kaisha-Database[6] and annual reports in compliance with the securities exchange law (the *yuka shoken hokokusho*). Because detailed explanations on the setting of the database are given in several papers and descriptions,[7] I shall restrict my remarks to within the setting of this sample. Financial data cover the period from 1985 to 1998 on a yearly basis. Investigated are 77 stock corporations from four industries: Automotive (AU), Electrical Machinery (EL), Machinery (MA), and Pharmaceuticals (PH). In order to eliminate outliers, all variables and work files containing financial data are truncated on the 1 percent and 99 percent level.

For this investigation, two kinds of definitions are used. One is a complete set of work files developed to investigate the networks from the history of the directors and their appointment to other institutions or firms. The other set is directly related to a firm's organizational structure, ownership, and investor relations.

The personal data concerning the *torishimariyaku* (directors) also come from the *yuka shoken hokokusho*. Starting in 1986, every third year was taken into account (i.e., the *torishimariyaku* data are from 1986, 1989, 1992, 1995, and 1998). Because of the tenure of directorships, this time span is sufficient. The personal data of the several directors gave detailed information on their biographies: year and university of graduation, degree, employment in other corporations, financial or state institutions, as well as their career tracks in the respective firm (cf. the section on board structures later in this chapter).

Definitions of Network Affiliation

Each firm is characterized by a set of attributes. The inter-firm networks are a major part of this. That means: to analyze a Japanese firm properly one has to clarify whether the firm is a member of one of the big six horizontal groups, an independent firm, or a subsidiary. But problems arise when a firm is a member of one of the horizontal *keiretsu* as well as part of a vertical relationship. In order to deal with these problems, the following definitions are used.

Horizontal (H): A company is considered horizontally-integrated when it is a member of a president's council (*shachokai*).[8] The firms of the horizontally-organized *keiretsu* groups are not only connected through the regular meetings of the firms' presidents but also through cross shareholding and directors dispatches. They use the same financial institutions and to a great extent, the same trading companies. We agree with the arguments that the presidents' councils fulfill a governing task.

Nevertheless, this definition may not be appropriate in cases when a firm is at the top of its own, vertically-integrated group. In these cases, the vertical dimension may dominate the other relationships. Therefore, we extend the definition and divide—where necessary—the group of H-firms into those at the top of a group (so-called horizontal core firms, HC-firms), and pure H-firms.

Vertical (V): A company is treated as vertically integrated if (a) another company owns more than 20 percent of its shares, or (b) a major owner owns more than 10 percent of the share and is at the same time a main customer. This definition was chosen to reflect the Japanese standards for subsidiaries (*kogaisha*) and related companies (*kanren gaisha*). They reflect the enormous potential for control and influence the owning company has, especially because stable shareholding was still common during the period investigated. One example of V-firm is Daihatsu, which belongs to the *Sansuikai*, the presidents' council of the Sanwa group, but its shares are owned to a large extent by Toyota (34.46%). Firms from the Sanwa group together own only 5.76 percent.[9] So in this case, the vertical effects dominate the horizontal ones.

Independent (I): A company is seen as independent when it belongs to none of the above stated groups (i.e., an independent company is not controlled by a presidents' council nor by a single other company). As with horizontally integrated firms, I-firms can also be on top of a vertical group. Therefore, we distinguish—where necessary—between independent core firms (IC) and pure independent firms (I).

Core Firms (C): Companies at the top of the 20 largest industrial groups are seen as core companies. Because all firms in our sample are listed on the first section of the Tokyo Stock Exchange, most of these have a certain number of subsidiaries. But in order to find the specific features of core firms, we have to take size into account and define "core" according to the standards set by the yearbook *Kigyo Keiretsu Soran*.[10] As already stated, the group of core companies consists of firms that are members of a horizontal *keiretsu* (HC, such as NEC, Toshiba, Toyota) and independent firms

(IC, for instance Sony, Sanyo, Matsushita Electric). The following figure shows an overview of these definitions and relations (Figure 4.1).

It should be noticed that for the present analysis, differentiation between horizontal and independent, as well as core and vertically integrated firms, is done.

Special Characteristics of Japanese Board Structures— A Basis for all Definitions

A striking peculiarity is the fact that in Japan the board of directors is the main governing body and, at the same time, top management. Moreover, it consists mostly of insiders (Baum & Drobnig 1994: 122). So, the appointment of personnel from other companies, financial and state institutions, and even from foreign countries has a certain impact on the performance of a firm, because this an important way to secure information that is otherwise not accessible to the firm.

The board of directors, which is (de jure) elected at shareholders' meetings, consists of directors of several levels, beginning with the chairman (*kaicho*), the president (*shacho*), senior managing directors (*senmu torishimariyaku*), managing directors (*jomu torishimariyaku*) and directors (*torishimariyaku*). Every position is not necessarily found in every firm. Representative directors (*daihyo torishimariyaku*) are chosen among the top-level directors. With relative independence, they fulfill the task of representing the company and often decide upon the firm's strategy and

Figure 4.1
Inter-Firm Networks According to the Definitions

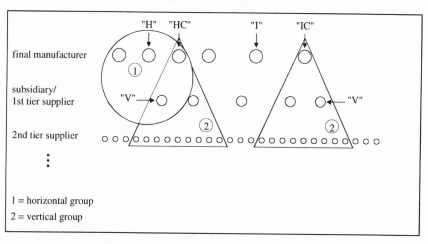

Source: Author's compilation.

business tasks (see Hirata 1996, and Otto 1997: 55, referring to an investigation of Keizai Doyukai of 1996). So even directors are not equal. The higher a certain person climbs in the hierarchy, the more influence he/she can exert. The position with the highest degree of freedom to decide things is the president (*shacho*). Figure 4.2 is a picture of de facto board structures in Japanese public corporations.

To the best of my knowledge, most investigations up until now have focused on current dispatches. The historical dimension (i.e., the employment of employees for more than four or five years in another company before entry into the particular firm), has not been taken into consideration. But, because Japan is very much a network society, these links should not be underestimated, because most of the connections are not cut when a person changes to another enterprise or organization. Further, one has to take into consideration that in the case of spin offs, the mother company often supports the new company with finances and personnel. Therefore, incorporating historical and contemporary dimensions allow us to observe the realities of personal ties in Japanese firms far more clearly than is possible using only reference works such as *Kigyo Keiretsu Soran*.

Figure 4.2
Japanese De-Facto Board Structures

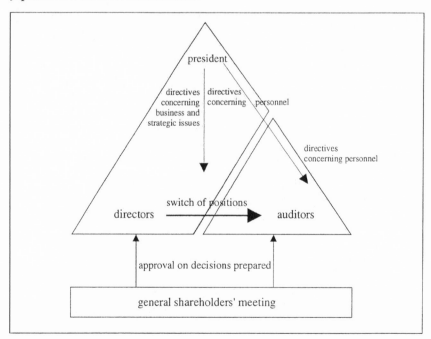

Source: Author's compilation.

Definition of Inter-Firm Networks in Japan

In order to analyze the personal ties (networks) and information flows within a group and to (Japanese) firms outside of this group, two indices were developed. The first one, GROUP, measures the intensity of the personal relations within a corporate group. The second, OUTSIDE, measures the personal links to enterprises outside the group. Companies are defined as belonging to the same group when they are connected through reciprocal shareholding. Information on shareholdings was taken from *yuka shoken hokokusho*. We compared the 10 largest shareholders of every firm to ensure that direct and indirect ownership came under consideration (for example, Toshiba Tungaloy and TEC are both connected via Toshiba Ltd.). If no ownership was found, the relation was seen as an outside link. The calculations were as follows.[11]

Index GROUP: In the first step (A), the (current and previous) posts for each director were counted. For every current interlock one point was given, for a previous one, 0.5 points. These were added up. In the next step (B), the rank of the director was included in the calculation. As already mentioned, the higher the rank, the more information a director receives and the more influence he/she has. Accordingly, we decided to give certain groups of ranks certain points, which were multiplied by the previously-mentioned number of mandates:

- 3 points for representative directors (*daihyo torishimariyaku*) and advisers (*sodanyaku*)
- 2 points for senior managing directors (*senmu torishimariyaku*) and managing directors (*jomu torishimariyaku*)
- 1 point for plain directors (*torishimariyaku*) and auditors (*kansayaku*)

The results of these calculations were related to the hierarchical structure (the sum of ranking points mentioned in B) of the whole board (C). Finally (D), to calculate the intensity of this network for the whole company, the values for each director were summed up.

Index OUTSIDE: The calculations for this index was done in the same way as for the index GROUP; the only difference was that the mandates in firms outside the corporate groups were taken into account.

Definition of Inter-Firm Networks outside Japan

As far as we know, not very much has been done to investigate the influence of foreign companies on Japanese corporations. But as the examples of Nissan and Mitsubishi Motors show, the influence from abroad can be rather strong. Even if we do not go as far as to say that only a major shareholder can exert influence, the role of foreign companies and their knowledge (and, among them, even subsidiaries) should not be underestimated. This is why an index FOREIGN was developed. It covers the connections of Japanese firms to foreign markets via the networks and experiences of its directors and is designed to show to what extent these foreign markets provide information to Japanese companies. Once again, it should be mentioned that we use unconsolidated data to show the effect on the Japanese side—which would be impossible in the case of consolidated statements. The calculation scheme of our index FOREIGN is practically the same of as that of the other indices.

First, every director's biography was checked to find out whether he/she is non-Japanese (in this case, three points were given). If the director had worked as an expatriate, two points were given. If somebody had been responsible for foreign markets at headquarters, one point was given. When several positions were held, associated points were summed.

These ranks were brought into the analysis (B), and then were related to the whole board (C). Finally (D), to calculate the intensity of the networks for each of the companies as a whole, the values for each director were summed.

Definition of Networks Involving Financial Institutions

Of course, main banks are an important institution for Japanese firms. But one must acknowledge that there are also relations to other financial institutions. In order to analyze the variety of links between the firms in my sample and financial institutions, the index FINANCE was developed. It takes the rank of directors into consideration as well as the roles these institutions play as lenders and shareholders and was calculated in the following manner.

1. I analyze whether the directors have a still existing link with a financial institution (two points), and whether they had been appointed by a financial institution in the past (one point).

2. Lending relations were investigated and points for their intensity were given: three points if a financial institution was the largest lender, two points for second or third lender, and one point in fourth to tenth place.

3. The ratios of shares held by banks or insurance companies were rated: three points if a financial institution was the largest shareholder, two points if one was the second or third largest shareholder, and one point if one was the fourth to tenth largest shareholder.

These three values were integrated in a radar chart and the square of this radar chart was calculated (index SQUARE). The index FINANCE was calculated as $1 + SQUARE$. The addition of the value one was necessary because the square value can be zero. Because we assume that humans act in a more or less economically rational manner, we assume that every director dispatch has a certain function and the value therefore cannot be zero.

In the next step (B), the rank of the director was included in the calculation. This was done in the same way for indices GROUP and OUTSIDE. The result of this had to be related to the hierarchical structure of the whole board (C). Finally, to calculate the intensity of the networks FINANCE for each of the companies as a whole, the values for each director in each company were summed (D).

Definition of Networks Involving State and Industry

In order to analyze the networks that involve companies and the state bureaucracy, the index BUREAUCRAT was developed. The biography (A) of every director was checked to clarify whether he/she had served in a state institution. First, the regulatory power of the state institutions was judged according to the industry to which the company belongs. Similar to the other indices, in the case of highest regulatory power three points were given, two points for medium level of power, and one point for less regulatory power. If a director had served in several institutions, the points for the regulatory power were summed. As with the other indices, the rank of each respective director was included into the calculation (B). Results were related to the hierarchical structure (the sum of the ranks analyzed in B) of the whole board (C). Finally (D), to calculate the network intensity of the whole company, the values for each director were summed.

Definition of the Management Production Function

A certain level of hierarchy characterizes every organization. In this context, important variables are organizational scale (the number of members), the number of hierarchical levels, and the control span resulting from this. An attempt to model dependencies in organizations was made by Martin Beckmann.[12] He developed a management production function, starting at the point that the output q of a firm depends on the input x.

$$(1) \quad q = f(x)$$

The variable x is the input of work related with production. It is possible to increase the productivity of x through input from the next managerial level of the hierarchy (input is understood here as information and knowledge). This is formulated as follows:

$$(2) \quad q = f(x_0, x_1, x_2, x_3, \ldots, x_R)$$

where: x_0 = object (production) related work,

$x_1, x_2, x_3, \ldots, x_R$ = controlling hierarchical levels,

R = number of ranks.

This is used to model the influence multiple networks have on the output of the targeted firms. Japanese corporations are connected with other organizations through the networks discussed previously. Each network is supposed to increase the productivity of a corporation. Therefore, the production function can be written as:

$$(3) \quad y_0 = f\,(A,\, y_1,\, y_2,\, y_3,\, y_4,\, y_5),$$

where: y_0 = output of the firm,

A = the number of employees of the firm,

y_1 = networks with intra-group firms (index GROUP),

y_2 = networks with inter-group firms (index OUTSIDE),

y_3 = networks with financial institutions (index FINANCE),

y_4 = networks with state bureaucracies (index BUREAUCRAT),

y_5 = networks with foreign firms and markets (index FOREIGN).

If we interpret equation (3) as a Cobb-Douglas production function, we then have to write the estimation equation as follows:

$$(4) \quad y_0 = a_0 A^\alpha \prod_{i=1}^{5} y_i^{\beta_i}$$

where: y_0 = the output of the firm,

A = the number of employees of the particular firm,

y_1 = the intensity of network i use,

α = the production elasticity of employees,

β_i = the production elasticity of network i.

We assumed that each of the networks investigated is indispensable. The impact on productivity, however, can differ.

EMPIRICAL INVESTIGATION

The empirical investigation was done in two separate steps. First, attention was given to the development over time of each of the indices defined above. Second, each firm's various networks were integrated into this management production function. The reason for this, as I have already mentioned in the Introduction, is that none of these networks exists separately from each other. As a matter of fact, they may overlap and influence each other, just as actions taken by different people in an organization do.

Empirical Investigation of the Personal Ties (Networks) inside and outside the Group (Hypotheses 1–3)

The following figures show how the GROUP and OUTSIDE indices developed over the period investigated. It is immediately noticeable that the levels of the two indices are very different (i.e., that intra-group connections were much stronger than connections to companies outside the group).

Obviously, firms that belong to one of the horizontal groups had relatively few directors that were dispatched from other group companies. For three out of the five years investigated, the ratio of the index for intra-group personal relations was the lowest among all subsamples. Therefore, hypothesis 1 was confirmed. It can be presumed that an institutionalized ex-

Figure 4.3
Development of Personal Networks with Corporations from the Same Group

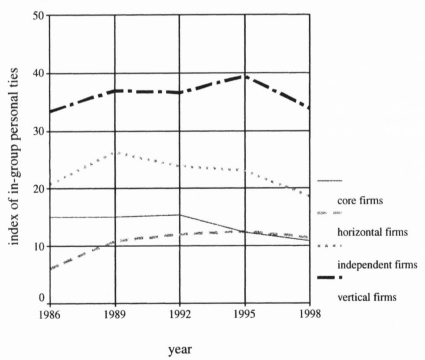

year

Source: Author's calculations.

change of information and coordination is done through the presidents' councils" and that this compensates to a certain extent for the need to employ widely networked directors.

Hypothesis 3 was tested by analyzing personal ties in vertical relationships. As seen in figure 4.3, vertically integrated corporations (subsidiaries) had a significantly higher degree of personal ties (and people with experience in another company from the same group) than core firms. Hypothesis 3 was confirmed. This higher ratio can be explained by the tendency of core firms to manage relationships for the whole group. Furthermore, in the case of Japan, spin-offs need to be taken into account. The mother company provides not only financial support but also human capital.

Figure 4.4 provides an overview of how networks to firms outside the group developed and confirms hypothesis 2 (independent companies have stronger ties outside the company).

The level of personal links of firms with no financial or ownership links

Figure 4.4
Development of Personal Networks with Corporations from Outside the Group

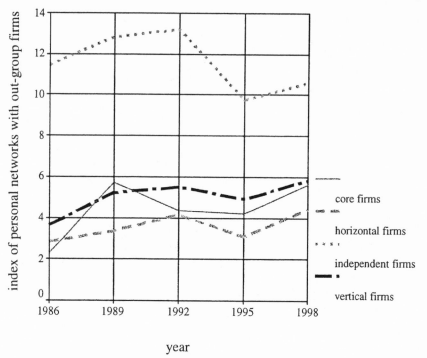

Source: Author's calculations.

is statistically different from other types of firms. This can be explained by their special situation. Independent firms have the highest equity ratio, and also a higher ratio of corporate bonds than other subgroups. That means that they depend much more on the capital market (whereas, *keiretsu* firms are, to a certain extent, isolated from the market—cf., Nakatani 1984). In order to act flexibly, independent companies create their own (personal) networks and secure a higher profitability.[13]

Empirical Investigation of Personal Ties (Networks) with non-Japanese Firms (Hypotheses 5 and 6)

With the exception of the pharmaceutical industry, all industries in this sample are quite export-oriented.[14] Also, the number of foreign firms investing in Japanese corporations (either in the form of a merger or total or partial acquisition) has been increasing over the last decade.[15] As such, it is not surprising that figure 4.5 confirmed hypothesis 5—personal ties with non-Japanese firms are increasing.

Figure 4.5
Development of Personal Networks with Foreign Firms and Markets

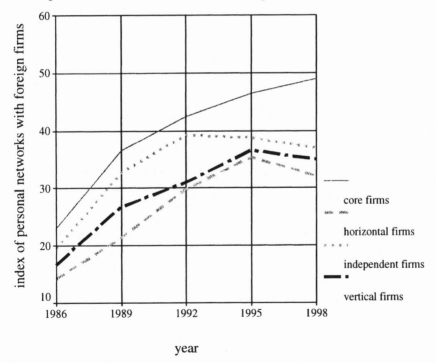

Source: Author's calculations.

The picture was even clearer when differences between the several kinds of firms were investigated[16] and hypothesis 6 was tested. Comparing horizontally integrated (*keiretsu*) and independent firms, it is interesting to note that through the years investigated, the horizontally linked firms had the lowest ratio of personal ties. This can be attributed to the corporate governance mechanisms used by the big six groups (i.e., the group management or the presidents' councils act as the platform for information and knowledge exchange). Furthermore, in the case of horizontal *keiretsu*, general trading companies act as intermediaries for business and relations in foreign markets. In vertically-integrated groups, (e.g., when comparing core firms and their subsidiaries), it is clear that core firms acted more directly than their vertically-integrated firms do. Therefore, hypothesis 6 was confirmed.

Empirical Investigation of Personal Ties (Networks) among Firms and Financial Institutions (Hypothesis 9)

Although different in their capital structure,[17] horizontal-integrated and independent core firms were similar with regard to their networks with financial institutions. They were also significantly different from the other subgroups.

Figure 4.6 clearly shows that the intensity of connections with financial institutions (including banks and insurance companies) has been increasing for independent and horizontally integrated companies. For core firms, the results fluctuated but the intensity in 1998 was only marginally higher than that in 1996.[18] Obviously, the group of vertically-integrated firms was very stable. Therefore, hypothesis 9 (loosing ties to financial institutions) was rejected.

What can be interpreted from these findings? The fact that vertically integrated companies constantly have the lowest ratio of personal ties might indicate a relationship management function within a vertical group (cf. also Görtzen, 2000). The core firm is, to a certain extent, also responsible for money supply and it acts on the capital market for the whole group. Because core firms are truly global players, they operate on international capital markets, issue bonds, and ask foreign banks for loans.

If one compares the networks of horizontal and independent companies, one clearly sees that after 1986 the firms of the big six *keiretsu* have closer connections with financial institutions. One interpretation is that banks have strengthened their monitoring activities. The crises of the Japanese financial system also influences bank-firm relationships within the horizontal groups. The poor financial situation of many banks and insurance companies has led to a credit crunch[19]; banks are becoming more cautious even toward firms of the big six *keiretsu*. The other interpretation is that firms—in order to strengthen their activities in the capital market

Figure 4.6
Development of Networks with Financial Institutions

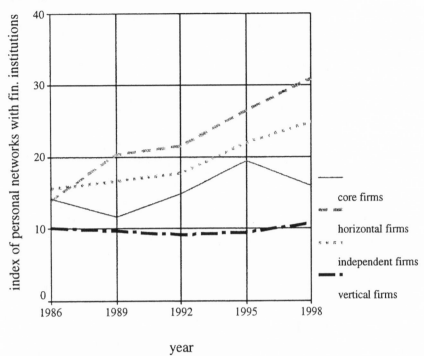

year

Source: Author's calculations.

and to reduce their dependence on bank finance—employ people from financial institutions with the necessary knowledge.

Empirical Investigation of Personal Ties (Networks) among Corporations and State Bureaucracy (Hypothesis 11)

As pointed out already, *keiretsu* firms (horizontal firms) were expected to be a favorite *amakudari* destination for bureaucrats. My investigation confirmed this. Figure 4.7 shows that the personal ties among corporations belonging to one of the big six groups and state institutions were at least more stable than that for the other groups (cf. also Nakano 1998). In contrast, independent firms were able to act more flexibly and loosen ties with state institutions,[20] reducing their dependence on the bureaucracy. The difference between core firms and subsidiaries was even clearer and statistically significant.[21] The results indicate that core firms were responsible for the relationship management of the group (cf. also Götzen 2000).

This includes the dispatch of ex-bureaucrats to subsidiaries—a fact that in my interpretation was responsible for the rising number and higher ranking of *amakudari* bureaucrats in vertically-integrated companies after 1995. The reason for these dispatches was that after so many recent incidences of scandals, the standing of the state bureaucracy has deteriorated rapidly.[22] Firms do not consider these *amakudari* useful and want to get rid of them. This statement was true for nearly every firm except the horizontal companies. Therefore, hypothesis 11 (i.e., *amakudari* pattern and group membership pattern are linked) was confirmed.

Empirical Investigation on the Integration of the Different Networks—Beckmann's Management Production Function (Hypotheses 4, 7, 8, and 10)

The most interesting part of the investigation may be the question of how networks influence each other and affect—in their reciprocity—the

Figure 4.7
Development of Networks with the State Bureaucracy

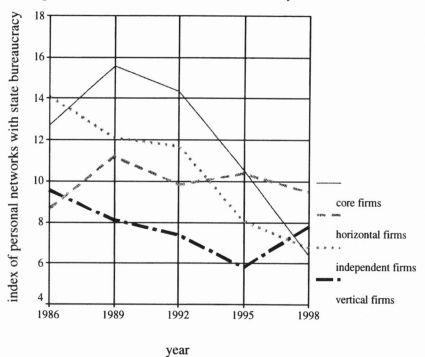

year

Source: Author's calculations.

economic results of a corporation. In other words, how effectively do Japanese firms use and manage personal ties (networks)?

Beckmann's Management Production Function gave an answer to this question. First, the model was tested for the whole sample over the whole time span. Then, in order to compare the subsamples, the same equation was applied to (1) the subsamples of horizontally integrated and independent firms, and (2) the subsamples of core firms and vertically integrated firms (the subsidiaries).

ESTIMATION FOR THE WHOLE SAMPLE OVER THE WHOLE TIME SPAN (1986–1998)

The following equation gives an overview of the influence of multiple networks on the output of a firm. For estimation, industry dummies were used. The results were as follows.

$$(7) \quad y_0 =$$
$$9.59 \cdot A^{1.048} \cdot y_G^{0.040} \cdot y_0^{0.0017} \cdot y_F^{0.003} \cdot y_B^{0.018} \cdot y_A^{0.091} \cdot d_m^{-0.049} \cdot d_e^{-0.016} \cdot d_a^{0.242}$$
$$(71.2) \ (78.8) \ \ (3.8) \ \ \ (1.5) \ \ \ \ (0.4) \ \ \ (2.0) \ \ \ (8.6) \ \ \ (-1.2) \ \ \ (-0.4) \ \ \ (4.2)$$

$$R^2 = 0.9338$$
$$DW = 1.9120$$

where
y_0 = output of the firm

A = number of employees

y_G = networks with intra-group companies (GROUP)

y_0 = networks with inter-group companies (OUTSIDE)

y_F = networks with financial institutions (FINANCE)

y_B = networks with state bureaucracy (BUREAUCRAT)

y_A = networks with foreign markets (FOREIGN)

d_m = industry dummy (machinery)

d_e = industry dummy (electrical machinery)

d_a = industry dummy (automotive).

By interpreting these figures, one can say that the first remarkable result is that connections to foreign firms have the strongest influence on the output of firms. Therefore, hypothesis 7 was confirmed. The elasticity of this type of network was high: for an increase in output of 1 percent, personal ties with foreign firms and markets (via dispatch, employment of board members from foreign countries, etc.) need to be increased by roughly 10 percent.

Next, the influence of networks within the same industrial group was evident. For the time investigated, intra-group connections had a positive impact on the output of a firm. In other words, as long as Japanese firms employ people on the board of directors with previous experience in other firms belonging to the same group, they support sales.[23] This may sound familiar but is nevertheless different from hypothesis 4 (good results are connected with less dense networks). To clarify this, I ran the regression analysis for two time spans—1986–1991 and 1992–1998. Unfortunately, the results were not sufficient in terms of statistical significance. Further research is necessary.

Interestingly, over the entire time span, the knowledge and personal ties of ex-bureaucrats on the board of directors had an influence on business results (statistically significant level of 5 percent). But at the same time, their influence was not anywhere near the impact of the first two networks mentioned. Exerting a positive influence on results is—in my opinion—an indication of pull (i.e., companies actively appoint, or appointed in the past, ex-bureaucrats to their boards). If they were pushed to do so without economic relevance, business results would have been affected as such. Therefore, hypothesis 10 should be rejected.

It is not surprising that the employment of managers from firms outside the same group had only a very vague influence. During the time investigated, the external labor market for managers in Japan was—and still is—underdeveloped. The structure of industry as a whole has not made it attractive for firms to hire real outsiders.

Astonishingly, networks with financial institutions did not seem to have a significant, positive influence on the performance of a corporation. Thus, monitoring should not be the main reason for strengthening ties between firms and financial institutions. The second supposition—the employment of experienced personnel to act independently in the capital market—is seen as the more realistic motive. Hypothesis 8 is partly confirmed insofar as strong ties with financial institutions usually occur when the results are bad. But, the question of why the situation of firms did not improve remains open. More research must be done to answer this question.

Next, horizontal and independent firms, as well as core firms and subsidiaries (vertically integrated firms), are investigated in the same way.

COMPARING HORIZONTALLY INTEGRATED (H FIRMS) AND INDEPENDENT FIRMS (I FIRMS)

When comparing H firms and I firms, the results differed in several respects (cf., Table 4.1). It is not surprising that for H firms (i.e., *keiretsu* firms), the elasticity of the intra-group networks is higher than that of independent firms, but a ratio of 10:1 is quite impressive. This result is contrary to the assertion of a MITI study group that stated that *keiretsu* firms do not prefer transactions with companies in their group (Uryu et al. 1993). They obviously do.

Table 4.1
Management Production Function for Horizontally-Integrated and Independent firms

Production elasticity (t-value)	Horizontally-integrated firms (the big six *keiretsus*)	Independent firms
- Number of Employees	0.910*** (20.198)	1.125*** (41.479)
- Index "GROUP"	0.111*** (7.015)	0.010 (0.711)
- Index "OUTSIDE"	0.043** (2.203)	-0.051*** (-2.793)
- Index "FOREIGN"	0.186*** (8.461)	0.083*** (5.673)
- Index "FINANCE"	-0.025** (-2.302)	-0.026** (-1.979)
- Index "BUREAUCRAT"	0.082*** (4.730)	0.048*** (3.499)
Constant	10.602*** (27.389)	9.425*** (39.442)
R^2	0.936	0.890
DW	1.873	2.069

***-Significance level $\alpha \leq 0.01$; **-$\alpha \leq 0.05$; *-$\alpha \leq 0.1$
Source: Author's calculations.

While the reasons for a lack of positive influence from networking with financial institutions have already been discussed, an explanation for networks with firms outside the group can—this moment—not be given. Examining the effects of ex-bureaucrats on output, the results (a value twice as high for H firms than for I firms) confirm Usui and Colignon (1997) findings that horizontal *keiretsu* are a favorite target for *amakudari* bureaucrats. Last but not least, networks with foreign firms and markets play an important role for both H and I firms. Especially in the case of horizontally integrated firms, the elasticity is high: if one were to increase networks with foreign firms by 10 percent, output would increase by about 2 percent.

COMPARING CORE FIRMS (C FIRMS) AND VERTICALLY INTEGRATED FIRMS (V FIRMS)

The results of the equations can be found in Table 4.2. Although not all of the results are satisfactory, they are nonetheless sufficient to give an impression of the differences between the two subgroups.

For core firms, networks with foreign firms have a significant and positive influence on sales. The employment of amakudari bureaucrats has significant but negative consequences. This result supports the view that, at least for these two subgroups, state institutions still have the power to send people to private firms (the so-called push perspective, stressed by Usui and Colignon 1997). I have already mentioned that the employment of directors with a background in financial institutions does not have a significant influence on sales. But it is interesting to see that such directors may even have a negative impact on core firms. So one has to ask why these firms still employ people from banks and insurance companies. One answer might be that financial institutions can strengthen their monitoring activities by sending personnel. Furthermore, in a society like Japan it is not easy to relax a relationship that was formerly important.

In the case of vertically integrated firms, core firms are responsible for their relationship management. Networks with foreign firms play an important role for this subgroup. But the production elasticity of this network type is only about one sixth of the value shown by core firms! Rather, networks with firms outside of their group and with financial institutions are characterized by higher production elasticity. Vertically integrated firms are smaller than core firms and are less active on the capital markets. This means that they do in fact depend more on know-how from and governance of financial institutions. The employment of directors from outside firms and the corresponding impact on V firms' output may hint that the relationship management of core firms is not perfect or sufficient.

SUMMARY AND CONCLUSION

This chapter set out to investigate two aspects of the network phenomenon. The first of these is the development of social (personal) networks maintained by large firms through their directors' networks. Because the aim was to investigate networks used for knowledge dissemination, it took into account directors' current position *and* previous experiences in other organizations. Second, an attempt was made to understand the influence of these networks on the economic success of corporations. To

Table 4.2

Management Production Function Estimated for Core Firms and Vertically Integrated Firms

Production elasticity (t-value)	Core firms	Vertically integrated firms
- Number of Employees	1.044*** (42.334)	1.062*** (41.480)
- Index "GROUP"	-0.020 (-0.903)	0.051 (1.388)
- Index "OUTSIDE"	0.016 (0.661)	0.123*** (5.835)
- Index "FOREIGN"	0.295*** (14.788)	0.052*** (2.626)
- Index "FINANCE"	-0.038** (-2.048)	0.068*** (4.125)
- Index "BUREAUCRAT"	-0.085*** (-4.679)	-0.006 (-0.363)
Constant	9.891*** (33.808)	9.747*** (33.916)
R^2	0.946	0.883
DW	2.234	1.596

***-Significance level $\alpha \leq 0.01$; **-$\alpha \leq 0.05$; *-$\alpha \leq 0.1$
Source: Author's calculations.

expedite this, I established a set of definitions on the density of ties to other firms (inside the group, outside the group, and outside Japan), to financial institutions and to the state bureaucracy. Analyzing and coding personal data for roughly 10,000 individuals according to those definitions were undertaken. This allowed for the application of a management production function that integrates the multiple networks of firms and showed the degree to which these networks influence each other and economic results.

To take group effects into account, I made a distinction between horizontally integrated and independent firms as well as core firms and their subsidiaries. This allowed for a different set of analysis to provide an even more detailed picture of networks during the last decade in Japan.

The results clearly show that one must clarify the existence of personal ties and their effect on economic relations. For example, the horizontally bound *keiretsu* firms and independent firms intensify their networks with financial institutions. But the effect of that is not necessarily positive—the results can actually be negative! Ties to the bureaucracy are fading away but the appointment of *amakudari* bureaucrats still has positive a influence on sales in the case of horizontal and independent firms. On the other hand, this influence is negative in the case of core firms and vertically integrated firms. Concerning inter-group networks, one can only conclude that the density of these networks is most intense in the case of subsidiaries but exerts most influence on results in the case of horizontally integrated firms. Not surprisingly, networks with corporations outside the group are strongest for independent companies—but these networks exert the most influence in cases of the vertically integrated firms. For all groups, connections with foreign firms and foreign markets are increasing—furthermore, these connections exert the greatest influence on economic results.

This analysis highlights the necessity of using networks when doing business with Japanese corporations. But patterns are changing, and Japanese firms are opening up to foreign managers and foreign firms.

ACKNOWLEDGMENTS

I would like to thank Horst Albach, Ulrike Schaede, Ulrike Stahlecker-Görtzen, and Rita Zobel for fruitful discussion and advice on the topic, as well as Ann Herring for help where my English reached its limitations. But of course, remaining errors are mine.

NOTES

1. Some examples of recent research are Iwanami (1999), Kikuchi (1996), the Fair Trade Commission's report Kosei Torihiki Iinkai (1992), and Nakata (1997). Cf. also Moerke (1999). This chapter borrowed heavily from my paper "Social Networks in Transition," Best Papers Proceedings of the Annual Meeting of the Association of Japanese Business Studies, St. Louis, 2002.

2. For instance, Aoki 1994, Fukuda and Hirota 1996, Horiuchi and Yoshino 1992, Nakatani 1984: 241 and Toyokeizai Shinposha 1996.

3. See Kato 1995: 69 and Shleifer and Vishny 1997: 757.

4. See Kaplan & Minton 1994: 227 and Kato 1995: 69.

5. On industrial policy and the role of state bureaucracy (especially on trade issues), cf. Tilton (1996).

6. The Kaisha-Database was compiled at the Science Center for Social

Research, Berlin (WZB) and is now hosted by the Otto Beisheim Graduate School of Management (WHU). It contains financial data from the annual reports of the biggest 111 firms in the following industries: automobile, chemical, electric machinery, machinery, and pharmaceutical from 1970 to 1998. Data for 1999 and 2000 is being input as of this writing. All firms are listed on the first section of the Tokyo Stock Exchange. Size was defined in terms of sales volume.

7. Cf. Albach et al. (2000).

8. This definition is often cited in literature. For instance, Gerlach (1992), Hoshi et al. (1991), Kosei Torihiki Iinkai (1992), Nakatani (1984), and TKD (1996).

9. See, TKD (Toyo Keizai Databank) (1998): Kigyo Keiretsu Soran '98. Tokyo: Toyo Keizai Shinposha.

10. TKD, (various editions) *Kigyo Keiretsu Soran*. Additionally, we treat Amada Corp. as a core company, because the group has been expanding very quickly and there are two subsidiaries in the sample.

11. For a more detailed description see Moerke (2001).

12. Cf., Beckmann (1977, 1978, 1983).

13. Return on sales for independent firms is 92 percent, whereas that for the big six firms is 4.11 percent. (The difference is statistically significant on a 10 percent level.)

14. In the case of pharmaceuticals the export ratio, measured as export over sales, reaches bottom at approximately 10 percent.

15. Think about the automobile industry: Ford extended its stake in Mazda, Renault invested in Nissan and DaimlerChrysler took over Mitsubishi Motors. The only independent automobile manufacturers left are Toyota and Honda.

16. Seen over the whole period, all differences in the mean values of the four subgroups were statistically significant on a 5 percent level.

17. To give an example: the difference in the ratio of equity over total capital between independent core firms and *keiretsu* core firms in this sample was about 25 percentage points! For detailed information, cf. Moerke et al., 2000: 19ff.

18. Because for all subsamples n >50, t-tests could be applied to check for differences. Looking over the whole period, with one exception, all means can be seen as different ($\alpha < 5\%$). The exception is the difference between independent firms and core firms, which was not statistically significant.

19. Cf. Miarka (2000) for this argument.

20. The differences of the means were not statistically significant.

21. This holds for the whole time span as well as for the periods 1985–1991 and 1992–1998, all on a 5 percent level.

22. As Schaede (2000) points out, state regulation is getting weaker— but self-regulation is playing a more important role.

23. It might be valid to check whether this holds for foreign firms in Japan. From the results stated above, one could suppose that it does.

REFERENCES

Abe, Y. (1997). *A Comparative Study of Labor Markets in the United States and Japan*. Princeton: University Microfilms International.

Albach, H., et al. (2001). Organizational Learning in Japanese Companies. Mimeo.

Albach, H., et al. (2000). Documentation of the Kaisha-Database—The Annual Accounts Database of Japanese Stock Companies 1970–1999. With a Detailed Glossary of Japanese Accounting Terminology. Discussion Paper, DP FS IV 00–10. Berlin: Science Center for Social Research.

Aoki, M. (1988). *Information, Incentives, and Bargaining in the Japanese Economy*. Cambridge: Cambridge University Press.

Aoki, M., et al. (1994). The Japanese Main Bank System: an Introductory Overview. In: Aoki, M., and Patrick, H. (eds.), *The Japanese Main Bank System*. Oxford, New York: Oxford University Press, pp. 3–50.

Beckmann, M. J. (1977). Management Production Function and the Theory of the Firm. *Journal of Economic Theory*, 14 (1): 1–18.

Beckmann, M. J. (1978). *Rank in Organizations*. Heidelberg: Springer.

Beckmann, M. J. (1983). Production Functions in the Analysis of Organizational Structure. In Beckmann, M. J., and Krelle, W. (ed.), *Technology, Organization and Economic Structure*. Heidelberg: Springer, pp. 2–14.

Calder, K. (1989). Elites in an Equalizing Role. Ex-Bureaucrats as Coordinators and Intermediaries in the Japanese Government-Business Relationship. *Comparative Politics*, 21 (4): 379–403.

Demise, N. (1997). *Kigyotochi Mondai No Keieigakuteki Kenkyu. Setsumeisekinin kankei kara no kosatsu*. Tokyo: Bunshindo.

Foljanty-Jost, G. (1989). Informelles Verwaltungshandeln: Schlüssel effizienter Implemetation oder Politik ohne Politiker? In Menzel, U. (ed.) *Im Schatten des Siegers*. Frankfurt: Suhrkamp, vol. 3, pp. 171–190.

Fukuda, A., and Hirota, S. (1996). Main Bank Relationship and Capital Structure in Japan. *Journal of the Japanese and International Economies*, 10 (3): 250–261.

Gerlach, M. (1992). *Alliance Capitalism—The Social Organization of Japanese Business*. Berkeley: University of California Press.

Görtzen, U. (2000). *Wissensgenerierung und -verbreitung als Wettbewerbsfaktor*. Wiesbaden: Deutscher Universitäts-Verlag

Göseke, C. (1997). *Information Gathering and Dissemination. The Contribution of JETRO to Japanese Competitiveness*. Wiesbaden: Deutscher Universitäts-Verlag.

Hirata, M. (1996). Die japanische torishimari-kai. Eine rechtliche und betriebswirtschaftliche Analyse. Zeitschrift für Betriebswirtschaft 3/96 (special edition), pp. 1–28.

Horiuchi, A., and Yoshino, N. (1992). *Gendai Nihon no Kin'yu Bunseki*. To-kyo: University of Tokyo Press.

Hoshi, T., et al. (1991). Corporate Structure, Liquidity, and Investment: Evidence from Japanese Industrial Groups. *The Quarterly Journal of Economics*, (Feb.) 33–60.

Ito, T., and Hoshi, T. (1992). Kigyo gurupu kessokudo no bunseki. In Hor-iuchi, A. and Yoshino, N. (eds.) *Gendai nihon no kin'yu bunseki*. To-kyo: Tokyo Daigaku Shuppankai, pp. 73–96.

Iwanami, F. (1999). The Structure of Inter-corporate Personal Relations Among Large Japanese Corporations. In, Albach, et al. (ed.), *Infor-mation Processing as a Competitive Advantage of Japanese Firms*. Berlin: edition sigma, pp. 193–210.

Johnson, C. (1989). Wer regiert Japan? Ein Essay über die staatliche Bü-rokratie. In: Menzel, U. (ed.), *Im Schatten des Siegers: Japan. Staat und Gesellschaft*. Frankfurt am Main: Suhrkamp, pp. 222–255.

Kang, J., and Shivdasani, A. (1995). Firm Performance, Corporate Gov-ernance, and Top Executive Turnover in Japan. *Journal of Financial Economics*, 38: 29–58.

Kaplan, S. N., and Minton, B. (1994). Appointments of Outsiders to Jap-anese Boards. Determinants and Implications for Managers. *Journal of Financial Economics*, 3: 225–258.

Kaplan, S. N. (1994). Top Executive Rewards and Firm Performance: A Comparison of Japan and the United States. *Journal of Political Econ-omy*, 102 (3): 510–546.

Kato, M. (1995). Meinbanku Kankei Ni Okeru Yakuin Haken No Keizai Bunseki. *Keizai To Keizaigaku*, 79: 69–92.

Kikuchi, H. (1996). Mitsubishi Kei Kigyo Yakuin No Shusshin Kaiso. *Seikei Kenkyu*, 67: 43–57.

Kosei torihiki iinkai (1992). *Nihon no Roku Dai Kigyo Shudan*. Tokyo: Toyo Keizai Shinposha.

Lincoln, J. R., et al. (1996). Keiretsu Networks and Corporate Performance in Japan. *American Sociological Review*, 61 (1): 67–88.

Lincoln, J. R., et al. (1992). Keiretsu Networks in the Japanese Economy: A Dyad Analysis of Inter-corporate Ties. *American Sociological Re-view*, 57 (5): 561–585.

Miarka, T. (2000). *Financial Intermediation and Deregulation—A Critical Anal-ysis of Japanese Bank-Firm Relationships*. Heidelberg: Physica.

Moerke, A. (2001). *Organisationslernen über Netzwerke. Eine empirische An-alyse der personellen Verflechtungen von Boards of Directors japanischer Industrieaktiengesellschaften*. Wiesbaden: Deutscher Universitäts-Verlag.

Moerke, A. (2000). Kanryoteki Keiei ka. Doitsu kara Mita Nihon no Kigyo Tochi. In Suzuki, W., et al. (eds.), *Keiei no Shihai to Kanryosei Soshiki*. Tokyo: Dobunkan, pp. 125–158.

Moerke, A. (1999). Performance and Corporate Governance Structure of Japanese Keiretsu Groups. In Albach. H., et al. (eds.), *Information Processing as a Competitive Advantage of Japanese Firms.* Berlin: edition sigma, pp. 211–238.

Moerke, Andreas, et al. (2000). Grundlegende methodische Überlegungen zur mikroökonomischen Forschung mit japanischen Unternehmensdaten. Discussion Paper, DP FS IV 00–07. Berlin: Wissenschaftszentrum Berlin für Sozialforschung.

Nakano, K. (1998). Becoming a "Policy" Ministry: The Organization and Amakudari of the Ministry of Posts and Telecommunications. *Journal of Japanese Studies,* 24 (1): 95–117.

Nakata, M., et al. (1997). *Kigyokan No Jinteki Nettowaku.* Tokyo: Dobunkan.

Nakatani, I. (1984). The Economic Role of Financial Corporate Grouping. In Aoki, M. (ed.), *The Economic Analysis of the Japanese Firm.* Amsterdam: North Holland, pp. 227–258.

Rixtel, A. v. (1995). Amakudari in the Japanese Banking Industry: An Empirical Investigation. Conference Paper, European Network and the Japanese Economy. Berlin: Wissenschaftszentrum Berlin für Sozialforschung.

Rixtel, A. v., and Hassink, W. H. (1998). Monitoring the Monitors: Amakudari and the Ex-Post Monitoring of Private Banks. Discussion Paper, DP No. 1785, London: CEPR.

Schaede, U. (2000). *Cooperative Capitalism. Self-Regulation, Trade Associations, and the Antimonopoly Law in Japan.* Oxford: Oxford University Press.

Schaede, U. (1994a). The "Old Boy" Network and Government-Business Relationship in Japan: A Case Study of "Consultative Capitalism." Occasional Papers No. 14, Center for Japanese Studies. Marburg: Philipps-Universität-Marburg.

Schaede, U. (1994b). Understanding Corporate Governance in Japan: Do Classical Concepts Apply? *Industrial and Corporate Change,* 3 (2): 285–323.

Shleifer, A., and Vishny, R. W. (1997). A Survey of Corporate Governance. The Journal of Finance, LVV (2): 737–783.

Tilton, M. (1996). *Restrained Trade.* Ithaka: Cornell University Press.

TKD (Toyo Keizai Databank) (various years). *Kigyo Keiretsu Soran.* Tokyo: Toyo Keizai Shinposha.

Toyo Keizai Shinposha (1996). *Nihon No Jinmyaku To Kigyo Keiretsu.* Tokyo: Toyo Keizai Shinposha.

Tsutsuumi, K., and Yamaguchi, J. (1997). *Kanryo Amakudari Hakusho.* Tokyo: Iwanami.

Uryu, F., et al. (1993). The Realities of "Keiretsu" Phenomena. A Review of Research and Arguments on "Keiretsu." Report, Research Institute of International Trade and Industry. Tokyo: MITI.

Usui, C., and Colignon, R. (1999). Serial Retirements of Administrative Elites—Wataridori. In AJBS (ed.), Annual Meeting of the Association of Japanese Business Studies, Best Papers Proceedings, 1999. Utah: AJBS, pp. 43–60.

Usui, C., and Colignon, R. (1997). The Ties That Bind the Japanese Polity and Economy,—Amakudari. In AJBS (ed.), Annual Meeting of the Association of Japanese Business Studies. Washington D.C.: AJBS.

Appendix
List of Firms, Keiretsu Membership, etc.

NAME	Code	Industry	Keiretsu
Aida Engineering, Ltd.	6118	MA	I
Aiwa Co., Ltd.	6761	EL	V
Amada Co., Ltd.	6113	MA	IC
Amada Sonoike Co., Ltd.	6107	MA	V
Amada Wasino Co., Ltd.	6108	MA	V
Asahi Diamond Industrial	6140	MA	I
Chiyoda Corporation	6366	MA	I
Chugai Pharmaceutical	4519	PH	I
Clarion Company	6796	EL	V
Daifuku Co., Ltd.	6383	MA	I
Daihatsu Motor	7262	AU	V
Daiichi Pharmaceutical Co., Ltd.	4505	PH	I
Daikin Industries, Ltd.	6367	MA	I
Dijet Industrial Co., Ltd.	6138	MA	I
Ebara Corporation	6361	MA	H
Eisai	4523	PH	I
Fuji Electric	6504	EL	HC
Fujisawa Pharmaceutical Co., Ltd.	4511	PH	H
Fujitsu General Ltd.	6755	EL	V
Fujitsu Ltd.	6702	EL	HC
Hitachi Construction Machinery Co., Ltd.	6305	MA	V
Hitachi Koki Co., Ltd.	6581	EL	V
Hitachi Ltd.	6501	EL	HC
Hitachi Seiki	6106	MA	I
Honda Motor	7267	AU	IC
Ikegai	6102	MA	I
Iseki & Co	6310	MA	H
Isuzu Motors	7202	AU	V
Japan Radio Co., Ltd.	6751	EL	V
Kenwood Corporation (Trio Kenwood Corp.)	6765	EL	I
Kokusai Electric Co., Ltd.	6756	EL	V
Komatsu Ltd.	6301	MA	I
Kubota Corporation	6326	MA	H
Kyushu Matsushita Electric	6782	EL	V
Makino Milling Machine Company	6135	MA	I
Makita Corporation	6586	EL	I
Matsushita Communication Ind. Co., Ltd.	6781	EL	V
Matsushita Electric Industrial Co., Ltd.	6752	EL	IC
Matsushita Refrigeration Company	6583	EL	V
Matsushita-Kotobuki Electronic Industries,	6783	EL	V

Appendix
List of Firms, Keiretsu Membership, etc. (continued)

Mazda Motor	7261	AU	V
Meidensha Electric Mfg. Co., Ltd.	6508	EL	I
Mitsubishi Electric Corporation	6503	EL	HC
NEC Corporation	6701	EL	HC
Nissan Motor	7201	AU	HC
Oki Electric Industry Company, Ltd.	6703	EL	H
Okuma Corporation	6103	MA	I
Omron Corporation	6645	EL	I
Osaki Electric Co., Ltd.	6644	EL	I
OSG Corporation	6136	MA	I
Pioneer Electronic Corporation	6773	EL	I
Sanken Electric Company, Ltd.	6707	EL	I
Sankyo Company, Limited	4501	PH	H
Sanyo Electric	6764	EL	IC
Sharp Corporation	6753	EL	H
Shionogi & Co., Ltd.	4507	PH	I
Sony Corporation	6758	EL	IC
Sumitomo Heavy Industries	6302	MA	H
Suzuki Motor	7269	AU	I
Tadano Ltd.	6395	MA	I
Taisho Pharmaceuticals Company Ltd.	4535	PH	I
Takeda Chemical Industries Ltd.	4502	PH	I
Tanabe Seiyaku Company Ltd.	4508	PH	H
Teac Corporation	6803	EL	I
Tokyo Electric Co., Ltd. (TEC)	6588	EL	V
Toshiba Ltd.	6502	EL	HC
Toshiba Machine Co., Ltd.	6104	MA	V
Toshiba Tungaloy Co., Ltd.	6139	MA	V
Toyo Engineering Corporation	6330	MA	V
Toyoda Automatic Loom Works, Ltd.	6201	MA	V
Toyoda Machine Works, Ltd.	6206	MA	V
Toyota Motor	7203	AU	HC
Tsugami Corporation	6101	MA	I
Tsumura & Co.	4540	PH	I
Victor Company of Japan, Ltd.	6792	EL	V
Yamanouchi Pharmaceutical Co., Ltd.	4503	PH	I
Yaskawa Electric Corporation	6506	EL	H

Abbreviations:

AU = Automotive; EL = Electrical Machinery; MA = Machinery; PH = Pharmaceuticals;

CHAPTER 5

Individual Networking for Internalizing Diverse Knowledge: A Case Study of Technology-Based Academic Societies

Kiyoshi Nosu

INTRODUCTION

Open-structured organizations and networking are playing increasingly more significant roles in knowledge-based economics by collecting knowledge and wisdom from a variety of individuals, institutes, and corporations. A technology-based academic society is a typical example of a nonprofit, open-structured interinstitute organization.

Technology-based academic societies internalize diverse technical knowledge of individual members beyond the limitations of an individual researcher's recognition capability. Researchers and engineers of competing corporations and institutes participate and contribute to various activities of a technology-based academic society so that collaboration and competition simultaneously coexist. Researchers collaboratively create new technical knowledge by exchanging new data and ideas.

Unlike traditional corporations, the organizational border and membership of an academic society is flexible and many researchers belong to different academic societies. Trust and reputation encourage and stimulate the activities of academic society members, while order and command determine the behaviors in hierarchical organizations such as large corporations or military troops.

In this chapter we will discuss the organizational structure of an academic society, taking the Institute of Electronics, Information and Communication Engineers, Japan (IEICE) as an example. Following the introduction, we will review the role of nonprofit organizations in a knowledge-based society. In the third section, we will discuss the organizational structure of technology-based academic societies from the viewpoint of collaborative organizational learning with competitors. We also discuss the roles of trust and reputation as key elements that activate an open-structured, nonprofit organization. In the fourth section, we will examine the collaborative knowledge creation and knowledge sharing processes at a technology-based academic society. In particular, we will focus on the research and development processes of fiber optic transmission technology. Finally, we will propose an effective participation strategy for technology-based nonprofit, nonhierarchical open-structured organizations from the viewpoint of corporate management.

THE ROLE OF NONPROFIT ORGANIZATIONS IN A KNOWLEDGE-BASED SOCIETY

Nonprofit organizations are occupying an important position in economics. For example, nonprofit organizations in the United States are estimated to produce more than 5 percent of the GDP of the United States (Drucker 1993). The following questions arise in connection with the activities of nonprofit organizations.

- Why have nonprofit organizations recently become so important?
- What are the major roles of nonprofit organizations in technological research and development?

In this section, we will examine the major roles of nonprofit organizations in knowledge creation by comparing the functions of private corporations and nonprofit organizations. The purpose of a nonprofit organization is to offer social and public solutions that private corporations cannot. Many volunteers contribute to nonprofit organizations. They do not seek ecumenical rewards and benefits but obtain satisfaction from serving the public and gaining a positive reputation within the community. There are other factors that distinguish nonprofit organizations from the private sector. These include:

1. stakeholders,
2. organizational governance,
3. organizational governance keeper,
4. organizational behavior principle,
5. human resources,
6. profit distribution.

The stakeholders of private corporations and firms are shareholders, executive officers, employees, and customers while those of nonprofit organizations include volunteers, donors, paid staffs, board members, and community members. The principal human resource of a private corporation is paid workers, while that of nonprofit organizations is unpaid officers and volunteers.

CEOs and executive board members usually manage the corporate governance of private organizations. On the other hand, the governance of a nonprofit organization is relatively weak. The management procedures in a nonprofit organization usually depend on the stakeholders and the purpose of the organization.

A private corporation usually seeks business efficiency with order and commands within a hierarchical system to win profits. A nonprofit organization behaves on a different principle: it emphasizes the freedom of volunteers and members as well as public and social benefits. As a result, a nondistribution constraint is applied to a nonprofit organization, although it can produce profits that can be used for further development of activities. This is a significant difference between nonprofit organizations and private corporations. Table 5.1 summarizes the differences between private corporations and nonprofit organizations.

Non-profit volunteers traditionally have supplied labor power to the activities of nonprofit organizations. For a knowledge-based society, the activities of knowledge-worker-based nonprofit organizations are becoming more and more important. Among nonprofit organizations, universities, academic societies, and other public corporations involved in science and technology fields are directly contributing to knowledge creation. Drucker describes a postcapitalist society where knowledge and information are more important than capital, natural resources, and labor, as follows (Drucker 1993).

Value is now created by "productivity" and "innovation," both applications of knowledge to work. The leading social groups of the knowledge society will be "knowledge workers"—knowledge executives who know how to allocate knowledge to productive use, just as the capitalists knew how to allocate capital to productive use; knowledge professionals; knowledge employees. Practically all these knowledge people will be employed in organizations. Yet, unlike the employees under Capitalism, they will own both the "means of production" and the "tools of production"—the former through their pension funds which are rapidly emerging in all developed countries as the only one owners; the latter because knowledge workers own their knowledge and take it with them wherever they go. The economics challenge of the post-capitalist society will therefore be productivity of knowledge work and the knowledge worker.

It has been said that nonprofit organizations complement both market failure and government failure. Because information and knowledge more or less gradually become public assets, institutions to stimulate knowledge creation are significant in a knowledge creation society. Along this line, nonprofit organizations, including universities and colleges, academic societies and intercorporate forums, are playing important roles in technical knowledge creation and technical research and development.

Figure 5.1 illustrates mutual relationships among key players in technology research and development. Government establishes industrial policy from a viewpoint of social welfare, to promote healthy economical growth and prosperity, while private corporations and firms offer market information and convey their requests to their governments so that they can enjoy business development. Principal players in a nonprofit sector include universities, colleges, academic societies, and other interorganizational forums. Individual members of universities and private corporations provide their research to academic societies. On the other hand, academic societies provide a place for organizational learning for its members from both private corporations and universities. Members can interactively discuss their research items, crossing organizational borders.

A government gives special preference to nonprofit organizations because it believes that the activities of the nonprofit sector, such as proposals, recommendations, and other public benefits improve the competitiveness of the economy. This knowledge-sharing chain that links the public, private, and nonprofit sectors helps meet public interest in promoting knowledge creation and economic growth.

ORGANIZATIONAL STRUCTURE OF A TECHNOLOGY-BASED ACADEMIC SOCIETY

Historically, technology-oriented corporations and firms have mainly conducted research and development internally to win their battle with competitors. Traditional strategies of research and development at high-tech corporations must deal with many issues and difficulties. These include:

1. Integration of wide varieties of rapidly growing high technologies,
2. Large financial budgets for high-tech research and development,
3. Uncertainties in markets,
4. Speedy business operation to catch up with the market and environmental change.

In this environment, high-technology corporations are shifting their research and development towards nonself-consistent styles, namely, collaboration with competitors. Technology-based academic societies and other intercorporate, nonprofit organizations are now providing places for collaboration among competing corporations and academic organizations so that they can respond to the trends previously described.

Figure 5.1
The Relationship among Government, Markets, and NPOs

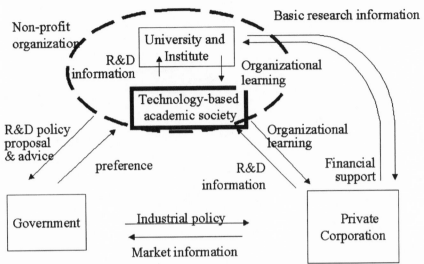

Members of a technology-based academic society present and exchange technical information and knowledge so that they can keep up-to-date positions in the technical fields. The information exchanges in a technology-based academic society are carried out by periodicals, technical journals, conferences, and conventions.

Interorganizational societies and associations exist not only for technical fields but also for other disciplines such as medical sciences, natural sciences, social sciences, and humanities. One feature of professional technology societies is that contributions from private corporations are fairly large. For example, researchers and engineers of private corporations usually present more than 70 percent of the technical papers at the National Convention of IEICE (Institute of Electronics, Information and Communication Engineers) in Japan.

There are many technology-based academic societies providing intercorporate linkages and collaborations. Some are national and others are global organizations. For example, the Institute of Electronics, Information and Communication Engineers (IEICE) in Japan has about 40,000 members and the Institute of Electric and Electronics Engineers (IEEE), which is headquartered in the United States, has more than 400,000 members throughout the world.

Figure 5.2 illustrates these interorganizational, technical knowledge chains that involve corporations and universities in a technology-based academic society. Like other nonprofit organizations, whose characteris-

Figure 5.2
Collaboration with Competitors through a Nonprofit Inter-Corporate Organization

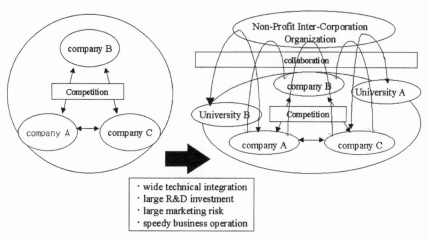

Table 5.1
Differences between Nonprofit Organizations and Private Corporations

	private corporation	non-profit organization
stakeholder	share-holder, executive officer, employee, customer	volunteer member, donor, paid staff, board member, community member
human resource	paid worker	unpaid officer and volunteer
governance holder	executive officer board	various stakeholder council/committee
organizational behavior principle	efficiency order and command	freedom voluntary public/social benefit seeking
profit distribution	dividend	non-distribution constraint

tics are summarized in Table 5.1, a technology-based academic society seeks public and social benefits and its members are not managed by an order and command-based organizational scheme. Therefore, one important factor for organizing members is the trust shared by members. Trust has received attention in several different disciplines—sociology, psychology, political science, economics, anthropology, and so on. Although trust plays a significant role in social processes, each discipline, or even each piece of literature, has it own viewpoint. Therefore, their perspectives regarding trust differ. Lewicki and Bunker (1996) aggregated the perspectives on trust for professional working relationships. Toshio Yamagishi (1998)integrated the various perspectives on trust more structurally and widely. Hereafter, we will develop a hierarchical structure of trust.

Lewicki and Bunker (1996) emphasized the dynamic process of trust in professional relationships (Lewick). We will discuss their theory for further rearrangement of the perspectives of trust.

The most important element in Boon and Holmes's description of the evolution of trust is their suggestion that trust dynamics are different at each of the three stages. This is a fundamentally different perspective on trust from the view that the essence of trust cannot be captured by a single "static" definition of its key elements and attributes. Trust is viewed as a dynamic phenomenon that takes on a different character in the early, developing, and "mature" stages of a relationship.

Lewicki and Bunker (1996) defined the early, developing, and mature stages of a relationship as follows:

1. calculus-based trust
2. knowledge-based trust
3. identification-based trust

Quoting Lewicki and Bunker's description, this paper will discuss the definition of the three stages of trust development (Lewicki).

Calculus-Based Trust

Shapiro, Sheppard, and Cheraskin identified the first kind of trust as deterrence-based trust. These authors argue that this form of trust is based on assuring consistency of behavior; that is, individuals will do what they say because they fear the consequence–of not doing what they say. Like any behavior based on a theory of deterrence, trust is sustained to the degree that the deterrent (punishment) is clearly possible and likely to occur if the trust is violated. Thus, the threat of punishment is likely to be a more significant motivator than the promise of reward. . . .

. . . Compliance with calculus-based trust is often ensured both by the rewards of being trusting (and trustworthy) and by the "threat" that if trust is violated, one's reputation can be hurt through the person's network of friends and associates. In a business relationship, the professional "reputation" of the other side can serve as a "hostage " If one party begins to violate the other's trust, the violated party can quickly let it be known, throughout the accused network, that the other is a disreputable individual. . . .

Knowledge-Based Trust

The second form of trust is knowledge-based trust. This form of trust is grounded in the other's predictability-knowing the other sufficiently well so that the other's behavior is anticipatable: Knowledge-based trust relies on information rather than deterrence. It develops over time, largely as a function of the parties having a history of interaction that allows them to develop a generalized expectancy that the other' s behavior is predictable and that he or she will act trustworthily. . . .

. . . In knowledge-based trust, regular communication and courtship are key processes. Regular communication puts a party in constant contact with the other, exchanging information about wants, preferences, and approaches to problems. Without regular communication, one can "lose touch" with the other—not only emotionally but in the ability to think alike and predict the reactions of the other. Second, "courtship" is behavior that is specifically directed at relationship development at learning more about a possible partner. Courtship is conducted by "interviewing" the other, watching the other perform in social situations, experiencing the other in a variety of emotional states, and learning how others view this behavior. Courtship permits actors to gain enough information to determine whether the parties can work together well.

Identification-Based Trust

The third type of trust is based on identification with the other's desires and intentions. At this third level, trust exists because the parties effectively understand and appreciate the other's wants; this mutual understanding is developed to the point that each can effectively act for the other. For example, Kramer argues that a certain form of group-based trust is linked with group membership and develops as individuals identify with the goals espoused by particular groups and organizations.

. . . A corollary of this "acting for each other" in identification-based trust is that as both knowledge and identification develop, the parties not only know and identify with each but come to understand what they must do to sustain the other's trust . . . In summary, identification-based trust develops as one both knows and predicts the other's needs, choices, and preferences and also shares some of those same needs, choices, and preference as one's own. Increased identification enables one to "think like" the other, "feel like" the other, and "respond" like the other.

The perspectives of trust developed by Lewick and Bunker are related to the expectations of a partners' will and threats. Yamagishi analyzed the concept of trust more widely. According to his structural model, there are two basic perspectives of trust (Yamagishi 1998).

1. Expectation on the order of nature
2. Expectation on moral order

He further classified expectation on moral order into the following two perspectives,

1.   Expectation on a partner's ability
2.   Expectation on a partner's will

What's more, he precisely analyzed expectation on a partner's will so that the structural model of trust covers not only working processes but also other social events. Because we are discussing the trust in nonprofit organizational activities, we also refer to Lewick and Bunker's perspectives on expectation on a partner's will. Although Lewick and Bunker were interested in only the dynamic aspect of trust, the static aspects of trust are also important for analyzing the activities of nonprofit organizations. Table 5.2 illustrates the hierarchical structure of trust, referring to Yamagishi's and Lewick and Bunker's theories.

The rest of this chapter examines the role of organizational learning in the creation of knowledge in intercorporate, technology-based societies. A case study on fiber-optic transmission system development is also described to illustrate the significance and effectiveness of semantic literacy in professional, high-tech societies. The case study indicates that organizational learning effectively contributes to research and development of both immature and widely integrated technologies.

INTERORGANIZATIONAL LEARNING IN A TECHNOLOGY-BASED ACADEMIC SOCIETY

Semantic Literacy

Joseph L. Badaracco Jr. classified knowledge into two groups (Badaracco, 1991):

1. Migratory knowledge and
2. Embedded knowledge.

Migratory knowledge can diffuse without aid from the person or organization having the original knowledge. Embedded knowledge is attached to a person or organization; it takes a conscious act to be transferred or learned. Thus, direct communication with the persons or organizations having the original knowledge is essential to obtaining embedded knowledge. Examples of embedded knowledge are know-how and other tacit knowledge that a person cannot obtain unless he/she is a member of a specific society or organization.

Following Badaraco's theory on knowledge, we can classify semantic literacy into

1. Migratory knowledge literacy and
2. Embedded knowledge literacy.

In technical fields, migratory knowledge literacy is literacy for understanding the contents of technical textbooks, manuals, technical journal

Table 5.2
The Hierarchical Structure of Trust

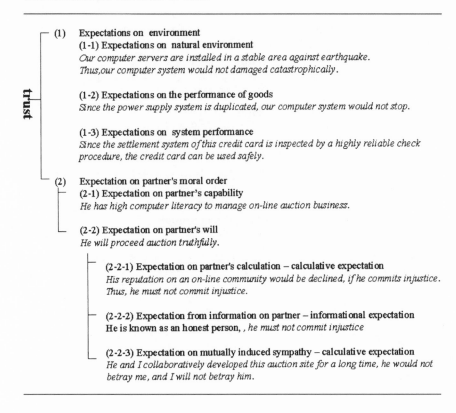

(1) Expectations on environment
(1-1) Expectations on natural environment
Our computer servers are installed in a stable area against earthquake.
Thus, our computer system would not damaged catastrophically.

(1-2) Expectations on the performance of goods
Since the power supply system is duplicated, our computer system would not stop.

(1-3) Expectations on system performance
Since the settlement system of this credit card is inspected by a highly reliable check procedure, the credit card can be used safely.

(2) Expectation on partner's moral order
(2-1) Expectation on partner's capability
He has high computer literacy to manage on-line auction business.

(2-2) Expectation on partner's will
He will proceed auction truthfully.

(2-2-1) Expectation on partner's calculation – calculative expectation
His reputation on an on-line community would be declined, if he commits injustice.
Thus, he must not commit injustice.

(2-2-2) Expectation from information on partner – informational expectation
He is known as an honest person, , *he must not commit injustice*

(2-2-3) Expectation on mutually induced sympathy – calculative expectation
He and I collaboratively developed this auction site for a long time, he would not betray me, and I will not betray him.

papers and conference presentations of technology-based academic societies. Through migratory knowledge literacy we can obtain some general knowledge. Formal education at schools, universities, and other educational institutes provide migratory knowledge literacy to those who want it. However, even for those individuals with migratory knowledge literacy the following questions arise.

- Is it possible to understand the relationship among leading-edge papers in technical journals and presentations at conferences of technology-based academic societies?
- How should we evaluate technical information in a proper and timely manner?
- Is it possible to recognize leading-edge technology trends?

Embedded knowledge literacy in a specific technical field is required to properly understand the trends of rapidly changing technology as well as the technical context. In a leading-edge technology field, the embedded knowledge is created and persevered in a tightly knit community such as a technology-based academic society.

Organizational Knowledge Creation

The knowledge shared by members of an organization is, hereafter, called organizational knowledge (Nonaka and Takeuchi 1995). We will discuss the process of organizational knowledge creation in a technology-based academic society so that we can understand the significance of embedded knowledge literacy. In a technology-based academic society, new pieces of information obtained by members are distributed to other members through periodicals, technical journals, and conferences. The new information is interpreted and evaluated by members who have a framework of organizational interpretation. The members of the society accept and share a common interpretation framework. The evaluated pieces of information are combined with and integrated into accumulated organizational knowledge.

The newly created knowledge affects the organizational interpretation framework, which is adjusted to the new knowledge environment. An abrupt change in an organizational interpretation framework reflects a paradigm change in a society. This is the basic concept of organizational knowledge creation in a technical society, whose schematic model is illustrated in Figure 5.3. It should be noted that the effective border of an

Figure 5.3
A Model of Interorganizational Learning at a Technology-Based Academic Society

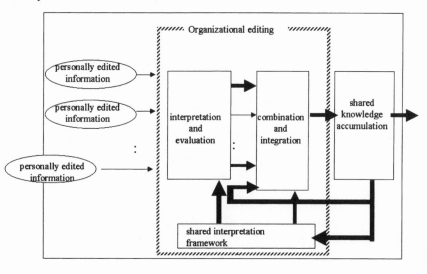

organization is defined by the accessibility of its embedded knowledge as well as its migratory knowledge.

For those who do not have the corresponding semantic literacy, especially embedded knowledge literacy, it is very difficult to share the organizational interpretation framework and some important organizational knowledge. Participation in a technology-based academic society provides the following opportunities (Powell and Brantley 1990):

1. Capability to understand the trends in leading edge technology,
2. Ability to evaluate technical achievements of members,
3. Chance to obtain competitors' information.

The above fruits are obtained when a researcher or an engineer has embedded knowledge literacy in a specific technical field. Embedded knowledge literacy can be captured when a researcher or engineer is deeply committed to organizational knowledge creation in a technology-based academic society. This is the reason why private corporations encourage their researchers and engineers to participate in technology-based academic societies, exposing the results of their internal research and development.

In summary, organizational knowledge creation in a technology-based academic society is the process that amplifies the outputs of its members through its communication media, such as journals and conferences, to create new combinations of knowledge and information so that members can accept the new knowledge to be shared. Embedded knowledge literacy is obtained only through actively participating in organizational learning at technology-based academic societies.

CASE STUDY OF INTERORGANIZATION LEARNING AT A TECHNOLOGY-BASED ACADEMIC SOCIETY—A CASE STUDY OF FIBER-OPTIC TRANSMISSION TECHNOLOGY DEVELOPMENT—(NOSU 93), (NOSU97)

A Knowledge Creation Process

We have discussed the importance of semantic literacy in a technology-based academic society. This section describes this literacy in a technology-based academic society focusing on long-haul fiber-optic transmission systems. The purpose of this study is to clarify the importance of organizational learning in a technology-based academic society.

We investigate two technology-based academic societies: the Institute of Electronics, Information and Communication Engineers (IEICE) in Japan (with 40,000 members) and the Institute of Electric and Electronics Engineers (IEEE) (with more than 400,000 members throughout the world). Members present and exchange technical information and knowledge through journals and conferences in order to keep up-to-date positions on both migratory knowledge literacy and embedded knowledge literacy.

Research and development on fiber-optic long-haul transmission systems started in the 1960s; the first commercial systems were introduced in Japan and the United States in 1981. Now fiber-optic transmission systems are deployed in domestic as well as international telecommunication networks. The research and development on these systems went through four phases:

1. Investigation period (1966–1974)
2. Preparation period (1975–1980)
3. Growth period (1981–1988)
4. Maturation period (1999)

Organization Model

Even in a technology-oriented society in which members share a common research target such as fiber-optic transmission technology, subnetworks of members form reflecting differences in members' knowledge interpretation frameworks. Fiber-optic transmission technology is based on the following three subtechnologies:

1. Transmission system,
2. Fiber-optic cables,
3. Optical devices, such as laser diodes and photo-detectors.

A wide variety of technical information is exchanged in an interorganizational network. Some is detailed information and some covers a broad scope of technology. Thus, we might be able to classify technology information based on technical scope. Hereafter, we define wide-scope information as upper-layer information and narrow-scope information as lower-layer information. For example, wide-scoped review papers written by opinion leaders of a technology society belong to the upper layer while detailed data presented on a specific experiment belong to the lower layer.

Three following factors characterize an interorganizational network.

1. Participating organizations,
2. Subtechnologies,
3. Organizational editorial layer determined by the technology scope.

Figure 5.4 shows a network model for interorganizational knowledge creation of fiber-optic transmission technology.

Bibliographic Research

Interorganizational knowledge creation was investigated by using the bibliographic data of IEEE Journals and Transactions, IEICE National Conventions, and patent applications submitted to the Japanese Patent Office. The sources of bibliographic data were as follows:

1. Papers by Japanese manufacturers and telecommunication service providers printed in IEEE Journals and Transactions during 1970–1972, 1980, 1985, and 1990 were collected and classified by corporation. These years correspond to the research and development phases defined previously.
2. Papers by Japanese manufacturers and telecommunication service providers presented at IEICE National Conventions during 1970–1972, 1980, 1985 and 1990 were collected and classified by corporations.
3. Japanese manufacturers' patent applications submitted to the Japanese Patent Office during 1970–1972, 1980, 1985, and 1990 were collected and classified into corporations.

Figure 5.5 indicates the knowledge interaction among subtechnologies obtained from the bibliographic data (1). The subtechnologies are optical fiber cable technology, optical device technology, and fiber-optic trans-

Figure 5.4
A Model of an Interorganizational Network for Development of Fiber-Optic Transmission Technology

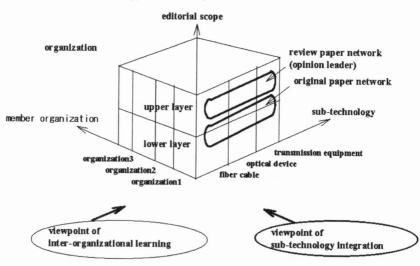

Figure 5.5
Knowledge Interaction among Fiber-Optic Transmission Subtechnologies

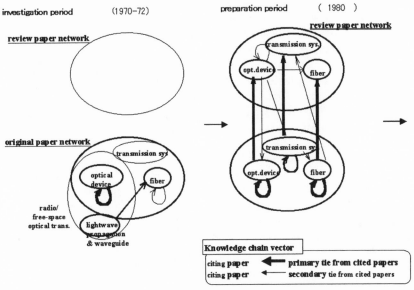

investigation period (1970-72)

preparation period (1980)

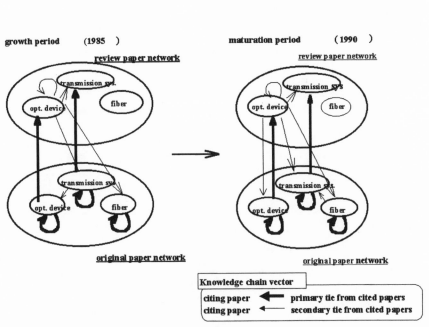

growth period (1985)

maturation period (1990)

mission system technology. In addition to these subtechnology categories, bibliographic data (1) were classified into an upper or lower layer in accordance with the scope of the paper as shown in Figure 5.4. An upper layer paper reviews technological trends and future perspectives while a lower layer paper describes individual original findings. Arrows indicates the knowledge chain from a cited (referred) paper to a citing paper. In other words, arrows indicate the knowledge chain between subtechnologies. Figure 5.4 suggests that knowledge interactions among different subtechnologies and different sublayers diversified in 1980 and 1985, which is near 1981, the year of the first commercial system installation. As technology matures, the interaction among different subtechnologies becomes weak.

The correlation coefficients between interorganizational learning and intraorganizational learning are shown in Table 5.3. The number of papers published in IEEE Journals and Transactions and the number of papers presented at IEICE National Conventions were used as indices of interorganizational knowledge creation, while the number of patents was used as indices of intraorganizational knowledge creation. As shown in Table 5.3.

1. The correlation between patents and papers of Japanese corporations for optical devices is large.
2. The correlation between patents and papers of Japanese corporations for optical-fiber cables is small.
3. The correlation between patents and papers of Japanese corporations for transmission systems is between those of the other two.

This indicates that the number of patent applications (intracorporation learning) is in proportion to a corporation's contribution to professional

Table 5.3
Correlation between Patent Applications and Papers/Presentations

		optical fiber cable	optical device	transmission system
1975	IEEE	–	–	–
	IEICE	0.17	0	0.2
1980	IEEE	0.38	0.17	–
	IEICE	0.31	0.83	0.31
1985	IEEE	−0.35	−0.05	0.18
	IEICE	0.49	0.49	0.49
1990	IEEE	−0.33	0.35	0.75
	IEICE	0.86	0.54	0.91

societies (intercorporate learning) in the fields of optical devices and transmission systems. This means that collaboration among corporations at technology-based academic societies is important in these fields. Researchers and engineers exchange technical information and knowledge through various activities of technology-based academic societies so that technical knowledge is organizationally created and accumulated.

Optical device technology development is still at the elementary stage in comparison to that of micro-electronic device technology. Major technological innovation in optical-fiber cables was completed in the 1980s. Development of transmission systems technology requires a broad integration of high-level subtechnologies.

These findings lead us to conclude that organizational learning in technology-based academic societies comprised of members from many corporations is useful for an immature technology and for a widely integrated technology, as illustrated in Figure 5.6. An effective strategy for participating in an interorganizational, technology-based academic society is to contribute and present papers on immature technologies as well as on widely integrated technologies so that effective use of the venue for interorganizational learning can be made.

A Long Term Knowledge Sharing Process at IEICE

We have discussed the development of long-haul transmission systems technology by examining activities at technology-based academic socie-

Figure 5.6
Technology Attributes Suitable for Interorganizational Learning

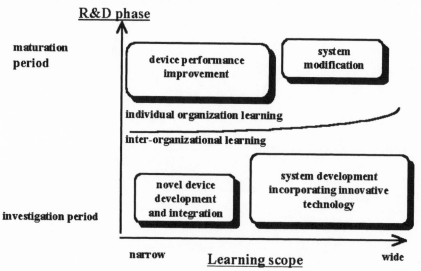

Figure 5.7
Presentations at the IECIE National Conventions of 1981, 1991, and 2001

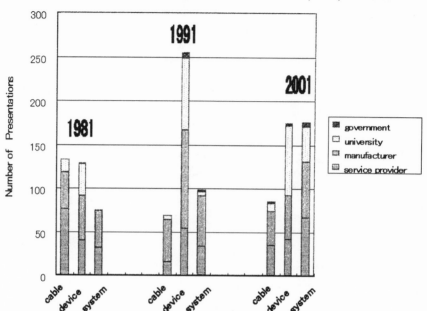

ties. As described in Fig. 5.5, research began in the 1970s and the first commercial systems were installed in Japan and the United States in 1981. Since then, the performance of long-haul, large-capacity fiber optic transmission systems has improved. In the early 1990s, the performance of fiber-optic transmission systems nearly met the telecommunication traffic requirements of the time. However, as the commercial use of the Internet penetrated into offices, factories, stores, schools, and homes after 1995, two new demands on fiber optic transmission systems emerged.

1. Even larger capacity of transmission systems
2. Broadband access systems, namely the fiber-to-the-home (FTTH) system

Figure 5.7 shows the number of presentations at the National Conventions of the Institute of Electronics, Information and Communication Engineers (IEICE) in 1981, 1991, and 2001. Presentations were classified into three categories.

1. Fiber optic cable
2. Optical device
3. Transmission systems

It should be noted that although we focused on long-haul, fiber optic transmission systems technology in the first part of this chapter, Figure 5.7 also includes fiber-optic access (Fiber-to-the-home, FTTH) systems.

In 1981, the number of presentations on fiber-optic cables and optical devices was greater than that of fiber-optic transmission systems. This was because the technologies of system elements, such as fiber-optic cables and optical devices, had not matured in 1991. Contributions from universities to the development of fiber optic transmission systems were very limited while universities made many presentations on fiber-optic cables and optical devices fields.

In 1991, although the total number of presentations on fiber-optic technologies increased, the number of presentations on fiber-optic cables decreased. This was because the basic structures of optical fibers and cables were nearly completed by this time. Presentations on novel optical devices for next generation systems, such as broadband access and very-large capacity, long-haul transmissions increased, owing to its advanced fabrication process. Although the total number of presentations in 2001 was almost the same as that in 1991, presentations on systems increased; particularly contributions from universities, which drastically increased. This might have been because system elements such as optical devices and optical fibers were maturing. In this manner, knowledge relating to fiber-optic transmission technology has been exchanged and diffused through the academic society, maintaining the technological competitiveness of our society.

CONCLUSION

We have investigated the role of interorganizational learning and embedded knowledge literacy in technology-based academic societies. A case study on fiber-optic transmission systems technology showed that interorganizational learning in a technology-based academic society is effective for immature technology and for a widely integrated technology.

ACKNOWLEDGMENT

Part of the research outlined in this chapter was carried out at the Graduate School of Systems Management, Tsukuba University in Tokyo under the supervision of Professor Yoshiya Teramoto (currently at Waseda University). The author sincerely expresses his thanks to Professor Teramoto for his advice and guidance.

REFERENCES

Badaracco. (1991). *Knowledge Link*, Harvard Business School.
Drucker, P. E. (1993). "The Ecological Vision—Reflections on the American Conditions." Transaction Publishers.

Lewicki, R., and B. B. Bunker. (1996). Developing and Maintaining Trust in Work Relationships, in R. M. Kramer and T. Tyler (eds.), *Trust in Organization,* Sage Publications.

Nonaka, Ikujiro, and Hirotaka Takeuchi. (1995). *The Knowledge Creating Corporation,* Oxford University Press.

Nosu, K. (1993). *Participation Strategy to Professional Technology-based Academic Society,* Master's thesis, Graduate School of Systems Management, Tsukuba University, Tokyo.

Nosu, K. (1997). *Semantic Literacy in Inter-Firm Technology Organizations— A Case Study of Fiber Optic Transmission Technology Development,* APEC Conference on Information Literacy '97, 1–3, Nippon University, The University of Queensland, APEC Human Resource Development (APEC HRD BMN and HURDIT).

Powell, W. W., and P. Brantley. (1990). Competitive Cooperation in Biotechnology: Learning though Networks?, in N. Nohia and R. G Ecoles, eds., *Networks and Organizations,* Harvard Business School.

Yamagishi, T. (1998). *Shinrai no Kouzou (Structure of Trust)* (in Japanese), Tokyo University Press.

CHAPTER 6

Open Sourcing as a Corporate Strategy: A Study of the Open Source Community from an Organizational Theoretic Perspective and the Development of R&D with External Resources

Midori Kato

INTRODUCTION[1]

Open Source[2] is a general term used to describe a method of software development on a network in which the source code is completely open to everyone. The Open Source movement, which started at the beginning of 1998, evolved in major companies and greatly transformed conventional R&D strategy, which was based on the thinking that unique and closed technology is the source of competitiveness. Implementation of Open Source projects by firms is new in terms of the use of external resources in R&D and business. Although the use of external resources for firms' R&D was performed in forms such as joint research, alliances, and outsourcing for many years, many focused on their own technology and complemented the external technology or resources through limited relations between companies. Alternatively, it was based on the strategic intention to control technology standards and make deployment of subsequent business advantageous. Open Sourcing by firms is different from conventional methods of R&D and business in that this process exhibits all technologies and uses many unspecified external resources.

This chapter clarifies the knowledge creation of engineers in a network through the case study of Open Source. In addition, it discusses the changing knowledge exchange among firms and individuals/communities as a case of meso-organization.

OPEN SOURCE

Historical Circumstances of Open Source

The Linux kernel[3] development project is probably the most famous Open Source project; however, the development method and its culture of sharing source codes have existed for many years, especially among Unix software engineers and on the Internet,[4] which is based on Unix. At the beginning of 1998, this method was officially named Open Source. The Open Source community has fully utilized communication on the network for social intercourse and business for many years. The programmers who participated in the Open Source project formed and shared their own culture called "hacker culture"[5] and have existed on the network as a community. Because the Internet was developed as a network connected throughout distributed environments, standard technology and the observance of operational rules by all persons concerned were required. Many of the standards of the present Internet are dependent on Open Source. Although the standard technologies of the Internet were mostly completed about 20 years ago, these were not necessarily called Open Source at that time. Crocker (1997) and others who made great contributions to e-mail technology explain in detail the situation of the technical development of ARPANET,[6] which is described as "standardization by free adoption." It is suggested that the technology that more people approve of because of its excellence became the standard. Moreover, all of the specifications and the requirements for various Internet technologies, which is called RFC (Request For Comment), are exhibited in written form. RFC was also made available to many people and has been refined by extensive comments and corrections.

Although Internet technology is developed on Unix, Open Source cannot be considered separately from the history of the Internet and the history of Unix programming.

The nature of the communication on electronic networks has also had a big influence on Open Sourcing. Mail, Net News, and ftp have mainly been used by the Open Source community.[7] Although the mailing lists that the community uses are similar to mass media in terms of their ability to send information to many people immediately and simultaneously, they are interactive, which is not a characteristic of mass media. Moreover, the cost of sending information on the Internet is very low. Furthermore, ftp and the Web have the feature that allows changes to become effective for all readers as soon as the change is made from one place. However, this feature of electronic networks can become a demerit in many cases.

The increase of information dispatch leads to an increase in S/N ratio (Signal Versus Noise Ratio) and cost of information searching. Furthermore, troublesome information can be sent as easily as helpful information whether it is sent by design or accident. In addition, because network resources are poor, a standard of manners called "netiquette"[8] has been recommended for those who frequently communicate on the Internet. Netiquette consists of the accumulated wisdom of the Internet community, which values conciseness.

The Open Source movement has been influenced by the enlightenment activities of Stallman[9] and others who founded FSF (Free Software Foundation) for the purpose of protection and encouragement of freeware and who started the GNU[10] project. FSF states that (FSF, accessed 1999) "Free software is a matter of users' freedom to run, copy, distribute, study, change and improve the software," which is a strict definition, reflecting anticommercialist thought. Based on this premise, FSF also proposed the concept of Copyleft,[11] which is the opposite of intellectual property rights, to free writings.[12] They also enacted the GPL (General Public License), which is often applied to freeware and Open Source projects. The influence of FSF on the Open Source community is very large. However, the definition of freeware is not necessarily unique and programmers' positions also vary. The present Open Source definition was set by the Open Source Initiative (OSI),[13] a nonprofit organization. Its purpose is to clarify differences with freeware, as described by Stallman, and to include the perspective of business use.

Various Open Source projects are being conducted all over the world. The Open Source movement does not stop at software. For example, an Open Source project (Morphy One) for mobile computers and open hardware (OHPA, 1999) was launched in Japan in 1999. This project was in the last stage of mass production at the end of 2001 and respects the ideas of the General Public License and applied these to the hardware.

Analysis 1: Open Source Community (OSC)

Here, we take the Linux kernel development community as a new model for R&D and consider this with literature review and interviews. Linux is a Unix-compatible OS (Operation System) that works on several platforms such as Intel chip, Alpha, SPARC, and PowerPC systems. Because the main targets were IBM PC/AT compatible machines that carried i386, or greater, chips, it is called PC-Unix, generically, with FreeBSD.[14] The development of Linux, which has over 10 million users as of March 2000, was started by Linus Torvalds in 1991 when he was a student at Helsinki University. Linux has been spreading as an alternative OS[15] to the Unix and Microsoft Windows NT platforms at a superior growth rate.[16] The Linux development community works mainly through mailing lists and is open to all persons. Although the kernel development community was small at the beginning, it has since expanded. Figure 6.1 shows the transition of the number of posts to the Linux-kernel mailing list since 1996. The number of posts increased rapidly in 1998 when Open Source became widely recognized by the general public.

The range of the OSC related to Linux is very wide and various persons outside kernel development contribute to the community. Figure 6.2 illustrates the structure of the Linux community. The elements in Figure 6.2, such as the development community and user groups, overlap but do not necessarily have a hierarchical structure.

This community developed autonomously and was self-organized into its present, refined form by the individuals who belong to it.

Organization Structure

Although several definitions of organizational structure exist, most of them suppose large firms that consist of complex divisions or companies, such as functional organizations. Since OSC is a single-function organization of research and development, we shall apply the classic definition of Chandler (1962).

1. The lines of authority and communication between the different administrative offices and officers.
2. The information and data that flow through these lines of communication and authority.

Figure 6.1
Transition of the Number of Contributions to the Linux-Kernel Mailing List

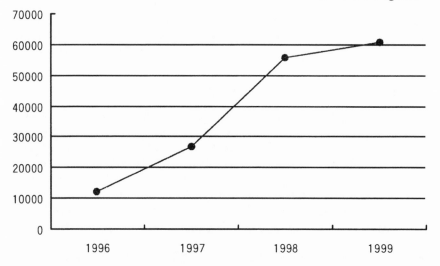

Source: Created from http://www.geocrawler.com/archives/.

Figure 6.2
The Linux Community

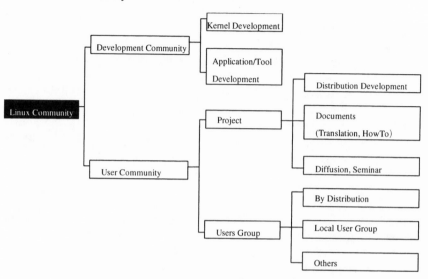

In "The Cathedral and the Bazaar," Raymond (1999a) likened the conventional method of developing software where the project proceeds under supervision of a capable leader to a cathedral. He explains that "centralized, a priori approach was required" and notes that development is "carefully crafted by individual wizards or small bands of mages working in splendid isolation, with no beta to be released before its time." On the other hand, he described the development style of Linus Torvalds, where people can enter and exit freely and powerful leadership does not necessarily work, as a bazaar and noted the stance of "release early and often, delegate everything you can, be open to the point of promiscuity." There is hardly any limitation for joining or leaving the community.[17] Nevertheless, this style does not correspond to the flat or network organizations in administrative organization theory. We can suggest the hierarchical structure shown in Figure 6.3, where Linus Torvalds is at the top and under him are core members, contributors, debuggers/testers, and users/audience (potential volunteers).

Torvalds explained in an interview (Nikkei Computer, 1999) that the core team is made up of ten people.[18] The core team is appointed by Torvalds and if there are no objections, confirmed by the consensus of the community. In the OSC, a core member is responsible for each subsystem. According to Raymond (1999a), decision-makers are core team members and Torvalds, and only Torvalds, is responsible for a final decision if opinions are divided in the core team.

In addition to the core team, there are MAINTAINERs who are in charge of each program. Although MAINTAINERs manage and arrange the program and its development process, decision-making power still belongs to the core team. For kernel version 2.2.14, there are 118 individuals described as MAINTAINERs in the MAINTAINERS file for 143 MAINTAIN items. There are 273 contributors whose names are on the CREDITS file because they contributed to the development of kernel version 2.2.14. A contributor is included in the contributor class not because he/she submitted a source code but because his/her code was adopted in the kernel. Contribution to the OSC involves not only making source codes that are adopted for the kernel but also other activities that are discussed later. However, this chapter defines MAINTAINERs and kernel contributors, excluding the core team, as contributors in the narrow sense.

The number of MAINTAINERs is shown in Table 6.1 by the number of items they are responsible for according to the MAINTAINERS file. The number of people whose names are included in the CREDITS file is presented in parentheses. The sum of the contributors to kernel version 2.2.14 is over 320.

The layer under contributors includes individuals who debug and re-

Table 6.1
MAINTAINERs and the Number of Items They Are Responsible For

The number of items	1	2	3	4	5
The numbers of MAINTAINERS	99 (52)	16 (12)	1 (0)	1 (1)	1 (1)

Figure 6.3
Organizational Structure of the Linux Kernel Development Community Hypothesis

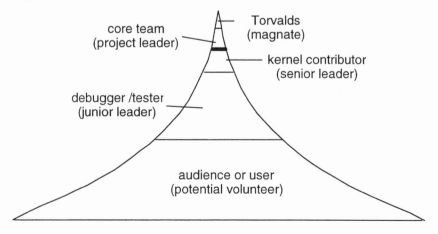

port results of the latest version used in their various circumstances as soon as it is released. The lowest layer is Read Only Members (ROM) who may later become contributors or core members.

Participants other than the core team and MAINTAINERs are not given responsibilities for specific tasks at first. They can choose their favorite kind and level of work. Originally, neither the core team nor MAINTAINERs were given responsibility. They were evaluated and identified as persons who should have that particular responsibility for the community as the result of their excellent work.

When it becomes impossible for them to fulfill their responsibility for certain reasons or when they lose interest in upholding the responsibility, they can resign from their positions by expressing their intention promptly and choosing a successor who has gained public legitimacy (Raymond, 1999b) with the consensus of the community.

Although Raymond (1999a) describes this community as "not centralized," the structure of decision-making at least is centralized considering that decision-makers are clearly specified and few compared to the whole community. In addition, the OSC has a common decision-making practice that is described as follows according to Raymond (1999b), "By custom, the 'dictator' or project leader in a project with co-developers is expected to consult with those co-developers on key decisions."

Communication in the OSC has several characteristic features. For example, members hate and avoid useless communication. The FAQ[19] of the mailing list, which should be read before subscribing to the kernel development mailing list, repeatedly calls attention to the importance of not causing problems with useless communication. However, this caution is typically observed not only by OSC but also on networks. Therefore, it is more appropriate to think that such cautions originated as a special feature of communication on networks rather than as a feature of OSC.[20]

Another feature is the direction of communication. Raymond (1999b) divides people in the mailing list into core members including Torvalds and others (periphery), and mentions, "Only communication between the core members and the circumference exists and the circumferences do not take communication each other." On the other hand, Torvalds supposes, "Since there is rarely the problem related to all the core members, who are responsible for their own sub area, the core team has no mailing list. When consulting, I do not use the exclusive mailing list." (Nikkei Computer, 1999). On the contrary, there is frequent inter-noncore member communication and inter-core member communication in the actual development mailing list. From preliminary observations of the digest version of the mailing list log[21] for 68 weeks for the development of the kernel 2.2, some communication patterns can be identified.

A. After both core and noncore members offer various opinions concerning a noncore member's proposal, a core member makes the final decision.

B. After several requests or revised ideas from noncore members concerning a core member's draft, the core member submits the formal development plan after considering their opinions.

Moreover, the top 10 to 20 people who posted messages within the above period were only those whose names are in the MAINTAINER or CREDIT files or who are recognized widely for their important responsibilities. It seems reasonable to consider Raymond's explanation of the typical type of communication between core and noncore members in some decision processes.

In this community, there are mainly two kinds of vertical communications: between Torvalds and core members and between core members, including Torvalds, and noncore members. In contrast, horizontal communications are secondary. We consider that the pursuit of rationality and efficiency of development has affected the direction of communication in OSC and in the networks mentioned previously. The likely reason that Torvalds is able to say that, "since there is rarely the problem related to all the core members, the exclusive mailing list does not exist" is his skillful division of the kernel into subsystems and significant delegation of authority to each core member. If someone does not "divide into each module which keeps its own independence" (Torvalds, 1999), it becomes "very difficult to promote a lot of projects concurrently." In addition, OSC members are obliged to have horizontal communication because they lapse into a situation in which they must check changed files one by one, and confirm one by one that these cause no bad side effects to other files. Therefore, the composition of core members and general participants was produced through observance of an organizational policy in which people whose knowledge is relatively less should not make unnecessary posts, and people who have knowledge or authority should make proper posts as expected.

It is likely that they avoid the confusion[22] that occurs from the communication of many persons who are not regulated and choose a development system that makes maximum use of an electronic network for communication. Although communication between Torvalds and the core team is occasionally secret, it is very easy for the all participants, even if they were not involved in the communication directly, to share the past process of development because all information required for development is disclosed. It is reasonable that the well-ordered communication in the Linux development community is fairly different from that in flat and network organizations, which are supposed to be more suitable for knowledge creation than hierarchical organizations or the crisscross communication that is assumed tacitly on the network.

Thus, the organization of the Linux development community has a hierarchical structure.

Moreover, it is interesting that this organization has many structural elements similar to ones found in a bureaucracy. These include the clear regulation of power hierarchy and administrative authority, the clarification of rules and procedures, posting with a strong focus on expert knowledge, and a documentation principle. It is reasonable that both organizations have many similar features because both aim to control the distribution of information to avoid unnecessary confusion and to improve the efficiency of the organization. However, there are several points that differ from conventional organizations including bureaucracy. These are freedom of affiliation selection, which allows members to quit the community, delocalization of information, low communication costs through effective use of electronic networks, and sharing of ideas. Based on observations, there are people who criticize the present development method and operating policy and even their own treatment. Such discussions invite many people and are often long and heated, although useless communication is disliked. These observations make it clear that they have the common view that free discussion including criticism is necessary. It is known that the more a bureaucratic organization pursues the structural elements mentioned above, the more unexpected dysfunctions, such as inefficiency, occur. According to Merton (1957), dysfunctions do not come from the organizational structure of bureaucracy itself but from the developing views and ways of thinking that excessively adapt to the bureaucracy. This community essentially differs from a bureaucratic organization in that the unique organizational culture in which autonomy is approved makes rationality possible; consequently, high efficiency is attained.

Organizational Culture

The members of the community are assenters of Open Source policy who are interested in Linux and have mastered the hacker culture and manners of the Internet that originated from Unix. The constituents of the community share a culture and a sense of values. For example, unspecified mailing list participants educate others who have not mastered the customs of the community.

Among the members, the participants with the most-advanced technology are the object of everybody's respect. It seems impossible for any company to employ such excellent engineers and have them participate in R&D. The members are very autonomous, and codes of conduct are disclosed as documents.

In the world of the Internet and Open Source, participants frequently mention, "we should appreciate the great efforts of predecessors and give our efforts to the community that raised us." This thought was taken up by those who became familiar with the Internet during its nonbusiness era, even if they did not actually develop software (for example, network administrators in Japanese firms) and spread further.

Although contribution to the community is greatly encouraged, coercion is not necessarily exerted. Moreover, members realize that contributions within his/her capability are enough. Not only the OSC but also communities focused on computers have huge archives (libraries) of past documents.[23] Linux development and user communities create these documents each corresponding to a specific purpose.

Documents by the development community cover almost all the knowledge required for development. Also, there are on-line manuals attached to the software and the various instruction documents. On the other hand, the volume and types of documents by the user community sometime exceed those of the development community, depending on the number of contributors. The documents created by user communities are relatively enlightening and helpful for beginners; for example, the translations of documents by the development community into different languages. The development communities recognize and evaluate the importance of such contributions by users.

The documents that are exhibited and accumulated are shared widely in the community. The same mechanism used for software development works in the development of documents; mistakes are corrected, information is accumulated, and the value of the documents are increased by being shown to many people.

Both the development community and user groups have their official or private portal Web sites and there are links on these that can be followed so that all official and useful documents can be found from these portal sites. Most of these sites have search functions for various documents. Moreover, from an educational point of view, the documents are prepared for newcomers, who are unfamiliar with a culture that avoids useless communication. Mailing list applicants are encouraged to register after reading such documents. Before making new posts, new subscribers are encouraged to read previous posts and search past discussions or documents. In a big community, documents and services are substantial and new users (i.e., potential codevelopers) are seen everyday.

In order to become a contributor in the development community, it is not necessary to follow complicated or implicit systematic procedures. An individual only needs to submit a report or source code of excellent quality following the exhibited procedures. After a submission, an authorized developer judges the work and if adopted, the submitter's name is listed in the CREDITS file as a contributor. If a person makes further contributions, his/her reputation will strengthen. If he/she continues further, a promotion will be prepared by the consensus of the community.[24] If there are many participants who judge the promotion as unsuitable, a lot of objections will be posted on the mailing list.

Thus, the mechanism, in which personnel assignment is based on the principle of "putting the right person in the right place," is realized through peer review (Raymond, 1999a).[25] Although there is the concern that if too many would-be contributors exist, there may be increases in confusion or evaluators' load, the community seems to avoid the worst situation by sharing an organizational culture of "disliking noise and appreciating the virtue of modesty" (Raymond, 1999b) and by appropriate responses to would-be contributors. The decision-makers are also directly or indirectly chosen by peer review. When someone makes a good contribution, it is the ironbound rule of the community that a decision-maker praises his/her work. We can say the principle of rewarding meritorious services and punishing faults is effective. Persons who contribute are given honor at public places, which is the most motivating factor. Moreover, his/her actions and evaluations are equally open to all participants. This means that the standards of evaluation are also open.

The characteristics of this organizational culture have been formed over the years to manage network-based development rationally and efficiently and to raise developers' motivations.

Management Control

According to Raymond (1999b), in the hacker culture, "most of the maintainer's job is going to be judging other people's code" and "the culture's 'big men' and tribal elders are required to talk softly and to humorously deprecate themselves at every turn in order to maintain their status." Many people claim that Torvalds is moderate and likable and not the strong leader type. It is thought that his leadership style fits closely with Raymond's description. Appropriate and fair judgment, high technical skills, and modesty are the fundamental elements of the leader of the OSC.

The development vision and design concept that a leader indicates are very important especially right after the start of a project because the success or failure of an Open Source project depends on how many people contribute. Although it is said that Torvalds wrote the program himself for a while after the development of Linux started, he does not issue detailed instructions for controlling the project now. At the moment, Torvalds' important business is considered to be announcing release timelines of upcoming versions, the planning of development and targets, and decision-making with regard to kernel adoption and other issues. Presently, when the project is progressing smoothly, Torvalds' existence, which imparts a vision of the community, is the most important leadership factor in terms of centripetal force.

Another important role of a leader is sorting valuable information and individuals. In the OSC, the strong authority of the decision-makers allows the radical sorting of source codes and individuals. A community whose leader begins to make unsuitable judgments has a higher probability of being disrupted faster than standard organizations.

The necessity of adjustments among members or among the community, its administration and the outside is relatively low. We can say that the reason decision-making authority is concentrated on the leaders of not only Linux but also of the general OSC is because it is widely recognized as a rational means for lean communication and quality software development. Torvalds (1999) mentions that,

If we took the same approach with Alpha, then I would have three different code bases to support in order to maintain Linux. Even if this had been feasible in terms of coding, it wasn't feasible in terms of management. I couldn't manage the development of Linux if it meant keeping track of an entirely new code base every time someone wanted Linux on a new architecture.

In this way, the branching of the project seems to have been avoided by the concentration of power on one leader. Originally, "There is strong social pressure against forking projects" and "customary practice clearly incorporates a premise that public legitimacy is important" (Raymond, 1999c) with the consensus of the whole community when a project leader changes.

According to Raymond (1999a), "Some very large projects discard the 'benevolent dictator' model entirely." For example, the Apache project, which 50 percent or more of today's web servers carry, adopts "turn the codevelopers into a voting committee" practice. In addition, the Perl project, a script language of high applicability, "is rotating dictatorship, in which control is occasionally passed from one member to another within a circle of senior co-developers."

The project leader's task for the development community is probably much smaller than what usual companies and conventional business administrations assume. Moreover, the so-called dilemma of leadership is almost eliminated. One reason is that community members are autonomous, organizational culture is shared, and the comings and goings of people are unrestricted. Though, for this reason, the evaluation of the leader is very severe. If a leader continues to make inappropriate posts or decisions, someone will correct the leader or valuable members may quit the community silently. In this event, the leader will be forced to resign or the project will decline.

Meaning of Management in OSC

Although the bazaar development system tends to be expressed as having neither management nor leadership, their management and leadership can be found. Still, the importance of strong leadership is relatively low because members are autonomous and organizational culture is shared; it seems that the culture of self-management substitutes for a part of the leadership role. However, all OSCs do not succeed as well as Linux. We may say that in comparison with the example of Mozilla.org, appropriate management and leadership are indispensable for general Open Source projects, in addition to technical quality, in order for the development to proceed smoothly (Kato, 2000).

The distinction between flat organizations and network organizations is frequently unclear. By describing them as typical organizations in management organization theory, Okumura (1996) compares hierarchical organizations and network organizations. In Table 6.2, a new perspective on OSC is added to Okumura's views of hierarchical and network organizations.

The distinction between flat and network organizations is often ambiguous. Okumura (1996) describes the flat organization as a knowledge-creating organization, in contrast to a pyramid type organization, which is ideal for executing a strategy of mass production and extensive sales. In flat and network organizations, members are typically not based in vertical relationships, such as vertical command and reports, but are in wide and versatile communication relationships. As described in this chapter, the organization structure of the OSC is a hierarchy. Although communication may be initiated from both upper and lower levels, it is controlled and mostly limited in the vertical direction. However, there is no limitation to the range that information is shared. Moreover, from the viewpoint that OSC members have a very high level of expertise and knowledge and that they are very autonomous, OSC is not classified under any conventional organization type in the field of business administration. In some respects, OSC is essentially different from the hypertext-type of organization that Nonaka and Takeuchi (1995) assert is good for creative work. The critical difference is communication. The communication of the hypertext organization, with its management style of middle-up and down, is characterized by Nonaka as "use of dialog, and metaphors/analogies." On the contrary, the OSC has actively induced the elimination of ambiguity and noise as much as possible.

The management of motivation is considered to be especially important for OSC. It is said that the motivations of OSC members are the satisfaction of having contributed to a significant community, satisfying intellectual curiosity on a high level, and honor. As Teramoto (1999) describes, the most important thing for people or organizations is how the circle of impression, sympathy, and resonance spreads; sharing the feeling of joy can be added to the above list of motivations.

However, open sourcing cannot fully explain the success of Linux development. There are both commercially successful and unsuccessful com-

Table 6.2

Differences among OSC and the Conventional Organization Types

Dimension and organization type	Hierarchy organization	Network organization	OSC
Determination of authority	Authority	Authority	Members' consensus
Behavior of members	Restrictive	Autonomous	Autonomous, but very restrictive to cultural observance.
Relationship among members	Vertical administration - dependency	Horizontal, equal	Vertical, no administration - dependency relationship
Integration of actions	Tight	Loose	Tightly bound to culture.
Combination and separation of elements	It takes time.	It is flexibly possible.	It takes time. Separation is avoided as much as possible. It requires the consensus of members.
Invitation of recombination	By authority	Emergently	Lack of rationality
Organized procedure of recombination	Un-explicit, By authority	Explicit to some extent By some persons	By explicit procedure and approval of members
Environmental conformity	Stable <- -- determinist-view of the world	Uncertainty <- -- probability theory-view of the world	Distribution <- -- sharing of an autonomous view of the world and culture
Economics	Scale, efficiency, few variations, mass production	Speed, diversity, creativity, variety, small-lot production	Efficiency, speed, Concurrent
Evaluation	One-sided from top to bottom	Partly interactive	Members' consensus
Source and character of information	Upper level information, static information <- by collection	Scene information, dynamic information <- by relation	Determination: upper level information; Report: scene information.
Flow of information	From top to bottom	Horizontally	Only in the vertical direction, shared by all, simultaneous and instant
Control of information	By authority to maintain status quo of power	Aiming at no control	Controlled autonomously as culture, to keep the rationality of development.
Paradigm of organization	(Heteronomous) division of work	Cooperation	Autonomous division of work (cooperation as a result)
Relationship between organization and strategy	From strategy to organization	From organization to strategy	From strategy and the quality of communication to organization
Organization center	One <- unified sense of fixed values	Plural or nothing <- multifaceted sense-of-value which change over time	Leader and organizational culture
Identity of members	Given from the organization	Members decide by choosing the organization	Through member's organizational selection and consensus of members
Reward	Money and status	Money and status	Honor, reputation among members

Note: Shaded cells are added by Kato.

munities smaller than Linux. Our finding that the organizational structure, culture, and communication of OSC are very characteristic means that there is a structure and management style suitable for Open Source and that these greatly contribute to the success of R&D projects. In addition, this is a new type of organization that does not fit into conventional classifications.

Analysis 2: R&D Project of an OSC

Difference between Linux Kernel Development and Firms' R&D Projects

Although the development speed of the Linux kernel is considered to be very fast, an appropriate evaluation must include the scale of members in connection with the project and improvement range of performance. Generally, efficiency of a project is defined as shown in the following formula.

$$Efficiency\ of\ the\ project\ = \frac{Return}{Invested\ Resource}$$

The development period is calculated in the cost and included in invested resource

In order to discuss the productivity of the Linux kernel development project, it is necessary to take into consideration the time spent on the development of rejected kernel parts as an invested resource. An exact result cannot be obtained if the time spent on the development of the rejected kernel is disregarded because it is surmised that the dropped resources are very large. The argument itself is almost impossible because this measurement is very difficult. However, in the Linux development community, it is certain that the version-updates and the release of a new kernel are frequent.[26] In addition, we may say that quality is high considering the development span.

Although communication and development techniques are highly sophisticated and development speed is also sufficiently high in the OSC, such abilities are different from the capability necessary to improve quality to a certain level under the major premises—limited resources and strict observance of development period—of firms' R&D projects. For OSC, it is not necessary to take into much consideration adjustments among entities inside and outside the project that are required in the case of firms' R&D projects.

Therefore, this section only covers the inside of the Linux kernel development community and focuses on the relatively quick development speed of the community compared to other collaborations on the electronic network and the mechanism that enables the development of high quality products, absent precise plans.

Circulation and Communication Cost of Knowledge

R&D speed is high because the circulation and transition speed of knowledge concerning development is large in the project, which is not an exclusive feature of OSC. To be open means that the absolute number of superior persons, that is those who have appropriate solutions for the problem, is large. The members of a development community generally have extensive knowledge of technology and community culture. Because the vision for development is specified by the core team, including Torvalds, it is easy to share. Therefore, members can adequately develop with their own judgment even if detailed directions are not given. When new knowledge is exhibited, it circulates among developers with unusual speed because of the large number of participants. Furthermore, new values are added to this knowledge in this manner. Simultaneously, this knowledge, whose value is updated by the minute, is eagerly shared among all members. Furthermore, prompt release and response lead to vigor and stimulation of the community. The more participants on the mailing list, the more posts are made—a process that forms a virtual cycle that invites even more participants.

On the other hand, a mechanism exists that helps to skillfully avoid the confusion and lessen the load of communication often seen in large development teams. Brooks (1995) comments that the case in the development of software where man and month[27] are fungible is only when the task can be shared without communication among many developers and points to the risk of the immoderate addition of developers prolonging instead of shortening development. The reason is that burden increases in two areas: education/training and communication.

Therefore, let us consider education and mutual communication in the OSC. As mentioned previously, the OSC has a custom of creating, sharing, and leveraging huge documents. This custom is very effective in reducing communication loads. Although the dispatch of useless information, such as in the case of duplication, is usually very much disliked, education is an exception in many cases. In order to take advantage of the merits of communication on electronic networks and to not aggravate demerits, when a newcomer commits a fault, instructions are repeated intentionally with the goal of educating other newcomers. There should be almost no need for the development community to educate most of those who are going to start communication because in such user groups, they have already mastered manners and procedures to learn the necessary technical information and prehistory of the development on their own before participating in the development mailing lists.

Moreover, although mutual communication is actually restricted by hierarchical structure and authority, there is rarely a shortage of information that is required for development because it is possible for everyone to grasp almost all past development processes by reading the mailing lists. Thus, the community has completed the scheme and existing developers do not have to pay educational costs. For such reasons, the large absolute number of participants converts into speedup of development without loss.

In the development of the Linux kernel, multiple projects proceed concurrently like in other OSCs. For example, there are two types of kernel[28]: one is the development version that Torvalds is responsible for and the other is the stable version that Alan Cox[29] is in charge of. Because new kernels are adopted to the development version one after another, there are frequent releases of the development version. As soon as a new version is released, many participants test and debug the software and results are reported one after the other. A policy of including in the stable only what has been evaluated in the development version is adopted.

The hierarchical structure is constituted rationally and autonomously and agrees with the characteristics of each R&D process. According to Vixie (1999), the elements of software engineering processes are generally enumerated as: (1) Marketing Requirements, (2) System-Level Design, (3) Detailed Design, (4) Implementation, (5) Integration, (6) Field Testing, and (7) Support.

There are few decision-makers who have responsibilities for subsystems in the Linux development community, as compared to the mailing lists, which can reach about 10,000 subscribers.

On the other hand, many people participate in debugging and testing, which requires a large number of people. The number of developers and the diversity of test environments in the field testing process have critical influence on the quality of products, including robustness, and on improvement of development speed. The community skillfully adapts this approach to each R&D process. In addition, it is able to sort out the best proposals at lower communication costs through the combination of freedom of discussion, the comings and goings of people, and powerful authority. It appears that members have designed the structure and process of the organization for decision-making, the most important issue, without worrying about internal and external coordination. The community combines such organizational structure and processes with the policy of giving priority to "Release Early and Release Often" (Raymond, 1999a) even if there are some bugs, over the practice of releasing products of high completeness, which takes time to achieve. In this way, the community promotes revisions by many hands and further accelerates the speed of generation and distribution of knowledge.

The modularization of the Linux kernel also plays an important role in improving results. Although modularization itself is not a new design thought, Torvalds's appropriate modularization resulted in the high independence of modules, the reduction of crosswise direction arrangements and of the additional development and communication generated in connection to these arrangements. Rich software development experience probably formed the rational organizational culture and conduct codes that have led to the excellence of their products.

The source code, which accounts for the large percentage of information required for the development of the software, requires no conversion cost for easy distribution on the media used for collaboration (e.g., electronic networks). This characteristic of knowledge also plays an important role in obtaining high results from the project.

The requirements for getting excellent results from a development project—which have been extracted from the consideration of the Open Source community—seem applicable to general collaborations using networks. Specifically, measures for reducing communication cost are helpful for improving the productivity of R&D projects on electronic networks.

For example, the case where more project members leads to better results is restricted to projects where the additional management cost of communication and education is within permissible limits. Although efficient communication is required for collaboration of any form, it is especially necessary with communication on electronic networks, which also has the demerits that are derived from easy dispatch of huge amounts of information. In R&D in fields other than software, the techniques of OSC are theoretically acceptable for knowledge that can be distributed on the main communication media for R&D projects, if developers can prevent the confusion mentioned previously. In addition, increasing the percentage of the knowledge that can be distributed on communication media, among all the required knowledge for R&D, also leads to the improvement of productivity. Knowledge regarding hardware R&D can be divided into those that can be directly exchanged on networks and those that must be converted for distribution on networks. Whether developers adopt OSC's techniques for commercial R&D depends on the cost of converting the knowledge required for the R&D into a form that can be distributed on the main media for the R&D.

OPEN SOURCE AS A CORPORATE STRATEGY

Firms' Involvement in OSC

Firms' participation in OSC is roughly divided into four patterns.

The first pattern is investment in or alliance to the distributors and development communities. When OSC was not yet recognized by the business world, firms recognized distributors as entrances to Open Source and as important business partners; they started investments and alliances one after another from around September 1998. Investments enabled existing companies to offer Linux-support businesses. On the other hand, distributors that received investments from the major firms were able to gain recognition in the market with Linux. Although Oracle and Netscape Communications built cooperative relationships with the Linux community early on, IBM was the first to officially form an alliance with an Open Source project, which was Apache.

The second pattern is support of Linux by major firms, which can be roughly divided further into two types. One is the correspondence of their products to Linux (software, porting, hardware, guarantee of operation) and the other is the so-called support service business ranging from the sales of preinstalled Linux machines to Linux-based solutions business. Because these major firms have formally offered support businesses, the number of business users of Linux increased rapidly.

Now, many hardware manufacturers offer information on their Web sites regarding the operation of their products in a Linux environment. Such companies exchange information with users. Although the community has created a list of hardware that operates on Linux in advance of these hardware venders, positive correspondence of a company's product is often reported to user group[30] mailing lists.

Firms' open source projects are the third pattern. Netscape Communications started the first open source project, followed by Sun Microsystems, Apple, IBM, and other companies. Whether the projects are true to Open Source depends on whether their license agrees to the OSI definition. There are examples of pseudo–Open Source licenses, such as the previously-mentioned Sun and Apple projects.

The fourth pattern is the adoption of Open Source as an official method of business. For example, some firms that have shown an understanding of the OSC have established new business sections that are involved in open source or have employed big names in OSC for full-time engagement in open source projects. Such measures lead not only to the improvement of corporate image but also to an increase in numbers of codevelopers and users. Persons famous in the OSC generally have the greatest support of system administrators; a ripple effect can be anticipated.

One feature of such movements is the inversion of knowledge between firms and individuals. In the past, firms commonly established their business using knowledge gaps of individuals. However, in the software industry, a community of people with far greater knowledge than engineers in firms has existed for many years. Thus, the influence of OSC on business has gradually become large, and firms have begun to recognize the community as a highly useful external resource.

Costs and Benefits of Open Source Projects by Firms

Although R&D with external Open Source resources is usually done to save time and costs, it is also known that such collaboration may markedly

increase costs and spoil efficiency, compared to the usage of internal resources for R&D. Table 6.3 shows two levels of transaction costs that are
frequently generated in R&D using external resources; one is managerial
concerning decision-making of managers and another is operational concerning activities of researchers and developers. Here, the conversion cost
of knowledge is the cost for changing R&D knowledge into a form that is
easily distributable on media used for communication with a partner. It
is thought that the size of the transaction cost is greatly influenced by the
property of technology and management, rather than the form of R&D-
using external resources. The transaction cost of Open Source is considered much lower than that of conventional collaboration.

In addition, Table 6.4 compares the characteristics of conventional col-
laborations/consortium and Open Source projects that are conducted by
firms from business and technical perspectives.

Some firms that have learned the merit of opening their technology
(e.g., businesses involved in Open Source movement) are beginning to

Table 6.3
Transaction Costs of R&D with the External Resources

Management level			Operational level	
Partner selection cost	Arrangement cost (between sections)	Results inspection cost	Communication cost	Knowledge conversion cost

Table 6.4
Comparison between Conventional Collaboration/Consortium and Open Source Project by Firms

		Conventional collaboration/consortium	Open Source project by firms
Partner		Specific and a small number (mainly firms)	Unspecific and a large number (community, individual)
Business	Making of business group (adding potential users)	Good	Excellent
	Avoidance of exhausting competition	Good, sometimes hard exhausting competition	Almost unrelated
	Corporate image improvement	Unrelated	Excellent
Both (Business and technology)	Time saving	Good	Excellent
	Cost saving	Good	Good--excellent
	Partner control	Possible and rather easy	Very difficult sometimes
Technology	Aim of technological complement	Emphasized and relatively easy to achieve	Usually subordinate
	Monopolizing the technology	Possible (monopolization is the premise)	Impossible
	Standardizing the technology	Possible	Easy to standardize (standardization is an aim)
	Gains from the technology	Possible, sometimes excellent	Impossible

open their technology during the beginning of development so that it may become their industry's center technology. IBM is one such example. Their strategy is similar to that of firms that distribute cellular phones for free, include customers in their communications network, and use telephone charges as the main source of profit. The strategy of open technology excels in the cellular-phone industry because improvement in quality and expansion of business is possible when the technology is shown to many people. This can be called a skillful strategy of invitation and enclosure using the open source movement. However, it differs from the conventional strategy of enclosure in that these firms do not intend to enclose partners and customers tightly; their relationships are looser and more flexible.

IMPACT OF KNOWLEDGE EXCHANGE AMONG INDIVIDUALS AND FIRMS

The Change of the Significance of Large Firms

There is a corporate fund operated by common firms among U.S. venture capitals. This fund intends to enclose the venture of rich possibilities that is under the category of a firm's strategy. However, investments to the Linux community differ from these small and tight enclosure situations.

As a typical example, let us consider R&D that attaches more importance to knowledge than to other business functions.

It is impossible for a firm to keep hold of the world's excellent human resources in all areas. On the contrary, in firms, which still have deep-seated customs of long-term employment (like Japanese firms), human resources can become nonperforming assets because of a mismatch of specialties and needs as the environment changes sharply with time. However, the situation changes completely if companies abandon their insistence of holding on to internal human resources. If the motivation of the best engineers' and researchers' is interesting work or valuable work, and if a firm can offer such work and suitable rewards for the work, firms will be able to find the necessary human resources throughout the world even if for only a temporary basis. For this open resource that assembles human resources from a wide range outside the firm, the displaying of knowledge is a major premise, even though the range of disclosure is limited.

The degree of flexibility of employment varies from the free situation of the Open Source movement to the formal situation of collaborations and contracts that can last for several months or several years. If a research theme cannot attract excellent developers, the quality of persons who are gathered is relatively low and good results cannot be expected. In other words, new competition between firms emerges, which is evaluation by external human resources.

Such a trend has been already partly actualized. Matsushita Electric Works announced the foundation of a virtual laboratory, New Business Open Process Network,[31] which invites public participation through its Web page. External experts evaluate the potential of the business proposals and Matsushita Electric Works jointly researches and develops those with high potential. Hewlett Packard (HP) and O'Reilly & Associates (a publishing company) conducted a test installation of SourceXchange, a Web site that mediates software developers and firms.[32] Moreover, Sun Microsystems has created a partnership with Collab.Net, an organization that has participated in SourceXchange, and they succeeded in attracting a large number of external developers and starting specific development projects of jxta[33] (CollabNet, 2002) and StarOffice.[34] Through Source-Xchange, HP sponsored, carried information on development projects, registered developers, and managed exchanges between companies and developers including the latters' remuneration. Moreover, HP managed quality, reliability, and other project areas.[35]

Although it is easy for software development to do well with Open Source and open resource because the knowledge, which is the product itself, can be distributed on the network freely, in the case of hardware development by small organizations or individuals, the availability of equipment for experiment or production can be a bottleneck. If large firms offer or lend such resources, a model for a new division-of-work may be possible.

In the near future, large firms will place importance not only on appropriate knowledge and resources to make profits but also on the exhibition of know-how and property that have been built to some extent to develop new businesses through coordination with individuals, community, and other firms and on their role as social infrastructure.

Relation between Individuals and Businesses—Time of Multi-Attribution

Diffusion of information and technology, including networks, has had an innovative influence on individual participation in business. Linux is the first example that showed it was possible for a noncommercial community or individuals to compete evenly with large firms at similar knowledge levels. Moreover, the case gave major firms the impetus to positively utilize multiple and unspecified external resources.

In *The Third Wave*, Toffler (1980) defines the "prosumer" as a possible future type of consumer who is involved in the design and manufacture of products. The prosumer is a sympathizer of the firm and is involved in promotion and campaign without pay.

In the future, it is believed that firms will actively adopt the strategy of users as codevelopers (Raymond, 1999a). The once clear boundary between firms and individuals is becoming ambiguous.

From the viewpoint of individuals, it is now possible to belong to multiple organizations or to be concurrently involved in plural business activities. In addition, the previous restriction that a company must chose a form for its business is being eased. It is possible for an employee to engage in various work opportunities from one place, even if the work that he/she finds valuable and what is necessary for making a living are not in agreement.

Change to a New Society

For industries with fast technical innovation, it has become almost impossible for one company to monopolize technology; the era in which only large firms lead technical innovation has come to an end. Teramoto (2001) describes a knowledge society as a society where various players can create value as equal partners. In the world of business, we have already rushed into an era of division of work and cooperation among firms, community, and individuals in some industries.

The formation of meso-organizations may have been started in technical fields where knowledge is most important. Such a movement can be considered a reconstruction of the industrial structure and is an effective use of resources, especially intellectual resources. In the new era of knowledge capitalism in which individuals can be involved with businesses, successful results can be achieved by firms offering a chance of intellectual symbiosis of individuals and community and providing many people with opportunities for interesting work.

NOTES

1. An early form of this chapter first appeared in Kato (2000).

2. See http://www.opensource.org/.

3. The kernel is the core part of the Operating System (OS).

4. It is the general term for the network used for scientific research that backboned the NSFNET, which is based on the technology cultivated in ARPANET. It became the parent organization of the current Internet, which is also used in business.

5. Although the media refers to Crackers (those who crack security and invade computer systems) as Hackers, this is inaccurate. RFC1983: In FYI (For Your Information) 18, 08/16/1996, a hacker is defined as "A person who delights in having an intimate understanding of the internal workings of a system, computers and computer networks in particular. The term is often misused in a pejorative context, where 'cracker' would be the correct term. See also: cracker."

6. The computer network that the Advanced Research Projects Agency

(ARPA) of the U.S. Department of Defense introduced in 1969. The form of interconnection of distributed Unix computers in various places by TCP/IP is just the prototype of the present Internet.

7. The WWW (World Wide Web) appeared relatively recently in the history of the Internet. Now, of course, WWW is used widely.

8. See http://www.edu.ipa.go.jp/mirrors/netiquette/fauj/netiquette.html.

9. See http://www.fsf.org/people/rms.html, and so on.

10. See http://www.gnu.org/home.html.

11. The copyright in which a user's freedom is secured, or its concept. See http://www.gnu.org/copyleft/copyleft.html.

12. FSF mentions, "Free software is a matter of the users' freedom to run, copy, distribute, study, change and improve the software." See http://www.gnu.org/philosophy/free-sw.html.

13. OSI is the voluntary organization founded in December 1998 to promote the Open Source movement. Perens and Raymond, big names in the community, are projectors.

14. FreeBSD follows in the wake of Berkeley Unix and also runs on a PC.

15. Although the comparison to Windows 95/98 is frequently made, they are client OS in a client-server system. On the other hand, because Linux is a server OS (so are Unix and NT), it is not valid to compare it to client OS. In addition, the movement to make Linux more popular as a client OS has already taken place with the construction of a GUI desktop environment, which can be operated intuitively, and free distribution of office-use applications software.

16. According to the International Data Corporation (IDC), the growth rate in shipments of Linux licenses in 1998 was 212.5 percent, Windows NT, 27 percent, and all other Unix-based systems, 4.1 percent.

17. As a matter of fact, the members of the core team and MAINTAINERs cannot quit without formal notice.

18. Both the election system and the existence of the members of Linux core team are considered too ambiguous as compared with those in other Open Source projects.

19. FAQ (Frequently Asked Questions).

20. Because most Internet users were scientific persons and network resources were significantly insufficient, restricted communication and cautions on writing (netiquette) were not special but disciplined strongly. Recently, because netiquette education has not caught up with the rapid increase in Internet users, the number of places that force such manners have decreased and netiquette has became a feature of veteran users.

21. We can read the precise arguments in past kernel development mailing lists in http://kernelnotes.org/, http://kt.linuxcare.com/kernel-traffic/, and so on.

22. When the number of persons communicate with each other, the communication path is expressed as $n(n-1) \div 2$. As the constituents increase, communication paths theoretically increase exponentially.

23. Personal computer communities, such as Windows and Macintosh, also have the behavioral pattern of accumulating huge documents and archives on the Internet and sharing them. There is a possibility that the personal computer communities would have done so spontaneously, even if the Unix community had not existed before, because accumulating documents is very logical on a media such as the Internet. However, it is reasonable to think the behavior of Unix or Internet communities was spread to personal computer communities considering the order of product appearance.

24. The Linux kernel development community has been criticized that the consensus of the community does not work because Torvalds assigns the core team.

25. This means the mutual evaluation by specialists of the field, as the constituents of the community here.

26. See http://www.linux.or.jp/kernel.html

27. Meaning, "man-hour."

28. The development version and the stable version are distinguished by the version number. The second number of the stable version's version number is odd, that of the development version's is even.

29. Alan Cox is a MAINTAINER of five items and his post number is always top in the mailing list. He has been a contributor from the first stage and is the most famous person in the development community.

30. Of course, firms that support Linux or actively offer information positively gain good reputations from general users.

31. See http://www.mew.co.jp/opn/index.html.

32. CollabNet reported, "As of April 6, 2001, SourceXchange officially closed its doors." in SourceXchange News. See http://www.collab.net/sites/sxc_redirect/.

33. Sun's framework technology that aims to offer an effective environment for development of P to P applications.

34. Office suite software.

35. However, IBM has been the most successful in the Open Source projects among firms.

REFERENCES

Brooks, F. P. (1995). *The Mythical Man-Month: Essays on Software Engineering, Anniversary Edition*. Massachusetts: Addison Wesley.

Chandler, A. D. (1962). *Strategy and Structure: Chapters in the History of the Industrial Enterprise*. Cambridge: The MIT Press.

CollabNet. (2002). Success Stories—JXTA Success Story. http://www.collab.net/customers/successstories/jxta_story.html (accessed February 22, 2002).

Crocker, D. (1997). *David Crocker and the Development of E-mail: The Soul of The Internet*. New York: International Thomson Computer Press.

Free Software Foundation. (1999). What is Free Software? http://www.gnu.org/philosophy/free-sw.html (accessed September 10, 1999).

Kato, M. (2000). Open Source as a Corporate Strategy—A study of the open source community from an organizational theoretic perspective and the development of R&D with external resources. NISTEP Discussion Paper no. 17 (in Japanese).

Merton, R. K. (1957). *Social Theory and Social Structure*. New York: Free Press.

Nikkei Computer. (1999). Syogyo-teki de nai Kaihatu Sutairu koso Honrai no Arubeki Sugata da (Non-Commercial Development Style Is the Just Ideal Situation), in, *Linux Perfect Guide for Corporate Users*. Tokyo: Nikkei BP (in Japanese).

Nonaka, I., and Takeuchi. (1995). *The Knowledge Creating Company: How Japanese Companies Create the Dynasties of Innovation*. New York: Oxford University Press.

OHPA (Open Hardware Palmtop Computing Association). (1999). Morphy One—The World's First Open Hardware Palmtop PC! http://www.morphyone.org/ (accessed December 24, 1999).

Okumura, H. (1996). Keiei Senryaku to Soshiki (Strategy and Organization) in, *Keiei Senryaku Ron (Theory of Business Strategy)*. Tokyo: Yuhikaku (in Japanese).

Perens, B. (2000). The Open Source Definition. http://www.hams.com/OSD.html (accessed January 10, 2000).

Raymond, E. S. (1999a). The Cathedral and the Bazaar. http://www.tuxedo.org/~esr/writings/cathedral-bazaar/ (accessed September 10, 1999).

Raymond, E. S. (1999b). "Open Source and the Impact of Linux on the Corporate system," Q&A in the memorial lecture of Nikkei Linux Publishing, Nikkei Hall in Tokyo, May 26, 1999.

Raymond, E. S. (1999c). Homesteading the Noosphere. http://www.tuxedo.org/~esr/writings/homesteading/ (accessed September 10, 1999).

Teramoto, Y. (1999). Sabisu no Honshitu to Sabisu Keiei no Kadai (Essence of Service and Problem of Service Management), in *Sabisu Keiei (Service Management)*. Tokyo: Doubunkan (in Japanese).

Teramoto, Y. (2001). Chishiki Stakai to Kachi Souzou (Knowledge Society and Value Creation), in *Chishiki Stakai Kouchiku to Rinen Kakushin (Construction of Knowledge Society and Policy Innovation)*. Tokyo: Nikkagiren (in Japanese).

Toffler, A. (1980). *The Third Wave*. New York: William Morrow and Company, Inc.

Torvalds, L. (1999). The Edge of Linux, in *OpenSource: Voice From the Open Source Revolution*. New York: O'Reilly.

Vixie, P. (1999). Software Engineering, in *OpenSource: Voice From the Open Source Revolution*. New York: O'Reilly.

PART III

Linking Knowledge among Organizations

CHAPTER 7

Promoting Competence and Reform with Global Groups

Caroline F. Benton

MESO-ORGANIZATIONS AND KNOWLEDGE SHARING IN THE GLOBAL ECONOMY

Introduction

Much has been written about the emerging borderless economy over the last decade. Management of global businesses, however, is still enigmatic in many areas and is growing more complex with the advancement of information technology. Companies are exchanging knowledge on a real-time basis with subsidiaries, customers, and business partners located in all corners of the globe. At the same time, our ability to transfer information has caused a rapid growth in the number of potential competitors, who are increasingly knowledge savvy. With the access to information and knowledge that are vital inputs into the value creation process is no longer limited to corporations with large budgets and human resources, making any one company's long-term position uncertain. IBM of the early 1990s, which was nearly left behind in the personal computer market, and the corporations of the last several years, which are now facing intensifying competition and a critical scarcity in funding, can testify to the dangers of standing still and the urgency of continued knowledge creation leading to innovation for sustained corporate survival.

The importance of knowledge for global businesses is heightened by the nonlinear relationship between knowledge and value. That is, the total value of an integrated and comprehensive set of knowledge is greater than the sum of the values of the individual pieces of the knowledge that comprise it. For example, the glue used in 3M's Post-it stickers does not have meaningful value by itself, but when it is combined with pieces of paper it is a useful marking system whose value is greater than the value of simple note pads added to that of removable glue. Not surprisingly, Post-it stickers readily became a global hit not long after launch.

In this manner, diverse and composite knowledge, such as those from different technical and cultural backgrounds, can lead to spectacular new knowledge and innovation. For instance, the combination of western manufacturing processes and Dr. W. E. Deming's theory on quality control with Japanese culture, which traditionally values teamwork, attention to detail, consensus building, and company loyalty, fueled the Japanese electronic and automobile manufacturers' rise from the economic devastation of World War II by being the basis for a unique form of production characterized by incremental improvements suitable to the rapid growth period from the 1960s to 1980s when efficiency was of paramount importance. Managers of global business groups who concern themselves only with the allocation and management of physical resources and with the unilateral integration of their organization's policy and knowledge into their subsidiaries and partners are missing the opportunity to capitalize on the latters' diverse knowledge set. Instead, in today's environment international managers need to focus on building a network that assimilates the knowledge creation processes of all group organizations to optimize the group's ability as a whole to produce unique value.

This chapter hopes to clarify how global businesses can build such a knowledge network that can be used to promote corporate competence and reform by presenting a theoretical framework for analysis and a case study of the recent rebirth of Nissan Motor, after its alliance with Renault. The first section introduces the concept of meso-organizations, or organizations that stretch their boundaries into the environment to embrace diverse and rich sources of knowledge. The second section discusses recent literature on networking and knowledge creation and analyzes the barriers to these processes in global meso-organizations. The third section is a case study of the Nissan, which was rescued from failure through the alliance that infused foreign knowledge. In the last section, I addresses how global corporations can compete in the borderless economy of the twenty-first century.

Emerging Prevalence of Meso-Organizations

For executives, business scholars and critics, the growing phenomenon of global knowledge exchange, which has led to increased rates of innovation and knowledge creation, requires new models and theories for understanding international businesses and their management. Traditional transaction cost analysis theories and models do not provide the tools that managers and executives need to develop proactive strategies for staying ahead of the competition, because they are focused mainly on the financial benefits of decisions, including alliance formation, that occur within the scheme of present business scenarios. In other words, they tackle issues dealing more with how and with whom things should be done within the current context of the business rather than with what should be done—the all-important question for today's businesses. This chapter discusses knowledge networks for creating new knowledge and value that answers this question.

Such new theories must take into account that the relationship between alliance and network partners has become much more involved and intricate over the last decade than acknowledged by traditional network and alliance theories in three ways. First, conventional theories approach and analyze networks and alliances as a means to share capital and tangible resources so that financial efficiency is achieved and physical limitations are overcome, whereas emerging forms of networks, like the Amazon.com community, which offers bibliophiles and the average reader feedback on tens of thousands of books, and the Human Genome Project, which is a collectivity of researchers, scientists, businessmen, and bureaucrats that is deciphering the human genetic sequence, are formed to pool and create knowledge. Second, the membership of networks discussed by these older theories is mainly profit-seeking enterprises and corporations; in contrast, today's networks bring together individuals, not-for-profit organizations, government agencies, as well as other businesses. Third, these theories deal with networks that are mainly fixed in space and time: contracts are drawn and deals are made between limited numbers of partners for prearranged deliverables and outcomes. The memberships of emerging networks are ephemeral in that participation is dynamic (not necessarily less devoted) and flexible. These networks are, thus, more loosely tied, maintaining diversity and autonomy for greater network value while promoting collaboration. One case is the eBay community, the largest on-line auction network, which is comprised of independent individuals and businesses that offer their products and knowledge and monitor each other's dealings through ratings as and when they see fit. (http://www.eBay.com; accessed June 3, 2001).

This book coins this new type of network *meso-organizations*, or networks that span into, and exchange knowledge from, all sectors of society fading the boundary between micro-socioeconomic issues (business) and macro-socioeconomic issues (societal). Formally, meso-organizations are non-self-contained networks that view the environment as an extension of themselves and that capitalize on diverse sources of knowledge through liberal exchange with other parties in the marketplace. Accordingly, our theory of meso-organizations differs from current networking theory in that it addresses the issues of wide-ranging and varying membership, fading organizational and sector boundaries, and network-wide knowledge creation and utilization processes for continuous innovation.

Examples of meso-organizations are the support mailing lists sponsored by computer software companies and organizations. Web sites linux.org and redhat.com host various mailing lists targeted at all levels of users that deal with all aspects of the Linux operating system (http://www.linux.org and http://www.redhat.com; accessed June 9, 2001). Through these lists, novices and experts alike have access to the wealth of information and knowledge harbored in the minds of users from all over the world. Users are able to communicate with software enthusiasts that enjoy volunteering advice and discussing the nitty-gritty details of the software and can avoid the paid support staff of corporations who can become disgruntled after enduring customer complaints day in and day out. What's more, because help can come from anywhere in the world, it is frequently given around the clock. From the perspective of software manufacturers, these volunteer mailing lists help maintain more satisfied

Figure 7.1
Flow of Knowledge

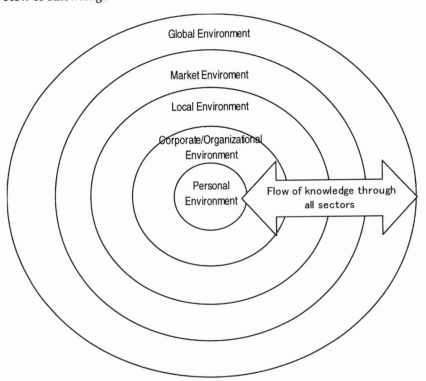

and loyal customers without the extra burden of an oversized support staff and are a source of real-time information on market needs and user perceptions. Such information can be vital input for development of subsequent product and service upgrades.

I have taken advantage of such mailing lists personally and have been rewarded with dozens of solutions to problems within a day, and more often then not, within hours. With input from respondents from diverse backgrounds such as freelance programmers, fellow users, and customer support representatives I had the chance to try different methods to solve my software problem and to ask for further clarifications for those that did not appear to work as suggested.[1] Such interactive mailing lists serve to build strong user networks and contrast sharply with pay-per-use customer support of many computer manufacturers for which users pay a not insignificant amount for each question session regardless of whether the problem is solved. Arguably more irritating to customers, for this type of support, users can spend hours waiting to get through to a support representative on the telephone or days for an answer to an e-mail request. Furthermore, one telephone call or e-mail query may not lead to a sufficient solution and the telephone calling and waiting—not to mention the additional cost—must be endured once again by the customer.

Our theory of meso-organization also recognizes that management cannot force innovation and knowledge creation; the change process must involve and take root at all interested levels of an organization for it to be fundamental. One reason for this is that status quo and organization inertia are addicting for both individuals and organizations as uncertainty tends to be intimidating. Without a vested interest in change, participants are not highly motivated to see the successful implementation of new strategies, ideas, and processes. Unmotivated employees are passive barriers to change and innovation and, hence, are a threat to long-term corporate success as they can be more difficult to detect or remove than employees who are aggressively antagonistic. Furthermore, recruiting active participation from all parts of the organization can lead to greater innovation as each member or organization of a network has a different set of knowledge that can be tapped into and utilized. This need for wide-ranged participation can be said of global businesses as well. A corporate group whose knowledge creation is inter-organizational, engaging subsidiaries and affiliates, can take full advantage of the tangible (physical) and intangible (knowledge) resources of group members to create greater value.

ANALYZING ORGANIZATIONAL INNOVATION

In this section, a review of theories of organizational innovation and knowledge creation, which are core characteristics of meso-organizations,

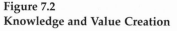

Figure 7.2
Knowledge and Value Creation

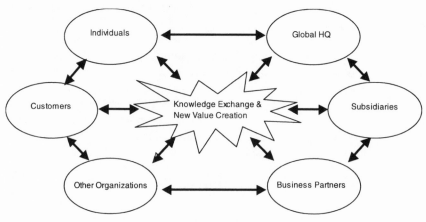

will be presented followed by a more detailed outline of these processes in global environments.

Revisiting Organizational Innovation

Although the recognition of the importance of knowledge-creating organizations is a relatively recent trend in the field of management and business research, the search for scientific understanding of business practices and their improvements goes back as far as Frederick Winslow Taylor's theory of scientific management. Taylor (1856–1915) believed that the practices of businesses and their workers could be scientifically analyzed to find optimal working conventions. In hindsight, however, management scholars and practitioners have since recognized that this theory is limited as it completely ignores the human factor in business operations including the needs, interests, and motivation of employees and have developed theories that incorporate a more humanistic and/or an organizational learning approach. Theories that were born from these efforts include Chris Argyris and Donald Schön's (1978) organizational learning, which recognizes the importance of learning on an organizational level and the existence of single and double-loop learning processes and Peter F. Drucker's (1993) proposition of a knowledge society in which knowledge workers are the most important resources of modern businesses.

Expanding on these works, Ikujiro Nonaka and Hirotaka Takeuchi (1995) developed a comprehensive theory of knowledge creation that examines the dynamics of two different types of knowledge, explicit and tacit, and knowledge creation processes. Explicit knowledge is one that is codifiable, or easily documented, and thus can be readily stored in databases and transferred to other parties. In contrast, tacit knowledge such as art, culture, and the intuition of craftsmen and experts, cannot be written down and is more innate and personal. It must be experienced firsthand. For example, German Meister bakers do not reach the level of expert baker by learning techniques from merely reading books. Rather, they spend years working with ingredients and dough, to gain an instinctive understanding of how such factors as the weather and the specifications of an oven can affect dough and the baking process and how these environmental variations can be overcome so that the highest quality can be achieved consistently.

Nonaka and Takeuchi also theorize that the exchange of tacit knowledge through direct human-to-human contact, a process termed socialization, and the conversion of tacit knowledge to explicit knowledge, a process coined externalization, are critical processes for knowledge creation. Tacit knowledge is individual expertise, know-how, and wisdom and requires genuine and extended interaction (socialization) to be passed from one employee to another. For this reason, tacit knowledge must be converted into explicit knowledge through verbalization and codification (the externalization process) for it to be conveyed on a wide scale throughout a global network or organization. Only in this manner can global businesses make maximum use of the knowledge found throughout its organization, which in turn can be used for the creation of the next generation of knowledge in a cyclic process of innovation.

The research of Yoshiya Teramoto, the business and management scholar to which this book is dedicated, has been focused on such knowledge-creating networks that pool and fuse knowledge resources from multiple entities for greater value. Many of these networks are flexible, dynamic, and temporary lasting only through the life of a project or product development cycle. The numerous IT companies that have formed alliances with multiple partners for the development of specific products and software are examples of such networks.

Figure 7.3
Tacit and Explicit Knowledge

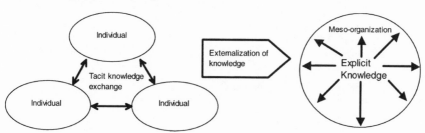

This pooling of network members' knowledge increases the diversity of knowledge in a corporate group, which is necessary to tackle the dynamic and varying needs of the global marketplace. Google, one of the leading Internet search engines of the world, has formed a joint project with BMW to develop a voice search system for the automobile manufacturer's 7 Series (http://www.salon.com/tech/feature/2001/06/21/goggle_ henziger/index1.html; accessed June 21, 2001). With this system, users will speak into a microphone to initiate an Internet search and will be given a list of matched entries. The user will then call out the number of the desired result to access the target information. Combining Google's expertise on searching information with keywords and phrases with BMW's automobile electronics expertise, the partnership is posed to develop a unique value for information-loving consumers.

Teramoto and Benton (2001) suggest that what enables such networks to spirally create new value are the following characteristics of knowledge: (1) the ease of transfer, or portability, over time and space; (2) the ability to be used by any number of persons simultaneously and repeatedly; (3) the malleability of context and form; and (4) the contextual dependence of meaning. These are discussed individually:

- Ease of transfer refers to the ability to exchange on a wide scale explicit knowledge that has been codified. In contrast, physical resources such as a plant or warehouse cannot be relocated without great cost and time. Tacit knowledge, on the other hand, must be codified for such transfer to be realized.

- Ability to be used simultaneously and repeatedly means knowledge can be used by an unlimited number of persons without being consumed. A computer program or database can be used by millions of persons unlike a tangible resource which usually has limits in terms of where it can be used, how many persons can use it, and how many times it can be used.

- The malleability of knowledge indicates that knowledge can be integrated and fused together to produce even greater value. Many oriental therapeutic practices, such as shiatsu, acupuncture, and moxybustion therapy are being combined with Western technology for holistic treatment of symptoms and diseases. For instance, low-level laser therapy is being used in Japan to treat wide-ranging conditions such as infertility, pain, and poor circulation by targeting the body points defined in traditional oriental medicine.

- Contextual dependence relates to how the meaning of a specific set of knowledge can vary by situation. For instance, the therapeutic agent derived from the Clostridium Botulinum bacterium, Botulinum Toxin A, which is marketed under the name of Botox by Allergan, Inc., is used for a variety of purposes. It is used as a muscle relaxant for treatment of medical conditions (cervical dystonia and strabismus) as well as for aesthetics purposes (removing wrinkles and furrows) and pain relief. It is also being clinically tested for use on toddlers/children with cerebral palsy to relax muscle constriction in limbs.

Global meso-organizations can take advantage of these characteristics of knowledge to develop effective and unique businesses. Ease of transfer makes it possible for information and knowledge to be transmitted and conveyed across geographic, market, and political boundaries on a real-time basis for exchange among meso-organization members. Companies like Microsoft Corporation support worldwide training, examination, and certification for its products with links to information and registration on its web page. These programs aim to recruit third-party system integrators, developers, and network administrators that can set up, maintain, and service Microsoft products globally (http://www.microsoft.com/traincert/default.asp; accessed August 10, 2001). Dell Computers' system provides users the ability to trace their orders throughout the order-production-delivery process, and links its procurement and delivery system with partners to keep average inventory levels to roughly four days, a feat that is remarkable considering that other manufacturers' levels reach over 30 days. Parts suppliers, factories, logistics partners, shippers, and import agents are all connected in this system and supply nearly real-time input into the order-tracing systems for customers to view on line (http://www.dell.com, accessed August 10, 2001).

For global meso-organizations, the ability to simultaneously use any piece of knowledge repeatedly makes it possible for all its members to use a particular set of knowledge, allowing for greater efficiency, value, and opportunities for new knowledge creation. For example, the knowledge embedded in the knowledge networks of Yahoo!, eBay, and Amazon are all accessed daily by millions of people throughout the world without being consumed. The characteristic of malleability means that knowledge can be fused with existing knowledge from a different market environment to create unique products and services that fit the needs of each market or even each individual. For instance, many Internet sites let customers customize the information displayed on its Web site. Viewers of ABCNEWS.com can arrange to have their customized financial portfolio displayed for up-to-date information on the performance of their stocks and funds (http://portfolios.abcnews.go.com/?=portfolios; accessed December 18, 2001). Contextual dependency of knowledge denotes that the products or services of global meso-organizations—which are all embedded with the knowledge used to create them—can have varying meaning depending on the cultural context of the market in which they are being sold. Accordingly, Hollywood movies that deal with conflicts in the Middle East are perceived differently in America, Europe, Israel, and the Middle East.

As we see, these characteristics bring flexibility to knowledge and make it possible for meso-organizations to exchange, create, and utilize diverse knowledge from and in a variety of markets. Multinational corporations,

Table 7.1
Characteristics of Resources

	Operation-based resources	Knowledge- based resources
Ease of transfer	Tangible operation-based resources like plants and offices are difficult and costly to transfer.	Non-tangible knowledge resources are easy to transfer over time and space barriers if made explicit.
Multiple usage	Tangible operation-based resources have a limit in terms of how many persons can use them at one time and how many times they can be used before being consumed.	Non-tangible knowledge resources do not get consumed and can be used by unlimited number of persons.
Malleability	Tangible operational-based resources tend to be created for limited usages.	Non-tangible knowledge resources can be adapted, fused and integrated with other knowledge sets to give new value and meaning.
Contextual dependency	The meaning or value of a tangible operational-based resource tends to have more limited contextual dependency.	The meaning or value of a knowledge-based resource can vary significantly depending on the contextual usage.

however, must actively develop a system of global knowledge creation as it will not naturally form ubiquitously in the network without a catalyst or inherent incentives for participants. The case study of Nissan that is presented in a following section will show how global knowledge can be incorporated for dramatic increase in performance and productivity leading to increased profitability.

Creating Knowledge for Organizational Innovation

This chapter addresses two obstacles to the knowledge creation process in global networks. These are the internal resistance to change and the difficulty in developing the trust that is necessary for fruitful socialization among persons of different cultural, environmental, or corporate backgrounds.

Internal Resistance to Change

Managing change and innovation has been difficult in any era. Status quo is very seductive as venturing out of the scheme of habit and familiarity into the realm of the unknown can be intimidating. Even when a corporation attempts change, it is often unsuccessful when the process is forced and does not receive acceptance from all affected parties. As Roman writer, Caius Petronius, stated nearly 2,000 years ago in A.D. 66,

We trained very hard, but it seemed that every time we were beginning to form up into teams, we would be reorganized. I was to learn later in life that we tend to meet any new situation by reorganizing, and a wonderful method it can be for creating the illusion of progress, while producing confusion, inefficiency and demoralization.

It is noteworthy that the same organizational and group dynamics still abound today, two millennia later. We are forced to acknowledge that unilateral implementation of change in an organization is not frequently successful in the long term due to internal resistance and top management's limited knowledge regarding the issues of day-to-day operations. For this reason, the best way to thwart failure is to have the change process, starting with knowledge creation, borne from the concerted efforts of every concerned level of an organization. The anxiety and uncertainly caused by change can be alleviated considerably by doing so. Also, because persons on the front lines of business have first-hand knowledge of the market, they will be able to provide vital information and knowledge for the innovation process. As Nissan's CEO Carlos Ghosn stated in a Japanese television documentary, aired on June 23, 2001 on Tokyo Broadcasting System which outlined the automobile manufacturer's recent success, the best learning is going to take place in the front lines of business.

In a global business, this means that all affected subsidiaries should feel involved in the processes toward change. In the blurring borders and boundaries of meso-organizations, this means that the knowledge and impetus behind wide-reaching innovation should involve input from all affected sectors of society. Rather than forcing change, top executives and management should conceive a grand scheme that is designed with input from all levels of the organization and that guides all organizational activities.

Developing Trust to Enable Socialization

As stated previously, socialization is the key to meaningful exchange of the tacit knowledge that is harboured in the minds of employees. Social-

Figure 7.4
Knowledge Creation and Innovation Spiral

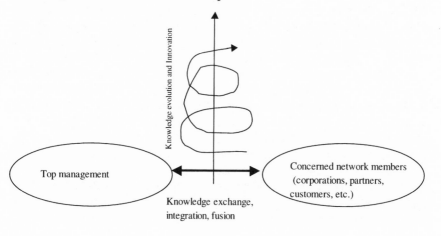

ization among individuals and groups from different countries, however, is difficult to accomplish as a result of cultural filters and language barriers and has been a major theme of research—although under varying names—in many academic fields including sociology, communications (cross-cultural communications), and political science (international relations). As such, managers and executives of international businesses must actively promote socialization through formal corporate initiatives as well as with a shared global vision and policy that will bind diverse groups, subsidiaries, and partners. A formal venue for dialogue, such as employee exchange programs and cross-functional/intersubsidiary projects, catalyzes understanding among employees from different regions who can then begin exchanging tacit knowledge. A shared global vision is vital for bringing together the goals and values of a diverse group with different cultural backgrounds by setting a framework or an umbrella theme by which all participants can direct their strategies and activities, including knowledge creation.

It is not sufficient to merely send knowledge workers aboard to visit foreign subsidiaries and partners as cultural barriers and filters will skew the internalization of the knowledge exchange. Rather, management must ensure that knowledge workers make conscious efforts to forge an understanding of the similarities and differences of the contextual meaning of the knowledge exchanged through earnest communication and direct experience; otherwise such trips will end up as little more than sightseeing tours for the knowledge worker. Knowledge workers should be assigned the clear goal of gaining an understanding of the subsidiaries' or partners' operations and market environment rather than unilaterally supervising activities and pushing their own agenda.

Ideally such exchange should include informal small-talk that promotes real understanding and trust among individuals. As several chapters of this book note, trust is important for socialization and the exchange of knowledge. Without trust, there is resistance to both conveying and receiving knowledge. Any knowledge that has been communicated will likely be perceived as not worthwhile or trustworthy by the recipient and will be wasted. Active development of trust is particularly necessary in cases where the persons participating in the exchange are from different backgrounds and cultural contexts. It is human nature for people to be wary of ideas that are not familiar or of those that they do not readily understand. These include foreign culture, behavior, and value systems that are new, unrecognizable, and confusing.

For example, an acquaintance told me that when she was a director of an international subsidiary of a European clothing manufacturer, she witnessed many instances where managers from the parent company would refuse to listen to the information and knowledge of subsidiary managers. At times subsidiaries were forced to import products that they did not deem appropriate for their markets leaving employees of the various subsidiaries aggravated. At one international meeting, she happened to hear the head of the parent company's international division tell his staff that they alone are the intellectual center of the company, thereby belittling the subsidiaries' management who were also participating and within earshot. Naturally, such statements did not help build respect for subsidiary staff on the part of the parent company's international division and inevitably the latter took on an air of superiority and tended not to listen to the needs and knowledge of the former.[2]

As we will see in the case study of Nissan in the next section, in an alliance of partners there must be a balance between independence and consolidation and between respecting each other's knowledge, culture and strategies and achieving consolidation and collaboration for operational, tactical, and strategic synergy. On one hand, respecting a partner's perspective is essential for building trust between alliance partners, but it must not be at a level that inhibits integration of the partners' strengths and capabilities. Too much shyness toward integration will cancel out the intangible benefits of the alliance as each partner will act as a completely independent entity with only capital ties to one another. Complete fusion of the partners' business models, strategies, and operations, on the other hand, can lead to efficiency and cohesiveness with the de facto creation of one organization but only at the expense of the operational and strategic diversity that is inherent in having two separate entities. Namely, there needs to be a balance between integrating the tangible and intangible resources of both partners and maintaining the independence that generates vital diversity for competing in a global market.

REFORMING NISSAN

In the Red

Less than three years ago, Nissan Motor Corporation, the second largest automobile manufacturer in Japan, was bound for corporate failure. Sales, profit, and market shares were plummeting while debt was increasing as Nissan continually failed to adapt to the recessionary economy plaguing the nation since the early 1990s. In the fiscal year ending March 1998, consolidated net unit sales decreased by 5.2 percent to 2,568 thousand units, while net sales decreased by 1.4 percent to 6,564.6 billion yen for a net loss of 14 billion yen, the second loss in three years. Nissan gave the sluggish economy and declining consumer demand and confidence as the major reasons for its dismal performance and stated that to rebuild its financial health it would "work to remedy a structural tendency toward high costs and to build a profit-oriented structure that does not depend solely on sales growth." The company's plans were to downsize business operations and reduce internal costs by changing its business approach to one of selection and concentration on heightened efficiency. Specific measures included focusing resources on highly profitable models, increasing production efficiency with a Flexible Manufacturing System, streamlining sales channels, and reducing interest-bearing debt (Nissan Motor Corp. annual report of fiscal year 1998).

However, these measures did not help to reverse the company's decline in the stagnant market as they did not lead to fundamental change in the behavior and perceptions of management and employees or create a sense of urgency among employees and only inhibited true reformation. Rather than a reformation plan that focused solely on slimming down operations, a plan that also creates new knowledge, leading to innovation and new value, was necessary to move the company away from status quo. As a result, the company's dismal performance continued. In the fiscal year ending March 1999, although the company's consolidated net sales rose very slightly by 0.2 percent to 6,580 billion yen, its net income decreased with a loss of over 27.7 billion yen, nearly double from the previous year. The situation deteriorated even further in the following fiscal year with a consolidated net sales decline of 10.1 percent to 5,977 billion yen and a net loss of 684 billion yen (Nissan's annual reports for fiscal years ending March 1999 and March 2000).

As Nissan's traditional reform efforts did not return the company to profitability, the company's executives had to make an extremely difficult decision for a proud, well-established Japanese company: it signed an alliance agreement in March 1999 with Renault, a major foreign compet-

Figure 7.5
Trends in Nissan's Consolidated Net Income

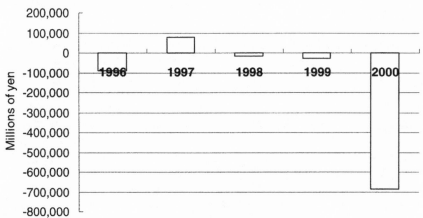

Fiscal year ended March

itor, to which it sold a significant portion of its stock. Under the arrangements, the company also consented to hand over operational control of the company to executives of the partner, a very embarrassing situation for a company that once could be said to represent Japan's economic miracle.

Rebuilding Business Philosophy with Knowledge Networking

Forming an Alliance Aimed at Knowledge Networking

Although it was a drastic decision for the company's executives, entering into the alliance proved to be a saving move for a company overburdened with debt and declining sales. By allying with a foreign automobile manufacturer with a different business culture and philosophy, Nissan was able to exploit a different knowledge set and knowledge creation paradigm to make a surprising performance comeback within the first year of the alliance, the initial terms of which were as follows (Nissan Motor's Annual Report for fiscal year ending March 1999).

1. Capital Participation

Renault purchases a 36.8 percent share of Nissan using allocation of new shares, while Nissan reserves the right of capital participation in the French partner. Renault buys a 22.5 percent share of Nissan Diesel and 100 percent of its partner's financial services business in Europe. In total, Renault invests over 643 billion yen in Nissan, making the partnership the fourth-largest automobile-manufacturing group with a worldwide market share of over nine percent. Each company, however, maintains its individual identity, thereby maintaining network diversity.

2. Management Exchange

Nissan takes three executives from Renault as members of the board of directors. Carlos Ghosn, Renault Executive Vice President, takes over as Chief Operating Officer of Nissan, to whom all executive vice presidents report. Patrick Pelata, Senior Vice President of Renault, fills the office of Nissan Executive Vice President in charge of Products and Corporate Planning, and Thierry Moulonguet, Renault Vice President, is appointed Nissan Senior Vice President and Deputy CFO. From Nissan's side, Yoshikazu Hanawa, Nissan Chairman, President and CEO, becomes a member of Renault's board of directors, and two Nissan executives join Renault as Senior Vice Presidents.

3. Business and Operational Cooperation

Both partners cooperate with tie-ups across a wide range of business functions and operations, such as research and development, production, purchasing, platforms, power trains, distribution and sales, and financial services to produce synergistic effects targeted at over 390 billion yen during a three-year period starting in 2000.

As announced by Nissan, the two strategic pillars of the global partnership, whose aim is to form a strong, two-country group that can achieve growth with balanced profit, are as follows: (Nissan Motor: http://www.nissan-global.com/JP/HOME/0,1305,SI9-LO4-MC92-IFN-CH120,00 .html, accessed June 29, 2001).

1. Form a world-class group to respond to the challenges of the globalization of the marketplace and intensifying international competition for higher quality, lower cost and shorter lead-time, and accelerating technological advancement.
2. Build a powerful complementary position. In particular, the three areas of product development (platform and common parts), procurement and regional cooperation (manufacturing, sales) are important.

As shown by the above two aims of the alliance, Nissan hopes that through the synergistic effects of pooling tangible (capital and human

Figure 7.6
Initial Alliance Agreement

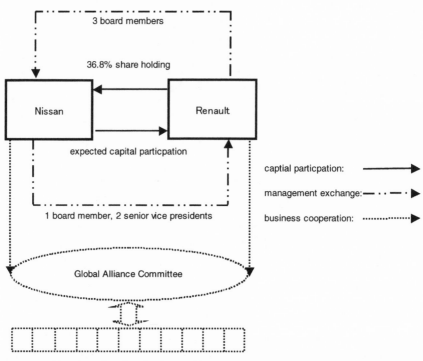

1 board member, 2 senior vice presidents

resources) and intangible resources (knowledge resources), the groups' consolidated value will prove to be greater than the sum of the value of the individual partners. Each company, however, will "respect each others' brand identities" and will "maintain its own identity and have its own corporate strategies (Nissan Motor's Annual Report for fiscal year ending March 1999)." In terms of our theory, this will promote both collaboration and diversity in the alliance.

To design the strategies and undertake the decision-making of the alliance, the partners established a Global Alliance Committee (GAC) consisting of both companies' top management. Eleven Cross Country Teams (CCT) made up of managers from both companies were created as well to bring together the partners' knowledge and develop plans and proposals for the GAC to consider. Each of the CCTs deal with one of four business areas (product planning and related strategy, power trains, purchase and supply, and vehicle engineering) or one of seven marketing and sales regions (Japan, Asia-Oceania, Mexico-Central America, South America, Europe, CIS-Turkey-Romania-North Africa, and Middle East/Sub-Saharan Africa), making their combined efforts far-reaching and comprehensive.

Promoting Knowledge Exchange with Mutual Trust

Nissan has stated that mutual respect of each other's corporate culture and brand identity was the essential for bringing together the two companies. Without mutual respect, which can be defined as a feeling of deference or consideration toward something or someone, neither partner would be open to learning from the other because the other's knowledge set or value system would be viewed as inferior or unworthy of study. That is, without mutual respect, the alliance partners would not trust each other's capabilities or accumulated knowledge, making futile the attempts at involved socialization, which is necessary for the exchange of tacit knowledge.

In order to construct and lead the reformation of Nissan, Carlos Ghosn, then vice president of Renault Europe, was recruited as COO by the partners who hoped that with his proven record of corporate rebuilding he would bring his extensive knowledge of cost-cutting and increasing productivity to Nissan. Ghosn himself, however, did not come to Nissan to implement merely the knowledge that he had acquired in other markets: he believed that the best learning was going to take place at the front lines of the business. He stated in an interview with *TIMEasia.com* magazine, "I had a very vague image, although a positive one, of Japan. But I considered it important not to start work with any preconceived ideas," and also that as a leader of a company or country "You have to listen deeply and not only to people reporting to you. You need to go deep into the organization." (TIMEasia.com: http://www.time.com/time/asia/features/ japan_view/int_ghosn.html; accessed June 10, 2001.) What this infers is that in order to effectively institute innovation, it is first necessary for managers to gain a genuine understanding of the situation through involved communication and networking before implementing change based on preexisting notions of how the business should be managed. Ghosn also put forth that building relationships between people is fundamental (to business) and that the sole pursuit of rationalization will not allow an organization to accomplish anything (Nihon Keizai Shinbum, October, 22, 2001).

One of Ghosn's first steps in reforming Nissan was not to force change based on his experience, but to exchange knowledge with Nissan management and employees and its partners. Shortly after his arrival, Ghosn visited all of the company's major suppliers and dealers to discuss the reasons behind the company's dismal situation and other major issues affecting the automobile market. In other words, Ghosn began his revival efforts by first taking advantage of and strengthening ties to the company's existing knowledge network.

Many, if not most, of the company's suppliers and dealers were surprised by this action, as no Nissan executive had made such an effort before to understand the situation of the front lines of the Japanese automobile market. Hiding behind the company's hierarchy, past Nissan executives had distanced themselves with the reality of the market and did not grasp the gravity of the situation. Ghosn, on the other hand, directly exchanged information with suppliers and dealers to access and internalize the first hand knowledge of important market players, while setting the stage for mutual respect and trust.

Likewise, to increase his ability to communicate and socialize with his colleagues and business partners, Ghosn has attempted to speak Japanese, a laborious effort that many expatriate managers do not choose to undertake. Ghosn shocked many stockholders by delivering his first major speech depicting his plans for Nissan in Japanese only months after his arrival, a formidable feat for even veteran foreign managers. With this effort, Ghosn conveyed his willingness to try and understand Japanese culture, since language is an essential element of any culture.

Creating a Revival Plan through Knowledge Networking

Within roughly half a year of the formation of the alliance, a wide-ranging and aggressive three-year plan, coined the Nissan Revival Plan (NRP), to rebuild performance was announced (October 18, 1999). The recovery plan itself was formed through collaborated efforts of employees and partners: two hundred of the company's global managers brought together their unique knowledge to design a plan that could achieve lasting and profitable growth for Nissan worldwide. The NRP focused on two initiates which are (1) growing business and market presence, and (2) reducing costs by 1 trillion yen and halving total debt to 700 billion yen by fiscal year 2002 (Nissan Motor: http://www.nissan-global.com/GCC/NRP/NEWS/news-e.html; accessed June 29, 2001).

The plan recognized that although cost and debt reduction is the first dire imperative, this alone cannot rebuild the company's position as a global leader. Ghosn noted that, "while cost cutting will be the most dramatic and visible part of the plan, we cannot save our way to success." This statement infers that after cost-cutting efforts establish a lean corporate composition that no longer bleeds, a foundation for sustained growth and innovation must be built.

In terms of specific efforts to increase sales, 22 new models were planned for the company in the short-term. The two alliance partners have agreed to share research, advanced engineering products, and common platform development to increase the group's technological and product development strengths. The first models jointly developed were the Micra and Cube, targeted for the Japan market. Nissan also planned to market four new models, including a next-generation version of Nissan's legendary Z sports car in the U.S., and to replace its product lineup in Europe by 2003 (Nissan Motor: http://www.nissan-global.com/GCC/Japan/NEWS/19991018_0e.html; accessed August 2000).

In terms of specific measures to increase efficiency and productivity

Figure 7.7
Knowledge Exchange and Creation

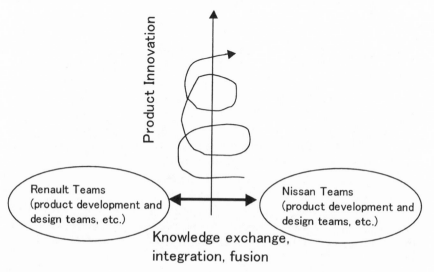

through the partnership, Nissan aimed to reduce costs by over 1 trillion yen with a focus on three business areas of global purchasing: manufacturing, sales, and administration. Planned efforts included the following:

1. Closing of three Japanese assembly plants in 2001
2. Closing of two power train operations in 2002
3. Closing of 300 unprofitable sales offices by end of fiscal year 2002
4. Reduction of world wide work force by 21,000 people
5. Globalization of key functions
6. Centralization of purchasing policy and execution
7. Reduction of suppliers from over 1,145 to 600
8. Forming common hubs, operation centers, and offices with Renault

The first four items on the above list are painful measures to slim down the company's operations and have received much media coverage and harsh criticism from employees. However, these alone are not enough to dramatically increase performance, as these are not forward-looking steps. The fifth and sixth items catalyze Nissan's accumulation of global knowledge regarding key functions, including procurement and purchasing, at the head office. In the past, these functions were carried out independently on a region-by-region or country-by-country basis, which made it impossible to maximize efficiency through synergy and lead to a huge loss of learning opportunities. With these efforts, Nissan hoped to reduce purchasing costs by 20 percent, for a 12 percent reduction of total costs over three years.

The seventh item will help Nissan achieve economies of scale and support knowledge exchange. By limiting the number of suppliers, Nissan can offer suppliers larger order volumes, leading to lower prices, and will be better able to exchange knowledge with important suppliers who will have a greater incentive to work closely with the automobile manufacturer. To fully exploit this new relationship with its suppliers, the company has developed a new program of cooperation. The program has been coined "3,3,3" in reference to three different types of partners (suppliers, purchasing agents, and engineering partners) working on a three-year plan in three different regions (Asia, the Americas, and Europe/Middle East/Africa), and calls for information and knowledge exchange on "worldwide best practices, technology, quality, cost and delivery." The intention is for the company to learn from its suppliers so that it "will challenge its own specifications and standards while protecting its established reputation for quality and reliability" through involved cooperation with suppliers in the areas of product development and design (Nissan Motor: http://www.nissan-global.com/GCC/Japan/NEWS/19991018_0e.html; accessed August 2000.)

The eighth item is aimed at increasing operational efficiently but also leads to knowledge exchange among group organizations. The common hubs and back offices in Europe promote inter-organizational communication and socialization. On the other side of the globe, Nissan will use Renault's organizations and infrastructure in South America to increase its presence on the continent: Renault Credit International will set up a Mexican sales finance company that will support Nissan's sales network in the region. Through these measures Nissan employees will have direct and routine communication with Renault employees, augmenting their insights into the unique factors of the European and South American markets.

These measures of the Revival Plan were intended to enhance the company's technological strength and boost research and development output while reducing the amount of resources necessary. As we have seen, the alliance is not merely a simple merger of two companies that saves one of the partners from financial ruin through the influx of capital and restructuring of inefficient operations; it calls for comprehensive collaboration to produce synergy leading to both operational efficiency and innovative product development and research. The alliance has preserved the independence of both partners while supporting the exchange of knowledge and increase the diversity of the network.

Returning to Profitability

Less than one year into the NRP, Nissan accomplished the seemingly impossible with Ghosn's leadership. The company was not only able to halt its downward inertia but surpassed its target income and returned to profitability. It posted its largest return in the company's recorded history: net consolidated operating income reached 290.3 billion yen, while net consolidated income was 3331.1 billion yen in the fiscal year ending March 2001. At the same time, the company reduced its automotive debt to less than one trillion yen for the first time in 15 years.

One key factor for this success was increasing the number of automobile models that achieved profits. In 1999 only 12 percent of Nissan vehicles generated profits; by 2001 this number increased to 42 percent by decreasing costs and streamlining suppliers (Nihon Keizai Shimbun, October 19, 2001). With these achievements under his belt, Ghosn became President and CEO of the company in June 2001. He is currently chairman of the management committee that was formed in March 2001 and is in charge of directly monitoring the management of the alliance (Nissan Motor: http://www.nissan-global.com/EN/STORY/0,1299,SI9-CH-LO3-TI226-CI237-IFY-MC109,00.html; accessed July 10, 2001).

In addition to streamlining costs, Nissan has recorded successes in the area of product development. Sales of its next generation Skyline model, which was launched in June 18, 2001, reached 4,200 units within the first two weeks, a figure more than twice its original monthly target of 2,000 units (Nissan Motor: http://www.nissan-global.com/EN/STORY/0,1299, SI9-CH123-LO3-TI395-CI342-IFY-MC109,00.html; accessed August 10, 2001). The company also achieved strong sales of its new Liberty model and introduced a series of its next generation vehicles, the new Z-car, Alpha trucks, and the Infiniti F45, for the North American market at a Detroit exhibition.

For the European market, Ghosn introduced three new concept cars that represent a "new phase" in the company's product and design strategy at the Frankfurt Motor Show in September 2001. The first of these automobiles is the mass production version of the futuristic Primera concept vehicle that combines the knowledge of Nissan's global subsidiaries: the vehicle was designed in Europe and is to be manufactured in the United Kingdom (Nissan Motor: (http://www.nissan-global.com/EN/STORY/ 0,1299,SI9-CH97-LO3-TI414-CI353-IFY-MC92,00.html; accessed August 10, 2001). Originally unveiled in October 2000 in Paris under the name Fusion, the car reflects the design philosophy of integrating themes: hard and soft styling; technology and humanism; and Western and Japanese styling. It has a high-tech theme with TV cameras for door mirrors and a humanistic styling with techno-tatami styling for flooring, integrating Japanese taste into the European-targeted vehicle. (Tatami is the woven straw floor covering used in traditional Japanese homes.) The two other concept cars that were unveiled are the mm.e, a compact, three-door hatchback with an all-new front-wheel drive platform developed jointly by the partners (to be built in the UK) for "young, free-thinking, style conscious individuals" that will be a key component to the company's strategy in Europe, and the Crossbow, a 4 × 4 vehicle with a combination of powerful off-road features and on-road practicality.

Ensuring Sustained Innovation

With the completion of the NRP in fiscal year 2002, the major restructuring efforts (closing of factories and 315 sales offices and layoffs) were implemented and Nissan will focus on growing sales globally. Nissan's major reformation measures for the future include (1) strengthening its brand image through new marketing programs designed with the knowledge gained from its customers and partners, (2) capitalizing on its investment in a key plant now under construction in Mississippi, U.S., and (3) making the most of its joint world wide purchasing organization that was established in April 2001, while continuing efforts to reduce costs and debts and to introduce new products.

The Mississippi plant is vital to making inroads into the American market, as it will be an essential venue for direct accumulation of market intelligence. The joint purchasing organization provides synergy development for the Nissan-Renault alliance through greater efficiency and effectiveness of tangible (physical resources and capital) and intangible resource (tacit and explicit knowledge) utilization. Initially, it will be responsible for roughly 30 percent of the partners' annual global purchasing needs, increasing to nearly 70 percent in the near future. It is hoped that the organization will lead to a 5 percent savings on common projects (Nissan Motor: http://www.nissan-global.com/EN/ASTORY/ 0,1301,SI9-CH-LO3-TI220-CI232-IFY-MC109,00.html; accessed July 16, 2001.)

To guide the strategic and operational course toward its goals for the three-year period starting fiscal year 2003, Nissan has crafted Plan 180, the successor to the original Revival Plan. The aims of this plan are to increase global sales by one million units, achieve a consolidated operating income ratio of 8 percent, and bring consolidated interest-bearing debt to zero (excluding debt from financial services) through increased profitability and careful management of investments and financial structures by fiscal year 2005. The catalysts for sales growth are the 22 new models, six of which were launched in Japan and seven in the United States in fiscal year 2002 (Nihon Keizai Shimbun, October 19, 2001, and Nissan Motor: http:// www.nissan-global.com/EN/HOME/0,1305,SI9-LO3-MC92-IFN-CH118,00.html; accessed July 10, 2001).

To further foster the alliance relationship, plans are being made for additional consolidation of sales offices and for Nissan to execute the original alliance stipulation of purchasing stock in the French partner. In seven European countries (France, Germany, England, Italy, Netherlands, Spain, and Switzerland), Nissan plans to decrease the number of sales offices/ companies from 1,500 to 500 by 2005 and to create sales hubs with Renault, which has over 2,000 sales companies in these regions. Ghosn shared in an interview with a leading Japanese business journal that the time for Nissan's investment in Renault might be approaching, but three conditions must first be met. These are (1) preserve clear independence of both companies' brands, (2) increase synergy, and (3) maintain a balance between both companies (Nihon Keizai Shimbun, October 17, 2001). By realizing these conditions, Nissan and Renault hope to have the best of both worlds—the enhanced resource (tangible and intangible) diversity that comes with maintaining separate, autonomous organizations, and the streamlining of operations and costs that comes with consolidation.

In spite of Nissan's remarkable success, no organizational situation or reformation plan can be the final solution for a company as both internal and external environments are in a constant state of change. In a television interview, Ghosn explained that there will be a time for him to leave Japan: he does not feel that it is healthy for one person to control a company for 10 or 20 years (Scoop aired on July 17, 2001, on Asahi Broadcasting Corporation). He also said that once he has taught the company all that he can and has learned all that he can from the company, he will resign and depart. To avoid stagnation, new management with new knowledge, insights, and experience must take over at some time to tackle the emerging issues of that time, sustaining a cycle of learning and innovation.

CONCLUSION

The global marketplace is growing more complex and sophisticated. As a result, today's consumers and customers are demanding more and more; it is no longer enough for organizations to produce good products or services. In such an environment, organizations and corporations must network with the external environment to integrate diverse knowledge and value to produce new and greater value. Moribund Nissan is in the midst of remaking its product lineup through networking with its French alliance partner, Renault. In January 2002 the manufacturers' first U.S. model launched under the NRP, the Altima, won the prestigious North American Car of the Year Award for its design, packing, and ergonomics.

As a result of Ghosn's accomplishments at Nissan, even the traditionally insular circle of Japanese corporations is beginning to understand the benefits of management diversity and the need for an influx of new human resources and knowledge. In the past, the old guards of Japanese management liked to believe that no one but a fellow Japanese could have sufficient understanding of the domestic culture to successfully lead a domestic corporation. In a survey of 1,711 newly appointed directors of publicly-traded corporations (with a response from 245) that was conducted by the Nihon Noritsu Kyokai in June and July of 2001, slightly less than 80 percent of the respondents replied that they were receptive toward having foreigners head Japanese companies. Nearly 25 percent of the respondents noted that a foreign head is necessary when a complete reform of management must be accomplished, while 53.9 percent stated that if a foreign candidate is highly capable, domestic corporations should try to actively recruit this person (Nihon Keizai Shimbun, August 7, 2001). Furthermore, two foreigners ranked in the top five in a poll of the ideal manager: GE former chairman Jack Welch placed third and Ghosn placed fifth behind Sony chairman Nobuyuki Idei (first) and Honda founder Soichiro Honda (second). This change in perceptions of Japanese managers reflects the growing awareness that even Japanese organizations cannot escape globalization and that new knowledge from abroad can be vital for technical, product organizational, and corporate innovation.

One of the most active areas of technological advancements in the early part of the twenty-first century will occur in the field of networking technology. Commonplace devices and equipment that have information and knowledge exchange functions will become ubiquitous: household appliances such as microwaves, television sets, and refrigerators will be networked. Advancements in and development of Internet and telecommunication infrastructures (such as broadband technology) is also occurring at unprecedented speeds. It is envisioned that a person will no longer have to be present to fully experience the sensory perceptions that come with actual physical participation in discussions, meetings or informal conversations, adding further possibilities for transferring of tacit knowledge over time and space barriers.

With such technology, meetings with indiscernibly real-life imagery among employees who are dispersed throughout remote locations and in different organizations can be conducted without second thought and as a matter of course. For global corporations, this means that the need for dealing with cultural and language barriers will become more acute as networking across national borders becomes routine in the general marketplace and among competitors. Both informal and formal processes of international and inter-organizational communications must be actively promoted: informal exchanges help build the necessary trust and understanding among global employees and partners located throughout dispersed locations and in different cultures that are necessary for optimal exchanges of knowledge during formal business interactions. For example, computerized corporate bulletin boards systems and Intranet and Extranet systems can be platforms for both informal and formal knowledge exchanges. It is likely that in the future most all global corporations will connect nearly all worldwide design, product development and procurement, and other operational teams with high-speed and high-value networking platforms to enable real-time, interorganizational, and cross-country collaboration.

In addition to networking business operations, we have discussed how networking functions will be widely embedded into products and services. Home electronics products with audio and video recognition interfaces will be widespread: consumers will set room temperatures, water the lawn, use the microwave from the telephone or other handheld devices. To create such multifunctional products, businesses will have to network with different market players to provide this diverse value.

Management of meso-organizations or networks made of independent entities, however, must be balanced so that both diversity and independence can be maintained while synergy and greater knowledge creation are achieved. Such balance is made possible by nurturing mutual respect of each network member's visions, goals, and cultural and environmental contexts while building compatible and complementary business models that enhance each other's capabilities. For true synergy in knowledge and value development to take place, meso-organization members must find a method of cooperation and interaction that does not sacrifice the strengths and knowledge resources of one member. This means that top management must not only design the alliance in a manner that ensures true collaboration and synergy, but they must also promote operational and strategic diversity among members.

NOTES

1. This is particularly helpful for novices like myself who cannot properly describe the situation or provide the necessary information up front and need prompting from more qualified users.

2. The company has since failed due to a variety of internal and external factors, one of which I believe was this inability to use the knowledge of its subsidiaries.

REFERENCES

ABC News: http://portfolios.abcnews.go.com/? = portfolios (accessed December 18, 2001).

Argyris, C., and Schon, D. (1978). *Organizational Learning: A Theory of Action Perspective*, Reading, MA: Addison-Wesley.

Dell Computer Corp: http://www.dell.com (accessed August 10, 2001).

Drucker, P. F. (1993). *Post-Capitalist Society*, Oxford: Butterworth Heinemann.

eBay: http://www.eBay.com (accessed June 3, 2001).

Linux.org: http://www.linux.org (accessed June 9, 2001).

Microsoft Corp: http://www.microsoft.com/traincert/default.asp (accessed August 10, 2001).

Nihon Keizai Shimbun (August 7, 2001). Gaikokujin Top Kamaimasen, Shinnin Torishimariyaku No 8 Warijaku Ga Younin, Noritsu Kyoukai Shirabe (loose translation; Do Not Mind Having Foreign Management, Slightly less than 80 percent of New Directors Reply to a Noritsu Kyokai Survey).

Nihon Keizai Shimbun (October 17, 2001). Nissan, Oushu de Renault to Hansha Tougou, 3 Bun No 1 No 500 Sha Ni Shuyaku, 2005 Nen Made Ni (loose translation; Nissan and Renault to Integrate Sales Companies in Europe).

Nihon Keizai Shimbun (October 17, 2001). Nissan, Renault Ni Shusshi He, Shacho Kaikenn, Jiki Sematteiru (loose translation: Nissan, To Invest in Renault, Presidential Interview, Time is Near).

Nihon Keizai Shimbun (October 19, 2001). Nissan Sekai Hanbai 100 Mandai Zo, Jiki Keiei Keikaku Plan 180 Sakutei, Nihon Keizai Shimbun (loose translation: Nissan to Increase Global Sales by 1 Million Units, Establishes Next Management Plan—Plan 180).

Nihon Keizai Shimbun (October 19, 2001). Nissan Ribaiburu Purann, Yotei

Wo Uwamararu Sokudo, Konjouki Renkestsu Eigyou Rieki 39 percent Zo (loose translation; Nissan Revival Plan, Proceeding Faster than Scheduled, Consolidated Operating Income Up 39 percent in First Half).

Nihon Keizai Shimbun (October 22, 2001). Nissan Jidosha Shacho Ken CEO Carlos Ghosn Shi—Watashi No Dairyokkan de Ketsudan, Nihon Keizai Shimbun (loose translation: Nissan Motor's President and CEO Carlos Ghosn—I make decisions based on my sixth sense).

Nissan Motor Corp. Annual Reports for fiscal years ending 1998, 1999, 2000, and 2001.

Nissan Motor Corp.: http://www.nissan-global.com/JP/HOME/0,1305,SI9-LO4-MC92-IFN-CH120,00.html (accessed June 29, 2001).

Nissan Motor Corp.: http://www.nissan-global.com/EN/IR/financial/2001/102.html (accessed July 10, 2001).

Nissan Motor Corp.: http://www.nissan-global.com/EN/IR/0,1294,SI9-LO3-MC78-IFN-CH86,00.html (accessed July 10, 2001).

Nissan Motor Corp.: http://www.nissan-global.com/GCC/NRP/NEWS/news-e.html (accessed June 29, 2001).

Nissan Motor Corp.: http://www.nissan-global.com/GCC/Japan/NEWS/19991018_0e.html (accessed August 2000).

Nissan Motor: Corp.: http://www.nissan-global.com/EN/STORY/0,1299,SI9-CH-LO3-TI226-CI237-IFY-MC109,00.html (accessed July 10, 2001).

Nissan Motor Corp.: http://www.nissan-global.com/EN/STORY/0,1299,SI9-CH123-LO3-TI395-CI342-IFY-MC109,00.html (accessed August 10, 2001).

Nissan Motor Corp.: (http://www.nissan-global.com/EN/STORY/0,1299,SI9-CH97-LO3-TI414-CI353-IFY-MC92,00.html (accessed August 10, 2001).

Nissan Motor Corp.: http://www.nissan-global.com/EN/ASTORY/0,1301,SI9-CH-LO3-TI220-CI232-IFY-MC109,00.html (accessed July 16, 2001).

Nissan Motor Corp.: http://www.nissan-global.com/EN/HOME/0,1305,SI9-LO3-MC92-IFN-CH118,00.html (accessed July 10, 2001).

Nonaka, I., and Takeuchi, H. (1995). *The Knowledge Creating Company*. New York, NY: Oxford University Press.

Salon.com: http://www.salon.com/tech/feature/2001/06/21/goggle_henziger/index1.html (accessed June 21, 2001).

Scoop, a news program aired on July 17, 2001, on Asahi Broadcasting Corporation.

Teramoto, Y., and Benton, C. (2001). Networking Knowledge for Value Creation, *Intangibles in Competition and Cooperation*. New York, NY: Palgrave.

TIMEasia.com: http://www.time.com/time/asia/features/japan_view/int_ghosn.html (accessed June 10, 2001).

CHAPTER 8

Knowledge Networks and the Restructuring of Competitive Superiority

Toru Takai

PREFACE

This chapter focuses on a new type of relationship between organizations, relationships developed between Japanese product manufacturers who have forged links specifically for a particular objective without crossing share-holding connections, and those who having reached their objectives, return to operation as separate, independent organizations. I seek to explain the importance of this new type of relationship, which is used to build knowledge skills and to create competitive superiority.

This new type of organizational relationship differs from the intermediate organizational forms found, for instance, in the Japanese motor industry. In other words, it is different from the situation whereby even without cross share-holding major automobile manufacturers support the management of suppliers with parts procurement, so that in practice they have no more independence than *keiretsu* supply chain manufacturers. Each separate company has its own independent technical resources, but through the coordination and unifying power of the "center" company, each company is able to table its knowledge so that innovation can occur, which is clearly a different intercompany relationship to the past practice found in *keiretsu* supply chains.

This chapter is structured as follows. In the first section, the importance of knowledge in strategy theory is emphasized. The second section shows the importance of continually monitoring the interaction of knowledge with the surrounding environment, because although knowledge is the source of continued competitive superiority it does not automatically confer competitive superiority on a company. The third section debates the role of corporate learning in knowledge management and clarifies the necessity to coordinate in-house knowledge management with programs between companies. The fourth section tackles the question of why attention should be paid to loose networks without financial links between companies. In the fifth section a case study of the new type of inter-company relationship involving the motor parts manufacturer Ohashi Technica (below Ohashi) is introduced. In the sixth section the case study is analyzed, revealing the organizational strengths necessary to manage the new inter-company relationship and also the corporate learning ability necessary to create such organizational strengths.

THE IMPORTANCE OF KNOWLEDGE IN STRATEGY THEORY

Recently, the field of strategy theory has seen the establishment of resource-based theory in which core competence and capabilities—the internal resource base of companies—are seen as the basis for building competitive superiority (Barney, 1991). Resource-based theory has arisen as the antithesis to strategy theory, which is built on analysis of the external environment such as the positioning approach.

Resource-based theory asserts that competitive superiority is rooted in the internal resources of a company. Placing analytical focus on the management resources of the company and recognizing that management resources are built up through the long-term application of competitive strategy, it holds that no two companies can have the same organizational culture or the same resources and skills (Collis and Montgomery, 1995). To the extent that built-up management resources are unique to each company, it is difficult for competitors to imitate them, and thus they create persistent competitive superiority.

Difficut imitation is a key factor in the building of persistently competitive superiority. For this reason, within the area of management resources intangible resources such as skills, management know-how, and other unseen techniques and tacit knowledge resources that create competitive superiority are important. In other words, tacit knowledge-based strategies are difficult for competing companies to analyze and identify as connected to success (Reed and Defillippe, 1990).

However, these days it is extremely difficult for a company to independently develop a unique management resources base. In fact, the alliance of Toshiba and Marsushita in the "holy ground" of the Japanese electrical appliance market illustrates an imperative, which is not limited to high-tech businesses but characterized by dynamic technological and market changes.

Resource-based theory has clarified how a company as a whole may acquire and sustain competitive superiority. Sufficient attention has not yet been paid to the subunit level of departments or subsidiary companies (Birkinshaw, 2000). In other words, resource-based theory has been applied only to models that view the company as a single organic entity. However, it is axiomatic that the unique resources of each organization are molded by the internal structure of the organization (Birkinshaw and Hagstrom, 2000).

Clearly, companies interact with their environment. This environment comprises a combination of environments such as competitive, market, and technological environments (Hakansson and Shehota, 1989). Through interaction with these environments, companies are able to receive learning signals and to accumulate knowledge resources. I make my analysis by focusing on knowledge as a key resource formed from the relationships between companies.

We place emphasis on knowledge as a resource, because in today's environment of dynamic changes in technology and market environments, knowledge resources are the source of persistent competitive superiority (Davenport and Pruck, 1998). Unlike material resources, which are depleted by use, knowledge resources can increase the more they are used. One idea spawns another, and shared knowledge benefits both the originator and the receiver. In effect, the knowledge of the entire company is broadened, and the company's ability to innovate is expanded (Barton, 1995).

From a close reading of the current economy, it may be said that 92 percent is knowledge-based. In fact, around 60–75 percent of all those employed in the manufacturing industry are engaged in knowledge-based activities including research, development, product design, management, and human resources (Ruggles and Holtshouse, 1999).

THE NECESSITY FOR CONTINUOUS LEARNING

Knowledge resources truly sustain the competitive superiority of companies, but knowledge itself does not produce competitive superiority. Specialty knowledge possessed by individuals cannot in this form constitute a base for the production of persistent, competitive superiority. Specialty knowledge resides with individuals who may move between companies. Also, the direct benefits of specialists' knowledge tend to reside with individuals rather than with companies. Therefore, the key to continuous creation of innovation through the integration of specialists' knowledge lies with the building of management systems (Grant, 1996). The integration of knowledge is necessary for organizations because of limits to the perceptive abilities of any one individual.

While knowledge resources allow companies to maintain competitive superiority, the useful life of any knowledge resource is becoming shorter.

Naturally, companies may hold some knowledge as patents, but it is a fact of the current state of the research environment that the value of patented knowledge may rapidly decline due to copying and deterioration. For instance, by reverse engineering companies may quickly copy new products or production processes and in practice it is impossible to prevent alterations.

Particularly in technology-intensive industries, the key to competitive superiority resides in not only patented knowledge itself but also in the ability to create fresh technical knowledge. Although technology alters the fundamentals of competition, technology itself ceases to be the basis of persistent, competitive superiority. In the case of service industries with knowledge as the basis of competitive superiority it is easy for competitors to imitate services or products. For instance, North American Bank is known to have copied competitors' products within 24 hours (Whitehill, 1997).

In addition to the problem of copying, the knowledge essential to competitive superiority in the present environment may actually impede the development of fresh knowledge. In other words, companies that excel in a particular field of knowledge tend to undervalue the development of new knowledge. This phenomenon of "core rigidity"[1] is concealed within many companies. They miss opportunities to gather fresh knowledge from the outside precisely because they excel in certain specialized areas of knowledge.

In order to build persistent, competitive superiority, rather than rest easy on the back of some successful application of knowledge, it may be necessary to leave that knowledge behind if it is judged to impede the progress of new knowledge development for the next stage of continuous, competitive superiority. In order to maintain competitive superiority, it is necessary to continually seek out and create fresh knowledge. If this is done, then even if competitors are able to match the price or quality of some service or product, the company that successfully manages a fund of knowledge will have moved onto a different level of product quality, creativity, and efficiency.

In order to achieve this, companies must have connections and space for the creation of knowledge (Teramoto, Iwasaki, and Takai, 1997). As noted above, companies exist and interact within competitive, market, and technological environments. By building connections within these environments a company may regularly access fresh knowledge sources. For instance, in recent years the sudden rise in strategic alliances between companies has enabled not only the joint exploitation of resources in product linkage but also the accumulation of such tacit knowledge as the management know-how and corporate culture of partners.

In fact, Japanese companies have made strategic alliances in many fields with European and American companies, which have strengthened their competitive position through knowledge accumulation.[2] In addition to the value gained through strategic links with competitors, companies may gain knowledge from contacts with customers and suppliers. For instance, it is said that 70 percent of production-related innovations come from interaction with customers (Utterback, 1994).

Companies can use their relationships to create knowledge resources. However this "knowledge network" is not limited to external links. Within an organization, by bringing together research and development, production, sales, and other functions into project teams, innovation can be organized. Multinational companies may use knowledge networks in conjunction with their subsidiaries to create innovation.

In order to clarify the learning process of knowledge networks, it is necessary to distinguish between in-house networks and links between companies (Birkinshaw, Hood, and Jonsson, 1998; Teramoto, Tackai, and Richter, 1994). Current theories of learning have not made any connection between internal and external sources. The following section reviews the need for linkage between the two types of learning, with reference to recent research.

ORGANIZATIONAL LEARNING POWER

It is necessary to use linkages between companies to gain fresh knowledge, which can be used to build up unique management resources. In other words, organizational learning power is required. Organizational learning is defined as the capability of an organization to respond to its environment (Hedberg, 1981). In an environment of increasing change, it is understood that organizational learning power is required of all organizations (Garvin, 1983). There is no consensus on organizational learning. Different researchers have employed different terms to describe the concepts relating to organizational learning (Crossan, Lane, and White, 1999).

However, some common characteristics may be seen among researchers in terms of explaining the purpose of organizational learning, the changes caused in perception and behavior, and the levels of organizational learning. For instance, research by March and Olsen (1975) has clarified the effect of managers' perception limits on organizational learning. Foil and Lyles (1985) have drawn a clear distinction between changes in perception and in behavior, asserting that perception changes are due to study while changes in behavior are due to application.

These researchers have clarified the interaction between individual learning and organizational learning, emphasizing that organizational learning is more than just the accumulation of individual efforts but a cause of perceptional changes and of behavioral changes in organizations. Research by Foil and Lyles (1985), Hedberg (1981), and Argyris and Schon (1978) have clarified the levels of organizational learning. These various researchers employ different terms for these various levels and distinguish organizational learning based on existing knowledge from that which has a completely different knowledge base and is tangential to existing knowledge.

Other researchers have approached the subject of organizational learning from the point of view of data mining and data processing. In contrast to analysis based on results (Osland and Yaprak, 1994), they explain the process of learning. For instance, Huber (1991) has characterized organizational learning as a data processing operation. He sees organizational learning as composed of the processes of knowledge mining, data distribution, data interpretation, and organizational memorization. Nonaka and Takeuchi (1995) have emphasized the creation of knowledge, its connection to product innovation, and how individual skills may bear fruit for the whole organization.

Research by Crossan (1999) made a more detailed assessment of the process model for organizational learning. He distinguished individual, group, and company-wide levels of learning and for each level identified four study processes: intuition, interpretation, collation, and systematization. He described the "feed forward" mechanism of individual-level learning-affecting groups and described group-level learning-affecting organizations as the process of searching for knowledge. The reverse process of "feedback" from organizational level to groups, and from groups to individuals, comprises the application of knowledge. The interaction of these levels and processes creates tension as strategic reform is undertaken.

While recognizing the context and purpose of studies, Bierley and Hamalainen propose that these research approaches have oversimplified the factors of organizational environment (1995). For instance, Huber (1991) proposed the term "grafting" as the process of using mergers with other companies or of forming long-term strategic alliances to increase the company's knowledge stock. Environments suitable for organizational learning are not universally present within all organizations.

For instance, according to recent surveys (Park and Ungson, 2001), if the management systems in two alliance partners are widely different (Daz, 1988) or if the partners have greatly different decision-making processes or corporate cultures, then organizational learning does not progress. Similarly, there are differences between the learning style and speed of partnerships between competing companies and between those that are not in competition with each other. The degree of control over subsidiaries also affects organizational learning.

Differences in learning styles between partner companies have not been sufficiently taken into account in current theories, and insufficient attention has been paid to the importance of a common base between companies participating in organizational learning (Bierley and Hamalainen, 1995).

Companies do not carry out their activities in an individual environment (Hakansson and Snehota, 1991). Organizational learning power is not only a matter of the learning skills within the company but is enhanced by interaction with competing companies, customers, and other entities. In fact, things that are learned are subject to the influence of things already learned (Parkhe, 1991). Learning performance is improved when the purpose of learning is related to things already known and by the existence of a common language as a basis for interpreting experience (Inkpen, 2000).

From the above examples it can be seen that organization learning, whether carried out within the organization or through connections with competing companies, customers, or other external parties, is not an independent process but a matter of interacting and complementing (Bierley and Hamalainen, 1995). In order to understand the learning power of an organization, it is necessary to understand the links between its in-house and external learning processes.

LOOSE NETWORK LEARNING

Organizational learning that occurs between alliance partners may be divided into those of tight alliances based on mergers and financial links, and those of looser alliances such as licensing or outsourcing where financial links are not involved. This section of the chapter analyzes the second type of alliance. One reason for this is that in this age of information-based companies, the trend is moving away from the pursuit of competitive superiority by accumulating all capabilities in-house and in seeking market share.

In contrast, through the concentration on specific strengths and the development of abundant knowledge by business development within a limited field, competitive superiority can be built. For instance, companies such as Microsoft or Amazon.com have overwhelmed their competitors with relatively small numbers of employees and fixed assets.

A second reason for the focus on loose alliances relates to the standpoint of academic research. Many studies have been made of organizational learning within joint ventures,[3] a relatively tight intercompany relationship. Much research has been made on strategic alliances, but looser alliances, such as those associated with outsourcing or nonfabrication (nonmanufacturing), have been understudied (Enatsu, 1995).

Of particular interest are those companies where repeated success through innovation occurs with loose relationships that are independent of financial links. These may be described as networked companies using knowledge as the key to their linkage.

This chapter discusses Ohashi, an automobile parts manufacturer that has built competitive superiority through concentration on development and design, with all fabrication outsourced. It has formed a network of 470 medium and small parts manufacturers. Ohashi's role is to match and integrate the skills of these 470 companies to meet customers' requirements.

Ohashi is completely independent from each of the companies in its network and maintains no special relationship with any single major automobile manufacturer. By concentrating on design and development, Ohashi acts as the nucleus of the network and has strengthened its position through its strong organizational learning power, as shown in its ability to integrate the specialized knowledge of the members of its network.

Answers to the question raised in this chapter regarding the linkage between external and in-house learning can be received through analysis of Ohashi. In order to make its strategy succeed, Ohashi made clever use of the opportunity to learn from its network of customers and cooperating manufacturers. At the same time, the fruits of its organizational learning were efficiently stored in-house as the company recognized the importance of both in-house and external learning. Analyzing Ohashi can also give insights into the possible implications for a theory on meso-organizations, the new type of organization proposed in this book.

CASE STUDY: OHASHI TECHNICA, INC.[4]

The automobile parts manufacturing industry consists of a pyramid of *keiretsu* companies, with the assembly automobile manufacturer at the peak. Due to this structure, it is said to be difficult for any independent company to forge new customer links within the industry. It is common knowledge within the industry that the fastest-growing company in the field has been Ohashi. Since its foundation, it has had a strategy of "non-fabrication," avoiding integrated manufacturing facilities and the received wisdom of the automobile car parts industry of complete in-house manufacturing. Presently, Ohashi has direct sales links with 7 of the 11 Japanese automobile manufacturers.

Acceleration of Business through Toyota

Ohashi has succeeded as an independent company and has grown using the new management technique of "non-fabrication," although it was founded in 1953. Throughout Ohashi's corporate history, the single greatest factor that accelerated its growth was its relationship with Toyota, which was promoted by its current president Ken Furuoya.

In order to succeed in the Kanto region, the company targeted its business with market leader Toyota, but was reputedly told initially that "Toyota does not need the skills of Ohashi." At that time, Toyota had its own major subsidiary, Toyota Susho, with a capital of two trillion yen, and had no particular need for business with Ohashi.

However, Furuoya was also told by his Toyota contacts that, "Many companies do need the skills of Ohashi. Dig through from the outer defenses." Therefore, Ohashi concentrated on appealing to Toyota *keiretsu* companies such as Denso and Aishin because of their high level of technical and problem solving ability. Furuoya considered that by forging business relationships with *keiretsu* manufacturers, their opinion of Ohashi would be transmitted to Toyota. During the following 10 years, Furuoya continued to approach Toyota.

During this time, the shift from mechanical to electronic controls began. Toyota began to search for companies who could control production precision in microns. But as Toyota's network of *keiretsu* companies was unable to respond to this requirement, chance arose for Ohashi. Toyota handed Furuoya a set of 15 drawings and demanded that he provide solutions to the production problems outlined within one week.

Furuoya surrounded himself with a group of precision engineers and managed to come up with solutions by working day and night. The results were mixed—but favorable. Toyota adopted only one of the solutions but as a result began procurement from Ohashi. In other words, a major shift in Toyota's manufacturing process gave Ohashi the opening it needed to pioneer a business relationship with the company.

At the time it began business with Toyota, 80 percent of Ohashi's sales were related to automobile parts. It is now again the time of rapid change and growth towards building an information-based society, and Ohashi is in the throes of a second major stage of growth in the information and communications market. Currently, Ohashi is increasing its sales of components related to information and communications. It is succeeding in turning a second major change in the environment into a business opportunity and a time for growth. It is worth examining how Ohashi is organizing itself for fresh rapid growth.

Turning Nonpossession into Strength

In general, component manufacturers manage technologies that involve press manufacturing and welding for a particular *keiretsu* manufacturer and carry out development and production at in-house factories. Ohashi, however, has never had its own factory or belonged to a *keiretsu* group.

The factor which enabled Ohashi to refute the accepted wisdom of the industry was its network of 470 companies,[5] each possessing some special skills in pressing, cutting, resin and ceramic fabrication (Figure 8.1). Ohashi set up six procurement centers around the country, which were used to set up a detailed database of all cooperating factories' equipment and technology. This network made possible Ohashi's competitive strength of being able to offer development solutions to production problems.

Ohashi's marketing of development solutions work as follows. First, sales representatives visit the design and development engineers of the automobile assembly manufacturers and ascertain their technical needs based on component specifications. Based on this information, procurement and sales teams plan a component. This process is no different from that of every other component manufacturer; but in the following stages, Ohashi uses its network to the full.

First, through studying customer's component specifications, Ohashi's procurement and sales teams determine what technology, material properties, and production processes might lead to cost reductions. For instance, conventionally, after a separate process of pressing and pinning, a component might require welding and heat treatment before completion. Ohashi might propose an alternative, integrated method of production that uses pressing only to reduce costs.

In order to implement such an alternative proposal, the database is used to determine which combination of companies hold the appropriate skills and methods. In the case described above, the company was able to propose the use of a delivery press which could make the piece at once, reducing the number of parts, eliminating a welding process, and resulting in approximately 30 percent cost reduction. This sort of production engineering development cannot be made solely by manufacturers that own the special presses but is possible in conjunction with molding manufacturers and other related technologies (Figure 8.2).

Companies owning their own plant and equipment naturally seek to increase production efficiency of that equipment. In contrast, Ohashi, having no equipment of its own, can consider how to achieve the best cost

Figure 8.1
Business System of Ohashi Technica, Inc.

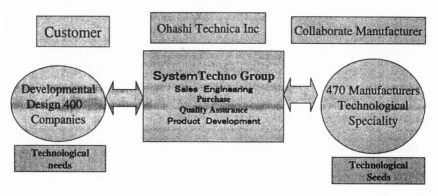

Figure 8.2
Product Development Process

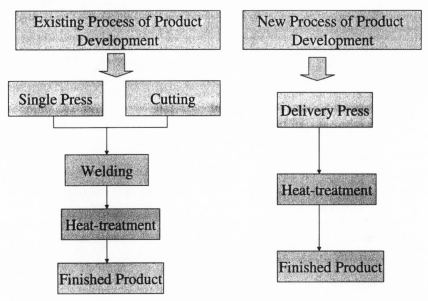

and quality combination for a component through the use of appropriate production methods and with the backing of a broad network of specialist factories. It can consider production problems from all angles.

For instance, even using a press, the question of whether to use forging or resin bonding as a less expensive way to achieve quality and functional performance, can be considered. Specialist fabricators are not able to break out of the mold of their field or to generalize; the more specialized the knowledge, the more it becomes a limiting factor.

Ohashi has not made its strength out of specialized technical knowledge but out of combining the specialist knowledge of others; it does not possess deep knowledge of operations such as pressing or fabrication. It makes a virtue out of general knowledge and avoids a rigidified approach to production problems. As a result, it has been able to develop unique production methods. "Non-fabrication" is typically considered an alternative word for "cost-reduction strategy." It, however, can be said that Ohashi has managed to combine the concept of "non-fabrication" with flexible development of production ideas.

Using the flexible development of ideas as a sales weapon, Ohashi has been able to function as a go-between for the technical needs of customers' development departments and the abilities of fabrication facilities. It has been able to turn the apparent weakness of a lack of production facilities into a strength.

Joint Ownership of Organizational Knowledge

In order for Ohashi to turn its lack of production facilities into a persistent strength, it must continually create new ideas. Components are not like JIS standardized products with a sales life of decades but are limited by regular model changes. In order to maintain competitive superiority, Ohashi needs to set up a mechanism for the continuous creation of organizational knowledge.

The key to Ohashi's business setup is the way in which its procurement and sales staff stay close to the needs and ideas of both customers and cooperating companies. By maintaining 12 sales centers across the nation, Ohashi is able to draw information from the wells of its customers and select appropriate technology from its six procurement centers, creating an environment in which needs and ideas can be integrated. The procurement centers are also tasked with sustaining and creating new relationships with companies holding innovative technology.

This setup alone efficiently links needs and ideas but is not enough to sustain competitive superiority. Passive holding of information may suffice to meet customers' immediate needs but does not identify or address their potential needs. For a company like Ohashi, without its own production facilities, it is necessary to identify the needs of customers in advance and to offer solutions.

Starting with automobile manufacturers, Ohashi has information on around 400 companies in various fields and on its network of 470 cooperating manufacturers. In order to make use of this wealth of information, the user of the data needs to have a clear sense of the problem at hand, and based on this he/she must be able to set targets for a solution, or else the volume of data may actually inhibit a timely response to customers' needs.

For instance, in the sales department, a contract may be established for theme A. Some part of the contract may involve theme B. The eventual solution in conjunction with the customer might address theme C. Each of these themes needs to be reported monthly in terms of cost and conditions. Within the field of theme A, there may be generic issues that can be turned into common knowledge within the company, if it is disseminated in the form of study materials or through the action of particularly skilled individuals.

Ohashi publishes such knowledge and rewards successful examples with bonus payments. For instance, when a new product is employed by a customer and one or more repeat orders are subsequently received, a special President's Prize is awarded. The success is also reflected in the amount of the next bonus payment. Ohashi has developed a system to share information and a result-based, compensation evaluation system in order to upgrade the knowledge of individuals to organizational knowledge.

The source of Ohashi's competitive superiority is rooted in its so-called techno-group approach, whereby the effective knowledge of the whole is greater than the sum of its individual parts. Naturally, in-house training courses and educational systems contribute to the skill development of individual employees.[6] But over and above this, the key to the company's competitiveness is its tacit knowledge. It is true that the head office's control of the detailed customer and cooperating company database and its accumulated knowledge, rather than training or the study process itself, has enabled its quick response to the problems of its customers.

The organization empowers its staff by giving them access to knowledge that others do not possess. This has the danger of leading to sectionalism within the company. Ohashi deals with this by common ownership of information and by giving appropriate rewards for turning individual knowledge into company-wide knowledge.

This thorough approach to commonality of knowledge and information in turn produces positive in-house competitive results. The ability to solve problems arising from customer needs and the ability to quickly identify appropriate manufacturing capacity and skills are made possible with common ownership of information by both procurement and sales centers. Each local procurement center will respond to a sales requirement for a particular order by giving arguments that support the use of a manufacturer from its own locality. In this way, in-house competition is fostered within the company.

Marketing is controlled centrally and direct orders to cooperating manufacturers are not permitted. In this manner, the company is able to decide which manufacturer is most appropriate. In order to determine this, the procurement centers compete with each other and direct associated cooperating manufacturers so that a high standard of technical ability is maintained.

Building Communal Relationships

The integration of fabricators' technology is not simply left to Ohashi procurement centers to grasp from studying the capabilities of cooperating companies listed in the database. Ohashi builds communal relationships between its cooperating companies. Most of them are small-scale companies; even though they possess excellent technical skills, they are weak in sales and cannot deal adequately with the development needs of major automobile manufacturers.

In contrast, Ohashi had no production facilities but its 12 procurement centers can develop close sales relationships with its customers. Consequently, it has plenty of information on customers' development needs. By combining these needs and its cooperating companies' technical skills, Ohashi has built a communal network.

The communal relationship among Ohashi's cooperating companies does not stop at mutually complementary behavior. Sales pitches to customers are made jointly. Described as exhibitions of new products and technology, Ohashi and its cooperating companies visit customers to explain their product characteristics and their production methods around 40 times per year. If, in the course of these presentations, technical questions or topics arise, it is possible to give direct answers since the cooperating company responsible for a technology is present.

Also, new cooperating companies who have formed business contracts with Ohashi are able to participate in study meetings and can carry out PR activities on their products, facilities, and track record. Through these activities, the sales staff of Ohashi can update its database regularly.

While Ohashi's "non-fabrication" strategy produces flexibility for production, it also has the drawback that the knowledge gained through technical proposals remains with the cooperating companies. However, Furuoya has stated that the reason for not maintaining fabrication facilities is as follows: "Development proposals are made not by us alone. Program saving proposals and similar technical developments come from our cooperating companies as ideas. If we maintained our own production facilities, we would become their direct competitors and would lose the benefit of their ideas" (Interview, 2001.6.25).

However, communal relationships can be easily and mistakenly turned into mutual, back-scratching situations. Ohashi's strength lies in its dependence on a large number of specialist manufacturers. In order to avoid losing the ability to form combinations of cooperating companies, Ohashi instructs its procurement centers to continually develop new relationships and to avoid carrying out more than 30 percent of their work with any single cooperating company.

Ohashi has managed to maintain tension in both internal and external relationships. If tension vanishes from a company, the organization stagnates and tends to become resistant to change. In a constantly changing environment, top companies must continually build new strengths. Furuoya says: "Once born, we must move on and change; if we have a fixed view, the company will fall apart. We want to be a company that maintains flexibility and fresh ideas" (Interview, 2001.6.25). It seems that the creative use of tension to maintain change has enabled Ohashi to function.

IMPLICATIONS

The Organizational Strength of Relationship Management

From the example of Ohashi, three organizational strengths can be shown to be necessary for skillful management and use of information in a network. The first strength is that of focused relationships. Many types of networks may be constructed, but it is necessary to consider how each will lead to true enforcement of a company's strength. Even if many relationships are constructed, the important question is which ones will give the best synergy for strengthening the company, and also which relationships will be potential triggers for change. Strength in focused relationships is necessary. For instance, within Ohashi's group of 470 cooperating companies, there were certain key partners at each stage of business growth.

In today's environment of growing rates of changing technical and market needs, there is no guarantee that the current nucleus of cooperating companies will continue to be important in the future. Ohashi makes changes concerning its network companies each year. In other words, in response to technical and customer needs, flexibility in forming and changing relationships is necessary.

Network relationships are not unchangeable; it is possible for companies that were formerly the center of Ohashi's strength to move to the periphery. It is necessary for Ohashi to regularly monitor and change its relationships to see which ones really contribute to its strength. This is the second organizational strength.

The third organizational strength requirement is the power to create mutually beneficial relationships. Companies must avoid making enemies of its partners in order to maintain the flexibility to alter relationships. For instance, if in a network relationship, the competitive position of one partner strengthens at the expense of other(s), the relationship is asymmetrical and is difficult to change. In practice, without mutually beneficial relationships and mutual trust it is impossible to share high levels of information or to interact for new knowledge creation (Dodgson, 1993) (Figure 8.3).

Figure 8.3
The Point of Relationship Management

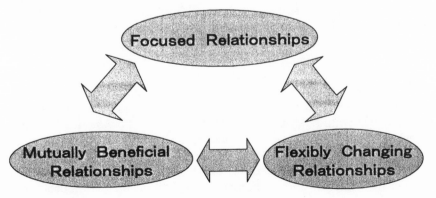

Ohashi has created a high level of trust with its partners, so that change and substitution of networking companies is possible. As explained above, Ohashi has chosen not to own any production facilities since its founding in order to avoid competitive relationships with networking companies and to maintain trust.

In the dynamic competitive and market environment of today, it has become extremely difficult for any single company to maintain all the resources necessary to respond to environmental changes. Therefore it has become important for companies to learn how to manage their relationships with other companies.

The Factors Composing Organizational Strength

How has Ohashi built its organizational learning ability so as to create the three organizational strengths noted above? First, in order to focus on relationships and to maintain the ability to flexibly change combinations of partners, it was necessary for the company to regularly renew its process of organizational learning (March, 1991). In other words, knowledge must be regularly learned and unlearned. The important point in building organizational learning power is to create tension within the company and with and between cooperating companies (Levinson and Asahi, 1995).

Once a company has succeeded, it becomes difficult for it to throw away the knowledge it has used to gain success—in other words it loses the ability to unlearn. Once a particular intercompany relationship has led to success in development of a new product, it is natural for the involved companies to continue the relationship for the next phase of product development. However, a continuing relationship may cause intercompany inertia, which may hinder further developments.

Because Ohashi has no production facilities, it will lose its competitive superiority and ability to make technical proposals to customers if it cannot continue to rely on the technical skills of its cooperating companies. It is necessary for Ohashi to regularly renew its learning. Its strategy of regularly changing partners is aimed at circumventing the problem of intercompany inertia. It has also avoided concentrating on any one cooperating manufacturer. This arrangement works by challenging manufacturers to continually improve their technical ability so that they can keep on responding to Ohashi's development proposals.

Within the organization, each manager of the local procurement center operates knowing that his work may be taken over by another procurement center unless he maintains a certain technical level amongst his cooperating companies and seeks continual improvement. This forms the motivation for continuous learning. This tension, deliberately created both within the company and in intercompany relationships, promotes organizational learning. It demonstrates that creative tension can promote learning.

Setting up tension inside and outside the company is possible given the common ground of knowledge shared between the cooperating companies. Whether in procurement or in sales, the technology possessed by all cooperating companies is known throughout the company. Furthermore, cooperating companies can easily understand what Ohashi expects of them through their participation in study meetings and customer presentations.

With a high level of common knowledge, a high degree of communication is possible between the partner companies. Without this, competition cannot be achieved and overall integration of the organization is hindered.

Even if higher levels of common knowledge are attained and communication is promoted actively to create new knowledge, success will not be achieved unless the results are correctly evaluated. As stated above, a common base of trust is needed among participants for interaction to result in new knowledge creation. Ohashi has provided financial incentives to individuals for success, thereby evaluating the results of individual knowledge creation in terms of benefit to the organization.

The fairness of the system is also demonstrated in intercompany relationships. This is the factor behind Ohashi's ability to create communal benefits. Ohashi carries out education and training in order to improve the technical skills of its cooperating companies, but, as an unwritten rule, does not interfere in the factory floor domain of each company. It also works to draw out the special skills of each cooperating company in product development. By fair evaluation of the technical skills of the cooperating companies and by sustaining mutually complementary relationships, a high level of trust has been built up.

The Integration of Knowledge Platforms

The factors behind Ohashi's ability to create its strengths have been described from the point of view of knowledge creation and organizational learning. A major influence on these abilities is the knowledge platform possessed by Ohashi. A knowledge platform may be thought of as the enveloping of separate increments of specialied knowledge.

Ohashi is able to keep developing fresh knowledge because of the breadth of its knowledge platform. Though it does not specialize in such operations as forging or cutting, it possess a wide knowledge platform encompassing these technologies. Innovation is made possible by combining various specialized elements of technology. In one sense, Ohashi's knowledge platform enables it to focus input from the most suitable cooperating companies to a problem and to change partners according to the needs of the problem. By offering technical advice, Ohashi builds not only trust but also broadens its knowledge platform.

Breadth of a knowledge platform in itself leads to complexity, which makes it difficult for competing companies to imitate Ohashi and enables continued competitive superiority.

An important element for integrating knowledge into a company's knowledge platform is the replication of information both inside the company and among cooperating companies. In other words, the staff of cooperating manufacturers, procurement centers, and sales departments all deliberately duplicate their information transfer so that the widest possible learning takes place, increasing the company's ability to integrate knowledge for future product developments.

Many of today's new products are the result of the integration of various specialist technologies to create innovation. The ability to integrate different specialized technologies determines whether a company will be innovative or not. Knowledge resources need not reside within a single company. A trend may be observed in recent corporate strategies towards outsourcing of functions that companies do not have competitive superiority, while concentrating investments in areas where it is strong.

The key to future competitive superiority lies in the integration of diffuse knowledge in a structured way to bring the company into contact with new strands of knowledge and to subsequently create increased knowledge integration ability. The case of Ohashi shows a new approach to the building of competitive superiority in a knowledge society.

NOTES

1. Firms that develop core competences that lose their dynamic quality over time may be less prepared to respond to environmental changes.

2. According to McKinsey Quarterly (1992), the aims of Japanese partners' tend to be to learn new skills, while those of their non-Japanese partners are usually to make money. On this subject, see Jones (1992), Lei and Slocum (1992), and Pucik (1998).

3. On this subject, see Hamel (1991, 1990), and Inkpen (1995, 2000).

4. The material in this case is derived from interviews and in-house data.

5. A comprehensive network of over 470 collaborative manufacturers work with Ohashi Technica to provide the most applicable technology (or combinations thereof) for the cost-effective production of quality parts to meet the changing needs of customers.

6. The backbone of Ohashi Technica is its unique employee education system. In order to stay on top of cutting-edge technology, Ohashi has adopted ranking examinations and certifications for product awareness and quotations for all its employees. Semiannually published technical

manuals, in-house R&D, and weekly seminars help employees stay on top of rapidly developing technologies in the precision components industry.

REFERENCES

Argyris, C., and A. Schon (1978). *Organization Learning.* Addison-Wesley.

Barney, J. B. (1991). Firm Resource and Sustained Competitive Advantage. *Journal of Management,* 17, pp. 99–120.

Barton, D. L. (1995). *Wellspring of Knowledge.* Harvard Business School Press.

Bierley, P., and T. Hamalainen (1995). Organizational Learning and Strategy. *Scandinavia Journal of Management,* 11, pp. 209–224.

Birkinshaw, J. (2000). *Entrepreneurship in the Global Firm.* Sage, 2000.

Birkinshaw, J., and P. Hagstrom (2000). *The Flexible Firm-Capability Management in Network Organizations.* Oxford University Press.

Collis, J., and A. Montgomery (1995). Competing on resource: Strategy in the 1990 *Harvard Business Review,* 73(4) 7–8, pp. 118–128.

Crossan, M., H. Lane, and R. White (1999). An Organization Learning Framework: From Intuition to Institution. *Academy of Management Review,* 24, pp. 522–537.

Davenport, T., and L. Pruck (1998). *Working Knowledge.* Harvard Business School Press.

Dodgson, M. (1993). Learning, Trust, and Technological Collaboration. *Human Relations,* 46, pp. 77–95.

Doz, Y. (1988). Technology partnerships between larger and smaller firms: some critical issues. In F. Contractor and P. Lorange (Eds.), *Cooperative Strategies in International Business,* Lexington.

Enatsu, K. (1995). *International Strategic Alliances,* Koyo Syobo.

Foil, M., and Lyles, M. A. (1985). Organization learning, *Academy of Management Review,* 10, pp. 803–813.

Garvin, D. A. (1993). Building a Learning Organization. *Harvard Business Review,* 7–8, pp. 78–91.

Grant, R. M. (1996). Prospering in Dynamically Competitive Environment: Organizational Capability as Knowledge Integration. *Organization Science,* 7, pp. 375–387.

Hakansson, H., and I. Snehota (1989). No Business is an Island: The Network Concept of Business Strategy. *Scandinavian Journal of Managemen,* 5, pp. 187–200.

Hallen, L., and J. Johanson (1989). Network of Relationships in International Industrial Marketing. In T. Cavusgil (Ed.), *Advances in International Marketing,* Vol. 3, JAI Press, Inc.

Hamel, G. (1990). *Competitive Collaboration: Learning, Power and Dependence in International Strategic Alliance.* UMI Dissertation Service.

Hamel, G. (1991). Competition for Competence and International Learning Within International Strategic Alliances. *Strategic Management Journal*, 12, pp. 83–103.

Hedberg, B. (1981). How Organizations Learn and Unlearn. In P. C. Nystrom and W. H. Starbuck (Eds.), *Handbook of Organization Design*. Oxford University Press.

Huber, G. P. (1991). Organization Learning: The Contributing Process and The Literatures. *Organization Science*, 2, pp. 88–115.

Inkpen, A. C. (2000). A Note on the Dynamics of Learning Alliance: Competition, Cooperation, Relative scope. *Strategic Management Journal*, Vol. 21, pp. 775–779.

Inkpen, A. C., and M. M. Crossan (1995). Believing is Seeing: Joint Venture and Organization. *Journal of Management Studies*, 32:5, pp. 595–618.

Jones, K. (1992). Competing to Learn in Japan. *McKinsey Quarterly*, 1, pp. 45–47.

Lei, D., and J. Slocum (1992). Global Strategy Competence-Building and Strategic Alliance. *California Management Review*, Fall, pp. 87–97.

Levinson, N., and M. Asahi (1995). Cross-National Alliance and Interorganizational Learning. *Organizational Dynamics*, pp. 50–63.

March, J. G. (1991). Exploration and Exploitation in Organizational Learning *Organization Science*, 2, pp. 71–87.

March, G., and J. Olsen (1975). Organizational Learning under ambiguity. *European Journal of Policy Review*, 3, pp. 147–171.

Nonaka, I., and H. Takeuchi (1995). *The Knowledge Creating Company*. Oxford University Press.

Osland, G., and A. Yaprark (1994). Learning through Strategic Alliances. *European Journal of Marketing*, 29, pp. 52–66.

Park, S., and G. Ungson (2001). Interfirm Rivalry and Managerial Complexity: A Conceptual Framework of Alliance Failure. *Organization Science*, 12, pp. 37–53.

Parkhe, A. (1991). Interfirm diversity, organizational learning, and longevity in global strategic alliances. *Journal of International Business Studies*, Fourth Quarter, pp. 579–601.

Pucik, V. (1988). Strategic Alliances, Organizational Learning, and Competitive Advantage. *Human Resource Management*, Spring, 21, pp. 775–779.

Reed, R., and R. Defillippe (1990). Causal Ambiguity, Barriers to Imitation, and Sustainable Competitive Advantage. *Academy of Management Review*, 16, pp. 88–102.

Ruggles, R., and D. Holtshouse (1999). Edited. *The Knowledge Advantage*, Capstone.

Teramoto, Y., N. Iwasaki, and T. Takai (1997). Strategic Alliances in Semiconductor Industry: New Strategy for Japanese Companies. *Malaysia Management Journal*, 2, pp. 73–85.

Teramoto, Y., T. Takai, and F. Richter (1994). Global Competitiveness through Strategic Alliance: The Case of the German and Japanese Chemical Industries. In H. Schutte (Ed.), *The Global Competitiveness of the Asia Firms*. St. Martin's Press.

Utterback, U. (1994). *Mastering The Dynamics of Innovation*. Harvard Business School Press.

CHAPTER 9

Exploration and Exploitation in Federated Networks

Tomoyuki Nishimura

INTRODUCTION

It is increasingly recognized today that business and other purposeful activities are not conducted by individual organizations but through cooperation among organizations. Phenomena such as interfirm strategic alliances, corporate group management,[1] and regional advantages through clustering have attracted the attention of many organization and management scholars. Thus, the main unit of organizational analysis has been shifting from individual organizations to interorganizational relationships (IORs).

Parallel with this shift, the study of organizational learning has expanded to interorganizational learning (Yoshida, 1991; Levinson and Asahi, 1995). Interorganizational learning refers to acquisition, exchange, sharing, creation, and utilization of knowledge in the fields of IORs. Organizations are understood as learning systems (Nevis et al., 1995), whereas IORs are understood as vehicles for organizations for accessing and acquiring partners' skills and know-how (Inkpen and Crossan, 1995).

IORs have been studied by using three distinct analytical levels (Van de Ven et al., 1979). The first and simplest level is the dyad. The second is the multiple dyads maintained by focal organization (i.e., the organization set originated from Evan, 1966). But IORs are so complex that these two approaches cannot adequately capture them. Accordingly, a third network perspective is used in which the whole IOR is the unit of analysis.

Existing literature on interorganizational learning focuses almost entirely upon individual organizations within IORs, but not upon IORs themselves (i.e., networks). In other words, the third approach to IORs has not been investigated in interorganizational learning studies. However, interorganizational networks compete with other organizations or networks for markets and innovation (Teramoto, 1990), so the competitiveness of overall networks should not be neglected. Jarillo (1988) claims that outcomes of networks need to be evaluated not only in terms of *efficiency* (the degree of satisfaction perceived by each organization joining in networks) but also in terms of *effectiveness* (the degree of achievement of the goal shared by network members) as stated by Barnard (1938).

This chapter attempts to examine how federated networks learn to enhance their effectiveness. A federated network is an interorganizational collectivity composed of legally independent affiliates and a federation management organization (FMO) that coordinates these affiliates (Provan, 1983). The formation of and the transformation to federated networks have been accelerating in recent years. Examples include the integration of European countries (EU) (Handy, 1992), proliferation of joint R&D through consortia (Evan and Olk, 1990), federalization of multinational corporations (Ghoshal and Bartlett, 1990), and franchising in retailing or food services (Bradach, 1998).

In a federated network, each affiliated organization has disparate goals. Affiliates and the FMO, however, set an inclusive formal goal (Warren, 1967), and mechanisms for coping with paradoxes (e.g., diversity versus unity of the goal, local versus global scope, and so on) are necessary (Handy, 1992). These issues need to be intimately tied to interorganizational learning research in federated networks.

The structure of this chapter is as follows. Firstly, the characteristics of federated networks are described and their types are introduced. Second, drawing on the resource-based view, learning in federated networks is conceptualized as a dualism of exploration and exploitation. Third, an ideal exploration-exploitation balance in federated networks is explored in comparison with unitary organizations. Finally, conclusions and implications are discussed.

FEDERATED NETWORKS

The Federated Network as an Interorganizational Network

Originally, studies on federated networks focused on nonprofit sectors, such as community agencies (Litwak and Hylton, 1962) and the United Way (Provan et al., 1980). Many studies on networks of nonprofit organizations have been undertaken before interfirm business systems were recognized as networks that are intermediate or hybrid arrangements of markets and hierarchies (Thorelli, 1986; Jarillo, 1988). For example, based on differences in patterns of interaction that exist within networks of nonprofit organizations, Warren (1967) illustrates four types of inter-organizational networks: unitary, federative, coalitional, and social choice (see Table 9.1).

As shown in Table 9.1, the interactive differences between the four types are (1) relation of units (member organizations) to an inclusive goal, (2) locus of inclusive decision making, (3) locus of authority, (4) structural provision for division of labor, (5) commitment to a leadership subsystem, and (6) prescribed collectivity-orientation of units. These six dimensions can be put together into one dimension, the intensity of networks (Miller et al., 1995). According to Miller et al., intensity means the degree of commitment and formalization in networks.

Whetten (1981) argues that there are three types of interorganizational

Table 9.1
Types of Interorganizational Networks

Dimension	Types Unitary	Federative	Coalitional	Social Choice
Relation of units to an inclusive goal	Units organized for achievement of inclusive goals	Units with disparate goals, but some formal organization for inclusive goals	Units with disparate goals, but informal collaboration for inclusive goals	No inclusive goals
Locus of inclusive decision making	At top of inclusive structure	At top of inclusive structure, subject to unit ratification	In interaction of units without a formal inclusive structure	Within units
Locus of authority	At top of hierarchy of inclusive structure	Primarily at unit level	Exclusively at unit level	Exclusively at unit level
Structural provision for division of labor	Units structured for division of labor within inclusive organization	Units structured autonomously; may agree to a division of labor, which may affect their structure	Units structured autonomously; may agree to ad hoc division of labor, without restructuring	No formally structured division of labor within an inclusive context
Commitment of a leadership subsystem	Norms of high commitment	Norms of moderate commitment	Commitment only to unit leaders	Commitment only to unit leaders
Prescribed collectivity-orientation of units	High	Moderate	Minimal	Little or none

Source: Warren (1967), p. 406.

networks along the continuum of intensity. The least intensive is the mutual adjustment network in which the network as a whole seldom has shared goals, and most relations are temporary and do not involve senior management of each organization. Therefore, mutual adjustment network is synonymous with the market, which is one mechanism of governance for organizing transactions (Williamson, 1975; Thorelli, 1986). The converse of mutual adjustment is the corporate relationship network in which member organizations are under the control of central management just like in a unitary organization. In these networks, rules and procedures are codified to a great degree and much attention is paid to an inclusive goal. Between these two extremes, Whetten positions the alliance networks. The alliance network is one that seeks to coordinate autonomous but interdependent member organizations without command. The alliance is subdivided into two types, federation and coalition networks. The federation network is a relatively more intensive alliance in which the central management unit (FMO) mediates interorganizational coordination. On the other hand, the coalition network is less intensive and does not have a centralized unit; roles of coordination are left to member organizations.

Besides these, there are other distinctive features of federated networks. According to D'Aunno and Zuckerman (1987), members of federated networks set criteria for membership and can exclude organizations that do not meet the criteria. As such, they can be distinguished from trade associations. In addition, federated networks involve more than two organizations and thus can be distinguished from dyadic linkages such as joint ventures. Evan and Olk (1990) state that because federated networks cannot be separated completely from member organizations and changes in membership may occur, they are different from joint ventures.

Formation of Federated Networks

A federated network is composed of affiliates that are legally independent organizations and the coordinating and mediating FMO. An interorganizational network in which coordination is left to member organizations and there exists no FMO, is a coalitional network as noted above and is distinguished from the federated network. Affiliated organizations to a federated network delegate partial rights of decisions to the FMO. In consequence, all affiliates must act on behalf of the interests of the overall network regarding those issues managed by the FMO but can keep their autonomy regarding other issues. Conversely, the FMO must act for the interest of all affiliates (Provan, 1983). Hence, using the agency theory framework (Eisenhardt, 1989) it is understood that affiliates are the principals and the FMO is the agent in a federated network (Fleisher, 1991). This state is opposite to an intracorporate relationship where the strategic apex (Mintzberg, 1979; Luke et al., 1989) is the CEO and those positioned in lower organizational layers are agents.

Why is the FMO created, and why does a federated network develop? The FMO is an organization that coordinates and mediates affiliates; it has also been called by other names, such as coordinating agency (Litwak and Hylton, 1962), focal organization (Evan, 1966; Metcalfe, 1976), or referent organization (Trist, 1983). According to Litwak and Hylton, a co-ordinating agency develops when (1) the number of independent organizations to be coordinated is moderate, (2) the degree of interdependence among organizations is moderate, (3) the interdependence is highly perceived, and (4) activities of organizations are standardized to some extent. Pfeffer and Salancik (1978) suggest that if many organizations seek to develop linkages with each other, then a centralized structure to facilitate and manage interdependence among these organizations will emerge. In short, the determinants of the formation of federated networks are the number of organizations and the degree of interdependence among them.

Provan (1983) was the first to examine federated networks comprehensively. Besides the number of organizations and their interdependence, he lists two causes that prompt organizations to set up federated networks: (1) a discrepancy between the expertise and the goal orientation of potential affiliates and the anticipated role of the federation management, and (2) external pressure that urges the organization of a network. A federated network is labeled *voluntary* when interdependent organizations perceive this discrepancy and establish the FMO. On the other hand, it is labeled *mandated* when a third party enforces organizations to participate in a federated network.

In their case study of hospitals, D'Aunno and Zuckerman (1987) propose a lifecycle model of federated networks in which interorganizational structures transit from a coalition, through a federation, to a hierarchy or dissolution over time. In the first phase of this model, organizations (hospitals) form a coalitional network to complement one another's resources. Critical contingencies of the coalition formation are environmental uncertainty facing each organization, the extent to which organizations share ideologies, and symbiotic rather than competitive relationships among organizations. In the next phase, the coalition transits to a federated network by forming a formal management group (i.e., FMO). The FMO is established when organizations gradually depend on the network for valuable resources and they discover that they do not have enough time to manage their dependencies nor to achieve an inclusive goal.

In addition to these studies on nonprofit federated networks, there have been reports on transformations of for-profit corporations to federations. For example, Ghoshal and Bartlett (1990) conceptualize today's multinational corporations as federated networks that consist of geographically dispersed and goal-disparate foreign subsidiaries (affiliates) and a headquarters (FMO). Handy (1992) claims that corporations have to handle paradoxes such as big versus small, global versus local, and diversity versus unity, so they adopt the federalist approach. He offers five principles for managing corporate federated networks: (1) subsidiarity,[2] (2) pluralism, (3) common law, language, and currency, (4) separation of the three powers (management, monitoring, and governance), and (5) twin citizenship to the local company and to the federation. Similarly, O'Toole and Bennis (1992) indicate universal characteristics of successful federated networks,[3] and suggest that because they allow affiliates to maintain their integrity while unifying for common purposes they are more advantageous than rigid, monolithic organizations.

To summarize, the characteristics of a federated network are as follows:

1. It is an interorganizational network that consists of affiliated organizations and an FMO. The existence of the FMO distinguishes the federated network from coalitional networks that do not have one.
2. The FMO attempts to simultaneously achieve both the diversity of affiliates and the sharing of the collective goal.
3. Different from an intracorporate relationship, affiliates are regarded as principals and the FMO an agent in a federated network.

Roles of FMOs

In a federated network, affiliates perform their own activities using their expertise and relinquish other tasks to the FMO. The main function of the FMO is to coordinate interdependence among affiliates. It is also important for the FMO to interact with external organizations or networks; the FMO represents the network.

The roles of the FMO outlined in existing literature are illustrated in Table 9.2. Though each study lists different roles, they share two elements: one relates to adapting to or maneuvering the external environment facing the federated network, and the other to internal management of the network. However, decisions that affect the overall federated network have to be ratified by affiliates (Warren, 1967). Hence, the FMO cannot play these two roles without approval by or negotiation with affiliates. The extent to which affiliates are involved in the FMO's activities, or the FMO in affiliates' activities, differs in every federated network. There are different types of federated networks, and each type has distinctive behavioral mechanisms and managerial requirements. In this respect, the above-noted five principles of federated networks by Handy (1992) might be applied situationally rather than universally.

Types of Federated Networks

In this study, federated networks are categorized into *voluntary* networks and *mandated* networks, corresponding to Provan (1983). As ob-

Table 9.2
Roles of FMO

Author	Given name	Roles
Metcalfe (1976)	Focal organization	Integration of the diverse expectations of organization set -Cultural integration: consistency of focal organization goal with organization set values -Normative integration: conformity of focal organization's behavior with organization set expectations -Communicative integration: mutual awareness among organization set members of expectations and interests -Functional integration: reciprocal exchange and power relations among organization set members
Trist (1983)	Referent organization	-Regulations of present relationships and activities: establishing ground rules and maintaining base values -Appreciation of emergent trends and issues: developing a shared image of a desirable future -Support of infrastructure: resources, information sharing, special projects, etc.
Provan (1983)	Federation management organization (FMO)	-Control the flow of resources among affiliates as well as between affiliates and elements outside the network -Reduce the complexity of the linkage network and improve their bargaining position relative to the external environment
D'Aunno and Zuckerman (1987)	Management group	-Increase the importance or non-substitutability of the management group for members -Attain objectives that benefit members -Build a shared understanding that individual interests sometimes must be compromised
Luke et al. (1989)	Strategic apex	-Strategic decision and implementation -Ensure a unity of effort among collaborating organizations -Determine and modify membership

served in nonprofit sectors, the former evolve from coalitional networks through the building of an FMO. The intensity of voluntary networks is relatively weak. The latter are developed by FMOs that are established in advance and call for affiliation later, or progress from hierarchical organizations through their decentralization. The intensity of mandated networks is relatively strong. While the loci of power are affiliates in voluntary networks, it is FMOs that hold relatively strong power in mandated networks. The voluntary and mandated networks are contrasted in Table 9.3.

Table 9.3
Mandated and Voluntary Networks

	Mandated	Voluntary
Formation	FMO → Affiliates	Affiliates → FMO
Intensity	High	Low
Locus of power	FMO	Affiliates

FEDERATED NETWORKS AND LEARNING

Resource-Based View and Capabilities of Federated Networks

A perspective that views firms as bundles of resources has a long history in firm theory (Penrose, 1959; Wernerfelt, 1984; Barney, 1991). This perspective is called the resource-based view (RBV) and has different implications for firm behavior than the industry structure view represented by Porter (1980).[4] According to RBV, firms can improve their competitiveness by having valuable, rare, imperfectly imitable, and nonsubstitutable resources or capabilities (Barney, 1991).

Although the definitions of resources and capabilities vary across RBV researchers, it is agreed that because resources are tradable in markets capabilities that firms accumulate internally can provide more competitive advantages for firms than resources can (Christensen, 1996). Firms are bundles of static and transferable resources, which are converted into capabilities through firms' idiosyncratic, dynamic, and interactive processes (Amit and Schoemaker, 1993). Amit and Schoemaker state that resources are inputs and capabilities defined as firms' capacities to deploy these resources. The scarcest and thus the most important resource is knowledge (Grant, 1996).

Capabilities can be classified into two levels, the managerial and the technical levels (Christensen, 1996). The former has to do with designing and managing organizational structures and processes. The latter are regarded as key factors for success in industries to which firms belong, and they are identical with the concept of core competences such as miniaturization (SONY) or logistics (FedEx) as noted by Hamel and Prahalad (1994) and are subordinate to the managerial-level capabilities.

When considering the capabilities of federated networks, we focus on the managerial level and not on technical capabilities. We are more concerned with the behavioral patterns and collective process of federated networks, although because federated networks settle themselves into certain industries it might be important to investigate the success factors as well. Hereafter, the technical-level capabilities are termed *competences* in order to be distinguishable from managerial *capabilities*. And large portions of organizational competences consist of knowledge related to knowing how (i.e., *procedural* knowledge). On the other hand, the above-noted knowledge inputs are related to knowing about something and are *declarative* in nature.

Thus, the capabilities of federated networks are defined as *their synthetic abilities to get things done through mobilizing procedural and declarative knowledge resulting in value creation.* Such capabilities can be explained by using two dimensions of learning: exploration and exploitation.

Exploration and Exploitation

RBV literature claims that organizations need to pursue both exploring and exploiting resources or competences (Penrose, 1959; March, 1991; Madhok, 1997). While exploration is to look for the unknown, such as innovation, risk-taking, and entry into new businesses, exploitation is to utilize and develop existing knowledge, such as *kaizen* and standardization (March, 1991). The relationship between exploration and exploitation is a trade-off, so organizations must balance these two types of learning. An overemphasis on exploitation without exploration will lead to eroding extant, competitive advantages. On the contrary, exploration not accompanied by exploitation cannot realize potential value through exploring and will lead to wasting resources (Madhok, 1997).

For individual organizations, one tactic for exploring new knowledge is to establish or enter into IORs. Explorative learning through IORs is called interorganizational learning, which is an extension of the concept of organizational learning (Yoshida, 1991; Levinson and Asahi, 1995).

The most frequently studied IORs in terms of interorganizational learning are joint ventures (JVs). Hamel et al. (1989) assesses performances of individual firms in joint ventures by asking whether they learn (explore) much from their partners and whether their partners learn relatively less. Hamel (1991) proposes three determinants of explorative learning from partners in joint ventures: the intent, transparency, and receptivity. Inkpen and Crossan (1995) also view joint ventures as opportunities for organizations to internalize partners' skills and know-how, and they claim that because learning relates to changes not only in behavior but also in cognition, managers' belief systems and interpretive complexity or flexibility must influence learning performances.

Those variables of interorganizational learning can be reconceptualized as absorptive capacity. The absorptive capacity refers to a firm's ability to recognize the value of outside knowledge, assimilate it, and apply it to commercial ends, and it is a function of the firm's level of prior related knowledge (Cohen and Levinthal, 1990, p. 128). This absorptive capacity is composed of three elements: (1) the firm's internal strength, (2) the structure of relationships between the firm and the external environment (i.e., other organizations), and (3) the quality and relevance of the external environment (Christensen, 1996). In other words, absorptive capacity is relative in nature (Lane and Lubatkin, 1998). We should pay attention to the fact that explorative learning in IORs depends on quality and relevance of knowledge held by other organizations. Organizations hardly explore if other organizations no longer develop new knowledge. After all, as it is for the whole IOR (networks), explorative learning by one organization is nothing but the exploitation of the fruits of others' learning (Levinthal and March, 1993).

Exploration and Exploitation in Federated Networks

The exploration-exploitation concept is also useful for analyzing federated networks. Exploration means that a certain organization develops new knowledge unknown to other members of the federated network. On the other hand, exploitation is to transfer knowledge from its original source to other organizations in the federated network. As well as for the case of single organizations, federated networks must pursue both exploration and exploitation. If exploration is not undertaken, present advantages of federated networks will disappear. Also, the development from scratch by one organization of things already explored by another organization is a duplication of effort. In order to avoid this waste, knowledge needs to be transferred from the holding organization and utilized by other organizations that pursue it.

In comparison with unitary organizations, exploration and exploitation of federated networks have the following characteristics.

Ease of Exploration

Generally, unitary organizations are myopic because of their hierarchy, cohesiveness, and high consistency of incentive structures. As a result, they tend to engage in too much exploitation and neglect exploration for which returns are more uncertain (Miner and Haunschild, 1995). In contrast, interorganizational networks including federated types are released from these structural constraints, and thus are prevented from inclining toward excessive exploitation and can focus upon exploration.

Inefficiency of Exploitation

Exploitation as knowledge transfer is achieved more easily within an organization than between organizations (Grant, 1996). The reasons are as follows: (a) in interorganizational networks, interactive patterns among actors are not stabilized and communications are not smooth as in unitary organizations; and (b) tacit knowledge that is hard to codify and is embedded within a person cannot be transferred without moving the person.

Unlike unitary organizations, personnel changes are uncommon in federated networks because each organization is self-governing. Thus, the transfer of tacit knowledge does not occur or the value of the tacit knowledge transferred is eroded (Madhok, 1997).

Therefore, the challenges for federated networks are to enjoy the merits of exploration and to overcome the demerits of exploitation.

Knowledge Flow Patterns in Federated Networks

How does knowledge flow in federated networks? There are two modes of interorganizational knowledge flow: contact and broadcast (Miner and Haunschild, 1995). While the contact mode is lateral and individualized, the broadcast mode has one hub and spokes. In the context of federated networks, contact is one mode of exploitation between affiliates, whereas broadcast is the other mode starting from the FMO to affiliates (see Figure 9.1).

It is supposed that patterns of exploitation and the preceding exploration are contingent upon the type of federated network. Since voluntary networks are less intensive and power resides within affiliates, the degree of affiliates' autonomy is high. Because of this, affiliates become differentiated from one another and explore knowledge individually in order to adapt to their local environments. Affiliates are motivated to learn from each other only if the knowledge of other members seems relevant and applicable to their own circumstances.

In contrast, mandated networks are more intensive and FMOs hold relatively strong power. FMOs attempt to control affiliates. In consequence, the activities of affiliates are standardized to a great degree. Thus,

Figure 9.1
Contact and Broadcast in Federated Networks

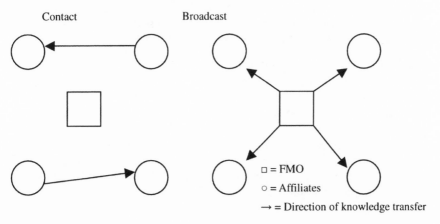

Contact   Broadcast

□ = FMO
○ = Affiliates
→ = Direction of knowledge transfer

new knowledge is usually developed by the FMO and knowledge is applied to affiliates that are treated in the same way.

To sum up, sources of exploration and modes of exploitation are aligned with each other. In differentiated voluntary networks, affiliates engage in exploration and exploitation is done in the contact mode. In standardized mandated networks, on the other hand, FMOs engage in exploration and exploitation is through the broadcast mode.

In addition, the notion of the exploration-exploitation alignment suggests that federated networks have to match their overall strategies with their learning processes. Here, overall strategies consist of the following dimensions, borrowed from studies on multinational corporations (e.g., Ghoshal and Bartlett, 1990; Porter, 1986):

a. Approach to environmental adaptation: whether a reaction to customer needs, technologies, and so on, is localized or comprehensive.
b. Resource distribution: whether ownership of resources (e.g., money, materials) is dispersed or concentrated.

For individual organizations to explore, they must have the ability to perceive environmental trends and to use resources with discretion. FMOs cannot engage in full exploration unless their approach is comprehensive and resources are concentrated at the FMO. Similarly, affiliates cannot explore fully unless their approach is localized and they have sufficient resources at their disposal. That is to say, the strategies of mandated networks are of the comprehensive approach and the resource concentration. In contrast, the strategies of the voluntary networks are of the localized approach and the resource dispersion. Both mandated and voluntary networks are so-called configurations in which multiple elements cohere (Miller, 1986; Meyer et al., 1993).

BALANCING EXPLORATION AND EXPLOITATION: COMPARING UNITARY ORGANIZATIONS WITH FEDERATED NETWORKS

As noted above, when compared with unitary organizations, the merit of federated networks is ease of exploration and the demerit is inefficiency of exploitation. It seems that federated networks can achieve superior performances in comparison to unitary organizations if they can manage the merits and the demerits.

In this section, a centralized organization with multiple units and a mandated network are first compared. Then a decentralized organization with multiple units and a voluntary network are compared in terms of exploration and exploitation.

Centralized Organization versus Mandated Network

In mandated networks, FMOs engage in exploring new knowledge that affiliates are to receive. This process can be seen in a centralized organization composed of multiple units as well. In centralized organizations, exploration is led by their headquarters (HQs) and knowledge is broadcasted from the HQs to their lower level units in order to realize value.

Most resources are concentrated at the FMO in federated networks. Perhaps the situation is the same for centralized organizations. That is, resources of centralized organizations are concentrated at their HQs. Hence, it is presupposed that FMOs and HQs have the right to decide how to allocate resources for exploration and exploitation.

The Centralized Organization

The optimal growth of an organization involves a balance between exploration and exploitation (Penrose, 1959; March, 1991; Madhok, 1997). This is explained as follows. For simplification, the unit cost of both exploration and exploitation is assumed to be 1. Scarce resources are invested simultaneously in exploration and exploitation. This trade-off can be written as:

$$T_c + U_c = R_c$$

where T_c and U_c are the levels of exploration and exploitation respectively, and R_c is the monetary value of resources as inputs.

The performance, P_c (in monetary value), of the centralized organization is written as:

$$(1 + S_c)(T_c + U_c)$$

where S_c is the synergy that is generated through combining resources divided between exploration and exploitation. Since $(T_c + U_c)$ is constant ($= R_c$), P_c is contingent upon only S_c. Suppose that S_c is proportional to $T_c U_c$ because of the complementarity between exploration and exploitation. If so, S_c is maximized when T_c is equal to U_c. Then, P_c is maximized when $T_c = U_c$ ($= R_c/2$).

The Mandated Network

As well as for centralized organizations, mandated networks have an initial resource of R_m (measured in the monetary value) and FMOs decide the allocation of this financial resource between exploration and exploitation. Set the level of exploration and exploitation to T_m and U_m, respectively. Considering the ease of exploration and the inefficiency of exploitation, it is supposed that the unit cost of exploration, a, is smaller than 1, and that of exploitation, b, is larger than 1. So:

$$aT_m + bU_m = R_m \qquad (1)$$

The performance, P_m, of the mandated network is written as:

$$(1 + S_m)(T_m + U_m) \qquad (2)$$

where S_m is the synergy achieved by combining resources divided between exploration and exploitation. S_m is assumed to be less than S_c for the following reason. A necessary condition for combination is exchange (Nahapiet and Ghoshal, 1998). Because federated networks are not as tightly interconnected as individual organizations there is some loss in exchanging resources.

As in the case of the centralized organization, it is supposed that S_m is proportional to $T_m U_m$. From (1),

$$U_m = -\left(\frac{a}{b}\right) T_m + \frac{R_m}{b} \qquad (3),$$

thus, $T_m U_m$ is

$$-\frac{a}{b}\left(T_m - \frac{R_m}{2a}\right)^2 + \frac{R_m^2}{4ab}.$$

Hence, $T_m U_m$ is maximized when $T_m = R_m/2a$, as the negative value in the above equation becomes zero. By substituting this into (3), we find that $U_m = R_m/2b$, so $T_m U_m$, accordingly S_m, is maximized when $T_m : U_m = b:a$. As T_m increases beyond the optimal level, S_m declines but $(T_m + U_m)$ in (2) grows.[5] Therefore, (2) is maximized in case of $T_m > U_m$. After all, mandated networks yield best results when emphasizing exploration over exploitation.

Comparison

The performances of the centralized organization and the mandated network are depicted in Figure 9.2. The curve P_c relates the exploration level of the centralized organization to its performance, and the curve P_m does so for the mandated network. While P_c is maximized when the exploration level is equal to that of exploitation, P_m is maximized when the exploration level is above that of exploitation.

Furthermore, if mandated networks reduce the loss generated in combining resources and increase synergy S_m, then P_m shifts upward (shown as P_m^* in Figure 9.2).

To summarize, the relative advantage of mandated networks over centralized organizations depends on the following:

a. Properly raising the level of exploration.

b. Improving the combinative effects of exploration and exploitation.

Of these two, (b) is also valid for centralized organizations. Therefore, the distinctive feature of mandated networks is (a).

Decentralized Organization versus Voluntary Networks

In voluntary networks, exploration is led by affiliates and exploitation is done through contact between affiliates. The dynamics of exploration and exploitation form spontaneously as affiliates interact with each other. Such dynamics are also seen in decentralized organizations that consists of multiple units.

These dynamics can be illustrated as follows. Levinthal and March (1993) refer to the upward spiral of learning in a population of organizations. R&D activities (i.e., exploration) by one organization create new knowledge. Part of this knowledge is pooled at the population level. Other organizations in the population begin to invest in R&D activities that access (exploit) the pooled knowledge, because the capacity to absorb external knowledge is a function of an organization's level of prior related knowledge (Cohen and Levinthal, 1990). This investment reinforces the organization's absorptive capacity and creates new knowledge. In turn, part of this new knowledge outflows to the above-noted pool and gives

Figure 9.2
Comparison of Performances of Centralized Organizations and Mandated Networks

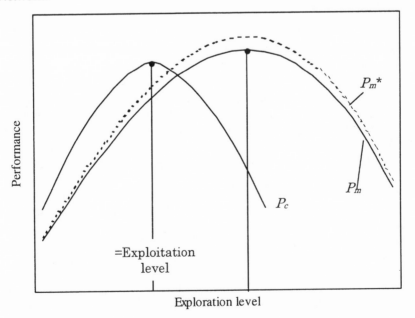

rise to investment by other organizations. In short, exploration has two roles: pooling of new knowledge at the population level, and enhancement of explorers' absorptive capacity. Thus, exploitation is not necessarily deliberate but emergent, and exploration coincides with exploitation. As a result, there are increasing returns to investing in exploration at the population level.

The increasing-returns effect can be seen in both voluntary networks and decentralized organizations. The more an affiliate (unit) explores, the more knowledge there is for exploitation by others. However, there also exist some structural differences between voluntary networks and decentralized organizations:

1. Units in a decentralized organization have relatively strong ties to one another, whereas affiliates within a voluntary network have relatively weak ties to one another. Although lean, explicit knowledge can be transferred through weak ties, tacit knowledge, such as know-how, is more difficult to transfer. In contrast, strong ties are good for transmitting tacit knowledge (Hansen, 1999). In short, decentralized organizations can carry out exploitation more efficiently than voluntary networks.

2. While units within decentralized organizations are sometimes called semi-autonomous, affiliates within voluntary networks are self-governing and legally independent. Semi-independent units are not as autonomous as self-governed affiliates. The less autonomy actors have, the more they tend to mimic others. In other words, the more autonomous actors are the more they engage in exploration. That is to say, affiliates can conduct exploration at higher levels than units.

In view of these differences, the relationship between exploration and performance is shown in Figure 9.3. The curve P_d is the performance of a decentralized organization and the curve P_v is that of a voluntary network. Each performance curve increases with exploration. But the curve P_v is below the curve P_d because affiliates in voluntary networks are interconnected with weaker ties than units in decentralized organizations are, and thus cannot exploit each other so efficiently. However, the voluntary network can offset this disadvantage by increasing exploration. And of course, if the voluntary network succeeds in more efficient exploitation by means of managerial structures or processes, such as shared culture, norm of reciprocity, or common language, the curve P_v shifts upward (shown as P_v^* in Figure 9.3). In contrast, if it underestimates the importance of exploitation, increasing returns does not take place and performance stagnates.

To summarize, the relative advantages of voluntary networks to decentralized organizations are dependent upon the following:

a. The extent to which affiliates engage in exploration.

Figure 9.3
Comparison of Performances of Decentralized Organizations and Voluntary Networks

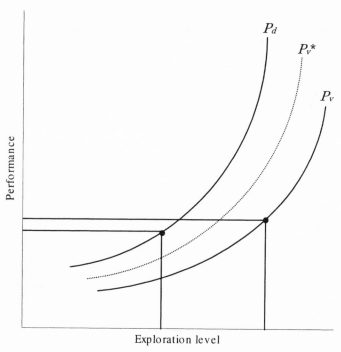

Exploration level

b. Overcoming the weakness of weak ties.

Among these, (b) can be imitated by decentralized organizations, which will shift the curve P_d in Figure 9.3 upward. Therefore, the distinctive feature of voluntary networks is (a).

CONCLUDING REMARKS

This chapter has attempted to analyze the effectiveness of federated networks in terms of exploration and exploitation. Federated networks have been classified into voluntary and mandated networks, and each has been compared with unitary organizations holding multiple units. Taken together, this chapter's main conclusion is that *federated networks are more effective when they emphasize exploration over exploitation.*

As with the case of unitary organizations, elements of federated networks such as strategies, structures, and behavioral patterns should complement each other and cohere into configurations. Federated networks that maintain and strengthen their configurations are thought to be more effective than those that do not. However, federated networks compete not only with other federated networks but also with unitary organizations. For example, voluntary chain stores compete with corporate chain stores, and R&D consortia compete with laboratories of large enterprises. If unitary organizations can imitate or make substitutions for the configurations of federated networks, then federated networks will lose their advantages. Thus, federated networks need to make good use of their distinctive strengths, which unitary organizations will find difficult to imitate or substitute. That is, they should emphasize exploration over exploitation. Of course, federated networks have to pursue both exploration and exploitation as unitary organizations do. Emphasizing exploration does not mean neglecting exploitation and excessively focusing on exploration; rather, it means to accentuate exploration while making efforts to exploit. One merit of federated networks is that it is relatively easier for them to promote exploration than unitary organizations. By utilizing this merit, federated networks can build competitive advantage over unitary organizations. For unitary organizations, keeping the level of exploration equal with that of federated networks leads to suboptimal performance, as shown in Figure 9.2, or is difficult, as shown in Figure 9.3.

Miles and Snow (1992) argue two causes of failure in interorganizational networks: extension and modification. Extension means that networks go beyond their limits as the result of trying only their favorite things; whereas modification means that they too try hard to overcome weakness, resulting in the destruction of their unique logic. In federated networks, extension is an overemphasis on exploration and it disregards exploitation, and modification is too much inclination toward exploitation and it disregards exploration.

Implications of this study are as follows. First, the roles of FMOs must be reconsidered. Existing literature on federated networks has emphasized the integration efforts of FMOs, as listed in Table 9.2. Integration is necessary but is not sufficient for effectiveness of federated networks. Integration is the process of exploitation that realizes value and that follows the potential-value creating process of exploration. Without exploration, exploitation is impossible, and, in such cases, there is an overload of integration efforts and a breakdown of federated networks. The FMO should play an important role in "fluctuation" as well as in integration. According to Teramoto (1990), fluctuation in interorganizational networks is created by: (1) changing membership, (2) diversifying and reorganizing subgroups within networks, (3) infusing external information, (4) making member organizations belong to more than one subgroup, and (5) linking the network with external networks. Fluctuation triggers exploration, after which order is created through exploitation.

Second, external linkages of federated networks can be reconceptualized in terms of capability building. In existing literature on the resource-dependence perspective (Pfeffer and Salancik, 1978), it is assumed that affiliates and FMOs are motivated to establish external linkages by considering power relationships within federated networks, and that external linkages affect internal power relationships (Provan et al., 1980; Ghoshal and Bartlett, 1990). The exploration-exploitation concept of this study sheds new light on the meaning of external linkages. Organizations conducting exploration in federated networks need to establish external linkages if exploration cannot be self-contained. Perhaps, FMOs are in a central position to discover external linkages because they represent their federated networks. However, in voluntary networks each affiliate, and not the FMOs, conducts exploration. So, the external linkages made by FMOs have to be shared with the affiliates. Alternatively, external linkages in mandated networks play the dual role of promoting exploitation as well as exploration. If outsourcing of some exploitation functions succeeds in reducing exploitation costs, then mandated networks can invest in the more crucial process of exploitation for creating value. They can correct the imbalance of exploration and exploitation costs and avoid becoming trapped by too much exploration.

As a next step, arguments in this study need to be tested empirically. Firstly, exploration and exploitation have to be defined more precisely. In addition, data on federated networks and comparable unitary organizations need to be collected. If future research tests and extends this study, our understanding of interorganizational relationships and learning will progress remarkably.

NOTES

1. In conventional Japanese corporate groups, control of affiliates (subsidiaries and associated companies) was divided and done directly by their parent companies, and they operated in isolation from each other. But in recent years, these one-on-one controlling systems have been replaced with "group management," which intends for the whole corporate group to grow and for implementation of collective strategies. See Teramoto (1990).

2. Subsidiarity means that power lies at the lowest point in the organization and can be taken away only by agreement. Accordingly, it is not the same as delegation but is a form of "reverse" delegation by which the center governs only with the consent of the governed (Handy, 1992).

3. These are noncentralization, negotiationalism, constitutionalism, territoriality, balance of power, and autonomy.

4. According to Porter (1980), firms can achieve superior performance by building a position in industries whose structures are attractive in terms of relative bargaining power, entry barriers, and so on.

5. From (3),

$$T_m + U_m = T_m - \frac{a}{b}T_m + \frac{R_m}{b}$$
$$= \frac{b-a}{b}T_m + \frac{R_m}{b}.$$

Because a is smaller than b, $(T_m + U_m)$ is not constant, but increases as T_m increases. The unit cost difference between a and b has a leverage on $(T_m + U_m)$.

REFERENCES

Amit, R., and P. J. H. Schoemaker (1993). Strategic Assets and Organizational Rent. *Strategic Management Journal,* 14, no. 1, 33–46.

Barnard, C. I. (1938). *The Functions of the Executive.* Cambridge, MA: Harvard University Press.

Barney, J. B. (1991). Firm Resources and Sustained Competitive Advantage. *Journal of Management* 17, no. 1, 99–120.

Bradach, J. L. (1998). *Franchise Organizations.* Boston, MA: Harvard Business School Press.

Christensen, J. F. (1996). Analysing the Technology Base of the Firm: A Multi-dimensional Resource and Competence Perspective. In N. J. Foss, and C. Knudsen (Eds.), *Towards a Competence Theory of the Firm,* London: Routledge.

Cohen, W. M., and D. A. Levinthal (1990). Absorptive Capacity: A New Perspective on Learning and Innovation. *Administrative Science Quarterly* 35, no. 1, 128–152.

D'Aunno, T. A., and H. S. Zuckerman (1987). A Life-Cycle Model of Organizational Federations: The Case of Hospitals. *Academy of Management Review* 12, no. 3, 534–545.

Eisenhardt, K. M. (1989). Agency Theory: An Assessment and Review. *Academy of Management Review* 14, no. 1, 57–74.

Evan, W. M. (1966). The Organization-Set: Toward a Theory of Inter-organizational Relations. In J. D. Thompson (Ed.), *Approach to Organizational Design,* Pittsburgh, PA: University of Pittsburgh Press.

Evan, W. M., and P. Olk (1990). R&D Consortia: A New U.S. Organizational Form. *Sloan Management Review* 31, no. 3, 37–46.

Fleisher, C. S. (1991). Using an Agency-Based Approach to Analyze Collaborative Federated Inter-organizational Relationships. *Journal of Applied Behavioral Science* 27, no. 1, 116–130.

Ghoshal, S., and C. A. Bartlett (1990). The Multinational Corporation as an Inter-organizational Network. *Academy of Management Review* 15, no. 4, 603–625.

Grant, R. M. (1996). Prospering in Dynamically-competitive Environments: Organizational Capability as Knowledge Integration. *Organization Science* 7, no. 4, 375–387.

Hamel, G. (1991). Competition for Competence and Inter-partner Learning within International Strategic Alliances. *Strategic Management Journal* 12, Summer Special Issue, 83–103.

Hamel, G., Y. L. Doz, and C. K. Prahalad (1989). Collaborate with Your Competitors—and Win. *Harvard Business Review* 89, no. 1, 133–139.

Hamel, G., and C. K. Prahalad (1994). *Competing for the Future*. Boston, MA: Harvard Business School Press.

Handy, C. (1992). Balancing Corporate Power: A New Federalist Paper. *Harvard Business Review* 70, no. 6, 59–72.

Hansen, M. T. (1999). The Search-Transfer Problem: The Role of Weak Ties in Knowledge across Organization Subunits. *Administrative Science Quarterly* 44, no. 1, 82–111.

Inkpen, A. C., and M. M. Crossan (1995). Believing is Seeing: Joint Ventures and Organization Learning. *Journal of Management Studies* 32, no. 5, 595–618.

Jarillo, J. C. (1988). On Strategic Networks. *Strategic Management Journal* 9, no. 1, 31–41.

Lane, P. J., and M. Lubatkin (1998). Relative Absorptive Capacity and Inter-organizational Learning. *Strategic Management Journal* 19, no. 5, 461–477.

Levinson, N. S., and M. Asahi (1995). Cross-National Alliances and Interorganizational Learning. *Organizational Dynamics* 24, no. 2, 50–63.

Levinthal, D. A., and J. G. March (1993). The Myopia of Learning. *Strategic Management Journal* 14, Winter Special Issue, 95–112.

Litwak, E., and L. F. Hylton (1962). Interorganizational Analysis: A Hypothesis on Coordinating Agencies. *Administrative Science Quarterly* 6, no. 4, 395–420.

Luke, R. D., J. W. Begun, and D. D. Pointer (1989). Quasi Firms: Interorganizational Forms in the Health Care Industry. *Academy of Management Review* 14, no. 1, 9–19.

Madhok, A. (1997). Cost, Value and Foreign Market Entry Mode: The Transaction and the Firm. *Strategic Management Journal* 18, no. 1, 39–61.

March, J. G. (1991). Exploration and Exploitation in Organizational Learning. *Organization Science* 2, no. 1, 71–87.

Metcalfe, J. L. (1976). Organizational Strategies and Interorganizational Networks. *Human Relations* 24, no. 4, 327–343.

Meyer, A. D., A. S. Tsui, and C. R. Hinings (1993). Configurational Approaches to Organizational Analysis. *Academy of Management Journal* 36, no. 6, 1175–1195.

Miles, R. E., and C. C. Snow (1992). Causes of Failure in Network Organizations. *California Management Review* 34, no. 4, 53–72.

Miller, D. (1986). Configuration of Strategy and Structure: Toward a Synthesis. *Strategic Management Journal* 7, no. 3, 233–249.

Miller, K., C. R. Scott, C. Stage, and M. Birkholt (1995). Communication and Coordination in an Interorganizational System: Service Provision for the Urban Homeless. *Communication Research* 22, no. 6, 679–699.

Miner, A. S., and P. R. Haunschild (1995). Population Level Learning. In L. L. Cummings, and B. M. Staw (Eds.), *Research in Organizational Behavior* 17, Greenwich, CT: JAI Press.

Mintzberg, H. (1979). *The Structuring of Organizations.* Englewood Cliffs, NJ: Prentice-Hall.

Nahapiet, J., and S. Ghoshal (1998). Social Capital, Intellectual Capital, and the Organizational Advantage. *Academy of Management Review* 23, no. 2, 242–266.

Nevis, E. C., A. J. DiBella, and J. M. Gould (1995). Understanding Organizations as Learning Systems, *Sloan Management Review* 36, no. 2, pp: 73–85.

O'Toole, J., and W. Bennis (1992). Our Federalist Future: The Leadership Imperative. *California Management Review* 34, no. 4, 73–90.

Penrose, E. T. (1959). *The Theory of the Growth of the Firm.* New York: Wiley.

Pfeffer, J., and G. R. Salancik (1978). *The External Control of Organizations.* New York: Harper & Row.

Porter, M. E. (1980). *Competitive Strategy.* NY: Free Press.

Porter, M. E. (1986). Competition in Global Industries: A Conceptual Framework, in M. E. Porter (Ed.), *Competition in Global Industries,* Boston, MA: Harvard Business School Press.

Provan, K. G. (1983). The Federation as an Interorganizational Linkage Network. *Academy of Management Review* 8, no. 1, 79–89.

Provan, K. G., J. M. Beyer, and C. Kruytbosch (1980). Environmental Linkages and Power in Resource Dependent Relations between Organizations. *Administrative Science Quarterly* 25, no. 2, 200–225.

Teramoto, Y. (1990). *Network Power.* Tokyo: NTT Press. [Japanese Language.]

Thorelli, H. B. (1986). Networks: Between Markets and Hierarchies. *Strategic Management Journal* 7, no. 1, 37–51.

Trist, E. (1983). Referent Organizations and the Development of Interorganizational Domains. *Human Relations* 36, no. 3, 269–284.

Van de Ven, A. H., G. Walker, and J. Liston (1979). Coordination Patterns within an Interorganizational Network. *Human Relations* 32, no. 1, 19–36.

Warren, R. L. (1967). The Interorganizational Field as a Focus for Investigation. *Administrative Science Quarterly* 12, no. 3, 396–419.

Wernerfelt, B. (1984). A Resource-based View of the Firm, *Strategic Management Journal* 5, pp: 171–180.

Whetten, D. A. (1981). Interorganizational Relations: A Review of the Field. *Journal of Higher Education* 52, no. 1, 1–28.

Williamson, O. E. (1975). *Markets and Hierarchies.* NY: Free Press.

Yoshida, T. (1991). Soshikikan Gakushu to Soshiki no Kansei. (Interorganizational Learning and Organizational Inertia.) *Organizational Science* 25, no. 1, 47–57. [Japanese Language.]

PART IV

Engaging Knowledge Globally

CHAPTER 10

The Talkative Company

John B. Kidd and Frank-Jürgen Richter

INTRODUCTION

For three millennia or more, individuals, firms, and representatives of nation-states have traded internationally and have had global reach. Yet, it is only in the relatively recent past that associations of firms (strategic alliances, multinational enterprises, corporate conglomerates, and so on) have grasped the need to have effective exchanges of their combined knowledge for the benefit of their members, and maybe altruistically for the good of others. Given the great reach of the modern organization, we agree with Yoshiya Teramoto (1993) that knowledge management is important and that organizations must learn how to better use their embedded knowledge.

Teramoto's publications on networks and on knowledge management indicate a pragmatic approach—yet it upholds a moral vision. The issues he is addressing require not just theoretical analysis but insights into the ways of the world. It is a happy coincidence that Teramoto is not from the West, but is from the East and has a clear grasp of the power of technology and of the influence of human networks. In this chapter we hope to be able to address some of the factors that have guided Teramoto throughout his life. We hope to do his scholarship justice. We commence by suggesting that knowledge management has three facets: technical (often entailing the use of computer and telecommunication systems); human; and organizational. This chapter concentrates on the latter two facets noting that knowledge flows through sharing or transfer, which raises the problematic issues of trust and culture. These issues apply even within a single organization and may be worse when explicit formal partnerships between two or more organizations are involved.

We acknowledge the contrast between the Eastern and Western concepts of trust at an individual level. A Westerner in negotiation might fall back on a morality stemming originally from Judaeo-Christian beliefs (McClelland, 1961); whereas an Easterner (in particular, a Chinese person) may rely on the ethics of *yi* (justice) and other internalized ethics derived from the edicts of Confucius (Lou, 1997). Although each may believe they are projecting a trustworthy image, the overt (even if unspoken) "trust me" of a Westerner may be perceived as arrogant or immodest by an Easterner. Conversely, an Easterner, even if truly an "expert," may appear too humble or self-effacing in a Westerner's eyes.

In this introduction we will set the scene, as it were, by considering the pace of change that is facing all of us in our daily lives; it matters little whether we are living in a developed country or in one that is developing. However we will exclude those who live frugally in deserts, jungles, or in frozen wastelands—though even here people are enveloped by many modern developments, especially those concerning the rest of the world's search for mineral reserves that may lie beneath their lands.

Economic Imperatives

The rising volume of Merger & Acquisitions (M&As) indicates that alliances, especially alliances that are often transborder alliances, are seen to be attractive to many firms. We note that total global foreign direct investment (FDI) in the four years preceding 2000 has risen almost four-fold to about 1100 billion U.S. (UNCTAD, Press Release TAD/INF/2875: 7 December 2000). The driving force behind the latest FDI expansion was cross-border M&As, especially between firms in Japan, North America, and Western Europe. Naturally the Asian financial crisis of 1998 affected FDI inflows into the Asian region, which recorded a fall of 11 percent in 1999. However, according to the year 2000 estimates (UNCTAD) FDI flows to Asia, contrary to a further anticipated decline, recovered quickly.

Figure 10.1 illustrates the rapid rise in both FDI and M&A global activity. We must note that UNCTAD states that there is no simple correlation between these two measures of economic activity, as underlying structural conditions are not constant over the years.

Commercial Imperatives

Western production organizations, once stable for many years, have evolved into complex and highly integrated global sourcing, assembly, and distribution systems that are observable in many manufacturing and service sectors today (Stock, Greis, & Kasunda, 1999; Chase, 1997). During

Figure 10.1
Global Economic Activity

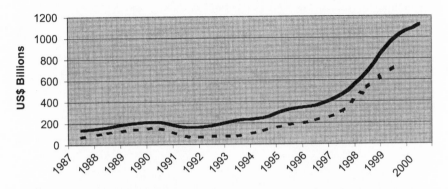

Global FDI Inflows and Cross-border M&A

Source: UNCTAD Press Releases—TDA/INF/2847 @ 15/4/2000 and TAD/INF/2875
@ 7/12/2000
Key   FDI, ——— M&A •••••

the decades between 1920 and 1980, there was pressure to only mass-produce in more effective ways. Since then we have moved to a regime that is "agile," in which alliances are made (and dissolved) rapidly, based on substitutable supply chains. Sometimes these chains are put in place to service a volatile market and then are reconstituted to serve another market. In these circumstances everyone in the supply chain has to learn quickly and effectively how to manage anew when a given customer will probably only order one item with no repeats (Peppard, 1996; Miyashita & Russell, 1994). The item will be unique—there are no mass markets now, but underpinning this item is the mass customization of nearly identical goods. Hence, there is a need to manage knowledge upstream and downstream in the supply chain (Drew & Smith, 1998; Chaston et al., 1999; Phan & Perdis, 2000).

Informational Imperatives

One might consider tiered supply systems as complex, but they are not unusual in many industrial, manufacturing systems. For instance, there are many in the automotive sector supporting the "big few"—GM, Ford, Toyota, for example. Herein the final assembly of the vehicle is dependent on hundreds of suppliers working in concert, often to a just-in-time (JIT) regime activated by integrated information technology and communications (ITC) systems (Angeles, 2000). Other examples may be found in

TRADENET or in TradeLink (see www.tradnet.gov.sg or www .tradelink.hk.com, respectively). The latter are just two examples of many government-initiated clearance portals set up to support thousands of local businesses in their relationships with overseas partners, as they "clear" their documents through ports (be they land, sea, or air).

Information technology and communications systems thus support manufacturing agility (Davenport, 1993; Davenport & Prusak, 1998). In addition, it is found that these complex systems are a necessary but not sufficient factor for supporting knowledge management and organizational learning. They enable the acquisition of data, they allow complex data analyses, and can, with the help of telecommunications networks, transmit data instantly across the globe. These systems may include databases freely available to all suppliers. Trusting one another, suppliers can reduce the overall cycle time by forecasting downstream demand so that they can initiate their own production before a formal order is placed by a higher tier in the system (Bhatnagar & Viswanathan, 2000). If a multinational enterprise (MNE) has undertaken detailed business network reengineering (BNR) of its supply chain, it will be in a good position to support flexible, agile organization learning. Otherwise only individual members of the chain might be willing to manage their learning processes—that is, if they can manage their data effectively (Clarke, 1998; Gupta & Govindarajan, 1991). Often, the new way involves data consolidation within an Enterprise Resource Planning (ERP) system, which also leads towards the downsizing of the workforce, thereby leading to the loss of intellectual capital (Kidd & Yau, 2000).

Ultimately in the global scene, we are focusing on the ability of individuals from different countries (having different beliefs and training) to trust each other and to understand that they have to share their knowledge with all others in the supply chain. For knowledge managers in MNEs, the big issues concern developing trust in (possibly) short-lived alliances amongst outsourced firms, and developing and maintaining knowledge across many major sectors of their firms' core competencies.

INDIVIDUALS, LEADERS, AND TRUST

The processes of M&A create much tension between the staff of partners because redundancies often occur as business functions are merged. This raises an outcome pertinent to this chapter—that is, in downsizing one looses organizational slack. Further, one disables access to the intellectual capital in the minds of those remaining as they have less time for contemplation and creative discussions. But more importantly, one cuts access to the tacit knowledge held in the minds of those fired from the firms (further reducing intellectual capital). Under this scenario, many staff in the West might attempt to withhold their knowledge in the hopes of being retained—they become strangely silent.

Due to the fairly rapid changes in global finances—for instance, during the recent Asian crisis or the earlier meltdowns in Mexico and Brazil—CEOs had to make and break alliances rapidly to save their MNEs. In these situations financiers move fast—much faster than the rationalization of the mental models of the persons caught up in the crisis of acquisition or divestment. It is natural, therefore, for these individuals to become confused and defensive and, thus, to not understand other parties. As a result they too become silent as frightened observers of the evolving scenarios. They halt the exchange of tacit data, information, and knowledge—they may even become aggressive or subversive.

Even if there are few redundancies, tension stems from the difficulty of understanding the newly acquired firms' culture—which is often quite distinct from ones' own firm. Understandably, little research has been addressed to knowledge management issues in far-flung MNEs (time, distance, and cost are reasonable deterrents). It is easier to focus on the local (Boyacigiller & Adler, 1991). To give an idea of the magnitude of the task, it has been estimated that there are more than 3,000 multinational enterprises operating in Asia (Islam & Chowdhury 1997). This may be an underestimate, as Lu (1998) found over 2,000 Japanese firms represented in China alone.

Proposition 1: If firms quickly form alliances simply because of financial or regulatory opportunism, it is likely the alliance will have difficulties in overcoming the lack of understanding on the part of local personnel "of why."

  •Simply put—if "they" with whom we are working, do not have sufficient cultural literacy they will not understand "us," creating conflicts that will detract from joint learning.

Sociomentrics

It is quite conceivable that in the process of merging, there will be fewer constraints if the firms involved are from the same (national) macro culture, than if they are from clearly different macro cultures. Hofstede (1980, 1991), Trompenaars (1993), and Hampden-Turner & Trompenaars (1997) have studied and measured culture over many years. The Hofstede Indices have been confirmed generally by Smith & Peterson (1994), Smith, Dougan & Trompenaars (1996), Yang (1988), and Smith & Bond (1993). Partial replications have been undertaken by Hoppe (1993), and Mcgrath, MacMillan & Sheinberg (1992) upon business persons; by Merritt (1998) on airline pilots; by Campbell (1998) on the relationships between business correspondence and cultural predisposition; and Ben-Ari (1997) notes how very young Japanese children learn what later becomes for them very strong culture-bound organization mechanisms. One further measure, with the appeal of representing cultural difference as a single number, is due to Kogut & Singh (1989). It is based on Hofstede's (op. cit.) four primary measures of culture; the 'Cultural Difference Index' gives quick insights into the potential for conflicts in proposed joint ventures between firms of different nations.

Proposition 2: If two firms from different nations wish to have an alliance, the greater their relative cultural difference the greater difficulty there will be in merging.

   • Here we are simply suggesting that firms should note the indices determined by Hofstede [and others], which refer to both organizational norms and societal inclinations. CEOs should be prepared to act accordingly. If there are predictable interorganizational difficulties, then the acquisition and dissemination of knowledge is likely to be difficult as well.

Leaders and Management Models

Greater Europe—if we consider this to be countries in the European Union (EU) aggregated with those in central Europe who wish to join the EU—comprises nation states with quite diverse histories and cultures. It is not surprising therefore that they have developed managerial styles which suit their indigenous populations (Calori & de Woot, 1994). We accept that the recent removal of many trade and organizational barriers in the EU has increased the permeability of national borders, with more and more people employed permanently in countries other than their birthplace. Yet, there will inevitably be a lag in the change and innovation processes that might improve the convergence of European management styles. It follows that there will be a lag in the realization of effective knowledge management processes—these differences are intensified when considering a globalized MNE (Berrel et al., 1999).

Leadership Models

The GLOBE program is a multiphased project designed to develop systematic knowledge of how national cultures and subcultures affect their perceptions of leadership and organizational practices. An introduction to this research program may be found in Advances in Global Leadership (Otazo, 1999).

Briefly, data for the GLOBE project were collected from over 17,000 executives in 61 countries using quantitative and qualitative methods. Qualitative aspects include interviews, focus groups, participant observation, unobtrusive measures, and content analyses of narratives: (for example, reviewing media, literature, and archival records). The quanti-

Figure 10.2
Schematic of a Firm

tative data were collected using the Societal Values Survey (SVS) ques-
tionnaire developed by the GLOBE research team. Over all countries, the
general findings of GLOBE are that attributes like charisma are widely
valued in leaders across the world; also seen as positive is being communicative, encouraging, and motivating. Risk-taking, ambition, and self-
centeredness are seen as culturally contingent—sometimes these are
acceptable traits, sometimes not. Kennedy & Mansor (2000) offer an interesting analysis of the GLOBE studies in Malaysia.

The concept of a leader must be grasped in our general discussion of
knowledge management and organizational learning. In Figure 10.2 we
assume there is one Chief Executive Officer (CEO) heading the operation,
and more and more junior managers are found as one cascades through
the classic pyramidal hierarchy to the shop floor where the workers are
located. These were once called "blue collar workers" due to their wearing
of a distinguishing (dirty?) uniform in contrast to suit-wearing managers.
The star indicates that at some midpoint of the organization there is a

potential for conflict. This is between the downward pressure to engage in knowledge management (KM) initiatives as promoted by the CEO and thus followed by the senior management, and the upwards pressure to engage in organizational learning (OL) from the groundswell of opinion of the workforce. The CEO's KM pressure is usually inspirational and promoted by edict. On the other hand, the OL activities of lower hierarchical levels derive from their common sense and their wish to cooperate with their fellow workers to jointly have an easier time than they would if they continued using old methods.

In our schematic, the star has further significance in that it would be the point of intense activity of a firm's Human Resource Management (HRM) group as it lends an ear to the words of workers and passes them to senior managers. In turn, the HRM group has a responsibility to interpret the discussions at board level and pass these on to workers. In advancing these two functions, the HRM group helps ensure that all staff maintain an alignment with the goals and aspirations of senior managers and board members. This is particularly important if the board has agreed to follow the path of chaos (Pascale et al., 2001) and has allowed many changes to disturb the stability that may be craved by the lower echelon staff.

Proposition 3: Suppose an MNE has set up a rapid response problem-solving team comprising one Chinese, one British, and one American (U.S.) person. It is likely that in the operations of one of the team member's home country, one or both of the other members will feel uneasy, as the member in whose country they are operating in will use a modeling system that is acceptable in that particular country but that excludes the other team members. Alternatively, if the other team members were to attempt to use their own modeling systems, the local staff would become silent due to their ignorance of these outsider processes.

• Intercultural confusion was noted in the 1980s in Japanese production subsidiaries located in the United Kingdom. The UK staff said it took them up to five years to become more comfortable working with their Japanese seniors. By the 1990s, this time span was reduced to about three years due perhaps to a wider accessibility of information (on both sides) on the other's works and expectations (Kidd & Teramoto, 1995). This relates to the difficulties of low context persons (in this instance, the United Kingdom managers) working with high context persons (their Japanese seniors). High and low contexts (HC/LC) are concepts developed by Hall, 1976, and Hall & Hall, 1987. It is not surprising that how information flows in a European subsidiary of a Japanese firm may appear fractured and intermittent to both Japanese and European staff, as a result of the mixtures of HC/LC and their differences of mono/polychronicity (Hall, op. cit.). Inevitably, this will make knowledge management more difficult as data and information flows become intermittent—too little or too much depending on the sender or receiver and their contexts.

- In a fully LC situation, we see that advisers to the CEO are important. They are gate keepers, becayse they not only filter information but do so according to their personal models—which may not conform to that of the CEO, to the vision of the organization, or to the model of the supplicant attempting to make a case to the CEO. Furthermore, a low context CEO sees only the LC persons that are relevant to his/her day's work, all of whom must have an appointment.
- Furthermore, modern Western management methods force everyone into a low context situation because they attempt to make all facts and aspects of a situation completely explicit. There is little acceptance of that which is already known tacitly by the people involved. In general, this is exacerbated by consultants who may not take the time to become fully aware of the contextual complexity of their clients' businesses (nor will clients pay for consultants' time spent on this process). There is another side to this argument. Very little credibility is given to the implementation of a complex solution; they have to be self-evident, simple, and thus of low context.

Trusting

The interaction mode within business networks must be one of mutual trust, which is perceived to be long-term and generated through commitment (Jarillo, 1988). Trust as experienced in East Asia is often a substitute for legally binding contracts, because most emergent problems between the economic agents are resolved through negotiation rather than resorting to law and litigation (Fukuyama, 1995). Indeed, as East nations still have only weak laws, and as these are interpreted freely by executives, businesspersons know they have no recourse to the law. Generally speaking, relationships in East Asia—business, political, and professional ones—are based on personal considerations and not on the kind of objective reasoning and contracts preferred by Westerners. The lack of an independent judiciary is the reason why lawyers are not nearly as common in East Asia as they are in the United States or Europe. Traditionally, business arrangements in East Asia were based on verbal commitments backed by trust, which, unlike detailed contracts, allows for considerable flexibility in interpretation and management as circumstances change.

The essence of trust in Asia revolves around the Confucian principle *ren*, which refers to the way people relate to each other. One cannot exist alone and one must be able to interact with others. Therefore, *ren* can be understood as being able to handle interpersonal or interorganizational relationships personally, having *renqing*—human feelings. Trust as a mode for corporate interaction is always based on long-term commitments.

Systems based on mutual trust ensure a return to a partner by imposing some form of power and influence over individuals or organizations being linked. It is important to note that mutual trust is not pursued out of purity or charity; and it is not altruistic in intent (Kao & Sek-Hong, 1993).

The self-interest lies in *hatake zukuri* (plowing the field) for future eventuality. You never know when you have to become indebted to others (*osewa ni naru*). Thus, long-term relationships can survive in environments where laws are poorly drafted and contracts are not easily enforceable by law (Luo, 2000). Central to mutual trust is the phenomenon of *market failure* characterized by Oliver Williamson (1975), the father of transaction cost theory. This is the predictable inability of market mechanisms to achieve maximum efficiency and to encourage growth when confronting economies of scale. Williamson believed that if market failure occurs and the normal economic pressure on economic actors to perform effectively breaks down, then other control mechanisms have to come into effect, hence *guanxi* in China (and the same concept is current in Japan).

Mutual trust and interorganizational relationships manifest themselves in a variety of different forms. On the interpersonal level, Japanese *nomunication* and Chinese *guanxi* relationships are the best known. *Nomunication* (Japanese: *nomu*, to drink; and English, communication) are informal meetings that take place at the end of the workday with the aim of building up a mutual group identity, thereby amplifying a spirit of *uchi* (in-group identity). Japanese salary men drink *sake* together at the many bars (*izakaya*), which specially cater to these groups of people. Thus, the staff grows closer to each other by sharing experiences and worries. *Nomunication* may include business partners such as suppliers, customers, and members of the same *keiretsu* to which the companies belong (Richter 2000). Similarly, when a Chinese entrepreneur seizes a business opportunity, he/she prefers to make a deal based on previously established *guanxi*, rather than seeking the anonymity of the market. Such a deal is based on opportunities arising from the *guanxi*, which are privileged contacts providing information not available to the public. Finally, for concluding a deal, the Chinese handshake is regarded to be highly valuable and invulnerable; deals are based on trust and are often promoted through banquets where business persons drink, chat, and evaluate their partners on a regular basis. This is not unlike the Japanese managers' use of banquets in discrete restaurants on the Ginza in Tokyo or of drinking at *izakayas*. We should note that the introduction of a new person to the (*guanxi*) group by a trusted agent gives this new person almost the same level of *guanxi* as the introducer has. This means the introducer has the responsibility to guarantee the debts of the new person if that person hints at defaulting. It also means the new person has great pressure brought on him by the group as a whole to behave honestly (I-Chuan Wu-Beyens, 2000).

In the West, contracts and associated prices determine the transactions that are undertaken—there is an old and strong belief in "rule by law." This results in a low level of mutual dependency by business partners in so-called arm's length transactions, rather than in a relationship-based system between Asian partners as mentioned above. As a result, institutional links matter less in the West and the market becomes the more important medium for directing and governing terms of transactions. For instance, "Bills of Lading" used by European merchants in the fourteenth century were simple receipts, but by the sixteenth century these had became a "proof of entitlement" and so evidenced a contract of carriage between shipper and ship owner. Since 1855 this proof transferred contractual rights and liabilities and is now incorporated in the Carriage of Goods by Sea Act of 1992.

There is a long history of Western studies of trust and its associated cognitive aspects from the late 1800s by Freud (see the archives at the Brill Library http://www.nypsa.org/) and Jung (see the C. J. Jung archive on http://www.cgjungpage.org/). In addition, there are, for instance, Eric Berne (1975) and the Transactional Analysis (TA) school of thought. Here we find that they suggest that we all have the right to assert ourselves (without being aggressive). There is also a more recent view on humanistic trust, which has been emphasized by Fukuyama (1995) and discussed by Richter and colleagues (2000). However, we feel that TA needs to be modified carefully when used in Asian cultures especially with the latter's stress upon consensuality (Albrecht, 2001).

LEARNING VIA TRUSTING

We have only fives senses (seeing, touching, smelling, hearing, and tasting) though some guru would say we have more—that we have an undefined sixth sense (or more). We use our five senses to create models of our environment, our world, as we perceive it to be. Moreover, we use these models, sometimes unconsciously, to make predictions and to sense our future. If that model yields good results we are happy; but if the results are in conflict with our belief we may be more or less disturbed and have to rebuild our model. Festinger gave us the concept of "cognitive dissonance" to explain our unease at finding our mental predictions at odds with our sensual perception—either because our model is wrong or because we have a poor perception of reality—as in a distorting hall of mirrors (Festinger & Carlsmith, 1959). We will develop this concept further by exploring how trust may be developed between two people.

In Figure 10.3 we suggest that B is passing to A sensual data pertaining to an issue that involves both of them. A receives this data and makes judgments regarding its quality. Also, A receives data about the models that B uses to make sense of that data (i.e., B's models of the world that are currently focused on this issue) (Edwards & Kidd, 2000).

The "triangles of trust" have certain characteristics. For instance,

a. If there is a lot of data passed but the height of the triangle is low, B is at pains to relate to A. He may state, "trust me," but we will find that A does not trust B.

Figure 10.3
"Triangles of Trust"

The strength of the relationship
... or "trust" is represented by the triangle's size

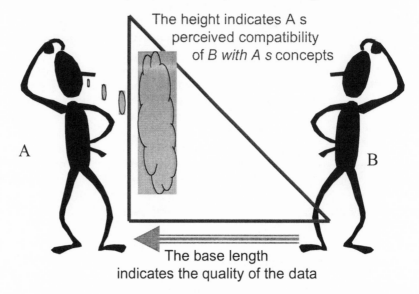

The height indicates A s
perceived compatibility
of *B with A* s concepts

A

B

The base length
indicates the quality of the data

b. If the height of the triangle is high, but little data is passed from B to A, we have a situation of "divine belief in B" on the part of A—this may in fact be a little foolish.

Naturally there are many variations on this theme and we must accept that we are multidimensional, even when focused on one issue. Note that our children often try to avoid getting into trouble by saying at length, "I did not do it, I was not there," yet we find our triangles of trust still tall: we still love our children, despite their data flows.

However, this may not be the case in a business context wherein the relationships are less personal and more contractual—at least, in Western business worlds where businesspersons can be described as low context. In contrast, there are nations where the people may be described as high context as they frequently exchange very detailed data, and there are often strong family connections at the business level (Hall & Hall, 1987). In Asian scenarios, especially those predicated on a Confucian background, we find *guanxi* relationships modify the triangle shape by involving networked groups as well as direct interpersonal A-B links.

The area of this "triangle of trust" between A and B need not be sym-

Figure 10.4
The Development of Trust between Two People

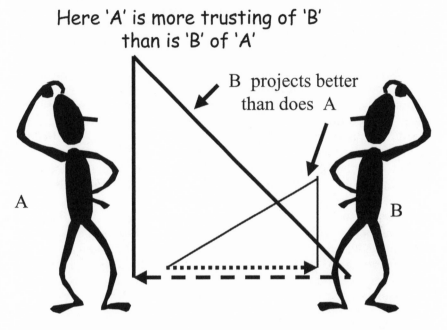

Here 'A' is more trusting of 'B'
than is 'B' of 'A'

B projects better
than does A

A

B

metrical (see Figure 10.4). Essentially, during the development of trust the different sizes of the two triangles held by A and B relate to being an insider or outsider. It is between *uchi* and *soto* (Japanese: within the group; outside the group). Although this can be seen as an underlying social principle that is hidden behind all business networks, it is highly subtle in Japan. Similarly in China, *ren chi ren* (Chinese: people eat people) is a common phrase. It is used to explain that individuals within their network (especially the family net) will act honorably towards each other, but against those outsiders they will be strongly competitive. There is a tendency for A (if *uchi*) to create a tall trusting triangle based on little direct data (with respect to the issue in focus) if the sender (B) is also part of *uchi*. But if the same restricted set of data is passed to one who is part of *soto*, then A (assumed now to be the outsider) will have a tiny flat triangle of trust towards B as he is not part of the rich chats that go on throughout the *uchi* crowd. How then might A and B learn to trust each other in such (culturally illiterate) circumstances?

There is a third effect, which is exacerbated in culture-crossing circumstances—namely the need to understand the rules and regulations that act upon B, which are unlike those pressing on A. We illustrate this in Figure 10.5. While acting between organizations person A must understand (1) with whom they usually interact (and vice versa) how person B relates to others in his/her hierarchy, and (2) how each of all the partner pairs A $\Leftrightarrow$ B (or B $\Leftrightarrow$ A) relate to their particular partner's organizational culture, which is often unlike that of their own operation. We see strong ties as relationships like A $\Leftrightarrow$ A^n or B^n $\Leftrightarrow$ B being the representation of how multiple persons relate to their colleagues in their in-house networks (Granovetter, 1973), and weak ties (op. cit.) (A $\Leftrightarrow$ B^n or A^n $\Leftrightarrow$ B and ultimately A^n $\Leftrightarrow$ B^n) as role-linkages across organizational boundaries.

Inevitably, the quality of the leadership of the firms involved in a supply chain is important. Leaders and subordinates have to understand the broad perceptions of "us and them" in joint alliances. We suggest that the management team of a firm being approached to join a supply chain is likely to have been drawn from the local population, while the acquiring firm's managers probably have an international background. This can result in clashes over the perceptions of the firm's leadership, which will have very important consequences for knowledge management (KM) and organizational learning (OL) in the joint alliance. It follows that the perceptions of "us and them" lower down the organizational hierarchy will also determine the quality of OL (Kidd & Edwards, 2000), as blue collar workers grapple with their perceptions of the "truths" being discussed by their leaders.

Proposition 4: People from different cultures bring with them their mental models—this is all they have with which to make sense of the contextual world in which they find themselves. When they are forced quickly into alliances it is

Figure 10.5
Interorganizational Trust Development via "Learning of the Other's Rules"

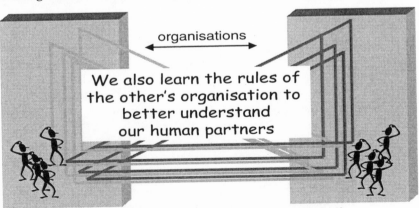

likely that there is little time put aside for contemplation of their joint situation or for exploring their different modeling processes.

- If an inappropriate process modeling technique is pursued, the result will be poor. The analysts will not be able to elicit the information needed nor will it be in the form desired. Quite possibly, the actors will not cooperate in the requisite manner. Chinese staff, for example, might become silent under the aggressive search for data by a U.S. or UK expatriate. In contrast, a Chinese expatriate might not ask questions in the U.S. and U.K. for fear of making local managers compromise themselves through over verbalization (i.e., lose face in the Chinese person's eyes).

However, for multinational clients, the Soft Systems (SSM) approach of Checkland may seem sloppy and not rigorous enough (the U.S. academic community that seems to prefer a data-rich scenario leading to a hard-science analysis of the problem might particularly seem so). In contrast, some Asians view SSM as too hard a science—they might prefer to commune and to use a Zen-like approach. In China there is silent communication between Chinese persons within an intangible *guanxi*. It is also said that Japanese persons engage together silently with *haragei*, wordless communication (Matsumoto, 1998). Both groups accept tacitly that "silence is golden," and become quiet, uttering no words so that neither they nor their partner loses face through an incautious phrase. By their logic, a person can also lose face if they have caused a problem for another person by making that person say imprudent words. Such wordless approaches are somewhat unfathomable for Westerners.

- The Westerner has a tendency to use externalized models and the Chinese, internalized models. As such, their joint interface will be problematical. Even so, when management gurus such as Prahalad "tell" Chinese managers that they, "should forget history, and do as Americans do—venture(!), as though there were no historical encumbrance," these gurus forget the innate sense of history that is alive and totally realistic for most Chinese, and it will make them hesitate (Prahalad, 1998).

We must admit that Prahalad has hinted at an interesting point—most Western managers come from a data-rich environment, and if they have passed through a formal business education program, they will have been instructed in data modeling. But the East is data-poor (in the sense of having a sufficient volume of publicly available, coherent, quantitative data). Formal analysis methods applied in the East will fail to generate statistically valid models; indeed many models may not be computable due to a lack of appropriate data (Haley & Tan, 1996). By data-poor we mean that there is often too little care placed on data consistency; there are too many regional differences and too many omissions in the data. Furthermore, local officials responsible for data collection may have quite simply lied to maintain good relations with senior officials, saying, in effect, that production targets were being met, if not exceeded, when the opposite was the truth.

- We perceive that Western persons look to public codification of explicit data at the start of a knowledge acquisition exercise, while persons in Asia remains strongly tacit and subjective. Haley & Tan suggest that Asian managers will tend to look to their personal networks to glean subjective qualitative data. These managers will busy themselves to obtain data directly more often and more deeply in the minutiae of their organizations than would a Western manager, who may rely more on secondary data sources and mathematical analyses.

• Each person's explicit processing of data is different. As such, it is very likely that their tacit systems are very different. They can only develop through a methodical exploration of their appreciation of a joint task can they develop. Once more, the joint acquisition of knowledge will be difficult to achieve.

SPECIFIC POINTS OF CONTRASTS BETWEEN KM AND OL

We have noted several factors that differentiate Eastern people from Western people and that will affect their management style—individualistic in the West, and more socially cohesive and familial, in the East (Bond & Forgas, 1984). At this stage, we wish to move to theories of Organizational Learning (OL) that appear culturally biased. Note that some scholars have described organizational learning as an oxymoron—saying that *only* people can learn and an organization cannot (Weike & Westley, 1996). Easterby-Smith (1997) argues that OL may be studied within a wide spectrum of disciplines—psychology, organizational design, management science, strategy, production management, sociology, and cultural anthropology. He proposes that as there is as yet no comprehensive theory of OL, inevitably emergent theories become entangled with the study of management of knowledge in a segment of a learning organization and become confounded with theories from psychology, anthropology, and so on.

A Western Approach

Huber (1991), whom Easterby-Smith classified as analytical within the management science discipline, has identified several aspects of OL. Huber suggested that when some unit of an organization acquires new knowledge it is a sign of the existence of learning, but as long as the knowledge rests only inside the unit there is no chance of organizational learning. He continued, saying that when other units interpret this information from their perspectives, the data is elaborated and is improved into a more thorough know-how. The key points in designing interaction patterns for OL are:

• to encourage individual units to acquire new knowledge
• to make each unit distribute its own knowledge to others

- to interpret the knowledge
- to make a database for organizational usage

Huber notes the basic start-up conditions for learning organization: it needs a data deposit that will be both qualitative and quantitative. This should be accessible through well conceived IT systems that allow individuals to search for data and to embed this in their personal mental models, leading to an enrichment of their own data and thus, learning. This represents a simple approach to learning where it is seen to be sufficient if the organization creates an open database. This condition is predicated perhaps upon the characteristics noted by Hofstede, Hall and others who suggest that the U.S. is a nation composed of short-term, individualistic persons who do not network (in the same way as Asian persons). The process of creating a database and an electronic network requires clarity of expression, an espoused strategy, and an innovation champion (Shane & Venkataraman, 1996) and trust (Shih, 1993). This environment is to be found in the noisy, argumentative and individualistic society of the United States that does not readily tolerate silence. However Huber (2000) has moved out of his focus on the "hard, database OL system" by acceding to the difficulty of eliciting some forms of knowledge. This process he describes as "sticky"—a phrase emphasized by Fruin (1997) from his research on Toyota (also note Baumard, 1999).

Other researchers present more complex learning models: embodied in forms of action research (Senge, 1990; Eden, Jones & Sims, 1983); carried by theories-in-use (Agryris & Schon, 1978); and the double loop learning approach (Argyris, 1993). In the last model, individuals are said to learn first from the observation of others and then from talking over their models with colleagues, which leads to greater learning and understanding and sets individuals up for another cycle of development. Checkland treats this learning process differently—he suggests that one has to "get into the mind of others in order to communicate meanings adroitly" (Checkland & Holwell, 1998). We worry over approaches that require that groups of individuals stay together long enough to benefit from the learning cycle, because there is often rapid interfirm personnel movement at managerial levels in Europe and in North America. These movements will inevitably break an individual's longer-term, group-focused learning cycle that is oriented to the cultural stance of a given organization, although it is enriching at the personal level.

An Eastern Approach

It is quite difficult to state explicitly what a knowledge-based system (KBS) is, although we each may have tacit feelings of what such a system might be in different organizations. In knowledge-based systems, we have to grasp the issue of *tacit* knowledge—that is, the knowledge which we have, which we all feel we understand, but which ultimately defies clear enunciation (Polanyi, 1958). Given that humans have basically the same needs, we might assume that we solve our problems in similar ways—yet this does not occur. We have seen above that process analyses differ: the outcome from one may lead to precise changes, and from another to holistic changes. These processes are modified according to the peoples involved (for instance, according to their Hofstede differences with respect to hierarchy, individualism, and long-term aims). How then are we to suggest how we approach or design a knowledge-based system?

Nonaka and his coresearchers describe tacit knowledge as having two dimensions (Nonaka, 1994; Nonaka & Takeuchi, 1995; Nonaka & Konno, 1998). First is the technical aspect, the know-how; the second is the cognitive aspect, comprising the beliefs and mental models we all develop and carry over the years and whose schema is hard to change as we often take them for granted. They propose a model for change and learning (SECI) that has four quadrants:

1. Socialization: The sharing of knowledge between two persons—a philosophical concept of "pure experience" which is related to Zen learning. Being together and sharing experience over time, not through written or verbal exchanges, fuels learning. We have to allow ourselves to empathize with others and not just sympathize—so we become larger through self-transcendence. We mentioned earlier *haragei,* wordless exchanges.

2. Externalization: This requires the expression of tacit knowledge through metaphor, analogies, or narratives. By so doing the individual can become integrated with the group's mental world. This process may also call for deductive or inductive reasoning, or creative inferences in order to make the sharing of knowledge clear and transparent.

3. Combination: Here, the key processes are communication and diffusion, which involve (a) collecting new externalized explicit knowledge, (b) disseminating this knowledge through meetings, for instance, and (c) editing of the new material to make it more usable.

4. Internalization: This is the conversion of explicit knowledge to an organization's tacit knowledge by identifying the knowledge needed for working in the organization. This is done by (a) being involved in training programs, and (b) engaging in simulations of learning-by-doing to trigger the learning process.

Nonaka and Konno (1998) advocate the study of the Japanese concept of *ba,* which can be translated to the English word "place"; it can be thought of as a "shared space for emerging relationships." This space can be physical like an office, virtual as in e-mail or teleconferencing, mental as in sharing ideas or expressions, or any combination of these. They stress that the differentiation between *ba* and an ordinary intervention is the concept of knowledge creation—it is *ba* that provides the platform for this.

They are saying that *ba* offers a transcendental perspective that integrates all needed information, and that is there is recognition of self in all this. Therefore, following existential theory, *ba* is a context, which harbors meaning. It follows, they say, that *ba* is the shared space which serves as a foundation for knowledge creation.

If knowledge is separated from *ba* it becomes simple information that can be transmitted independently from *ba*. Information resides in media and networks, it is tangible; but knowledge resides in *ba*, which is intangible. More realistically, *ba* is grounded in sharing. So individuals in knowledge creating firms should have *ba*, and *ba* will unite teams, informal groups, and even organizations. The self is embraced by the collective when an individual enters the *ba* of teams. Later, in the spiral of SECI, the organization is the *ba* for these teams, and the market environment is the *ba* for the organization. It may be seen that the concept of *ba* is quite close to those of WSR (*wuli, shili* and *renli*)—they emphases the wholeness of the perspectives in the (Chinese) study of issues in a firm (Zhu, 1998a).

Proposition 5: It is likely that cultures will only embrace learning systems that are appropriate for them. Thus, noisy, individualistic LC cultures look to databases, while HC cultures look for better ways to enhance internalization.

- Although Nonaka et al., propose *ba* as a model appropriate for Asian cultures—and maybe only specifically Japan. It is akin to the WSR process embracing space and reflective silence in the form of *Fù Găo* (Chinese) or *Haragei* (Matsumoto, 1988). For instance, when Japan looked to use the eclectic SSM, in the form of *Shinayakana* methodology (Nakamori & Sawaragi, 1997) it was perceived to be too aggressive.

In contrast, Western societies do not tolerate silence or noncommunication, as they desire contextualization. This can only be achieved, they believe, through conversations conducted face-to-face, using e-mail, or through accessing an electronic database.

- Both the Western and the Eastern models are embedded in and empowered by trust that must be nurtured in a way sensitive to the groups' ability to understand the relationships between tacit and explicit knowledge. The people have to be able to work within their individualistic (or collectivist) goals with respect to data sharing.

DISCUSSION

The five propositions with their bulleted notes were given above to prompt thought and inquiry. Essentially, they are concerned with factors that might delay the development of knowledge management processes in fast-moving alliances. For instance, in the global supply chain—which can be described as multiserviced and having tiers of manufacturers connected by logistics providers—we have seen that some MNEs have outsourced most functions, except core competences which are their distinct intellectual capital. CISCO Corporation was a good example of this through the late 1990s, before the dot-com shakeout of the early 2000s. We would contend that even in this firm, one of the world's richest, there might have been room for improvement, as key knowledge is unlikely to have been transferred smoothly from one partner firm to another. Simply because, in short-term strategic alliances individuals do not trust others to behave ethically with knowledge—that which can be made explicit may be copied!

It should be obvious also that the technical implementation of information technology and communications solutions do not ensure the smooth working of a networked alliance—though the absence of an electronic network will surely hinder growth and hamper the timely delivery of goods to the end customer. Many of the world's largest firms have striven to provide electronic networks to exchange data and other information of benefit to its corporate membership. Sometimes, this data is made available to customers in the form of Question & Answer databases, or downloadable files (of up-to-date software code, for instance). These solutions for customers save a great deal of money for the hosting firms (HP has suggested that downloading a printer driver file costs about $0.40 compared to about $40.00 for a person-to-person conversation to elicit the required information. Rick Wagoner, CEO of GM, suggests their drive to Internet purchasing, retailing, and distribution might save U.S. $5,500 per vehicle [*Financial Times* May 29, 2000: 11]). Thus, providing Q&A database access is a move towards a knowledge management process that is independent of time, location, or culture of the enquirer.

However, deeper, less codifiable knowledge is much more difficult to elicit. It takes time to gather persons together, to allow them to feel comfortable in the company of others, and to let them judge the truth of the mission statement of the alliance in comparison with their personal constructs and models. After this, they may begin the socializing process that moves them toward the exchange of mental models with one another— they begin to trust, as individuals. Later, as a person engages more deeply with more persons in a partner's firm, organizational trust can flourish, and with this, a deeper translation of tacit knowledge into explicit knowledge becomes possible.

All this takes time. It would seem that time is not freely available for today's global alliance, or even for local alliances. To solve this problem, new solutions in the new alliance are often old solutions from elsewhere, transported in the hopes that they will be accepted for their new organizational framework. Perhaps they become solutions operating at the lowest common denominator (as we may describe a committee decision)—they are understandable, they may be better than what was originally present, they offer promise of something better later, and they might not offend the local culture. To address the promise of the future, the alliance needs time to translate its tacit knowledge into explicit knowledge and to open this up to its corporate membership. Above all, the individuals concerned with this process have to learn to trust—if they do not, they may promote antipathy.

Silence . . .

We titled this chapter "The Talkative Company," and we noted early that "Words are silver silence is golden," that it may be better not to be a chatterbox, since words may be valueless (one *shekel*) when compared to holding one's (silent) council (worth *two shekels*). Of course, in the vicinity of the Tower of Babel there was the cacophony of multiple languages— but herein we mean something deeper. It is about the problem of discerning value or truths in the conversation rather than simply accepting meaningless data exchange. The latter links to the adage of "garbage in, garbage out"—since poor data brought into one's mental model will lead inevitably to poor information (in a Zuboff, 1988, sense). However, if an informant is silent, we have another difficulty—one that carries the possibility of lying by omission, which, if proven true will break down any trust that has developed.

Thus, we have to ask—why are people silent? Often the reasons lie in cross-cultural issues, and the lack of players' cultural literacy (Merry 2000). However, in the global village in which we now find ourselves, some persons may not have the linguistic ability to converse in the various languages current in an MNE, and understandably remain silent.

Western Specificity

An essential feature of Western cultures is the high esteem given to words. Because of the diversity of Western worlds' peoples and their lack of homogeneity it has always been necessary for explicit explanation of opinions and intentions and for striving for consistency in order to make oneself understood. In ancient Greece, the word *logos* also played a central role, acquiring the additional meaning of logic. Greek philosophers developed the art of speech, rhetoric, argumentation, dialectics, and logically consistent conversation and discourse. These techniques in the use of language were taught at Western universities, and are still a living part of today's European culture.

Eastern Inscrutability

In Japan, society developed from small village communities, undisturbed by foreign contacts for centuries (in stark contrast to the countries of Europe that experienced population migrations and many wars over their history). Because of the homogeneous nature of the Japanese people, explicit and coherent expression in speech was not necessary. Rules of rhetoric and logic did not develop. Instead, *sasshi* (empathy), *ishindenshin* (telepathy) and *haragei* ("belly talk") became accepted aspects of gesture-free body language and have become forms of communication considered characteristically Japanese. In Japanese literature, it is not the precise term that is esteemed but the *oku fukai* (deep and wide) and *ganchiku no aru* (suggestive) expressions that are. This particularly Japanese way of conducting silent discussion is disturbing to Western businessmen (Matsumoto, 1988).

The Influence of Confucius

We note that Confucius' five cardinal relationships and their accompanying moral code established the importance of hierarchy that survives across Asia to this day; he established rules of engagement between ruler and minister, father and son, husband and wife, elder and younger brother, and between friends. These codes offers many opportunities for silence: the junior may not interrupt the senior; at all costs, the junior must not cause the senior to lose face in public; and all must maintain decorum in public. Frequently, silence may be observed in Asian group processes, as any utterance would be an affront to the accepted status quo, and to break rank would cause one or more persons to lose face. Many have written on this facet of Asian society (Bond on China, 1994; Holmes & Tangtongatavy on Thailand, 1997; Backman on the darker side of Asian business where maintaining face leads to corruption, 1999).

There is one relationship that Confucius missed—the one between an individual and an outsider. Outsiders don't fit readily into the Confucian hierarchy; indeed, they represent a challenge to it (Li & Kidd, 2000). Effectively, Confucius left an ethical vacuum with respect to dealings with outsiders—those, for instance, who are expatriates. It is not surprising that he did not address this issue, because in his day, there were very few true outsiders. As such, he did not establish a sixth rule of behavior. In modern situations, the Chinese, who are normally rule-followers, are confused when there is no internalized rule to follow or break, as the case may be. To cover this confusion, they may engage in silent behavior, such as *Fù Gǎo*, keeping words in the stomach before uttering them too soon, as they have learned that "when a word has left the mouth, not even the swiftest horse can catch it" (Chinese proverb). On the other hand, a Japanese person might remember the proverb—"*Kiji mo nakazuba utaremai*—even a pheasant will not be shot if it keeps quiet" (Takashima, 1985: *Kotowaza no izumi*—Fountain of Japanese Proverbs).

The Need for Conversation

We accept the view of Richter (1999) that smooth working of an alliance may be best guaranteed by the exchange of staff. However, in today's fast and loose alliances, who should be exchanged with whom is a difficult question, because mixing management teams from different cultures carries risk. This risk is dependent on the magnitude of the cultural difference as described by Hofstede or Kogut & Singh. If the perceived cultural difference is small, the players may be too blasé; within a scenario of a big cultural difference there will be issues that won't go away, even though the players can perceive them. They may be unable to make the steps necessary to accept their partner's cultural identity and thus, method of working. Equally problematic is their different perception of leadership (Brodbeck op. cit., 2000).

We understand that we are the product of our early training—new data, procedures, and situations present threats to our self-image. In some cultures, leaders are protected by ritual and by silence so their (public) face is saved. If they are intuitive, they, themselves, may offer routes for subordinates to follow in a new scenario situation and to begin to harvest new knowledge. There are many ways to do this, but all involve conversations and the correct, local networking etiquette in order to inform the local society.

Even so, following this argument we suggest firms in the West might be advised to generate more conversations internally. Normally, they would be operating as low context, low networking firms; but with the initiation of Q&A databases, they have the opportunity to engage in more complex conversations as the baseline of their knowledge has been raised. We can liken this to the term "informating" presented by Zuboff (1988), wherein she describes how shop-floor workers, once they became aided by IT, could reformulate their personal models of their firm's operations and join these with those of their coworkers. It is quite likely that the knowledge-managing firms of the West have reengineered their firms so that their newly freed workers (normally to be made redundant) can engage in knowledge work. Western CEOs can direct their employees to hold conversations to exchange tacit knowledge, thereby mimicking high context networks (Inkpen, 1996).

The Need for Trust

Business-modeling systems, such as WSR and SSM, are inward looking (with respect to their concentration on modeling China and the UK, respectively). This leads them to be somewhat incompatible in their focus, thus, an inevitable compromise has to be made by each side. Consequently, following this argument, managers of all firms in a supply chain

must have a deep understanding of the other firms' psychological processes in order to become more trusting and better able to critique the
merging of their business processes. This is very important when cross-
border alliances are undertaken. For example, McIvor, Humphries &
Huang (2000) note the interactions of a group comprised of businesspersons from Hong Kong and southern mainland China. Those persons from
Hong Kong, having been exposed longer to Western ways, acted as bro-
kers for both mainland Chinese persons and for Western managers, the
outsiders. Since the Hong Kong persons better understood the mores of
the West (than the mainland Chinese), they instilled trust in each side of
the partnership through their actions. There has to be very sensitive management practiced along the reach of the global supply chain, because
what is acceptable behavior in one place may not be so elsewhere, and
some actions may even be unethical (Ralston, Egri, Stewart, Terpstra, &
Kiacheng, 1999; Backman, 1999).

It is vital for corporate leadership to be seen as having a supporting
role in the alliance. We are finding, as research data has revealed, that
leadership perception is culturally bound. It is important to understand
that the Hofstede implications (maybe in the form of the Kogut & Singh
measures) need to be linked to the leadership factors (GLOBE studies).
Brandt (1990) found that for success in U.S.-Japanese ventures, it was vital
to develop a high degree of trust early on. Allert & Chatterjee (1997) re-
viewed how corporate communication engenders trust by which the individuals involved can maintain their relationships. They say it is vital to
have a leader who can be a listener, a communicator, and an educator to
help develop a positive organizational culture. Similarly, Madhok (1995)
urges a shift in focus from ownership issues to relational dynamics and
social processes within an alliance culture.

In China there is the universal practice of *guanxi*, the maintenance of
which will involve gift giving (note the same word and social process is
endemic in Japan). It is, however, instructive to note the (Western-biased)
observations of Collins (1997); she sees *guanxi* as "probably not much
different from the old-boy network and other associations." We think this
view does not fully grasp neither the potentially infinite time base of the
obligation, nor the fact that the obligations extend through family ties.
More recently, as China opens up, *guanxi* has become known as "social
capital." The exchanges of favor involving *guanxi* are not strictly commercial in nature; they are also social, involving *renqing* (social or human-
ized obligation) and the giving of *mianzi* (the notion of face) (Lou, 1997;
Yang, 1994). Taking a Western view on this, social capital is used to "make
tidy" the commercial contracts between corporations and may lead the
innocent Westerner towards an over reliance on gift giving and banquet-
ing as a means of conducting business in China. These activities are both
normal facets of Chinese *guanxi*, but many Western firms' go too far and

operate too close to bribery. Western individuals can become known as "meat and wine friends," defeating the object of true *guanxi*, which is the offering of favors during the development of a personal relationship, naturally promoting business between Chinese businesspersons.

Spontaneous Groupings

Kautz & Vendelø (2001) have recently explored the spontaneous gathering together of individuals for the purpose of knowledge sharing. They refer back to the work of Hayek (1973) who described the ordering of individuals as being "designed" or "spontaneous". In our context, we find that Kautz & Vendelø echo much of what has been said above—that persons low in an organizational hierarchy are likely to strive for organizational learning spontaneously unless their leader is despotic. Even in this extreme case, the cultural backgrounds of the players may modify leadership pressure by protecting the workers and thereby allowing them to maintain their individuality through their inclination to abide by (local) consensus. However, if leaders attempt to design a knowledge management initiative, it is likely that HRM has to work hard to explain why this initiative is being promoted top-down or even across organizational boundaries, in order to engage the workers in organizational learning.

It is at this point that Kautz & Vendelø invoke the concepts of the "strong and weak ties" researched by Granovetter (1973) that we mentioned earlier. Granovetter suggested that sometimes we learn better from our weak ties as these relative strangers introduce novelty to our stable world; and for the firm, chaos is a force for the good, according to Pascale et al. (2001). On the contrary, we are said to learn more deeply from our strong ties, because we best understand the models of those close to us (cf., the Nonaka *ba* processes). Teramoto et al. (1994) and Teramoto (1993) state that companies lead according to the principles of a pluralistic network culture exhibit far better achievement than a conservatively lead company.

CONCLUSION

We suggest that silence between individuals is disruptive, although silence within a person may generate strength, wisdom, and may even enhance the personal development of some individuals. Essentially, it is said that this inner strength comes from a Vedic tradition and is promoted by modern transcendental meditation. Herein, silence is used privately by individuals to regenerate their inner strength each day; once this is in place, these persons have a vitality that engages urgently with others (Heaton & Harung, 2000). These individuals do not use silence between individuals as a learning device, instead they become assertive; the TMenabled person has the ability to stand outside his/herself to better see the whole situation. In this respect, they can uphold a system similar to *haragei* or *Fù Gǎo*. However, this silence is not a form of communication with others; it is an internal conversation—but once done, individuals can rapidly make use of words and conversation to engage others in meaningful learning.

The conversations in this chapter do not seek to provide answers; we have sought to raise many issues that can result in silence in multinational organizations, strategic alliances, and joint ventures. In the end, we have learned that understanding another is a long and subtle process, and like Yang (1994) we do not believe that the modernization of society will soon eliminate cross-cultural issues. However, precisely because it is such a long process, there is nothing to be gained by delaying an alliance: there is much to be gained by being talkative.

A firm's HRM function must nurture interfirm organizational learning so that knowledge management at a group level in the multinational enterprise can be initiated and maintained. This is very important when the supply chain becomes dynamic and satisfies niche markets. Without a knowledge management program supporting broad organizational learning, the firm will (relatively) atrophy under intense competition, which is now seen as having global reach. As the ultimate factor governing KM and OL is trust, we must stress that a detailed understanding of the many contextual aspects within the chain (across interfirm barriers) is needed to nurture this trust.

We suggest that encoding of personal knowledge in open databases will lead to a first level of learning (aka Huber), whereas through an organizational culture supportive of learning we may find deeper learning (aka Nonaka). This is possible through the deployment of Internet, Intranet and Extranet technologies, but we advocate starting off the process through face-to-face exchanges. Thereafter, learning must be managed by humans, though may be mediated by IT. To this end, it can be useful to exchange IT personnel in MNEs, so they become multi-hybrid—not only skilled in bridging IT and business concepts but also accomplished in cross-cultural issues.

To support this purpose, we see the need to fatten up firms a little. This would be through employing more staff to regenerate real organizational slack, so as to rekindle the organizational learning that once was nascent when there were spare individuals able to indulge in conversations. Employees, when they are not pressed for time, can develop several useful metaphors of a firm's operation, enabling others to grasp new knowledge. Of course, IT can be used very effectively for passing messages within learning teams, but this is only one aspect of the manner in which IT supports exchanges. Another aspect is now the outputs from Enterprise Resource Planning (ERP) software could be brought to a wide audience via IT links, to generate new ideas and to rekindle the interpretative learning lost after the initiation of ERP and the subsequent downsizing of the firm.

We are not suggesting that the Japanese model of organizational learning is the only one. Yet, the theses of Nonaka et al. have merit. However, this can only be so if there are sufficient spare individuals to be generative and interpretative with data, which surely is coherently, algorithmically and swiftly aggregated by the ERP software. Yet, we believe that neither in the West nor in the East can software be any match against two humans who merge their creative thoughts together; data networks are good for command and control purposes, but it is human networking that will smooth out differences, hopefully before they inflame into aggression.

REFERENCES

Albrecht, D. (2001). Culture and BrainStyles®℗: New Alternatives for Human Resource: Strategies to Develop Chinese-Western Cooperation. In J. B. Kidd, X. Li, & F.-J. Richter (Eds.). *Advances in Human Resource Management in Asia*. London & New York, Palgrave Press.

Allert, J. R. & Chatterjee, S. R. (1997). *The role of corporate communication in building trust in leadership*. Working Paper 9706. School of Management, Curtin Business School, Curtin University of Technology, Perth, Western Australia.

Angeles, R. (2000). Revisiting the role of Internet-EDI in the current electronic commerce scene. *Logistics Information Management 13*, 45–57.

Argyris, C. (1993). Knowledge for Action: A guide to overcoming barriers to organizational change. San Francisco: Jossey-Bass.

Argyris, C. & Schön, D. A. (1978). Organizational Learning: A theory of action perspective. Reading, MA: Addison-Wesley.

Backman, M. (1999). The Asian Eclipse: Exposing the dark side of business in Asia. Singapore: Wiley

Baumard, P. (1999). Tacit Knowledge in Organizations. London: Sage.

Ben-Ari, E. (1997). *Japanese childcare: An interpretative study of culture and organization*. London: Kegan Paul International.

Berne, E. (1975). *Transactional analysis in psychotherapy, a systematic individual and social psychiatry*. London: Souvenir Press.

Berrel, M., Wright, P. & Tran, T. V. H. (1999). The influence of culture on managerial behavior. *Journal of Management Development 18*, 578–589

Bhatnagar, R. & Viswanathan, S. (2000). Re-engineering global supply chains: alliances between manufacturing firms and global logistics services providers. *International Journal of Distribution & Logistics, 30*, 13–34.

Bond, M. H. (1994). *Beyond the Chinese Face: Insights from psychology*. Hong Kong: Oxford University Press.

Bond, M. H. & Forgas, J. P. (1984). Linking person perception to behavior intention across cultures: The role of cultural collectivism. *Journal of Cross Cultural Psychology 15*, 337–352.

Boyacigiller, N. A. & Adler, N. J. (1991). The parochial dinosaur: Organizational science in a global context. *Academy of Management Journal 16*, 262–290.

Brandt, S. A. (1990). Perspectives on Joint Venturing with the Japanese in the United States. *Advanced Management Journal 55*, 34–36, 47–48.

Brodbeck, F. C. (2000). Cultural variation of leadership prototypes across 22 European countries. *Journal of Occupational and Organizational Psychology 73*, 1–29.

Calori, R. & de Woot, P. (1994). *A European management model: Beyond diversity.* New York: Prentice Hall.

Campbell, C. P. (1998). *Beyond Language: cultural predisposition in business correspondence.* Presentation to Region 5 STS conference, Fort Worth: Texas, 5th February.

Chase, R. L. (1997). Effectively using Intranets for Knowledge Management. *International Journal of Business Transformations, 1* 30–40

Chaston, I., Badger, B., & Sadler-Smith, E. (1999). Organizational Learning: Research issues and application in SME sector firms. *International Journal of Entrepreneurial Behavior and research 5*, 191–203

Checkland, P. & Holwell, S. (1998). *Information, Systems and Information Systems.* Chitchester: Wiley.

Clarke, M. P. (1998). Virtual Logistics: an introduction and overview. *International Journal of Physical Distribution and Logistics Management 28*, 486–507.

Collins, P. (1997). Postcard from China. *Management Services 41*, 36–38.

Davenport, T. H. & Prusak, L. (1998). Working Knowledge: how organizations manage what they know. Boston: Harvard Business School Press.

Davenport, T. (1993). Process Innovation: Re-engineering work through information technology. Boston: Harvard Business School Press.

Drew, S. A. W. & Smith, P. A. C. (1998). The New Logistics Management: transformation through organizational learning. *International Journal of Physical Distribution and Logistics Management 28*, 666–681.

Easterby-Smith, M. (1997). Disciplines of Organizational Learning: contributions and critiques. *Human Relations 50*, 1085–1113.

Eden, C., Jones, S., & Sims, S. (1983). *Messing about in problems.* Oxford: Pergamon.

Edwards, J. S. & Kidd, J. B. (2000). *"Trust me! I'm a CKO": Multi-national issues in Knowledge Management.* In R. Dale, H. Scarborough, J. Swan (Eds.), *Knowledge Management: concepts and controversies.* BPRC Conference, Warwick University: UK; 10–11 February.

Festinger, L. & Carlsmith, J. M. (1959). Cognitive consequences of forced compliance. *Journal of Abnormal and Social Psychology 58*, 203–210.

Fruin, W. M. (1997). *Knowledge Works: Managing intellectual capital at Toshiba*. London: Oxford University Press.

Fukuyama, F. (1995). *Trust*. New York: The Free Press.

Granovetter, M. S. (1973). Strength through weak ties. *American Journal of Sociology 78*, 1360–1380.

Gupta, A. K. & Govindarajan, V. (1991). Knowledge flows and the structure of control within multinational corporations. *Academy of Management Review 16*, 768–79.

Haley, G. T. & Tan C.-T. (1996). The Black Hole of South East Asia: Strategic decision making in an informational world. *Management Decision, 34* 37–48.

Hall, E. T. (1976). *Beyond Culture*. New York: Doubleday.

Hall, E. T. & Hall, M. R. (1987). Hidden differences: Doing business with the Japanese. New York: Doubleday.

Hampden-Turner, C. & Trompenaars, F. (1997). Mastering the Infinite Game: how East-Asian values are transforming business practices. Oxford: Capstone.

Hayek, F. A. V. (1973). Law, Legislation, and Liberty: Vol 1: Rules and Order. Chicago: University of Chicago Press.

Heaton, D. & Harung, H. (2001). Awakening Creative Intelligence for Peak Performance: Reviving an Asian Tradition. In J. B. Kidd, X. Li, & F.-J. Richter (Eds.), *Advances In Human Resource Management In Asia*. London & New York: Palgrave Press.

Hofstede, G. (1980). Culture's Consequences: international differences in work-related values. London: Sage Publications.

Hofstede, G. (1991). Cultures and Organizations: software of the mind. London: McGraw-Hill.

Holmes, T. & Tangtongtavy, S. (1997). *Working with the Thais*. Bangkok: White Lotus.

Hoppe, H. M. (1993). The Effects of National Culture on the Theory and Practice of Managing R&D Professionals Abroad. *R&D Management 23*, 313–325.

Huber, G. P. (1991). Organizational Learning: the contributing processes and the literatures. *Organizational Science 3*, 383–397

Huber, G. P. (2000). *Transferring Sticky Knowledge: Suggested solutions and needed studies*. In J. S. Edwards & J. B. Kidd (Eds.), *Knowledge Management beyond the Hype: Looking towards the new millennium*. Proceedings of KMAC 2000, Aston Business School, 17–18 July.

I-Chuan, W.-B. (2000). *Hui: Chinese business in Action*. In Chan Kwok Bun (Ed.), Chinese Business Networks. Singapore: Prentice Hall.

Inkpen, A. (1996). Creating Knowledge through Collaboration. *California Management Review 39*, 123–141.

Islam, I. & Chowdhury, A. (1997). *Asia-Pacific Economics: A survey*. London: Routledge.

Jarillo, J. C. (1988). "On Strategic Networks," *Strategic Management Journal* 9, 31–41.

Kao, H. S. & Sek-Hong, N. (1993). Organizational commitment: From trust to altruism at work. *Psychology and Developing Societies*, 543–60.

Kautz, K. & Vendelø, M. T. (2001). *Knowledge Sharing as Spontaneous Ordering: On the emergence of strong and weak ties*. In C. Carter, H. Scarbourough & J. Swan (Eds.), *Managing Knowledge: Conversations and critiques*. Leicester University, 10–11 April.

Kennedy, J. & Mansor, N. (2000). Malaysian Culture and the Leadership of Organizations: A GLOBE Study. *Malaysian Management Review*, December 2000.

Kidd, J. B. & Edwards, J. S. (2000). *Fast Moving global supply chains: how organizational learning may offer bridges in crossing cultures*. In the proceedings of ECKM 2000. D. Remenyi (Ed.), *First European Conference on Knowledge Management; Bled, Slovenia*. 26–27 October.

Kidd, J. B. & Teramoto, Y. (1995). *Can the Japanese Localize?—A study of Japanese production subsidiaries in the UK*. In Park S-J & M. Jovanovic (Eds.), *What is behind the Japanese miracle?* London: Megatrends I.E.C.

Kidd, J. B. & Yau, T. Y. L. (2000). Management Integration Through Software Applications: Japanese manufacturing firms in the UK exert control. *Journal of Global Information Management*, Oct-Dec.

Kogut, B. & Singh, H. (1988). The effect of national culture on choice of entry mode. *Journal of International Business Studies, 19* 411–432.

Li, X. & Kidd, J. B. (2000). *The Realization of Meanings: Understanding expatriates' needs in a novel environment*. In U. C. V. Haley & F.-J. Richter (Eds.), *Asian Post-crises Management—Corporate and Governmental Strategies for Sustainable Competitive Advantage*. Forthcoming.

Lou, Y. (1997). Guanxi: Principles, philosophies and implications. *Human Systems Management 9*, 1–9.

Lu, J. (1998). *Characteristics and Performance of Japanese FDI in China*. A presentation to the 13th LVMH Conference, INSEAD. *Asian Foreign Investment in Asia*. 6–7 February, 168–190.

Luo, Y. (2000). *Guanxi and Business*. Singapore: World Scientific.

Madhok, A. (1995). Revisiting multinational firms' tolerance for joint ventures: A trust-based approach. *Journal of International Business Studies 26*, 117–137.

Matsumoto, M. (1988). *The Unspoken Way Haregei: Silence in Japanese business and society*. Tokyo: Kodansha International.

McClelland, D. C. (1961). *The Achieving Society*. Princeton: van Nostrand.

McIvor, R., Humphreys, P., & Huang, G. (2000). Electronic Commerce: re-engineering the buyer-supplier interface. *Business Process Management Journal, 6* 122–138.

Merritt, A. C. (1998). *Replicating Hofstede: A study of pilots in eighteen countries*. In proceedings of the *Ninth International Symposium on Aviation Psychology*. Columbus, OH: The Ohio State University.

Merry, P. (2001). *Cultural Literacy – its link to Business success in Asia-Pacific*. In J. B. Kidd, X. Li, & F.-J. Richter (Eds.), *Maximizing Human Intelligence Deployment in Asian Business: The sixth generation project*. London & New York: Palgrave Press.

Miyashita, K. & Russell, D. W. (1994). *Keiretsu: inside the hidden Japanese conglomerates*. New York: McGraw-Hill

Nakamori, Y. & Sawaragi, Y. (1998). *Systems approach based on Japanese intellectual tradition*. In proceedings of ICSSSE'98: J. Gu (Ed.), *Systems Science and Systems Engineering*. Beijing: Scientific & Technical Documents Publishing House. August 25–28.

Nonaka, I. & Konno, N. (1998). The concept of "Ba": building a foundation for knowledge creation. *California Management Review, 40* 40–50.

Nonaka, I. (1994). A Dynamic Theory of Organizational Knowledge Creation, *Organizational Science 5*, 16–35.

Nonaka, I. & Takeuchi, H. (1995). *The Knowledge-creating Company*, Oxford: Oxford University Press.

Otazo, K. L. (1999). *Global Leadership: The Inside Story—Advances in Global Leadership*. New York: JAI Press Inc.

Pascale, R., Millemann, M., & Gioja, L. (2001). *Surfing the Edge of Chaos*. New York: Texere.

Peppard, J. (1996). Broadening visions of business process re-engineering. *Omega 24*, 255–270.

Phan, P. H. & Perdis, T. (2000). Knowledge creation in strategic alliances: another look at organizational learning. *Asia Pacific Journal of Management 17*, 201–222.

Polanyi, M. (1958). *Personal Knowledge*. Chicago: Chicago University Press.

Prahalad, C. K. (1998). *Internationalization, Globalization and Chinese Firms*. A presentation to the China Europe International Business School [CEIBS] Annual Conference, *Competing in Chinese Markets*. Shanghai, 27 July.

Ralston, D. A., Egri, C. P., Stewart, S., Terpstra, R. H. & Kiacheng, Y. (1999). Doing Business in the 21st Century with the New Generation of Chinese Managers: A study of the generation shifts of work values in China. *Journal of International Business Studies 30*, 415–428.

Richter, F.-J. (1999). Business Networks in Asia: Promises, doubts, and perspectives. Westport, CT: Quorum Books.

Richter, F.-J. (2000). Strategic Networks: The art of Japanese interfirm co-operation. New York: The Haworth Press.

Senge, P. (1990). *The Fifth Discipline: The art and practice of the learning organization*. New York: Doubleday.

Shane, S. & Venkataraman, S. (1996). Renegade and rational championing strategies. *Organization Studies, 17* 751–771.

Shih, C. (1993). Trust is a prerequisite for innovation. *International Journal of Public Administration 11*, 1693–1698.

Smith, P. B. & Bond, M. H. (1993). Social Psychology across Cultures: Analyses and perspectives. Hemel Hempstead: Harvester-Wheatsheaf.

Smith, P. B. & Peterson, M. F. (1994). Leadership as Event Management: A cross-country survey based upon middle managers from 25 countries. Presentation to a symposium at the *International Congress of Applied Psychology*, Madrid.

Smith, P. B., Dougan, S., & Trompenaars, F. (1996). National culture and the value of organizational employees. *Journal of Cross-Cultural Psychology 6*, 231–264.

Stock, G. N., Greis, N. P., Kasunda, J. D. (1999). Logistics, Strategy and Structure: a conceptual framework. *International Journal of Physical Distribution and Logistics 29*, 224–239.

Teramoto, Y. (1993). Gakushu suru soshiki (The Learning Organization), Tokyo: Shobunsha.

Teramoto, Y., Richter, F.-J., Iwasaki, N., Takai, T., Wakuta, Y. (1994). Global Strategy of Japanese Semiconductor Industry: Knowledge Creation through Strategic Alliances. In N. Campbell & F. Burton (Eds.), *Japanese Multinationals: Strategies and Management in the Global Kaisha*. London: Routledge.

Trompenaars, F. (1993). *Riding the Waves of Culture: Understanding cultural diversity in business*, London: The Economist Books.

UNCTAD (2000). *World Investment Report*. United Nations Conference on Trade and Development. Geneva.

Weike, K. E. & Westley, K. (1996). *Organizational Learning: Affirming an oxymoron*. In S. R. Clegg, C. Hardy & W. R. Nord (Eds.), *Handbook of Organizational Studies*. London: Sage Publications.

Williamson, O. E. (1975). Markets and Hierarchies: Analysis and Antitrust Implications. New York: Free Press.

Yang, K. S. (1988). Will societal modernization eventually eliminate cross-cultural psychological differences? In M. H. Bond (Ed.), *The Cross-Cultural Challenge to Social Psychology*, Newbury: Sage.

Yang, M. (1994). *Gifts, Favors and Banquets: The art of social relationships in China*. Ithaca, NY: Cornell University Press.

Zhu, Z. (1998a). Confucianism in Action: recent developments in Oriental systems methodology. *Systems Research and Behavioral Science 15*, 111–130.

Zhu, Z. (1998b). *Cultural Imprints in Systems Methodologies: the WSR Case.* In J. Gu (Ed.), *Systems Science and Systems Engineering,* proceedings of the 3rd International Conference [ICSSE'98] August. Beijing: Kedya Press. 402–407.

Zuboff, S. (1988). *In the age of the smart machine: The future of work and power.* Oxford: Heinemann.

CHAPTER 11

Cross-Cultural Co-opetition among Organizations

Rasoava Rijamampianina and Claire Gordon-Brown

ABSTRACT

With great rapidity, the dynamics of the business world are changing. Increasingly, companies are called upon to form alliances and forge productive working relationships with their competitors to achieve competitive advantage in the global economy. This new environment is one that is characterized by a combination of competition and cooperation: something that has been termed "co-opetition." However, such arrangements are not easily formed and managed. Indeed, national and organizational cultures are crucial variables in today's business setting. Firms engaged in alliances have to deal with each other's cultural norms and quirks. Cross-cultural alliances have frequently been aborted due to the fact that issues pertaining to culture are often neglected by managers at various stages of the alliance formation process. Given that interorganizational and cross-border alliances are growing rapidly, managers and researchers should be taking a closer look at culture. Moreover, culture is not the only factor that plays a critical role in alliance success. Organizational competencies and alliance drivers also have a defining role. A framework that considers the interaction of these variables is necessary to make co-opetition work effectively across cultures.

WHY CO-OPETITION?

Ever since the 1980s the trend towards alliances between businesses, both within national borders and across borders, has been marked. Mergers, acquisitions, joint ventures, and nonequity cooperative strategies like technological licensing and marketing agreements have become increasingly popular. It has been an era of global evolution (Chan & Wong, 1994).

The basis for the growing number of business alliances lies in the rapid advancement of technology and the uncertainties and complexities of today's business environment. These partnering approaches allow organizations both to compete and collaborate with each other. Cooperating to compete in any form gives participants greater opportunity for growth and a stronger competitive edge (Amin, Hagen & Sterrett, 1995). Baranson (1989) notes that companies that fail to form alliances may, in fact, be jeopardizing their prospects. By forming alliances with strategically well-chosen competitors, companies will find that they can shorten development cycles, share the financial risks, and increase their access to markets. A technology-sharing alliance conducted between E. J. Lilly and Denmark's Novo Company, for example, produced a new insulin product that leapfrogged Squibbs' efforts. Baranson (1989) indicates that mutual dependence and mutual learning, rather than cost avoidance, should be the objective of interorganizational alliances. Moreover, if companies content themselves to work in the old way (internal development), then they will find that in 90 percent of the cases their market position will be eroded and threatened by foreign or domestic competitors.

Chan & Wong (1994) comment that global competition requires a simultaneous need for global-scale efficiencies, worldwide learning, and local responsiveness. Ghoshal (1987) and Harrigan (1987) add that multinational alliances are critical mechanisms for competing in global markets and dealing with rapid change. Indeed, single firms are unlikely to have all the resources and strategic capabilities to achieve global competitiveness. In other words, interorganizational alliances are essential to achieve these strategic capabilities more quickly.

The result has been that companies have formed alliances with marketplace competitors and collaborators *alike* (Dowling, Carlin, Roering & Winieski, 1993).

In most modern theories of business, competition is seen as one of the key forces that keep firms lean and drive innovation. Adam Brandenburger of Harvard Business School and Barry Nalebuff of Yale School of Management have challenged that emphasis. In part using some of the ideas of game theory, they suggest that businesses can gain advantage by means of a judicious mixture of competition and cooperation. Cooperation with suppliers, customers, and firms producing complementary or related products can lead to expansion of the market, formation of new business relationships, and perhaps even the creation of new forms of enterprise (Brandenburger & Nalebuff, 1996). They chose the term "co-opetition" for this concept (a blend of cooperation and competition).

A new environment that is characterized by a combination of competition and cooperation has emerged and companies are increasingly called upon to form alliances and forge productive working relationships to achieve competitive advantage in the global economy.

The relationship between Intel and Microsoft is a leading example of co-opetition. The two companies have some conflicting interests. Microsoft wants computers to be inexpensive. Intel wants software to be cheap. But they also have mutual interests. Microsoft's software requires faster computers, while Intel's computers allow customers to run more complex programs. By cooperating in designing new chips and software rather than competing destructively, the two companies expand each other's opportunities (Henricks, 1996).

IMPACT OF CULTURE ON INTERORGANIZATIONAL ALLIANCES

Yet history is riddled with examples of failed alliances. Often the blame is laid on inadequate understanding of and incompatibility between the cultures of the partner companies. Knowledge of organizational culture is crucial to the success of any joint venture note, Chan & Wong (1994). Interorganizational alliances can stretch the ability of alliance partners to integrate their cultures or adapt to each other's culture. Whether it is for a short-term project or a long-term business venture, the cultures of alliance partners will have to integrate or adapt at an innterorganizational level and possibly even at a cross-national level. Firms engaged in alliances, therefore, have to deal increasingly with the vagaries of each other's cultural norms. Yet managers often neglect issues of culture at various stages of the alliance formation process (Rao & Swaminathan, 1995).

Interorganizational alliances can take a number of formats:

- *Strategic alliances.* In this type of relationship, interorganizational cooperation occurs without the formation or joint ownership of a separate legal entity. The probability of culture clash in this situation is high at the level of both organizational and national cultures. This is why strategic alliances frequently turn into mergers or acquisitions, bringing cultural issues to the fore.

- *Marketing/Supply/Buy-back agreement.* In this case, organizations cooperate at the product-market level. Culture impacts both at the organizational and national levels. However, its effects can be mitigated if the degree of overlap is low.

- *Cross-licensing agreement.* This is an alliance in which each of the partners licenses the other's competence. Mutual access and knowledge are allowed in this case. As a result, cultural integration and adaptability are required at the levels of competence and organizational values.

- *Technology transfer agreement.* This happens usually when large multinational organizations set up operations in developing countries. Culture is likely to impact significantly at the national level.

- *Joint venture.* This type of alliance involves interorganizational cooperation with joint ownership of a separate legal entity. A distinct culture (not necessarily based on parent cultures) may emerge over time.

- *University-Industry linkage.* In this case, researcher(s) at an institution may be sponsored by a corporation that may have ultimate rights to the product or process developed.

From all of the above-mentioned structures, one can deduce that culture can be an important variable that has an impact on alliance performance (Chakravathy & Lorange, 1991). Rao & Swaminathan (1995) say that uneasy alliances rest on the shaky foundations of incompatible cultures.

THE CONCEPT OF CULTURE COMPATIBILITY/ INCOMPATIBILITY

From a narrow perspective, culture can be defined as ". . . that complex of activities which includes the practice of the arts and of certain intellectual disciplines, the former being more salient than the latter" (Trilling, 1978). Most management researchers subscribe to a view of culture that sees it as a set of ideas shared by members of a group (e.g., Allaire & Firsirotu, 1984). Culture is therefore not an individual characteristic but rather a set of common theories of mental programs (Hofstede, 1991) that are shared by a group of individuals.

Harris and Moran (1987) define culture as the cumulative deposit of knowledge, beliefs, values, religion, customs, and mores acquired by a group of people and passed on from generation to generation. It includes not only arts and letters, but also ways of lives, value systems, traditions, and beliefs. Kohls (1981) defines culture as an integrated system of learned behavior patterns that are characteristic of the members of any given society. It includes everything that a group thinks, says, does, and makes—its customs, language, material artifacts, and shared systems of attitudes and feelings.

Rijamampianina (1996) says that the best definition of culture combines those of Harris & Moran (1987) and Kohls (1981): "Culture is created, acquired and/or learned, developed and passed on by a group of people, consciously or unconsciously, to subsequent generations. It includes everything that a group thinks, says, does and makes—its customs, ideas, mores, habits, traditions, language, and shared systems of attitudes and feelings—that help to create standards for people to coexist."

This definition of culture encompasses a wide variety of elements, from the visible to the invisible, from core to peripheral values. It embraces national and organizational boundaries.

The core values are more important, enduring, and resistant to change, particularly if they are invisible. They may be highly valued within an

Figure 11.1
The Structure of Culture

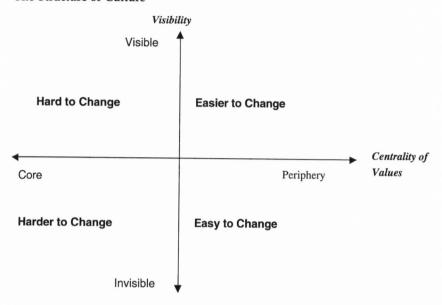

In an interorganizational alliance, cultures are therefore compatible when cultural differences are not significant (mostly characterized by peripheral values). In this case, cultural change, and therefore cultural integration or adaptation, is likely to be smooth.

organization and therefore more likely to cause clashes in interorganizational alliances. Resistance to change softens when core values become visible. Values of low priority, low consensus and less importance—the peripheral values—are relatively susceptible to change—even more so when they are visible. They are more easily changed and are less likely to cause conflict when they are visible than when they are not.

In an interorganizational alliance, cultures are therefore compatible when cultural differences are not significant (mostly characterized by peripheral values). In this case, cultural change, and therefore cultural integration or adaptation, is likely to be smooth.

On the other hand, cultures are incompatible when cultural differences are significant (mostly characterized by core values). This situation is likely to make cultures change, thus, cultural integration and/or adaptation difficult.

Cartwright & Cooper (1995) point out that cultural change is a long and difficult process that realistically can take as long as three to five years, and possibly even longer. The consequences of an unsuccessful culture fit can spell disaster for an interorganizational alliance.

Companies that deal with foreign organizations must understand and work with different cultures at the national and organizational levels, as well as adapt their own cultures to suit each other (Levinson & Asahi, 1995). In alliances that transcend international borders there is an array of cross-cultural differences that companies have to deal with. Horror stories abound of firms failing to adapt to a host culture (Rao & Swaminathan, 1995).

Yet cultural compatibility is not the sole determinant of alliance success. Alliances may still be successful even if the cultures of the partner firms are not compatible. This allows a smaller firm to partner with a bigger firm while maintaining its independence and resisting the adoption of the bigger firm's professional management practices. Rao & Swaminathan (1995) contend, "a mere difference in firm cultures need not necessarily indicate possibilities of failure . . . strong strategic complementarity's can single handedly carry an alliance forward. Alliances are often structured based on the objectives and the level of competencies embedded in the firm." Murray & Siehl (1989) say that it is the match between the parent firms' cultures and their competencies that indicate the potential for success or failure in a joint venture. Alliances, they say, cannot succeed without cultural similarities or strategic complementarities. Where two cultures are totally dissimilar, culture has to take second place to strategy.

There is a finely balanced interplay between culture, organizational competencies, and alliance drivers that lays the foundation for the nature and success of strategic alliances. Therefore, a framework that considers this interplay is necessary to make co-opetition work across cultures.

CULTURE COMPATIBILITY & COMPETENCE SIMILARITY/COMPLEMENTARITY

Organizations' competencies are either similar or different. If they are different, they are either complementary or noncomplementary. According to Mason (1994) organizations have to be clear on what their core competencies are before entering an alliance. Alliances should support and leverage a company's core competencies. Core competencies are those competencies that give an organization its competitive advantage. They define the nature of the organization. They cannot be outsourced. Doing this would sign the death warrant of the organization.

Together cultural compatibility and organizational competency define the nature of the business relationship that potential alliance partners should consider.

Figure 11.2 indicates that organizations with compatible cultures and similar competencies (area A) have the potential to enter into co-opetitive relationships. In this case, however, the degree of competition will be higher than the degree of cooperation. The business relationship between those with similar competencies but incompatible cultures (area B) will remain in the realm of pure competition. No cooperation will be possible. Where cultures are compatible and competencies are complementary

Figure 11.2
Organizational Relationships According to Organizational Culture and Competencies

		CULTURES	
		COMPATIBLE	INCOMPATIBLE
COMPETENCIES SIMILAR		COOPETITION Competition > Cooperation (A)	PURE COMPETITION (B)
DIFFERENT — COMPLEMENTARY		PURE COOPERATION (C)	COOPETITION Competition < Cooperation (D)
DIFFERENT — NON-COMPLEMENTARY		NO BUSINESS RELATIONSHIP (E)	

(area C), the relationship between the alliance partners can be one of pure cooperation. Where cultures are incompatible but competencies are complementary (area D) there is scope for co-opetition. In this relationship, however, cooperation will be greater than competition. If it is found that the competencies are noncomplementary (area E), then no business relationship is possible, regardless of whether cultures are compatible or incompatible.

FRAMEWORK FOR EFFECTIVE CROSS-CULTURAL CO-OPETITION AMONG ORGANIZATIONS

This section starts by considering the two areas (A and D) of figure 11.2, which are related to co-opetition, and suggests that the real success of cross-cultural co-opetition depends on the in-depth understanding and management of the following drivers: motivation drivers, interaction drivers, vision drivers, and learning drivers (figure 11.3). These four drivers are interlinked. In other words, they affect each other.

Motivation Drivers

The motivation drivers of any alliance define the identity of the alliance and cause the organizations to come together in the first place. The motivation to come together could be anything from creating or discovering a new market, enhancing an existing market or cocreating stronger competencies to become larger, stronger, and agile enough to act in the global market.

Porter (1985) suggests that firms usually cooperate because they have reciprocal dependencies, such as the following: gaining access to new technologies or markets; benefiting from economies of scale in joint research, production and marketing; and gaining complementary skills by tapping into sources of know-how located outside of the boundaries of the firm. Moreover, advantages of cooperation include (Amin et al., 1995):

- sharing the risks of activities that are beyond the scope or capability of a single organization
- gaining synergy by combining the strengths of firms in ventures that are much broader and deeper than a simple supplier relationship, marketing joint venture or technology licensing agreement

In an environment of increasing global competition alliances can assist organizations to achieve sustainable competitiveness. These partnerships

Figure 11.3
Framework for an Effective Cross-Cultural Co-opetition

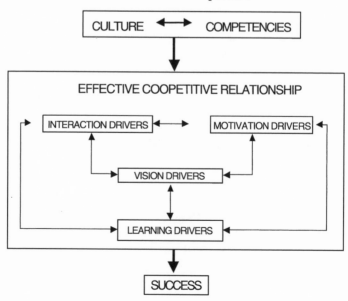

allow companies access to the competencies and resources of other parties to strengthen competitive advantages. These strategies are effective in overcoming the competency and resource gaps needed to gain access to global markets. However, they may fail if allying partners do not carefully consider the culture variable.

Companies must identify and understand why joining forces with competitors would be beneficial for them. It is essential to conduct a thorough alliance cost-benefit analysis as well as culture, competencies, and resources audit before making any decision about co-opetition.

Cross-cultural co-opetition however will not take place outside of the areas A and D (see figure 11.2) and will only be effective if, in the first place, the motivation drivers include:

- *Mutual dependency.* This is the recognition that allying partners need each other. It is the recognition that organizations achieve goals through and with others and that co-opetition is therefore vitally important. An interdependent organization knows that no one is an island.

- *Mutual interests.* This is the acknowledgement that allying partners have interests in the business (though their interests might not necessarily be the same) and that each organization has interests in what their partners are doing or contributing.

- *Mutual benefits.* This is an important tool in aligning the partners' interests with those of the alliance. When benefits are mutual, both parties get what they need from the relationship. Each helps the other. It generates a win-win situation. Moreover, it is the underlying force that gives rise to critical success components, such as identity with, involvement in, and commitment to the business.

These motivation drivers are:

- the foundation of any cooperative relationship
- the conditions that transcend all cultural differences and
- the only conditions that may shift a competitive intention into a cooperative one

To support these drivers, the alliance, of course, must provide all partners with an open and equal opportunity environment and with just and fair systems.

Interaction Drivers

The willingness to enter into an alliance and the potential for success of the alliance will depend on the nature and outcome of the historical relationship between the potential alliance partners. If they have not worked together before the alliance will take place on a trial basis. This situation has its pros and cons. For example, it is beneficial for both allying partners because the relationship is still more or less similar to that of all just-dating couples. The willingness to be together and to sacrifice a certain amount is still high. Each partner is very careful in nurturing the new relationship. However, such a situation may also slow down the interaction process, which is necessary to lead the partners into a relationship of mutual understanding, trust and commitment. Indeed, this type of relationship requires repeated and continuous interaction, and therefore it requires time!

If the potential partners already have a relationship history and if their past interactions have been unsuccessful, this would militate heavily against successful co-opetition. Indeed, common life experiences show and confirm that once a relationship is unproductive it is hard (and sometimes impossible) to keep that relationship moving forward! This is usually the case when

- allying partners' cultures are incompatible
- partners think that their competencies are similar rather than complementary
- none of the partners is truly willing to rework the interaction and/or
- the motivation drivers are unclear, and therefore not strong enough to support the interaction drivers

If, on the other hand, there is a history of successful co-opetition between two potential partners and a relationship of trust and commitment has been established, then the potential for success in a new co-opetitive relationship is high. Indeed:

- Successful past history increases the potential costs to a defector in any single transaction. By acting opportunistically within one transaction, a partner places at risk the benefits it expects to receive from other transactions in which it is currently engaged, as well as the benefits from future transactions.
- A successful relationship history facilitates communication and improves the flow of information, thus boosting trust between the partners.
- Past success at collaboration can provide a culturally defined template for future collaboration.

The formula for managing any relationship involves the similar basic elements to those, which motivate the relationship in the first place:

- *Mutual understanding.* Usually mutual understanding takes place after repeated interaction between the parties. Due to cultural differences that exist between organizations, this interaction driver may take a much longer time to develop when the partners' cultures are incompatible than when they are compatible. When there is mutual understanding each partner understands the reasons why the other acts in a particular way and accepts the other's behavior as legitimate and authentic, despite the tension or inconvenience it might cause. Each partner understands the other's motives and accepts the role of the other with greater empathy (Rijamampianina, 1996).

- *Mutual trust and respect.* The mutual confidence that no party will exploit the other's vulnerability is today widely regarded as a precondition for success. If trust and respect is absent, no one will risk moving first. All will sacrifice the gains of cooperation in order to remain safe. Mutual trust and respect eases collective life. The greater the level of trust and respect within an alliance, the greater the likelihood of cooperation (Rijamampianina, 1996).

- *Mutual commitment.* Usually mutual commitment emerges when partners find that the motivation drivers are clear, when they understand each other, and when the level of mutual trust and respect is fairly high. In other words, in the great majority of cases, the foundation of mutual commitment depends on the expectation, the durability, and the quality of the relationship. Nevertheless, it is worth noting that cross-cultural collaboration always implies changes on everybody's part (Rijamampianina, 1999).

As everything is interconnected, a relationship that is characterized by these interaction drivers will strengthen the motivation drivers of the allying partners. Thus, the partnership will have a greater chance of success.

Vision Drivers

The vision that drives the alliance can only be achieved if the motivation and interaction drivers are in place. Yet it is dependent on the overall visions of the individual partners and how similar or different these are. The allying partners have to be able to cocreate a common vision for the alliance. The common vision may or may not derive from the parent visions. The point is that the vision is cocreated and takes into account the partners' interests in the alliance. If they can do this, then the potential for successful co-opetition is high. If no common vision can be created, then the motivation for and the interaction between the two companies may be negatively affected and the companies may revert to a competitive relationship.

Usually, organizations with incompatible cultures have incompatible orientations. And since visions are shaped by these orientations, one can deduce that organizations with incompatible cultures may have incompatible visions. Frequently, however, weak motivation drivers and unsuccessful past relationships are more important factors in making common vision difficult than incompatible cultures.

The process of creating a vision is a collective one; and a vision can only be a power when it is shared between the partners. A shared vision is the inner power that enables an organization to win the battle, but it is also the cement that links and binds the partners to both succeed and win the war.

Learning Drivers

The main goals of any alliance are the exchange of new information, knowledge, skills, and abilities, and the cocreation of new competencies. Crossan & Inkpen (1995) contend that being able to extract knowledge and skills may become vital to the survival of alliances. Morrison and Mezentseff (1997) argue that learning facilitates the partners' motivation in achieving the objectives of the alliance relationship. Moreover, they say, alliances will achieve sustainable competitive advantage only if they involve learning and knowledge transfer.

Co-opetition encourages a learning environment that provides benefits through mutual transfer of knowledge, skills, and competencies. Organizations in a co-opetitive alliance, therefore, have to take a serious look at their ability to learn. Indeed, in reality, in any interorganizational relationship, learning takes place at both the intra- and interorganizational levels.

To make a co-opetitive relationship successful, allying partners need to:

• Understand that intra- and interorganizational learning must be directed toward a common vision

• Cocreate a learning culture

• Understand that organizations may have different approaches to learning. A fairly open and flexible interorganizational learning process would then be required

• Determine work responsibilities and boundaries and make interorganizational arrangements for (Levinson & Asahi, 1995):

  • the types of information, knowledge, skills, and competencies that are to be mutually transferred

  • how these learning elements are going to be mutually transferred (formal/informal face-to-face meetings, electronic interactions, digital communications, etc. . . .)

  • in what form they are to be conveyed and received

  • how much these learning elements could be modified and adapted

Though compatible cultures may be viewed as facilitating interorganizational learning (Levinson & Asahi, 1995) in reality, it is rather the existence or the absence of learning cultures in the allying partners that can either promote or hinder interorganizational learning. Indeed, since difference is a natural condition for learning, culture incompatibility is an opportunity for learning rather than a threat. The challenge is to develop mechanisms to capture, save, and share this learning and the benefits that come from it.

If motivation, interaction, and vision drivers are satisfied, an environment that fosters competence creation through interorganizational learning can be generated effectively and easily.

The following steps of interorganizational learning should take place:

1. *Awareness of the need for acquiring one or more new learning elements (information, knowledge, skills, and competencies).* This is usually due to the fact that the business environment is continuously changing. Consequently, individual partners are aware that there is a gap between their current information, knowledge, skills, and competencies and what they will need. Huber (1991) refers to organizational learning as the development of insights or awareness, which is a change in states of knowledge that expand the range of potential behaviors. Without this awareness, the motivation driver for an organization to seek an alliance will be weak.

2. *Identification and search for the new learning elements.* In this step, individual partners need to carry out a learning element audit to facilitate the search for and identification of the required learning elements. These learning elements may come from inside or outside the industry, inside or outside national boundaries or through formal and/or informal channels and sources. Normally, this step requires time. It may occur quite by chance or it may be the result of careful planning. Moreover, it is often difficult to know the relevance of possible learning elements in advance of when they are needed (Rijamampianina, 1999).

3. *Exchange of new learning elements.* Once the needed learning elements are identified, allying partners have to transfer them along a selected and agreed pathway. Indeed, this is the main purpose of establishing the alliance! The objective of this step must therefore be twofold: to exchange the learning elements for the benefit of each partner; and to produce the joint product of the alliance. The critical part of this step is the ease of access to all necessary learning elements.

4. *Adaptation of the new learning elements to the partners' and/or alliance's competencies.* Newly acquired learning elements do not always fit easily with the existing elements. Hence, there may be a need to adapt them. Adaptation involves both exploitation and exploration. Exploitation refers to improving, refining, routinizing, and elaborating existing learning elements, and then tying them to other newly acquired elements to produce a joint product. Exploration refers to experimentation with new learning elements in the hope of finding alternatives that improve upon old ones. Exploitation and exploration are linked in an enduring symbiosis. Each is dependent on the other to contribute effectively to an organization's and alliance's survival and prosperity. This step may take time if the partners' cultures are incompatible. Indeed, an organization's culture will shape the way it transfers, receives, interprets, and adapts new learning elements.

5. *Improvement of existing learning elements.* This activity involves scientific and nonscientific methods simultaneously, through formal and informal conversations.

6. *Cocreation of new learning elements.* At this stage, partners work together with constant determination to improve on what has been and what should be done and to create new learning elements that will contribute towards achieving the shared vision. Nonaka (1994) believes that successful companies are those that consistently create new knowledge (learning elements), are able to disseminate it (them) throughout (and among) the organization (the allying partners) and embody it (them) in new technologies and innovation.

It is worth noting that before genuine interorganizational learning occurs, genuine intraorganizational learning needs to happen. Indeed, in both cases, individual and group learning are the starting point. Support structures for continuous learning and an overall organizational attitude that encourages learning are also crucial for creating a learning culture.

Morrison & Mezentseff (1997) state that managers within a learning alliance must provide an environment that stimulates the exchange of ideas across all sections of a partner's organizations. Osland & Yaprak (1995) say that firms that excel in interpartner learning are better able to adapt to dynamic environmental changes and improve their ability to meet customer requirements.

If one of the purposes of cross-cultural co-opetition is to improve the potential for learning, beyond of the development of interorganizational learning mechanisms, partners also need to build (Morrison & Mezentseff, 1997) the following:

- *A conducive learning culture.* A learning culture is one where people are creative in their working relationships and experiences. Managers within a learning alliance will need to create the right organizational climate for learning.

- *Learning relationships.* A critical success factor of long-term learning alliances is the ability to create learning relationships. However, building a learning relationship can be a difficult process. Individual organizations involved in the process may have a firm commitment to their own agenda and not to that of the alliance. This may worsen if the allying organizations' cultures are incompatible.

- *Joint learning structures, strategies, and processes.* These are reward systems that encourage individual, group, and organizational learning, thus making the learning elements available throughout the alliance for continuous learning. The shared learning within the alliance will enable the partners to incorporate the learning elements into future generations of products/services.

CONCLUSION

Today's business environment compels organizations (including competitors) to join forces in various forms because global competition requires a simultaneous need for global-scale efficiencies, worldwide learning, and local responsiveness (Chan & Wong, 1994). This chapter has argued that co-opetitive relationships can only exist under two situations:

1. When the cultures of allying partners with similar competencies are compatible.
2. When the cultures of allying partners with complementary competencies are incompatible.

The chapter suggests that the success of cross-cultural co-opetition will depend on the in-depth understanding and effective management of allying partners' motivation, interaction, vision, and learning drivers. It is, however, naïve to assume that all organizations initiating co-opetition will easily adapt to the proposed framework. Indeed, it requires the following:

- mutual dependency
- mutual interests
- mutual benefit
- mutual understanding
- mutual trust and respect
- mutual commitment
- a shared vision
- intra- and interorganizational learning mechanisms
- intra- and interorganizational learning cultures
- interorganizational learning relationships
- joint learning structures, strategies, and processes

Nevertheless, it is worth noting that if organizations that are looking for long-term co-opetitive alliances incorporate the key elements of the suggested framework, then they will gain advantage over their competitors by developing a unique relationship. This relationship will increase the organizations' intelligence, which will ensure a secure future and sustainable, competitive advantage.

REFERENCES

Allaire, Y. & Firsirotu, M. E. (1984). Theories of Organizational Culture. *Organization Studies, 5,* 193–226.

Amin, S. G., Hagen, A. F. & Sterrett, C. R. (1995). Cooperating to Achieve Competitive Advantage in a Global Economy. *SAM Advanced Management Journal, 60,* 37–51.

Baranson, J. (1989). Form Alliances Now or Forfeit Future. *Research and Development,* 15–16.

Brandenburger, A. M. & Nalebuff, B. J. (1996). *Co-opetition.* New York: Currency/Doubleday.

Cartwright, S. & Cooper, C. L. (1995). Organizational Marriage: Hard Versus Soft Issues? *Personnel Review, 24,* 32–42.

Chakravarthy, B. S. & Lorange, P. (1991). *Managing the Strategy Process.* Englewood Cliffs, NJ: Prentice Hall.

Chan, P. S. & Wong, A. (1994). Global Strategic Alliances and Organizational Learning. *Leadership & Organization Development Journal, 15,* 31–36.

Crossan, M. & Inkpen, A. (1995). The Subtle Art of Learning Through Alliances. *Business Quarterly, 60,* 68–78.

Dowling, M., Carlin, B., Roering, W. & Winieski, J. (1993). Multifaceted Relationships Under Co-opetition: Description and Theory, Working Paper: University of Georgia.

Ghoshal, S. (1987). Global Strategy: An Organizing Framework. *Strategic Management Journal,* 425–440.

Harris, P. R. & Moran, R. T. (1987). *Managing Cultural Differences.* (2nd ed.). Houston: Gulf.

Henricks, M. (1996). Joining Forces: Work With Your Competitors—Not Against Them—And Soon You'll Be Succeeding With the Enemy. *Entrepreneur,* 76–79.

Hofstede, G. (1991). *Cultures & Organizations: Software of the Mind.* London: McGraw-Hill.

Huber, G. (1991). Organizational Learning: The Contributing Processes and Literatures. *Organization Science, 2,* 88–115.

Kohls, L. R. (1981). *Developing Intercultural Awareness.* Washington: Society for Intercultural Education, Training & Research.

Levinson, N. S. & Asahi, M. (1995). Cross-national Alliances and Interorganizational Learning. *Organizational Dynamics,* 50–63.

Mason, D. (1994). Scenario-based planning: decision model for the learning organization. *Planning Review,* 6–11.

Morrison, M. & Mezentseff, L. (1997). Learning Alliances: A New Dimension of Strategic Alliances. *Management Decision, 35,* 351–359.

Murray, A. I. & Siehl, C. (1989). *Joint Ventures and Other Alliances: Creating a Successful Co-operative Linkage.* Financial Executives Research Foundation.

Nonaka, I. (1994). A Dynamic Theory of Organizational Knowledge Creation. *Organizational Science, 5,* 14–37.

Osland G. & Yaprak, A. (1995). Learning Through Strategic Alliances: Processes and Factors That Enhance Marketing Effectiveness. *European Journal of Marketing, 29,* 52–66.

Porter, M. E. (1985). *Competitive Advantage.* New York: Free Press.

Rao, B. P. & Swaminathan, V. (1995). Uneasy Alliances: Cultural Incompatibility or Culture Shock? Proceedings of the Association of Management, 13th Annual International Conference, Vancouver BC, Canada, 1–13.

Rijamampianina, R. (1996). Effective Management in Multicultural Organizations. *Economic Journal of Hokkaido University, 25*, 119–167.
Rijamampianina, R. (1999). *Developing Core Competence Through Multicultural Learning.* Parkland, FL: Universal Publishers.
Trilling, L. (1978). *Beyond Culture.* New York: Harcourt Brace Jovanovich.

CHAPTER 12

The Metastrategy: A Systematic View of the Theory of Corporate Internationalization Strategies

René Haak

INTRODUCTION

The internationalization of entrepreneurial activity is one of the biggest strategic challenges facing management at the beginning of the twenty-first century. All companies doing or wanting to do business beyond their national borders are asking which internationalization strategy they should chose, given their competitive situation and the resources available to them. Which internationalization strategy will achieve their objectives, taking into consideration the company's strengths and weaknesses? This chapter is not intended to give a complete overview of the complex and multifaceted results from previous research on the many entrepreneurial internationalization strategies. Its concern is with offering an initial approach to a theoretical understanding of a new strategy level, the metastrategy, which this chapter presents for scientific consideration by international and strategic management. This new strategy level is developing against the background of discussion on centralized internationalization strategies from a systematic, theoretical perspective.

In this chapter it is argued that in addition to the three traditional, logically interrelated forms of strategy—corporate, business, and functional strategies there is a requirement for a fourth, a "metastrategy," to accord theory with the real situation we find in today's internationalization process. This is happening increasingly in business networks.

The metastrategy should be seen as super ordinate, which in its formulation and implementation is related to the subordinate strategies, creating a framework for discovering further strategies. The metastrategy can be seen as a paradigm for entrepreneurial activity or for how international management imagines the company of the future will look like. It describes the spirit of the company and its fundamental alignment.

THE FORCES DRIVING THE PROCESS OF INTERNATIONALIZATION

Over the last few decades, profound changes have taken place in the corporate environment. These changes have accelerated the process of entrepreneurial internationalization. New, dynamic businesses from the small tiger states of South Korea, Taiwan, Hong Kong, and Singapore, and the increasing presence on the international market of globally active businesses from Western Europe, Japan, and the U.S. are examples of the rapid change in international competition (Perlitz, 1997). The collapse of the planned economy systems in Central and Eastern Europe, the subsequent political and economic transformation in these countries, the realignment of the economy in the People's Republic of China (Hilpert and Haak, 2002; Haak and Hilpert 2002) with its impressive rates of growth since the end of the 1970s, and the evolution and establishment of large, unified economic blocs such as the European Union (EU), the North American zone (NAFTA), and the ASEAN states are defining processes for the global economic map (Dülfer, 1997; Ohmae, 1985), to which company management needs to respond as part of its strategic considerations. Concepts such as globalization and internationalization highlight this process, which is presenting international management with new challenges with regard to gaining and maintaining market position and competitive advantage.

However, it is not only the global changes described above that are confronting businesses to an increasing degree with tasks for restructuring long-established business models (Okumura, 1998). We are seeing intensified pressure on competition in old domestic markets, saturation of traditional market segments, the emergence of new aggressive competitors, the decline, for example, of traditional leads over competition on the part of successful high-tech companies (Spur, 1998a), and increasing technical complexity of industrial products with a simultaneous reduction in innovation cycles (resulting in a demand for international cooperation on research and development (Haak, 2000; Inkpen, 1995). All these are forcing industrial companies to rethink their palette of products and services, and in particular, their international direction and presence.

INTERNATIONALIZATION—A MULTIFACETED CONCEPT

The concept of internationalization can be defined in different ways. It is frequently taken to be an umbrella term for many entrepreneurial activities and processes. In a broader sense, internationalization is seen as the equivalent to long-term activities abroad that are of significance to the company. The internationalization of a business can, for example, be characterized by a global network of subsidiaries (Sydow, 1993; Schacher, 1998), company-owned sales organizations and production plants, and partners in international alliances. A high proportion of exports relative to total company sales can also be a feature of internationalization.

In order to formulate a scientific theory it is desirable to quantify and measure the degree of entrepreneurial internationalization; there have been many contributions towards this (Schmidt, 1991; Perlitz, 1997; Bartlett, 1989), which have not resulted in a uniform view or a binding definition. Familiar indicators for entrepreneurial internationalization include, for example, the number of employees abroad, the turnover they achieve, involvement of foreign management and the amount of foreign investment and export turnover. However, the degree of entrepreneurial internationalization is demonstrated better by a company's targets, strategies, culture, and existing thought and decision patterns exhibited by management. This is where the new concept of a metastrategy comes into play: it should be defined as a manifestation of management thought and action models. In this context, internationalization can also be understood as the shaping of a metastrategy rooted in the models for decision-making. In other words, the internationalization strategies of a company can be described by the concept of a metastrategy, which is based on innovative structuring of the complex relationships between technology and management, formulates specific corporate, business and functional strategies (Spur, 1998b; Bullinger, 1994; Zahn, 1995), and manifests itself in increased corporate activity abroad.

THE PROCESS OF INTERNATIONALIZATION AND LEVELS OF STRATEGY

Business and management teachings have already provided solutions to many of the problems associated with international management on a theoretical level. In particular, these tackle questions of strategy formulation: *why* companies should do business on an international level and the conditions under which a specific internationalization strategy is preferred (Albach, 1981; Pausenberger, 1981; Lück and Trommsdorf, 1982; Macharzina and Welge, 1989; Welge, 1990; Welge and Böttcher, 1991; Dülfer, 1985). It must be recognized, however, that business and management theories have paid hardly any attention to questions concerning the relationship among the different strategy levels (corporate, business, and functional) in entrepreneurial internationalization. The metastrategy brings a new perspective to these relationships. As a super ordinate strategy that manifests management thought and action patterns it creates a frame of reference for the formulation of further strategies.

Management is confronted with the central questions of which form of internationalization should be chosen to fulfill market and competition requirements and help the company grow into a position of technology and market leadership. Management is consequently faced with a series of questions that go beyond its abilities, competence and knowledge on a national level. Hence, one of the most important questions for the management of an internationally active company is whether, in the course of the entrepreneurial internationalization process, direct investment should be made in foreign markets or an export strategy might be more productive. If the company decides on an export strategy, it must give consideration to questions about the market and to competition and cultural conditions. If company management chooses the direct investment strategy, it must clarify which company functions should be realized abroad. For example Would it be beneficial to set up its own sales operation?, Is it worth acquiring foreign production plants?, and how should it proceed with research and development? This decision process encompasses all the phases of a classic management process, from planning, organization, personnel deployment, and management to control, and the three strategy levels considered in traditional management teachings:

- corporate strategy
- business strategy
- functional strategy

Corporate strategy defines, amongst other things, the environment in which a company wishes to engage. The central strategic question at the corporate level is in which areas should the company do business, and how should these be positioned in relation to each other. Realistically, this means that strategic management on a corporate level deals with structuring the so-called business portfolio. This is intended to achieve an optimum orientation for the whole company. In contrast to this, there is the *business strategy,* which addresses how the company and its various areas of business stand in relationship to the competition (for example, cost leadership or product differentiation). The central question at the business level is, therefore, how the business intends to operate in each business area to succeed in the market and against competition. In other words, how to create and exploit advantage over the competition and achieve business targets. One thing is certain: competition strategies must be developed separately for each business area. The *functional strategy* is the basis for working out the corporate and business strategies in individual functional areas (Wheelen and Hunger, 1995; Johnson and Scholes, 1997).

The functional strategy attempts to address, amongst other things, the most flexible and economical production methods as possible and appropriate marketing concepts for customer care.

This chapter will introduce an enhancement, giving a new overall perspective on the discussion surrounding the relationship between these three strategy levels for entrepreneurial internationalization: the metastrategy. An overall perspective, such as the metastrategy, can be beneficial in association with the internationalization of corporate activities, particularly in the areas of global strategic alliances (Bronder and Pritzl, 1991; Kreikebaum, 1998) and networks.

It is the task of strategic management at the meta-level to structure the company and cooperating and/or network partners that are not part of the hierarchical coordination and integration functions of the company—and hence are not part of the three traditional strategic levels—and to provide the systems, such as those for information and control, required for management from an overall point of view. A central role for management at the meta-level is therefore to define the strategic self-image of the company.

THE NEED FOR A METASTRATEGY IN THE PROCESS OF ENTREPRENEURIAL INTERNATIONALIZATION

The process of entrepreneurial internationalization, which is described here using ideally typical internationalization strategies, is leading increasingly to transnational businesses with a network-like organizational structure and diverse forms of international cooperation. (Dathe, 1998). Unlike earlier forms, such as export-based strategies, this new complex form of entrepreneurial internationalization makes a higher-level perspective indispensable: on the metastrategy level it is possible to coherently express the complex processes in modern trends towards internationalization. To explain the concept of the metastrategy further we shall examine the historical development of corporate internationalization in the following sections. In addition, we must investigate the relationship of the three traditional strategy levels and also the functions of the metastrategy in their interaction. Last but not least, we must ask whether the metastrategy plays a significant role in all forms of corporate internationalization (e.g. export strategy, international strategy in a more restricted sense, multinational strategy, global strategy, transnational strategy, and corporate networks).

Viewed from a historical perspective, corporate international activity in the eighteenth and nineteenth century extended mainly to the colonies. Closer examination shows that this international corporate business was trade of a highly national nature within an area frequently under political and military control or rule (Perridon and Rössler, 1980). Towards the end of the nineteenth century, business activity in these still nationally oriented companies began to develop in the direction of increasing internationalization in work and trade processes. A liberal economic policy, the emergence of new technologies (railway, ships, telegraph, telephone, etc.), and the increasing political independence of the trading partner nations all greatly benefited this development. From the point of view of the colonial powers, this early phase of international entrepreneurial activity was limited principally to the export of manufactured products but also to a large degree to exploiting valuable raw materials in the colonies, which functioned simultaneously as sales markets. To secure raw materials long-term for production at home represented a key factor in this early form of entrepreneurial internationalization. Described in this way, this export-oriented strategy was an early stage of internationalization, which has since receded before other internationalization strategies. However, it is still pursued by many companies as a promising strategy for internationalization (Sydow, 1993).

The export strategy is cross-border marketing of manufactured goods that presents itself when domestic markets are saturated and scale effects become necessary. The export strategy is the right choice for gathering experience abroad while risking little. A requirement for using the export strategy is that nothing hinders or limits international trade. In general, it can be seen that the export-oriented companies are usually insufficiently sensitive to the peculiarities of foreign markets, largely because of the domestic limitation of corporate structure. Furthermore, exporting companies cannot realize the benefits of global resource allocation, which limits its growth potential (Dülfer, 1982).

With the increase in activities beyond national boundaries, selected productive foreign markets were supplied with manufactured goods within the framework of an international strategy in the narrow sense. However, it must be stressed that this happened without any particular attention to country-specific peculiarities or alternatively without any adaptation. This is what characterizes the core of the international strategy (Sydow, 1993).

In theory, the internationalization of a company (internationalization strategy in the more narrow sense) via direct investments (e.g., in building up new branch operations, representative offices, and production and research plants) represents the second stage of internationalization. In the course of this process, the traditional international enterprise emerges. This is characterized by a headquarters or home-country dominated strategy. According to Meffert (1986) the limited ability of companies to adapt to country-specific particularities is typical at this stage of internationalization (ethnocentric orientation).

When can the headquarters or home-country dominated strategy be considered successful? When foreign markets still need developing and competitors have not yet adjusted strategically or organizationally to the specific conditions in the foreign markets. Many enterprises, however, will have already gathered initial experience in foreign markets, possibly in the course of applying an export strategy.

It must be born in mind that the organizational structure of the international enterprise in the narrow sense is characterized by a high degree of centralized decision-making. The management of foreign subsidiaries often reports directly to a member of the board of the parent company. However, foreign branches frequently have a great deal of autonomy (Sydow, 1993), which can be attributed principally to the way they were developed and to local expertise. Bartlett and Ghoshal (1990) use the term "co-ordinated federation" in this context where many resources, responsibilities, and decisions are decentralized but over which the head office exerts much control via strictly formalized planning and monitoring systems (Sydow, 1993).

Unlike the strategies described above, the multinational strategy accommodates the particularities of the country in which the company is active to a great degree. With the multinational strategy, advanced internationalization of the enterprise is seen as a rule, and production, research, and development functions are added to the initial sales functions in foreign markets.

The multinational enterprise pursues a multinational or country-specific strategy, instead of internationally-oriented headquarters or home-country dominated strategy (Porter, 1989). Often, the multinational enterprise is the result of progressive internationalization, as seen particularly in U.S., European, and increasingly in Japanese companies of the 1990s. In what context is the multinational strategy successful? The answer to this is: when the foreign markets are strongly differentiated and dissimilar from the domestic market. The motivation for pursuing this strategy can be found in certain company-specific traditions, but also in differences in culture, legal systems, and government regulations.

The characteristic organizational structure of multinational businesses is the decentralized federation: the parent company controls and organizes the federation, which is broken down into regional sections. This organizational structure thus forms the basis for strategically required adaptation to country-specific particularities of products, advertising, sales, and possibly the manufacturing process (Sydow, 1993). On the management level, the decentralized structure is the counterpart to the polycentric orientation described in Perlmutter (1969).

A distinction should be drawn between multinational businesses, with multinational internationalization strategy, and global businesses, with their strategy. According to Porter (1989), the latter type of enterprise pursues strategies oriented towards the global market and has a global organizational structure. The global enterprise does not follow the route of country-specific differentiation in its business activities. At the heart of the strategy are global standardization and configuration of marketing, production, logistics, for example., and a conscious acceptance of nationally suboptimal strategies (Meffert, 1996). There are two versions of the global strategy: the broad market approach and the niche strategy that focuses on specific and selected market segments.

It should be emphasized that with the simple global strategy the world market is supplied with largely standardized goods. Perfect examples of this are the brands of Coca Cola, Levi's, and Sony Walkman. The global strategy assumes a progressive homogenization of living standards and life styles, international legal systems, and technologies. However, one should not see this strategy in the context of just a response to increasing globalization. Global businesses are also contributing to further homogenization of products and levels of expectation.

Formally, a feature of the organizational structure of the global enterprise is the centralized nodal point structure. (Bartlett, 1989). This organizational structure is characterized by the fact that strategic decisions are taken by the parent company, which as a rule is structured into product sections. These are put into practice with formal plans and increasingly personal integration mechanisms, and these are controlled by the staff of the parent company (Sydow, 1993). The result is a lack of autonomy for the foreign companies.

There is an intensive flow of resources between the parent and subsidiary companies. These are not limited to capital but also include products, services, technology, expertise and much more. Japanese companies (Abegglen and Stalk, 1989; Dirks, 1995; Ohmae, 1986) prefer this organizational model, which apart from centralization is based mainly on the worldwide standardization of products and production strategies (Sydow, 1993), as their form of comparatively late internationalization strategy (Bartlett, 1989).

The centralized nodal point structure allows the global enterprise to realize economies of scale and scope and to exploit comparative cost benefits. Global businesses can be more flexible than other types of organizations or strategies with regard to decisions on the international distribution of individual manufacturing tasks and on the resources necessary to carry out activities. Country-specific differences on sales and input markets are used to optimum purpose by global enterprises (Ghoshal, 1987; Porter, 1989).

Theoretical discussion is broadened by the dual internationalization strategy. A dual strategy is an attempt to accommodate both the requirements of global coordination of activities and also country-specific differentiation (Sydow, 1993). The term "transnational strategy" has been coined for this dual strategy (Barlett, 1989).

The transnational enterprise embraces efficiency, flexibility, and receptivity as equally valid strategic goals. At its core is a network-like organizational model (Bartlett, 1989; Barlett and Ghoshal, 1990). The transnational strategy concentrates on market proximity, whereby market proximity is understood primarily to be an instrument for reacting quickly to international business deals (Barlett and Ghoshal, 1990). Learning processes involving all organizational units in the business are made possible by market proximity. For example, specific expertise can be concentrated at selected locations to allow exploitation of advantages in cost or knowledge. Other resources and expertise are held in readiness at decentralized locations and are used as required through cooperation between individual units. For example, this means that with redundant structures transnational enterprises can reduce their susceptibility to breakdown over the whole system (Staehle, 1999).

Transnational enterprises vary the role of their foreign branch operations, as company-specific adjustments are not necessary in every foreign market. In some foreign markets, the branch operations deal in globally standardized products. As such, they essentially have the role of efficiently implementing the decisions taken at the central office. In contrast, differentiation may be required of other branch operations. This means, for example, that some branch operations will develop products that will be handled by other branches. In this case, the headquarters hands over its management role to the branch offices in question. One of the most important identifiers of a transnational enterprise is that there are no clear role assignments in the system (Bartlett and Ghoshal, 1990).

Today, the real business world shows that realizing a transnational strategy with its contradictory requirements of differentiation and integration is resulting in a network-like organizational model, the integrated network (Sydow, 1993). The integrated network is characterized by largely reciprocal and cooperative relationships among organizational units, which enjoy equal status.

According to Sydow, business network are polycentric organizational structures of economic activity that target competitive advantage and are strategically managed by one or more enterprises. These are characterized by a special type of (network) relationship, express a certain degree of reflexivity, are based on a trade logic that is different from that of the market, and a hierarchy (Sydow, 1998; Sydow, 1992; Sydow and Windeler, 1998).

The strategic network is an organizational model that can also be used for internationally active businesses, which consist of a structurally, culturally, and relatively close-coupled kernel (e.g., the transnational enterprise itself) and is surrounded by a loosely bound periphery of relationships (strategic alliances, value-added partnerships, and subcontracting arrangements). Self-organizing processes triggered by a model of this kind amidst conflicts between corporate autonomy and control should be considered diverse in their effects. On the one hand, they reduce the requirement for management of the network; on the other, they need to develop mechanisms and strategies that ensure integration. Some authors describe networks as an organizational form, some even as a postmodern organizational form (Clegg, 1990; Reed, 1992; Clegg and Hardy, 1997). Sydow refers to the network as a fluid organization, both internally and interorganizationally (Sydow, 1998). More than with other organizational forms, a strategic network makes it possible to pursue, for example, multinational, global, cost leadership, and differentiation strategies.

Internationalization processes in today's businesses are characterized by a trend towards the network form. This creates new demands on management, which needs to act in a network-oriented fashion, to realize international competitive advantages. The trend towards network management means that the traditional levels of corporate, business, and functional strategies can no longer meet the needs of economic reality: this economic reality is characterized by existing or emerging business networks and globalized markets. The metastrategy presented in this chapter should be deployed.

The metastrategy should be understood as a paradigm for business activity. It integrates by performing different functions that are relevant to success and production of goods and services that are distributed over networks. The functions of the metastrategy of a business can be defined as follows: identification function, where the metastrategy demonstrates to employees the deeper meaning and benefit of their work, making it easier for them to identify with the company; motivation function, where the metastrategy encourages employees to pursue company objectives as a common goal; and finally, the identity function, where the metastrategy describes a future view of the company that is perceived as unique. More than other organizational models, the metastrategy can lead to greater cultural integration in the form of shared values, visions, style and philosophies. An international human resource management system adjusted to international business activities characterizes the personnel economics of the metastrategy model.

A sound metastrategy should aspire above all to serve as a guideline for business development for as long as possible. In these network structures, management is less responsible for direct leadership and control than indirect control via the metastrategy. The metastrategy creates a framework for the development of independent corporate, business, and functional strategies for subsidiaries of networks or international collaborations.

In formulating the metastrategy, international management has the difficult task of integrating different perspectives and philosophies that exist in the enterprise while maintaining differentiation. The objective of the metastrategy, derived from the company vision, should be to build up productivity and commitment in different parts of the company that can be used for the whole business. With the metastrategy, the foreign subsidiaries and the companies integrated in or associated with the network are considered active participants in the global competition arena. They will develop their own corporate, business and functional strategies within the framework of the metastrategy. It should also be noted, however, that the metalevel and its subordinated strategy levels work retroactively through their creative autonomy on the formulation and implementation of the metastrategy.

The description of the typical stages of the internationalization process up to the business network model, which is seen to dominate today, demonstrates that strong centrifugal forces act on networks. The model of the business network, hence, implies the requirement for an element like the metastrategy to impose order and meaning. With the metastrategy, internationally active management has an instrument to work against the centrifugal forces in the network with newly defined shared values, visions, and style for the network members. This should be qualified however: not every internationally active business goes through the process described above. It would also be wrong to assume that transnational businesses or business networks can be considered successful just on the basis of their nature.

Indeed, differences in national, industrial, and company-specific contingencies allow internationally active companies to develop their activities in different configurations and become successful. As such, it should not be assumed that a metastrategy is required in every case.

SUMMARY

In the course of corporate internationalization, management of companies active on an international level are facing new kind of problems arising from contact with foreign cultural, economic, and social systems; and these problems go much beyond the demands made on the management of a company doing business on a national level. Seen as a process developing from traditional national business activity, internationalization is currently being driven by three key factors.

These include the following factors: the tendency towards market saturation, which is becoming particularly apparent in the industries of mass production; the progressive globalization of markets and the success of suppliers of cheap goods on an international level with structural cost advantages, particularly in the production of both consumer and of investment goods; and the growing pressure on these markets for flexibility, quality, reliability, service, and innovation, which also extends to other components.

Companies are responding to these challenges with a bundle of market, production, and organizational strategies. It has been seen here that the many different corporate strategies amount to further internationalization of a company. Yet another point becomes obvious: some companies are reacting not only to different environmental conditions but are also actively contributing to their formation with appropriate internationalization strategies. Other businesses, on the other hand, are adapting to the existing market and competition requirements and are pursuing proven internationalization strategies.

Today's internationalization process seems to result increasingly in a transnational business with structures equivalent to the business network organizational model. The result of this trend is the need for a new strategy form at a higher level than the three traditional strategies: corporate, business, and functional strategies. This is the metastrategy presented in this chapter. The metastrategy aspires, based on the assessment of the strengths and weaknesses of the company, to act as a guideline for further development. By using identification, motivation and identity functions on dynamic networks in similar environmental demands, it can fulfill the contradictory demands of differentiation and integration of operations and information processes in a network-like organizational model.

REFERENCES

Abegglen, J. C. and Stalk Jr., G. (1989). Kaisha. München: Wilhem Heyne Verlag.

Albach, H. (1981). Internationlae Betriebswirtscahftslehre. Ergänzungsheft 1/81 der Zeitschrift Betriebswirtschaftslehre.

Bartlett, C. A. (1989). Aufbau und Management der transnationalen Unternehmung: Eine organisatorische Herausforderung. In M. E. Porter (Ed.), Globaler Wettbwerb. Wiesbaden: Gabler.

Bartlett, C. A. and Ghoshal, S. (1990). Internationale Unternehmensführung. Frankfurt and New York.

Bronder, C. and Pritzl, R. (1991). Strategische Allianzen zur Steigerung der Wettbewerbsfähigkeit. io Management Zeitschrift, 60, pp. 27–30.

Bullinger, H. J. (1994). Einführung in das Technologiemanagement. Stuttgart: B.G. Teubner.

Clegg, S. R. (1990). Modern organizations: Organization studies in the postmodern world. London.

Clegg, S. R. and Hardy, C. (1997). Organizations, organization and organizing. In S. R. Clegg, C. Hardy, and W. R. Nord, (Eds.). Handbook of organization studies. London.

Dathe, J. (1998). Kooperationen. Leitfaden für Unternehmen. München: Hanser.

Dirks, D. (1995). Japanisches Management in internationalen Unternehmen. Methodik interkultureller Organisation. Wiesbaden: Gabler. 1995.

Duelfer, E. (1985). 'Die Auswirkungen der Internationalisierung auf Fueh-
rung und Organisationsstruktur mittelstaedischer Unternehmen,
Betriebswirtschaftliche Forschung und Praxis 3 (6), pp. 493–514.

Dülfer, E. (1982). *Projektmanagement—International*. Stuttgart.

Dülfer, E. (1997). *Internationales Management in unterschiedlichen Kulturber-
eichen*. München und Wien: R. Oldenbourg Verlag.

Ghoshal, S. (1987). Global strategy: An organizing framework. *Strategic
Management Journal, 8*, pp. 425–440.

Ghoshal, S. and Bartlett, C. A. (1990). The multinational corporation as an
international network. *Academy of Management Review, 15*, pp. 603–
625.

Haak, R. (2000). Zwischen Internationalisierung und Restrukturierung—
Kooperationsmanagement der japanischen Industrie in fortschrit-
tlichen Technologiefeldern. *Industrie-Management, (6) Globalisierung
und Regionalisierung*, pp. 64–68.

Haak, R. (2002). Japanese Business Strategies towards China. A Theoreti-
cal Approach. In H. G. Hilpert and R. Haak (Eds.), *Japan and China.
Cooperation, Competition and Conflicts*. Houndsmills, Basingstoke,
Hampshire: Palgrave.

Haak, R. (2002). Strategy and Organization of International Enterprises—
Japanese-German Business Cooperation in Third Markets: The Case
China. In R. Haak and H. G. Hilpert (Eds.), *Focus China—The New
25. Challenge for Japanese Management*. München: Iudicium Verlag
(forthcoming).

Haak, R. and Hilpert, H. G. (2003). *Focus China. The New Challenge for Japanese Management*. München: Iudicium (forthcoming).

Hilpert, H. G. and Haak, R. (2002). *Japan and China. Cooperation, Competition and Conflict*. Houndsmills, Basingstoke, Hampshire: Palgrave.

Inkpen, A. (1995). *The Management of International Joint Ventures. An Organizational Learning Perspective*. London and New York.

Johnson, G. and Scholes, K. (1997). *Exploring Corporate Strategy*. London.

Kreikebaum, H. (1998). *Organisations management internationaler Unternehmen. Grundlagen und neue Strukturen*. Wiesbaden: Gabler.

Lück, W. and Trommsdorff, M. (1982). *Internationalisierung der Unternehmung als Problem desr Betriebswirtschaftslehre*.

Macharzina, K. and Welge, M. K. (1989). *Handwörterbuch Export und internationale Unternehmung*. Stuttgart.

Meffert, H. (1996). Marketing im Spannungsfeld von weltweitem Wettbewerb und nationalen Bedürfnissen. *Zeitschrift für Betriebswirtschaft, 56*, 689–712.

Ohmae, K. (1985). *Die Macht der Triade*. Wiesbaden: Gabler.

Ohmae, K. (1986). *Japanische Strategien*. Hamburg: McGraw-Hill Book.

Okumura, H. (1998). *Japan und seine Unternehmen*. München and Wien: Oldenbourg.

Pausenberger, E. (1981). *Internationales Management*. Stuttgart.

Perridon, L. and Rössler, M. (1980). Die internationale Unternehmung: Entwicklung und Wesen: *Wirtschaftswissenschaftliches Studium 9*, 211–217.

Perlitz, M. (1997). *Internationales Management*. Stuttgart: Lucius & Lucius.

Perlmutter, H. V. (1969). The Tortutous Evolution of the Multinational Corporation. *Columbia Journal of World Business, 1*, 9.

Porter, M. E. (1989). *Globaler Wettbewerb*. Wiesbaden.

Reed, M. (1992). *The sociology of organizations*. Hemel Hempstead.

Schacher, D. (1998). Vernetzte Zusammenarbeit—Neue Formen der Organisation in globalen Produktionsunternehmen. In L. Krause and E. Uhlmann, (Eds.), *Innovative Produktionstechnik*. München and Wien: Carl Hanser Verlag.

Schmidt, R. (1991). Zur Messung des Internationalisierungsgrades von Unternehmen. In W. H. Wacker, H. Hausmann, and B. Kumar, (Eds.), *Internationale Unternehmensführung. Management probleme international tätiger Unternehmen*. Berlin 1991.

Spur, G. (1998a). *Technologie und Management. Zum Selbstverständnis der Technikwissenschaften*. München und Wien: Carl Hanser Verlag.

Spur, G. (1998b). *Fabrikbetrieb*. München und Wien: Carl Hanser Verlag.

Staehle, W. H. (1999). *Management*. München: Verlag Franz Vahlen.

Sydow, J. (1991). Strategische Netzwerke in Japan—Leitbild für die Gestaltung interorganisationaler Beziehungen europäischer Unternehmungen? *Zeitschrift für betriebswirtschaftliche Forschung, 43*, 238–254.

Sydow, J. (1992). *Strategische Netzwerke. Evolution und Organisation*. Wiesbaden: Gabler.

Sydow, J. (1993). Strategie und Organisation international tätiger Unternehmungen—Managementprozesse in Netzwerkstrukturen. In H.-D. Ganter and G. Schienstock, (Eds.), *Management aus soziologischer Sicht*. Wiesbaden: Gabler.

Sydow, J. and Windeler, A. (1998). Organizing and evaluating interfirm networks: A structurationist perspective on network processes and effectiveness. *Organization Science, 9*, 265–284.

Sydow, J. (1998). Postmoderne Konzerne?—Zum Verhältnis von Konzern und Netzwerk. Schriftenfassung eines Vortrages auf dem 22. Workshop der Kommission "Organisation " im Hochullehrerverband für Betriebswirtschaftslehre an der Freien Universität Berlin, 26–28 Februar 1998. FU Berlin http://www.wiwiss.fu-berlin.de/w3/W3SYDOW/Neuersch/index.htm.

Welge, M. K. (1990). *Globales Management*. Stuttgart.

Welge, M. K. and Böttcher, R. (1991). Globale Strategien und Probleme ihrer Implementierung. *Die Betriebswirtschaft 51*, 435–454.

Wheelen, T. and Hunger, D. (1995). *Strategic Management and Business Policy*. Reading.

Zahn, E. (1995). *Handbuch Technologiemanagement*. Stuttgart: Schäffer-Poeschel.

Index

About the Contributors

CAROLINE F. BENTON is a professor at the University of Wales validated MBA programme in Japan. She earned her MBA degree from Tsukuba University and her PhD degree in Management Engineering from the Tokyo Institute of Technology. She has held positions as a director of a Japanese subsidiary of a European manufacturer and chief consultant of a marketing consulting firm for foreign-affiliated firms in Japan.

FRANK-JÜRGEN RICHTER is Director, Asia, of the World Economic Forum, Geneva. He was educated in business administration and mechanical engineering in Germany, France, Mexico, and Japan. Prior to joining the World Economic Forum, he gathered high-level management experience in Asia and Europe. He was based in Beijing for several years developing and managing a European Multinational's China operations. An active scholar, he has authored and edited several books on Asian economies and international business.

TORU TAKAI specializes in international management and management strategy. He is currently Professor of Strategic Management at the Faculty of Commerce, Nihon University. He has written many papers on strategy for small/medium companies and international management.

CLAIRE GORDON-BROWN is a research associate and case writer at the Wits Business School. She holds a BA from the University of Cape Town and a Higher Diploma in Personnel Management from the Wits Business

School. She has a background in business journalism and her interests lie in leadership and organizational change.

SYUICHI ISHIDA is an Associate Professor of Product Development at the Hokkai-Gakuen University in Sapporo, Japan. His research interests have centered on knowledge-based networking for scientists and engineers and in finding markets for new technologies.

RENÉ HAAK studied business administration, production technology, and human engineering. In 1992, he took the position of researcher at the Fraunhofer Institute for Production and Design Technology. In 1995, he transferred to the Institute for Machine Tools and Factory at the Technical University of Berlin and was the project leader of the aerospace-work group. He joined the German Institute for Japanese Studies in Tokyo in 1999, and is currently economics group manager and deputy director of the business and economics department of the German Institute for Japanese Studies.

MIDORI KATO holds an MBS from Tsukuba University and a PhD in Management Engineering from the Tokyo Institute of Technology. She was formerly a chemical engineer of a Japanese large fine chemical manufacturer and a Domestic Research Fellow at the National Institute of Science and Technology Policy, Science and Technology Agency. She is currently an associate professor of Tokyo Keizai University.

JOHN B. KIDD worked in industry for about 10 years before he moved to Birmingham University, and later still, to his present position at Aston Business School. His publications include essays on Japanese management methods (funded by the Japan Foundation). This work has broadened to include all Asian managers following a period at the China Europe International Business School, Shanghai.

ANDREAS MOERKE has an MA in Japanese Studies and a PhD in Management Science. He studied at Humboldt University (Berlin, Germany) and Tokai University (Hiratsuka, Japan), and received a Mombusho Scholarship for research at the University of Tokushima, Japan. He has over six years experience as Research Fellow at the Science Center Berlin (Market Processes and Corporate Development Section). He is currently working as a research fellow at the German Institute for Japanese Studies in Tokyo. His main areas of research are Corporate Governance, Industrial Organization, and (Personal) Networks in Japan. He set up his own consulting firm in 2000, focusing on market entry strategies in Japan and Germany.

AKI NAKANISHI is an associate professor of Information Network Society at the Tokyo Metropolitan Institute of Technology. She earned an MBA from Tsukuba University and a PhD in Value and Decision Science from the Tokyo Institute of Technology. She has written many books and papers on organizational learning and business management in the knowledge network era.

TOMOYUKI NISHIMURA is an assistant professor of Management at Kushiro Public University of Economics in Japan. His research interests include interorganizational relationships, knowledge, and governance, and he is currently focused on interactive patterns between autonomous and cooperative systems in federated networks.

KIYOSHI NOSU received his MS and degrees in electronics engineering from the University of Tokyo, Japan, in 1974 and 1977, respectively. He also received an MBA degree from University of Tsukuba, Tokyo, Japan, in 1993. Formerly, he worked at NTT Laboratories where he engaged in research in the area of fiber optics and broadband communication network services. In 2001, he joined the Department of Information and Communication Technology, the School of High-Technology for Human Welfare at Tokai University in Numazu, Japan.

RASOAVA RIJAMAMPIANINA is an associate professor of diversity and change management and the Director of the Senior Executive Programme for Southern Africa at the Wits Business School, South Africa. He holds a DSSC and a DESCA from the National Institute of Accounting Science and Business Administration, Madagascar, an MBA from Otaru University of Commerce, Japan, and a DBA degree from Hokkaido University, Japan. He was formerly a senior research associate at Hokkaido University, Japan. He has also been an auditor-consultant at Delta Audit Deloitte & Touche, Madagascar for many years and an overseas consultant of the Indian Ocean Resources for Quality.

JIN-ICHIRO YAMADA is an associate professor of Small & Medium Sized Firm Management at the Faculty of Economics, Kagawa University and a visiting scholar in Cranfield University School of Management. His main interest is strategic management of high growth firms from a knowledge-based perspective. His current work focuses on the coevolutionary relationship between entrepreneurship and regional activation.